Real-Time Design Patterns

The Addison-Wesley Object Technology Series

Grady Booch, Ivar Jacobson, and James Rumbaugh, Series Editors
For more information, check out the series web site at www.awprofessional.com/otseries.

The Component Software Series

Clemens Szyperski, Series Editor
For more information, check out the series web site at www.awprofessional.com/csseries.

Real-Time Design Patterns

Robust Scalable Architecture for Real-Time Systems

Bruce Powel Douglass

Addison-Wesley

Boston • San Francisco • New York • Toronto • Montreal
London • Munich • Paris • Madrid
Capetown • Sydney • Tokyo • Singapore • Mexico City

Many of the designations used by manufacturers and sellers to distinguish their products are claimed as trademarks. Where those designations appear in this book, and Addison-Wesley was aware of a trademark claim, the designations have been printed with initial capital letters or in all capitals.

The author and publisher have taken care in the preparation of this book, but make no expressed or implied warranty of any kind and assume no responsibility for errors or omissions. No liability is assumed for incidental or consequential damages in connection with or arising out of the use of the information or programs contained herein.

The publisher offers discounts on this book when ordered in quantity for bulk purchases and special sales. For more information, please contact:

U.S. Corporate and Government Sales
(800) 382-3419
corpsales@pearsontechgroup.com

For sales outside of the U.S., please contact:

International Sales
(317) 581-3793
international@pearsontechgroup.com

Visit Addison-Wesley on the Web: www.awprofessional.com

Library of Congress Cataloging-in-Publication Data

Douglass, Bruce Powel.
    Real-Time Design Patterns : robust scalable architecture for Real-time systems /
Bruce Powel Douglass.
        p.   cm.—(The Addison-Wesley object technology series)
    Includes bibliographical references and index.
    ISBN 0-201-69956-7 (alk. paper)
    1. Real-time data processing. 2. Software patterns. 3. Computer architecture.
    I. Title. II. Series.

qa76.54 .D68 2003
004'.33—dc21

                                                                2002074701

Text printed on recycled and acid-free paper.

ISBN 0201699567

6 7 8 9 DOC 08 07 06

Text printed in the United States at RR Donnelley, Crawfordsville, Indiana

6th Printing   November 2006

For Sarah. With all my heart, I dedicate this book
and the following haiku to you.

Mist
cool forest mist
subdued hues, shrouded souls
walking, touching, sigh

Contents

Foreword

In this book, Bruce Douglass illustrates for the first time how two important contemporary software engineering advances—patterns and the UML—can be applied advantageously to the concepts and techniques traditionally used in mainstream real-time software. Most other publications about software patterns (such as [1]) have not addressed real-time systems per se in any depth, or have focused on the narrower and more advanced topic of real-time middleware ([2]), or have been application domain specific ([3]).

This book offers a significant benefit to the practice of real-time computing, because software patterns and the UML enable potentially lower software costs in many systems. Real-time software spans the entire range of complexity and costs. In some real-time systems, the software is so small and simple, and the hardware is so complex and/or expensive, that software costs are a small fraction of the system costs (for example, software in a laser gyroscope). In other real-time systems, the software is so large and complex that regardless of the hardware costs, the software costs are a major part of the system costs (for example, software in a military or commercial aircraft). Barry Boehm, in his recent book updating the ubiquitous Cocomo software cost model [4], assigns an effort multiplier of 1.74 (the highest one) to all lifecycle phases of this latter kind of software, compared to "nominal" software (depending on the project circumstances, that multiplier can easily be a major underestimation). Most real-time software lies between these two extremes, and it is that mainstream audience of practitioners who will benefit the most from this book.

Historically, developers of real-time software have lagged behind other developers in using the most contemporary software engineering methodologies. There are several reasons for this.

One is, as mentioned above, that some real-time software is so simple that only the most elementary methodologies are needed.

A more common reason is that many real-time systems with non-trivial software suffer from hardware capacity constraints (due to size, weight, power, and so on). Software structured for purposes such as re-usability, modularity, or flexibility does tend to consume additional time or space resources. This is sometimes compensated for by the fact that commodity computing system hardware cost is always declining and its performance is always increasing. But in many real-time systems, hardware cost is still an easily measured quantitative factor that is thought to outweigh the hard-to-measure qualitative factors of software quality and costs.

Yet another reason is that real-time software practitioners are frequently application experts who are not always educated enough in modern software engineering to understand and employ it properly. New computer science and engineering graduates rarely enter the real-time field, because their formal education has not exposed them to much if any significant realistic real-time practice (real-time is a uniquely disadvantaged aspect of computer science and engineering in this respect), and what little real-time theory they may have learned is still of very limited practical relevance.

This book provides an introduction to software patterns and the UML—by one of the most authoritative contributors to those topics—as applied to mainstream real-time software, in a manner that is easily understood by practitioners in that field without prerequisite knowledge. Those who make a modest investment in learning this material can expect to discover how to cast much of their hard-earned professional experience in a framework that can make their real-time software designs more predictable—not just in terms of their timeliness (timeliness predictability being the raison d'être of real-time computing), but also in terms of their lifecycle costs.

Another prospective benefit for many real-time software designers of becoming familiar with software patterns and the UML is that these issues are of rapidly increasing importance to building larger scale, more dynamic and complex, and more distributed real-time computing systems. Such systems offer highly significant (albeit as yet not always fully appreciated) added value to many enterprises, and hence offer perhaps the most challenging and rewarding career development opportunities in the field of real-time computing systems. This book is an excellent starting point toward that future.

—E. Douglas Jensen
Natick, Massachusetts
July 2002

Doug Jensen is widely recognized as one of the pioneers of real-time computing systems, and especially of dynamic distributed real-time computing systems. He is credited with the research leading to the world's first deployed distributed real-time computer control system product. He has over three decades of hardware, software, and systems research and technology development experience in military and industrial real-time computing, and was on the faculty of the Computer Science Department of Carnegie Mellon University for eight years. He is currently in a senior technical leadership position at The MITRE Corporation, where he conducts research and technology transition on real-time computing systems for projects of strategic national interest. Doug Jensen's Web site is http://www.real-time.org.

References

1. Boehm, Barry, Ellis Horowitz, Ray Madachy, Donald Reifer, Bradford Clark, Bert Steece, A. Winsor Brown, Sunita Chulani, and Chris Abts. *Software Cost Estimation with Cocomo II.* Upper Saddle River, NJ: Prentice Hall, January 2000.
2. Gamma, Erich, Richard Helm, Ralph Johnson, and John Vlissides. *Design Patterns: Elements of Reusable Object-Oriented Software.* Reading, MA: Addison-Wesley, 1995.
3. Lea, Doug. *Design Patterns for Avionics Control Systems,* http://st-www.cs. uiuc.edu/users/patterns/patterns.html, 1994.
4. *OOPSLA 2001, Workshop on Patterns in Distributed Real-Time and Embedded Systems,* ACM, October 2001.

Preface

Goals

Real-time and embedded systems (RTE systems) must execute in a much more constrained environment than "traditional" computer systems such as desktop and mainframe computers. RTE systems must be highly efficient, optimally utilizing their limited processor and memory resources, and yet must often outperform systems with significantly more compute power. In addition, many RTE systems have important safety-critical and high-reliability requirements because they are often used in systems such as avionics flight control, nuclear power plant control, life support and medical instrumentation. The creation of RTE systems to meet these functional and quality of service requirements requires highly experienced developers with decades of experience. Yet, over the years, these developers have encountered the same problems over and over—maybe not exactly the same problems but common threads. The very best developers abstract these problems and their solutions into generalized approaches that have proved consistently effective. These generalized approaches are called *design patterns*. They are often best applied at the level of the system or software architecture—the sum of design decisions that affect the fundamental organization of the system. *Real-Time Design Patterns* is an attempt to capture in one place a set of *architectural* design patterns that are useful in the development of RTE systems.

Audience

The book is oriented toward the practicing professional software developer and the computer science major in the junior or senior year. This book could also serve as an undergraduate- or graduate-level text, but the focus is on practical development rather than a theoretical dissertation. The book assumes a reasonable proficiency in at least one programming language and a basic understanding of the fundamental concepts of object orientation, the Unified Modeling Language (UML), and real-time systems.

Organization

Part I consists of three chapters. Chapter 1 provides a very brief review of the major concepts in the Unified Modeling Language. Chapter 2 introduces the fundamental concepts of architecture as they are defined in the Rapid Object-oriented Process for Embedded Systems (ROPES), including the primary division of architecture into logical (design-time) and physical (run-time) aspects, and the five important architectural views. In the third chapter, the book gets into a discussion of design patterns and their role in defining architecture. Because it is difficult to discuss architecture in a process-free environment, the ROPES process, and the key technologies it tries to optimize, are introduced to provide a background in which design patterns may be effectively discussed. Once process has been introduced, design patterns are next. Their various aspects are explained, and the fundamental organization of design patterns used in this book is provided. The chapter finishes with a discussion of how design patterns can be applied in the development of real systems.

Part II contains the *architectural design patterns* that reify the ways that large-scale system components are organized and structured to optimize some set of general system criteria.

The patterns in Part II are organized around the architectural concept they address. Chapter 4 is dedicated to high-level structural patterns—focused around what is called the Subsystem or Component architecture. Because concurrency and resource management is so crucial to real-time and embedded systems, Chapter 5 focuses on the common patterns of concurrency. Memory management is crucial for many systems in this domain, and it is the subject of Chapter 6. We see even more general resource management patterns in Chapter 7. Chapter 8 presents a number of common distribution architecture patterns that define how objects can be distributed across multiple address spaces and computers. Finally, Chapter 9 provides a number of patterns that deal with building safe and reliable architectures.

Two appendixes appear at the end of the book. The first is simply a summary of the UML graphical notation, and the second is an index of the patterns by name.

The CD-ROM provides a number of interesting and useful tools. It contains a full copy of the Rhapsody UML tool with instructions on how to get a temporary license from I-Logix. Other additional potentially useful tools for developers of real-time systems are also provided. The Papers chapter contains some papers on various topics as well as some useful OMG specifications.

More Information

Additional information on the UML, object-oriented technology, and the development of real-time systems can be found at *www.ilogix.com*. In addition, the current UML, MDA, and CORBA standards can be seen at *www.omg.org*. For more information on using the UML in real-time systems, *Real-Time UML, 2nd Edition* is also available from Addison-Wesley, as is the more comprehensive *Doing Hard Time: Developing Real-Time Systems with UML, Objects, Frameworks and Patterns*. Many other well-written and useful books on the UML and software engineering are similarly available.

Acknowledgments

A book like this is always a joint effort, not only of the direct contributors, such as the editorial staff of Addison–Wesley Professional (and I'd especially like to thank my editor, Paul Becker, for the sometimes less-than-gentle pushing to complete the book!) but of many others who in their own way have raised the bar for all of us. The core team members working on the UML—Cris Kobryn, Eran Gery, Jim Rumbaugh, Bran Selic, and many, many others are certainly among those who should be acknowledged in bringing forth a useful standard language for capturing and manipulating models of systems. Also, Erich Gamma, Richard Helm, Ralph Johnson, and John Vlissides deserve recognition for bringing the concept of design patterns into common use with their wonderful book *Design Patterns: Elements of Reusable Object-Oriented Software.* David Harel (inventor of statecharts, the semantic basis for all behavior in the UML) and Werner Damn continue to make significant contributions to the state of the art, especially with respect to formal verification of systems modeled with the UML.

My two boys, Scott and Blake Douglass, continue to delight and amaze me—and keep me humble at the same time—and make all this effort worthwhile.

Part  I

Design Pattern Basics

Introduction

Several prerequisites are necessary to be successful in the application of design patterns into your own designs. First, in this book we will use the Unified Modeling Language (UML) to represent the patterns and the sample models. To make sure everyone starts on more or less the same footing, Chapter 1 introduces the basic semantics and notation of the UML. (Appendix A provides a notational summary for a quick reference.) Both structural and behavioral aspects are discussed well enough so that if you are a beginner, the patterns presented in Part I will at least make sense. It is not meant to be a full-blown UML tutorial—there are many other books available for that. If you need such a tutorial, then the reference section in Chapter 1 gives a list of suggested titles. Chapter 1 also talks a little about what a design pattern is and why its use is justified.

Once you know a little about the UML, it behooves us to understand what we mean by the term *architecture*. There are many different uses of the term as applied to software, so Chapter 1 explains how the term is used in this book, including the two basic types of architecture (logical and physical) and within physical architecture, the important architectural views or aspects that are subject to pattern analysis. Chapter 2 goes on to discuss how architectures may be implemented and describes the Model-Driven Architecture (MDA) initiative of the Object Management Group (OMG), the standards organization that owns the UML specification.

Once we have an understanding of architecture under our cognitive belts, the last thing we must understand before delving into the patterns per se is how patterns fit into design and how design fits into an overall development process. Of course, there are many different viable development processes, so this chapter will focus on one—the Rapid Object-oriented Process for Embedded System (ROPES)—and use this to explain how design in general, and patterns in particular, fit into the development of real-time and embedded systems. The first part of Chapter 3 introduces the ROPES process, and the latter part discusses the structure and use of design patterns, including the identification, use, and application of design patterns.

Chapter 1

Introduction

This chapter discusses the following.

- Basic modeling concepts of the UML; overview of the UML; definition of design patterns

- Class and object models—what they are; how classes and objects work together in collaborations; collaborations; packaging of logical elements

- Component and deployment models; representing run-time artifacts and localizing them on processor nodes—State machines and behavioral models

- Use case and requirements models; capturing black-box behavior without revealing internal structure

1.1 Basic Modeling Concepts of the UML

The Unified Modeling Language (UML) is a third-generation object-modeling language standard, owned by the Object Management Group (OMG). The initial version of the OMG UML standard, 1.1, was released in November 1997. Since then, a number of minor revisions have been made. As of this writing, the current standard is 1.4 [1] and is available from the OMG at *www.omg.org*.

The response from the development community to the introduction of the UML has been overwhelming. The UML is now the de facto standard for software modeling. There are a number of reason for this, and it is the totality of all of them that, I believe, accounts for the phenomenal success of the UML.

First, the UML has a well-defined underlying semantic model, called the UML metamodel. This semantic model is both broad (covering most of the aspects necessary for the specification and design of systems) and deep (meaning that it is possible to create *executable models* that can be executed as-is or be used to generate source-level code for compilation). The upshot is that the developer can fairly easily model any aspect of the system that he or she needs to understand and represent.

Second, the notation used by the UML is easy to master and, for the most part, simple to understand. Although some people claim that the UML has *too many diagrams*, in reality there are only a few: structure (class) diagrams, deployment diagrams, statecharts, activity charts, and use case and sequence diagrams. They work in the obvious way and use a few common principles. Although the breadth of the notation can be a bit overwhelming to newcomers, in reality, complex systems can be easily developed with three core diagrams: class diagrams, statecharts, and sequence diagrams. The other diagrams can be used to model additional aspects of the system (such as capturing requirements or how the software maps onto the underlying hardware).

Third, the UML is a *standard*, rather than most modeling languages that are both proprietary and single-sourced. Using a standard means that the developer can select both tools and services from many different sources. For example, there are at least a couple of dozen different UML modeling tools. The availability of different modeling tools enables the developer to find tools that emphasize the aspects of development that may be important to them at a cost point that makes sense for their business or project. For example, Rhapsody from I-Logix emphasizes the deep semantics of the UML, allowing the validation and testing of the user's models via execution of the model using the UML notation. This execution can take place on the host development machine or on the final target hardware, and the generated code can then be used in the final delivered system. Other tools emphasize other aspects, such as drawing the diagrams but permitting more flexibility for a lower price point. The availability of so many different tools in the market gives the developer a great deal of latitude in tool selection. It also encourages innovation and improvement in the tools themselves. Because the UML is such as well-adopted standard, many companies provide training in the use and application of the UML. Indeed, the UML is taught in many college courses. My previous books [2, 3] are in use in undergraduate and graduate courses in many different universities throughout the world.

Last, the UML is *applicable*. Being a third-generation object-oriented modeling language, we now have person-centuries of experience applying object-oriented methods to the development of systems, including real-time and embedded systems. We have strengthened support for ideas that have worked well in the Darwinian world of systems development and removed those things that weren't useful. The UML is used today to model and build systems that vary in scope from simple one- or two-person projects up to those employing literally hundreds of developers. The UML supports *all* the things necessary to model timeliness and resource management that characterize real-time and embedded systems. That means that the developer need not leave the UML to design the different aspects of their system, regardless of how complex or arcane those things might be.

In this chapter, we introduce the basics of the UML. This is not meant to supplant other books about the UML but to provide enough information to understand and utilize the concepts and patterns that form the main content of this book. For a more in-depth discussion of the UML, the reader is referred to the references at the end of the chapter. Additionally, there are many whitepapers available on the I-Logix Web site: *www.ilogix.com.*

1.2 Models

The purpose of the UML is to allow the user to define a model of the system. A model is an integrated, coherent set of abstractions that represents the system to be designed. The model consists of both the semantics and the user views of those semantics. The important part of the user model is the definition of the semantics of the system under development. These semantics have three primary aspects: structural, behavioral, and functional. The structural aspect of the model identifies the "things" that make up the system. For example, a set of objects and their relations represents the state or condition of the system at some point in time—a "snapshot" view. The set of classes and their relationships specify the possible sets of objects and object relations that may exist at run-time. The difference is that the objects exist at run-time while the classes (being a specification) exist only at design time. At a larger scale, subsystems (basically big objects or classes) and components (also basically big objects or classes) form larger-scale abstractions for more complex systems. These concepts allow you to think about and manipulate the system at different levels of abstraction, which is *required* to build today's more complex and comprehensive systems.

The behavioral aspect of the model defines how the structural elements work and interact in the executing system. Behavior can be modeled and viewed for individual structural elements or for assemblies of structural elements working together to achieve larger-scale behaviors. For individual structural elements, such as objects, classes, subsystems, components, or use cases, the UML provides statecharts and activity diagrams to specify the actions and their permitted sequencing. Interactions are used to model how assemblies of structural elements, called *collaborations,* work together over time to achieve larger-scale behaviors. The UML uses two kinds of interaction diagrams: sequence and collaboration diagrams. Of these, sequence diagrams are by far more commonly used.

Finally, system functional aspects refer to required behavior without regard to the implementation of that behavior. In the UML, functional aspects are modeled as use cases; the detailed requirements of use cases are modeled using statecharts and interaction diagrams.

With the use of the UML, the user creates the application model. The goal is to create an application model that is complete, consistent, and accurate. If done properly, this model can be verified via analysis or execution and can (and should!) be used to generate the source level code to implement the system. This code can be automatically generated if you're using a tool such as Rhapsody, or it can be generated by hand. There are many advantages to automatic code generation, such as reduction of effort and the maintenance of consistency between the UML model and the code, but either approach can be used to create the final system.

As mentioned previously, the application model consists of the semantics and all the views. The views reflect some particular set of the system semantics shown at some specific level of abstraction. The semantics are the sum of the semantics represented in the multitude of views, so it isn't necessary to show all the semantics in a single view. The views, however, are very useful. For one thing, they provide a very usable approach for the entry of the semantic information into the model. By drawing the classes on class diagrams, for example, we can define the structural semantics of that part of the system. By drawing the statechart for those classes, we enter the behavioral semantics for those elements. Thus, there is *in principle* a tight coupling between the set of diagrams you draw and the semantic model you construct of the system. That is one of the primary advantages of using a design automation tool as opposed to a drawing tool, such as Visio or Powerpoint. The design automation tool not only allows you to draw the diagrams but also manages the semantics of the application, making sure that they are consistent, performing checks on those semantics, and even validating the model through simulation or execution.

Now that we understand, in general terms, what a model is, let us discuss the semantic elements of the model and how to represent them on UML diagrams.

1.3 Structural Elements and Diagrams

The UML has a rather rich set of structural elements, and it provides diagrammatic views for related sets of them.

1.3.1 Small Things: Objects, Classes, and Interfaces

There are a number of elementary structural concepts in the UML that show up in user models: object, class, data type, and interface. These structural elements form the basis of the structural design of the user model. In its simplest form, an *object* is a data structure bound together with operations that act on that data. An object only exists at run-time; that is, while the system is executing, an object may occupy some location in memory at some specific time. The data known to an object are stored in *attributes*—simple, primitive variables local to that object. The behaviors that act on that data are called *methods*. These are the services invoked by clients of that object (typically other objects) or by other methods existing within the object.

A class is the design-time specification of a set of objects. That is, the objects are *instances* of the class. A class may have many instances in the system during run-time, but an object is an instance of only a single class. A class may specify a statechart that coordinates and manages the execution of its primitive behaviors (called *actions*, which are often invocations of the methods defined in the class) into allowable sets of sequences driven by the different events received. Statecharts are discussed later in this chapter.

For example, a *Sensor* class may contain attributes such as *value* (of the physical thing it is monitoring) and *calibrationConstant* and have methods such as *acquire* (to get a sensed value), *getValue* (to return the last acquired value to the client on request), and *setCalibrationConstant* (for the calibration of the sensor). Diagrammatically, the *Sensor* class can be shown as it is in Figure 1-1. This view option shows three segments. The first gives the name of the class—in this case, *Sensor.* The middle segment gives a list of the attributes. The bottom segment shows the methods. The lists of attributes and methods don't need to be complete; in fact, it is very common to only show the features of the class relevant to the purpose of the diagram and not show those unrelated to the purpose of the diagram. Other features of the sensor class might be shown on other diagrams or appear in no diagram at all, being visible only when browsing the object repository of the UML tool or in a report generated from that repository.

Figure 1-1 shows two other classes as well with a line (called an *association*—more on that later) connecting them to the *Sensor* class. The first is the *Filter* class. This class offers services for filtering the data acquired by the *Sensor* class. It is shown in the figure using the same display format as the *Sensor* class. The other is the *SensorClient* class; its features are hidden. In this view, called the *canonical form*, only the class name is shown on the diagram. To view its features, it is necessary to browse the model repository or look on another diagram.

An *interface* is a named collection of operations. While it is not required to do usable modeling, interfaces allow you to separate out a set of services that may be called on a class from the implementation of those services. As we've seen, a class contains *methods*, which include the lines of code that implement the service. An operation is a specification of the service that does not include this implementation. To be well formed, the operation should define the signature for invoking the service, including the required parameters and return value (if any), plus the preconditional and postconditional invariants of the operation. Preconditional invariants are things that must be true prior to the invocation of the service, while

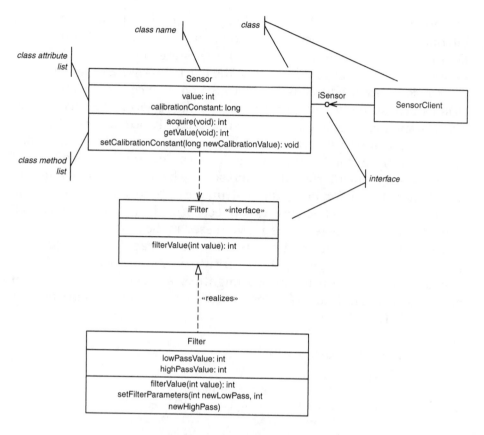

Figure 1-1: *Basic Class Diagram*

postconditional invariants are things that the operation guarantees are true upon its completion.

Interfaces may not have attributes or methods, and they are not directly instantiable. A class is said to *realize* an interface if it provides a method for every operation specified in the interface and those methods have the same names, parameters, return values, preconditions and post-conditions of the corresponding operations in the interface.

Interfaces may be shown in two forms. One looks like a class except for the key word interface placed inside guillemet, as in «interface». This form, called a *stereotype* in UML, is used when you want to show the oper-ations of the interface. The other form, commonly referred to as the "lol-lipop" notation, is a small named circle on the side of the class. Both forms are shown in Figure 1-1. When the lollipop is used, only the name of the interface is apparent. When the stereotyped form is used, a list of operations of the interface may be shown. In the figure, the *Sensor* class is said to *depend* on the interface *iFilter,* while the *Filter* class *realizes* that interface.

Interfaces are used to ensure interface compliance—that is, the client class can consistently and correctly invoke the services of a server class. There is another means to ensure interface compliance that uses the generalization relation from what is called *abstract classes* (classes that may not be directly instantiated). Abstract classes define operations but not methods, just as an interface does, and so may be used to ensure interface compliance. Either (or both, for that matter) approach can be used to ensure that the clients and servers connect correctly at run-time. Generalization and other class relations are discussed in the next section.

Of course, the UML model must ultimately map to source code. In Java and C++, the mapping is straightforward. The source code for such a class diagram in Java is the most straightforward because Java contains interfaces as a native concept. The Java source code would look like the Java code in Code Listing 1.

Code Listing 1: Class Diagram in Java

```
public SensorClient {
     protected myISensor iSensor;
     public void displayValue(void) {
          int sensedValue = iSensor.getValue();
          System.out.println(value);
     };
}; // end class SensorClient

interface iSensor {
     int acquire(void);
     int getValue(void);
     void setCalibrationConstant(long
          newCalibrationConstant);
}; // end interface iSensor

public class Sensor implements iSensor {
     protected iFilter myIFilter;

     int value;
     long calibrationConstant;

     public int acquire(void){ /* method here */ };
     public int getValue(void) {
```

```
              return myIFilter.filter(value); };
        public void setCalibrationConstant(long
            newCalibrationConstant) {
            calibrationConstant = newCalibrationConstant;
            };
}; // end class Sensor

interface iFilter {
    public int filterValue(int value);
}; // end interface iFilter

public class Filter implements iFilter {
    int lowPass;
    int highPass;
    public int filtervalue(int value) {
        /* method here */
    };
    public setFilterParameters(int newLowPass,
        int newHighPass) {
        lowPass = newLowPass;
        highPass = newHighPass;
    };
}; // end class Filter
```

In C++, the code is almost as straightforward as the Java code, but not quite, because an interface is not a native concept in C++. There are two common approaches to implement interfaces is C++. The first, shown in Code Listing 2, is to create an *abstract base class* by declaring the interface operations as pure virtual. The other common approach is to use the *Interface* or *Façade* pattern. This involves creating the interface class as an instantiable class that associates to a separate implementation class.

Code Listing 2: Class Diagram in C++

```
class SensorClient {
protected:
    iSensor* myISensor;
public:
    void displayValue(void) {
        int sensedValue = iSensor.getValue();
        cout << value << endl;
    };
};

class iSensor { // abstract class
```

```
public :
      virtual int acquire(void)=0; // pure virtual
      virtual int getValue(void)=0; // pure virtual
      virtual void setCalibrationConstant(long
            newCalibrationConstant)=0;

};

class Sensor : public iSensor {
protected :
      iFilter* myIFilter;
      int value;
      long calibrationConstant;
public :
      int acquire(void);
      int getValue(void){
            return myIFilter->filterValue(value);
      };
      void setCalibrationConstant(long
            newCalibrationConstant) {
            calibrationConstant =
                  newCalibrationConstant;
      };
};

class iFilter {
public :
      virtual int filterValue(int value)=0;
            // pure virtual
};

class Filter : public iFilter {
public :
      int filterValue(int value) {
            lowPass = newLowPass;
            highPass = newHighPass;
      };

};
```

In summary, an object is one of possibly many *instances* of a class. A class has two notable features: attributes (which store data values) and methods (which provide services to clients of the class). Interfaces are named collections of operations that are *realized* by classes. Interfaces need not be explicitly modeled. Many useful systems have been designed solely with classes, but there are times when the additional level of abstraction is useful, particularly when more than a single implementation of an interface will be provided.

1.3.2 Relations

Classes, objects, and interfaces are little things. To do anything system-wide, many of these small things need to work together. And to work together, they must relate in some way.

1.3.2.1 Associations

The UML defines a number of different kinds of relations. The most important of these are association, generalization, and dependency. The most basic of these is called the *association*. An association is a design-time relation between classes that specifies that at run-time, instances of those classes may have a *link* and may be able to request services of one another.

The UML defines three distinct kinds of associations: association, aggregation, and composition. An association between classes means simply that at some time during the execution of the system, those objects may have a link that enables them to call or somehow invoke services of the other. Nothing is stated about *how* that is accomplished, or even whether it is a synchronous method call (although this is most common) or an asynchronous message transfer. Think of associations as conduits that allow objects at run-time to find each other and send messages. Associations are shown as lines connecting classes on class diagrams.

There are a number of aspects of an association between two classes that can be specified. For example, the ends of the associations may have *role names*. These name the instances with respect to the other class. It is a common practice to give the role name on the opposite end of the association to the pointer that points to that class. For example, in Figure 1-2, the *Switch* class might contain two pointers—one named *primarySource* and one named *backupSource*—that would be dereferenced at run-time to send the instance of the *Charger* and *Battery* classes messages, such as to enable or disable them.

Although somewhat less common, *association labels* may also be used, such as between the *Power Subsystem* and *Display Subsystem* classes. The label is normally used to help explain why the association exists between the two classes. In this case, the label "displays messages for" indicates that is how the *Power Subsystem* intends to use the *Display Subsystem.* To get the directionality of the label (is the *Power Subsystem* displaying messages for the *Display Subsystem*?), you can add an arrowhead next to the label to show the speaking perspective.

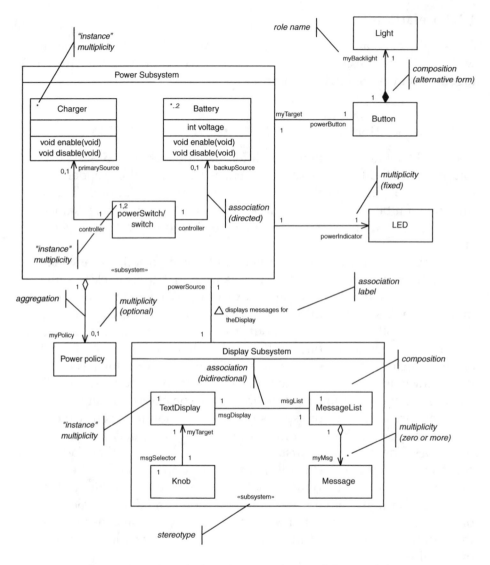

Figure 1-2: *Association, Aggregation, and Composition*

The *multiplicity* is probably the most important property of an association end. The multiplicity of an association end indicates the possible numbers of instances that can participate in the association role at run-time. This may be any of the following.

- A fixed number, such as "1" or "3"
- A comma-separated list, such as "0,1" or "3,5,7"
- A range, such as "1..10"
- A combination of a list and a range, such as "1..10, 25", which means "one to ten, inclusive, or 25"
- An asterisk, which means "zero or more"
- An asterisk with an endpoint, such as "1..*," which means "one or more"

In Figure 1-2, we see multiplicities on all the associations. Multiplicity is shown at the role end of the class to which it applies. Thus, each *Switch* object associates with zero or one *Charger* object, but each *Charger* object associates with exactly one *Switch* object.

Finally, the directionality of the association may be specified. A normal line with no arrowheads means that the association is bidirectional; that is, an object at either end of the association may send a message to an object at the other end. If only one of the objects can send a message to the other and not vice versa, then we add an *open arrowhead* (we'll see later that the type of arrowhead matters) pointing in the direction of the message flow. Thus, we see that a *Switch* object can send a message to a *Battery* object, but not vice versa. This does not imply that the *Switch* object cannot retrieve a value from a *Battery* object because it can call a method that returns a value. It means, however, that an object of type *Battery* cannot spontaneously send a message to a *Switch* object.

All of these adornments, except for perhaps multiplicity, are optional and may be added as desired to further clarify the relationships between the respective classes.

An association between classes means that at some point during the lifecycle of instances of the associated classes, there *may be* a link that enables them to exchange messages. Nothing is stated or implied about which of these objects comes into existence first, which other object creates them, or how the link is formed.

1.3.2.2 Aggregation

An aggregation is a specialized kind of association that indicates a "whole-part" relation exists between the two objects. The "whole" end is marked with a white diamond, as in Figure 1-2. For example, consider, the classes *Message List* and *Message.* The *Message List* class is clearly a "whole" that aggregates possibly many *Message* elements. The diamond on the aggregation relation shows that the *Message List* is the "whole." The "*" on the *myMsg* association end indicates that the list may contain zero or more Message elements. If we desired to constrain this to be no more than 100 messages, we could have made the multiplicity "0..100."

Since aggregation is a specialized form of association, all of the properties and adornments that apply to associations also apply to aggregations, including navigation, multiplicity, role names, and association labels.

Aggregation is a relatively weak form of "whole-part," as we'll see in a moment. No statement is made about lifecycle dependency or creation/destruction responsibility. Indeed, aggregation is normally treated in design and implementation identically to association. Nevertheless, it can be useful to aid in understanding the model structure and the relations among the conceptual elements from the problem domain.

1.3.2.3 Composition

Composition is a strong form of aggregation in which the "whole" (also known as the "composite") has the explicit responsibility for the creation and destruction of the part objects. Because of this, the composite exists before the parts come into existence, and it exists after they are destroyed. If the parts have a fixed multiplicity with respect to the composite, then it is common to create those parts in its constructor (a special operation that creates the object) and destroy them in its destructor. With nonfixed multiplicities, the composite dynamically creates and destroys the part objects during its execution. Because the composite has creation and destruction responsibility, each part object can only be owned by a *single* composite object, although the part objects may participate in other association and aggregation relations. Composition is also a kind of association, so it can likewise have all of the adornments available to ordinary associations.

Composition has two common presentations: nested class boxes and a filled-in diamond. There is no semantic difference between the two, and individual preferences vary. Personally, because composition is so distinct from aggregation, I prefer to nest the class boxes on the diagrams, but your mileage may vary.

Figure 1-2 shows both forms. The *Power Subsystem*, for example, is a composite class that contains parts of type *Charger*, *Battery*, and *Switch*. The *Button* class is also a composite that contains a single *Light* part. With the containment presentation, there is an issue as to how to show the multiplicity of the part (by definition, the multiplicity on the whole end of a composition is exactly "1"). Since there is no line on which to place the multiplicity, it is common to put the multiplicity in one of the upper corners of the part class. This is called *instance multiplicity.* We see that the *Power Subsystem* contains either one or two objects of type *Switch*, zero or more objects of type *Charger*, and zero to two objects of type *Battery.*

There is also the issue of how to show the role names. The common way is to use a class role name. A class role name precedes the class name and a slash (/) separator. In the figure, instances of class *Switch* have a class role name of *PowerSwitch*. As an aside, we can also show object names if we like, independently from the class role names. An object name is shown as preceding the class name, with a colon (:) separator. Thus,

PowerSwitch/ thePowerSwitch: Switch

shows a role called *PowerSwitch* that is played by an object named *thePowerSwitch*, which happens to be an instance of class *Switch.*

The most common implementation of an association, as seen in the previous code examples, is an object pointer (in C++) or an object reference (in Java). This is true regardless of which kind of association it is, whether it is an ordinary association, an aggregation, or a composition. There are many other ways of implementing an association—including nested class declaration, object identifier reference (as in a MS Windows handle or a CORBA object ID), an operating system task ID, and so on—but using a pointer is the most common.

A Word About Stereotypes   Figure 1-2 has a couple of places where a class has a special adornment called a *stereotype*. A stereotype is a way of tailoring the UML to meet a specific need or purpose. It is part of the lightweight extension mechanism defined within the UML. A stereotype is a user-defined kind of element that is based on some already defined element in the UML, such as *Class, Operation, Association,* and so on. Stereotypes are usually shown by attaching the stereotype name in guillemets with the stereotyped element or shown using a user-defined icon. In the example figure, a class box is used for a large-scale element called a *Subsystem*. To indicate that this is that special kind of element, we attach the stereotype «subsystem» to the class box. Subsystems are discussed later in this chapter.

1.3.2.4 Generalization

The generalization relation in the UML means that one class defines a set of features that is either specialized or extended in another. Generalization may be thought of as "is a type of" relation and therefore only has a design-time impact rather than a run-time impact.

Generalization has many uses in class models. First, generalization is used as a means to ensure interface compliance, much in the same way that interfaces are used. Indeed, it is the most common way to implement interfaces in languages that do not have interfaces as a native concept, such as in C++. Also, generalization can simplify your class models because a set of features common to a number of classes can be abstracted together into a single superclass, rather than having to redefine the same structure independently in many different classes. In addition, generalization allows for different realizations to be used interchangeably. For example, one realization subclass might optimize worst-case performance, while another optimizes memory size, while yet another optimizes reliability because of internal redundancy.

Generalization in the UML means two things. First, it means *inheritance*—that subclasses have (at least) the same attributes, operations, methods, and relations as the superclasses they specialize. Of course, if the subclasses were *identical* with their superclasses, that would be boring, so subclasses can differ from their superclasses in either or both of two ways: specialization or extension.

Subclasses can *specialize* operations or state machines of their superclasses. Specializing means that the same operation (or action list on the statechart) is implemented differently than in the superclass. This is commonly called *polymorphism.* In order to make this work, when a class has an association with another that is a superclass, at run-time an instance of the first can invoke an operation declared in the second, and if the link is actually to a subclass instance, the operation of the subclass is invoked rather than that of the superclass.

This is much easier to see in the example presented in Figure 1-3. The class *MsgQueue* is a superclass, and it defines standard queue-like behavior, storing *Message* objects in a FIFO fashion with operations such as *insert()* and *remove().* *CachedQueue* specializes and extends *MsgQueue* (the closed arrowhead on the generalization line points to the more general class). The *Communicator* class associates with the base class *MsgQueue*. If it needs to store only a few messages, a standard in-memory queue—that is, an instance of *MsgQueue*—works fine. But what if some particular instance of

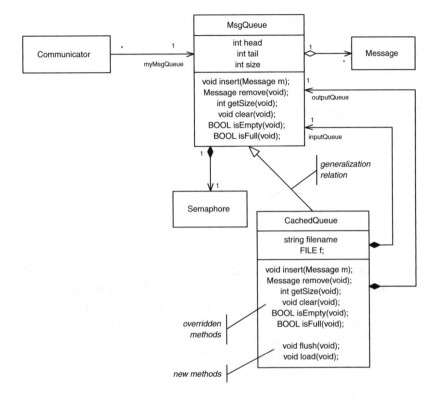

Figure 1-3: *Polymorphism*

Communicator needs to store millions of messages? In that case, the instance can link to an instance of the *CachedQueue* subclass. Whether Communicator actually links to an instance of *MsgQueue* or one of its subclasses is unknown to the instance of *Communicator.* It calls the insert() or remove() operations as necessary. If the connected instance is of class *MsgQueue,* then the correct operations for that class are called. If the connected instance is of class *CachedQueue,* then the operations for that class are invoked instead, but the client of the queue doesn't know which is invoked.

It is common not to show inherited methods in the subclass unless they override (redefine) methods inherited from the superclass, but this is merely a stylistic convention. Remember that a *CachedQueue* is a *MsgQueue,* so everything that is true about the latter is true of the former, including the attributes, operations, and relations. For example, *CachedQueue* aggregates zero or more *Message* objects and has a composition relation to the class *Semaphore* because its superclass does. However, in this case, the operations for insert and remove are likely to work differently.

For example, *MsgQueue::insert()* might be written as shown in Code Listing 1-3.

Code Listing 1-3: MsgQueue::insert() operation

```
void MsgQueue::insert(Message m) {
        if (isFull())
                throw OVERFLOW;
        else {
                head = (head + 1) % size;
                list[head] = m;
                };
        };
```

However, the code for the insert operation in the subclass must be more complex. First, note that the subclass contains (via composition) two *MsgQueues:* one for input buffering and one for output buffering. The *CachedQueue::insert()* operation only uses the *MsgQueue* instance playing the *inputQueue* role. If this is full, then it must write the buffer out to disk and zero out the buffer. The code to do this is shown in Code Listing 1-4.

Code Listing 1-4: CachedQueue::insert() operation

```
void CachedQueue::insert(Message m) {
        if (inputQueue->isFull()) {
                // flush the full queue to disk and then
                // clear it flush();
                inputQueue->clear();
                };
        inputQueue->insert(m);
        };
```

Similarly, the operations for *remove(), getSize(), clear(), isEmpty(),* and *isFull()* need to be overridden as well to take into account the use of two internal queues and a disk file.

Note that in the UML, attributes cannot be specialized. If the superclass defines an attribute of time *sensedValue* and it has a type *int,* then all subclasses also have that attribute, and it is of the same type. Subclasses can also *extend* the superclass—that is, they can have new attributes, operations, states, transitions, relations, and so forth. If you need to change the type of an attribute, you should use the «bind» stereotype of dependency, discussed in Section 1.3.2.5.

The other thing that generalization means in the UML is *substitutability*. This means that anyplace an instance of the superclass was used, an instance of the subclass can also be used without breaking the system in any overt way. Substitutability is what makes generalization immensely useful in designs.

Figure 1-4 shows the previous queue example in a larger context. In this example, *CachedQueue* is still a subclass of *MsgQueue*. We see that *MsgQueue* also has a composition relation to a semaphore to ensure its integrity if it is called in the presence of multiple threads. We see the *MsgQueue* superclass has two different kinds of clients: end user clients (who want to send and receive messages), which are types of *Communicating Object*, and *Communicators*, which use the queue to do transmission and reception of the queues. Both of these are abstract, which means that they define at least one operation for which they do not supply a corresponding method. In C++ terms, they are *pure virtual* classes. The intended usage of these classes is that a class that wants to be able to send and receive messages will subclass from *Communicating Object*, and a class that wants to be able to use queues to perform transmission and reception will subclass *Communicator*.

1.3.2.5 Dependency

Association, in its various forms, and generalization are the really key relations defined within the UML. Nevertheless, there are several more relations that are useful. They are put under the umbrella of *dependency*. The UML defines four different primary kinds of dependency: Abstraction, Binding, Usage, and Permission. Each of these may be further stereotyped. For example, «refine» and «realize» are both stereotypes of the Abstraction relationship, and «friend» is a stereotype of Permission. All of these special forms of dependency are shown as a stereotyped dependency (dashed line with an open arrowhead).

Arguably, the most useful stereotypes of dependency are «bind», «usage», and «friend». Certainly, they are the most commonly seen, but there are others. The reader is referred to [1] for the complete list of "official" stereotypes.

The «bind» stereotype binds a set of actual parameters to a formal parameter list. This is used to specify parameterized classes (templates in C++-speak or generics in Ada-speak). This is particularly important in

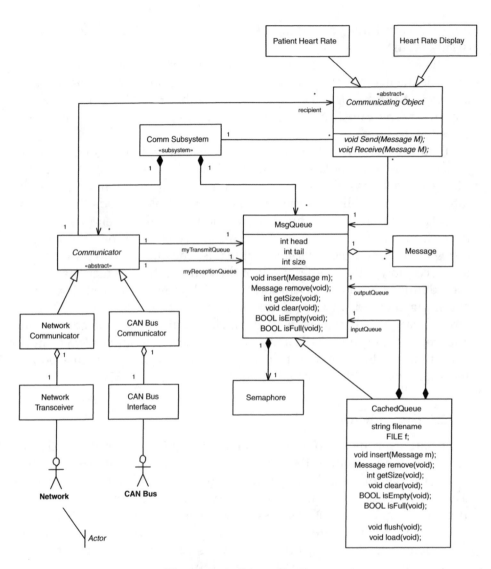

Figure 1-4: *Generalization*

patterns because patterns themselves are parameterized collaborations, and they are often defined in terms of parameterized classes.

A parameterized class is a class that is defined in terms of more primitive elements that are referred to symbolically without the inclusion of the actual element that will be used. The symbolic name is called a *formal parameter,* and the actual element, when bound, is called an *actual parameter.* In Figure 1-5, *Queue* is a parameterized class that is defined in terms of two symbolic elements: a class called *Element* and an int called *Size.* Because the exact elements that these parameters refer to are not provided in the definition of *Queue, Queue* is not an instantiable class; those undefined elements must be given definitions. The «bind» dependency does exactly that—binding a list of actual elements to the formal parameter list. In the case of *MsgQueue, Element* is replaced by the class *Message,* and the int *Size* is replaced by the literal constant 1000. Now that the actual parameters are specified and bound, *MsgQueue* is an instantiable class, meaning that we can create objects of this class at run-time.

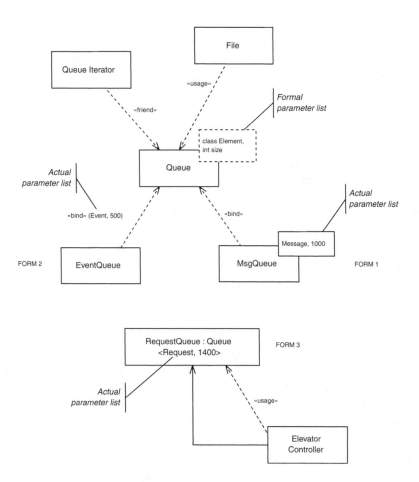

Figure 1-5: *Dependency*

The diagram shows three common forms for showing the «bind» dependency. Form 1 is the most common, but the other forms are prevalent as well.

The Usage relation indicates some element requires the presence of another for its correct operation. The UML provides a number of specific forms, such as «call» (between two operations), «create» (between classifiers, e.g., classes) , «instantiate» (between classifiers), and «send» (between an operation and a signal). Of these, «call» is common, as well as an unspecified «usage» between components, indicating that one component needs another because some of the services in one invoke some set of services in the other.

The Permission relation grants permission for a model element to access elements in another. The «friend» stereotype is a common one between classes, modeling the *friend* keyword in C++. «access» is similar to Ada's *use* keyword, granting access of a namespace of one Ada package to another. The «import» relation adds the public elements of one namespace (such as a UML package) into another.

1.3.3 Structural Diagrams

UML is a graphical modeling language, although, perhaps surprisingly, the notation is nonnormative for the language. Nevertheless, there is a common set of graphical icons and idioms for creating these views of the underlying model. We call these views "diagrams." UML has been unjustly criticized for having too many diagram types—class diagrams, package diagrams, object diagrams, component diagrams, and so on. The fact is that these are all *really the same diagram type*—a structural diagram. Each of these diagrams emphasizes a different aspect of the model, but they may each contain all of the elements in the others. A package diagram may contain classes, and a class diagram may contain objects, whereas a component diagram might have objects, classes, and packages. In truth, the UML has a *structural* diagram that we call by different names to indicate the primary purpose of the diagram.

We use diagrams for a number of different purposes: as a data entry mechanism, as a means to understand the contents of the model, and as a means to discuss and review the model. The model itself is the totality of the concepts in your system and their relations to one another. When we use diagrams as a data entry mechanism, we add, modify, or remove elements to the underlying model as we draw and manipulate the diagrams.

The most common diagrams you'll draw are the class diagrams. These diagrams emphasize the organization of classes and their relations. The other aspects are drawn as needed, but class diagrams provide the primary structural view.

In real systems, you really cannot draw the entire system in a single diagram, even if you use E-size plotter paper and a 4-point font. As a practical matter, you must divide up your system into different structural views (behavioral views will be described later). How, then, can we effectively do this? What criteria should we use to decide how many diagrams we need and what should go on them?

In the ROPES process [3], we use a simple criterion for decomposing the views of the system into multiple diagrams. The ROPES process introduces the concept of a *mission* of an artifact—its "purpose for existence." For diagrams, the mission is straightforward: Each diagram should show a *single important concept.* This might be to show the elements in a collaboration of objects or classes realizing a use case, or a generalization taxonomy, or the contents of a package. Usually, every element of your model appears in some diagram somewhere, but it is perfectly reasonable for it to appear in several diagrams. For example, a class might be involved in the realization of three use cases (resulting in three different diagrams), be a part of a generalization taxonomy, and also be contained in a package of your model. In this case, one might expect it to appear in five different diagrams. It is also not necessary for all aspects of the class to be shown in all views. For example, in the class diagrams showing collaborations, only the operations and attributes directly involved in the mission of that collaboration would be shown; in a diagram showing generalization, only the features added or modified by that class would be shown; in a diagram showing the contents of the package that owns the class, you probably wouldn't show any attributes or operations.

Which of the views is right? The answer is *all of them.* Just because a feature of a class or some other element isn't shown doesn't mean or imply that the feature doesn't exist or is wrong. The semantics of the class or model element is the sum of the semantic statements made in *all* diagrams in which it appears. Indeed, you can define model elements without explicitly drawing them on diagrams at all. One of the most valuable things that modeling tools provide over simple drawing tools is the maintenance of the semantic information about the structure and behavior of your system.

Normally, you don't draw object diagrams directly. Most often, classes and class relations are drawn, and these imply the possible sets of objects and their relations. If for some reason you want to depict particular configurations of the run-time system, the object diagrams are the appropriate venue.

1.3.4 Big Things: Subsystems, Components, and Packages

Classes, objects, and interfaces are little things. It takes collaborations of many of them to have systemwide behavior. Because of the complexity of today's systems, it is unusual to find a system that can be effectively developed and managed without thinking about larger-scale structures. The UML does provide a number of concepts to manage systems in the large scale, although most of the literature has not effectively explained or demonstrated the use of these features. And, to be honest, the UML specification does not explain them and how they interrelate very well either.

Since the focus of this book is architectural design patterns, we will use these concepts extensively in the patterns that form the bulk of this book, so it behooves us to be clear and precise about these concepts and how we'll apply them.

Packages are model elements that can contain other model elements, including other packages. Packages are used to subdivide models to permit teams of developers to manipulate and work effectively together. Packages cannot be instantiated and can only be used to organize models. They do define a namespace for the model elements that they contain, but have no other semantics. The UML does not provide any criterion as to whether a class should go in this package or that; it merely provides packages as a model building block to aid in whatever organizational purpose the developer desires.

The ROPES process recommends that packages be used with a specific criterion: "common subject matter or common vocabulary." This is similar to the Shaler and Mellor concept of a *domain,* and the ROPES process uses the stereotype «domain» to indicate this particular usage of packages. Indeed the Layered Architecture Patterns in Chapter 4 use «domain» packages to organize a model. This is a special case in which the subsystem organization maps one-to-one to the package structure. However, packages can be used to organize the application model in any desired way.

A package normally contains elements that exist only at design-time—classes and data types—but may also contain use cases and various diagrams, such as sequence and class diagrams. These design pieces are then used to construct collaborations that realize systemwide functionality. Packages are normally the basic Configuration Items for a configuration management tool, rather than the individual classes. Figure 1-6 shows that packages are drawn to look like a tabbed folder and may optionally show the elements that they semantically contain.

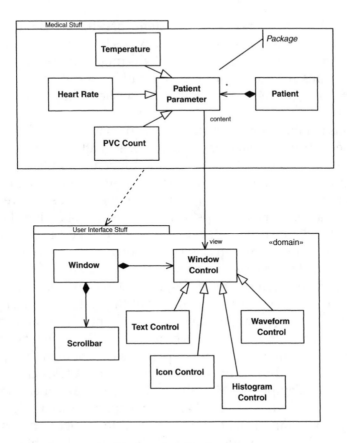

Figure 1-6: *Packages*

Subsystems are different animals, although in the UML 1.4 they are partially based on packages. A Subsystem is a stereotype of both Package and Classifier. This makes subsystems instantiable, meaning that you can create an instance of the type that occupies memory at run-time. A subsystem is used to organize the run-time system consisting of instances; the criterion for inclusion in a subsystem is "common behavioral purpose." The real work of a subsystem is implemented by the run-time instances contained within the subsystem; the subsystem offers up the collaborative behavior of those elements. Subsystems don't do any "real work" in and of themselves. The "real work" is done by what is sometimes called the *semantic objects* of the system—the primitive objects that actually perform the bottom-level functionality. A subsystem is at a higher level of abstraction of the system than these primitive semantic objects, and this level of abstraction allows us to view and manipulate the structure and behavior of complex systems much more easily.

Subsystems have three aspects: operation, specification, and implementation. The operations are the set of services directly offered by the Subsystem.

Various notations for subsystems are shown in Figure 1-7. One notation shows the «subsystem» stereotype of a package with segments for the specification and realization elements (a fork can be used in lieu of the stereotype). However, because a Subsystem is *also* a subclass of Classifier, it is also reasonable to show Subsystems as a stereotype of Class as well. And, in fact, this is a common way to show subsystems—showing the run-time instances that do the real work of the subsystem as being contained via the composition relation between classes, as shown at the bottom of the figure.

Like the metatype *Class,* a *Component* is also a kind of *Classifier;* it can have methods that realize interfaces, have statecharts and use cases. It is used to represent the replaceable pieces of the system. Typically, components have language-independent opaque[1] interfaces and may have «usage» dependencies on other components. Components are coarse-grained elements that are usually replaced as a whole in the application. Components usually fit into a component framework, such as COM+, CCM (CORBA Component Model), or EJB. These component frameworks provide the means to load or unload the components as needed and standard ways for components to find each and to invoke services on them. As the UML 1.4 specification states, "There are only subtle differences between the semantics of components and classes."

So how, then, are components different from classes and subsystems? The answer is "usage." While components are certainly larger scale than most classes, they differ from both subsystems and classes in that they are used as replaceable building blocks. Components are often purchased, such as math libraries, TCP/IP protocol stacks, or databases, or they may be specially constructed, such as configuration tables or static or dynamic link libraries. In typical usage, they are also designed to work within a specific component framework, and this is less true with subsystems. Finally, Component-Based Development (CBD) approaches use the metaphor of construction through assembly (of existing parts) rather than construction via invention. Where possible, CBD can provide a tremen-

---

1. By "opaque" we mean that the underlying implementation is not visible, just a way to invoke the service.

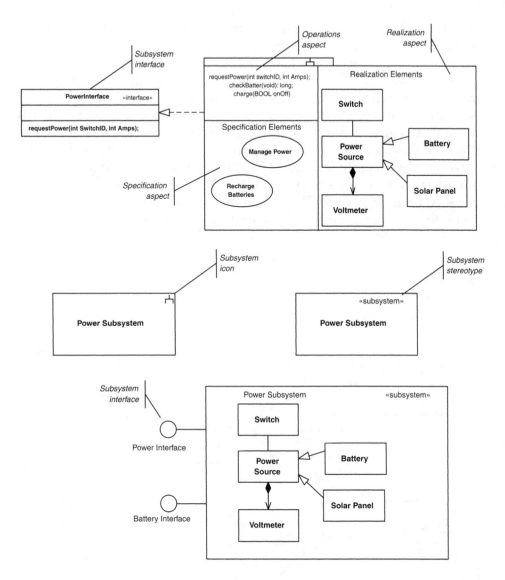

Figure 1-7: *Subsystems*

dous savings of effort and time. That presumes, of course, that the component framework runs on your target hardware environment, suitable components are available for you to purchase, and these components meet your quality of service constraints, such as worst-case performance, memory size, and predictability.

Often, components and subsystems are mixed in with the deployment model, particularly for asymmetric deployment architectures—that is, where the processor location of a component or subsystem is known at design time. Nodes are the only three-dimensional icon in the UML notation and represent the hardware environment on which one or more software entities run (the «processor» node stereotype) or a piece of hardware that is just used but doesn't itself execute software that you write (the «device» node stereotype). Figure 1-8 shows components with the «usage» stereotype. In the figure, the components are placed on processor nodes, but this isn't necessary. Note also the stick figure in Figure 1-8. This is called an actor. An *actor* is an object that is outside the scope of concern but interacts with the element under development in ways that we care

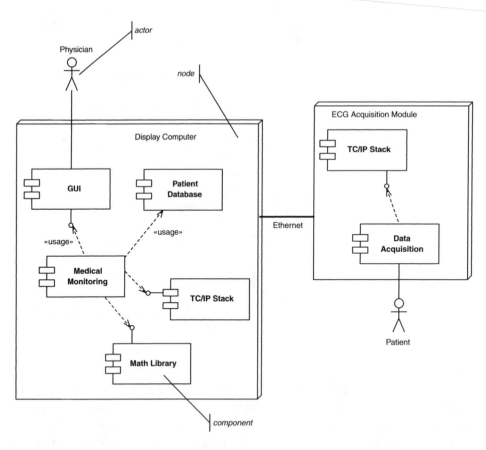

Figure 1-8: *Components*

about. We will see actors used more extensively later in the section about use cases and requirements modeling.

While the concepts of System, Subsystem, and Component are sufficiently flexible to support most any organizational schema you would like to employ, I generally find it useful to use these concepts in a particular sizing. The System (shown with the «system» class stereotype) represents the entire system under development. The largest-scale pieces of the System are «subsystem» objects. Subsystems may in turn contain Components. Components may contain multiple threads, modeled with «active» objects. And the passive or *semantic* objects that do the real "work" of the system run within the «active» objects. For really large projects, you may have all of these levels and perhaps even multiple at one or more levels—for example, you may have multiple layers of subsubsystems before you get to the Component level. For simpler systems, you may not require all of these levels. You might skip Subsystem level and just have Components. You may even find that for very simple systems, you need only the System, «active» objects, and semantic objects. Your mileage may vary in terms of how you apply these concepts, but I have found this a useful way to use the organizational concepts in practice. This size hierarchy is shown in Figure 1-9.

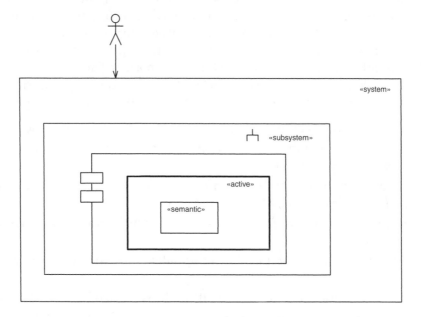

Figure 1-9: *System, Subsystem, Component, and Active Objects Organized by Size*

1.4 Behavioral Elements and Diagrams

What we've discussed so far is the definition of structural elements of the system: classes and objects (in the small) and systems, subsystems, and components (in the large). As developers, we are usually even more concerned about how these structural elements behave dynamically as the system runs. Behavior can be divided up into two distinct perspectives: how structural elements act in isolation and how they act in collaboration.

In the UML metamodel, *ModelElements* are the primary structural elements that have behavior. *Classifiers* (which are types of *ModelElements*) also have *BehavioralFeatures*, specifically *Operations*, and the realization of operations, *Methods*. In practice, we are primarily concerned with the specification of the reactive behavior of only certain *Classifiers* (classes, objects, subsystems, components, and use cases) and certain other *ModelElements* (*Actions, Operations*, and *Methods*).

1.4.1 Actions and Activities

An action is "a specification of an executable statement that forms an abstraction of a computational procedure that results in a change in the state of the model, and can be realized by sending a message to an object or modifying a link or a value of an attribute" [1]. That is, it is a primitive thing, similar in scope to a single statement in a standard source-level language, such as "++X" or "a=b+sin(c*PI)". The UML 1.4 specification identified a number of different kinds of actions such as the following.

- CreateAction—action that results in the creation of an instance
- CallAction—action that results in the synchronous invocation of an Operation or Method
- ReturnAction—action that results in the synchronous return of control to a caller Operation, Method, or Action
- SendAction—action that results in the asynchronous transmission of an event
- TerminateAction—action that terminates the behavior of an ActionSequence
- DestroyAction—action that results in the destruction of an instance
- UninterpretedAction—action that does something unspecified
- ActionSequence—action that has parts, each of which is an action

Actions are normally computationally simple things and, by far, are most commonly represented using an *action language.* The UML does not define an action language because most developers want to use the implementation source level language for the action language. That is, almost all of the time, actions in a UML model are provided in the implementation language of that system. A more abstract action language is possible, providing the ability to generate code in multiple target languages, but the UML does not define one.

Actions have "run-to-completion" semantics, meaning that once an action is started, it will run until it is done. This does not mean that an action cannot be preempted by another action running in a higher-priority thread, only that when the context executing that action returns from preemption, it will continue executing that action until it is complete. This means that if an object is executing an action, that action will run to completion even if that object receives events directing it to do something else. The object will not accept the incoming events until the action has completed.

An *Activity* is an action that runs when a Classifier is in a state and is terminated either when it is complete or when the Classifier changes state. That is, Activities do not have run-to-completion semantics. An object executing an activity may receive an event that triggers a transition, exiting the state and terminating the activity. Thus, the UML allows the modeling, at a primitive level, both interruptable and noninterruptable behaviors.

1.4.2 Operations and Methods

An Operation is a specification of an invocable behavior of a Classifier, whereas a Method is the implementation of an Operation. That is, an Operation is a specification of a Method. Operations are synchronously invoked and are logically associated with CallEvents in the UML metamodel. Operations have typed parameter lists, as you might expect, and can return typed values. It is common to use an operation call as an action on a state behavior.

Modeling of the behavior of an operation is done primarily in two ways. First, and most common, is to simply list, in a textual fashion, all of the actions comprising the internals of the operation or method. The second, which will be described shortly, is to model the operation with a synchronous state machine or with an activity diagram.

1.4.3 Statecharts

A finite state machine (FSM) is a machine specified by a finite set of conditions of existence (called "states") and a likewise finite set of transitions among the states triggered by events. An FSM constrains the behavior of a model element by explicitly stating which events are handled for each of the states of that element, as well as what actions are performed under what conditions.

Actions, such as the invocation of an operation, may be specified to be executed when a state is entered or exited, or when a transition is taken. The order of execution of actions is exit actions of the predecessor state, followed by the transition actions, followed by the entry actions of the subsequent state.

The UML uses statecharts as its formal FSM representation because of their expressiveness and scalability. Statecharts have these notable improvements over "classical" Mealy-Moore FSMs.

- Nested states for specifying hierarchical state membership
- And-states for specifying logical independence and concurrency
- Pseudostates for annotating commonly needed specific dynamic semantics

Figure 1-10 shows some of the basic elements of a statechart—basic or-states and transitions—as well as a few less elementary concepts, including nested states and conditional, initial, and terminal pseudostates.

Transitions are arrowed lines coming from a predecessor state and terminating on a subsequent state. Transitions usually have the optional *event signature* and *action list.* This is the basic form of an event signature.

event-name '('parameter-list')' '['guard']' '/' action-list

The event-name is simply the logical name of the event class that may be sent to an instance of the Classifier at run-time, such as "Send" or "tm" in Figure 1-10. The UML defines four distinct kinds of events that may be passed or handled.

- SignalEvent—an asynchronously sent event
- CallEvent—a synchronously sent event
- TimeEvent—an event due to the passage of an interval of time (most common) or arrival of an epoch
- ChangeEvent—a change in a state variable or attribute of the Classifier

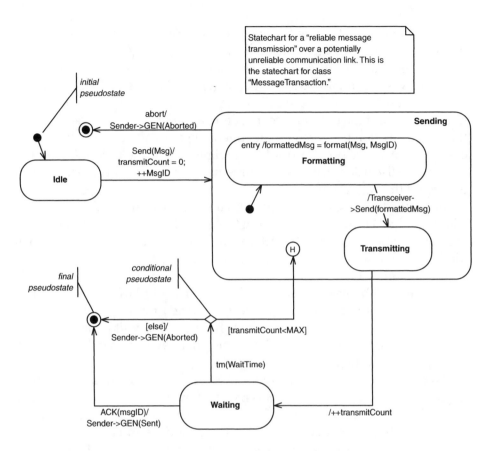

Figure 1-10: *Simple Statechart*

Asynchronous event transfer is always implemented via queuing of the event until the Classifier is ready to process it. That is, the sender "sends and forgets" the event and goes on about its business, ignorant of whether the event has been processed. Synchronous event transfer executes the state processing of the event in the thread of the sender, with the sender blocked from continuing until that state processing is complete. This is commonly implemented by invoking a class method called an event handler that executes the relevant part of the state machine, returning control to the sender only when the event processing is complete.

Events may have parameters, which are typed values accepted by the state machine that may then be used in the guard and actions in the processing of the event. The statechart specifies the formal parameter list, while the object that sends the event must provide the necessary actual parameters to bind to the formal parameter list.

Time events are almost always relative to the entry to a state. A common way to name such an event (and what we will use here) is "tm(interval)," where "interval" is the time interval parameter for the timeout event. If the timeout occurs before another specified event occurs, then the transition triggered by the timeout event will be taken. If another event is sent to the object prior to the triggering of the timeout, then the timeout is discarded. If the state is reentered, the timeout interval starts over from the beginning.

If a transition does not provide a named event trigger, then it is activated by the "completion" or "null" event. This event occurs either as soon as the state is entered (which includes the execution of entry actions for the state) or when the activities complete, if the state declares activities to be executed.

A guard is a Boolean expression that returns only TRUE or FALSE and does not have side effects. If a guard is specified for a transition, then if the event trigger (if any) occurs, then the transition will be taken if and only if the guard evaluates to TRUE. If the guard evaluates to FALSE, then the triggering event is quietly discarded.

The action list for the transition is executed if and only if the transition is taken. That is, the named event is received by the object while it is in the predecessor state, and the guard, if any, evaluates to TRUE. The entire set of actions—that is exit actions, transition actions, and entry actions—is executed in that order and is executed using run-to-completion semantics, as noted previously.

In addition to entry and exit actions, states may also have activities that, as noted previously, are actions that may be interrupted by incoming events that trigger named reactions in the specified state.

Figure 1-11 shows an important additional concept in statecharts: and-states. While or-states are disjoint and exclusive, and-states are disjoint but not nonexclusive. Given a set of or-states, the object must be in one and only one or-state in a state context. Given a set of and-states, the object must be in *every* active and-state simultaneously. In Figure 1-11, the object only has a single high-level state: Operating. The Operating state, however, has two and-substates: Processing and Testing. The fact that these are and-states is denoted with the dashed-line separating them. This means that while in the Operating state, the object must be in *both* Processing and Testing state. Since each of these two substates have sub-or-

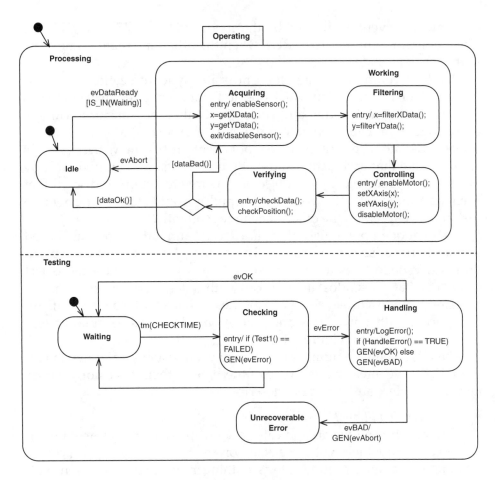

Figure 1-11: *And-States*

states, any combination of a single or-state from each of the two and-states is semantically correct. For example, the object could be in Idle and Checking or Handling and Controlling at the same time. This is, of course, logically concurrency, albeit concurrency "in the small."

When the and-states are truly independent, life is pretty easy and care-free. However, just as in other kinds of concurrent systems, when the and-states are *not* completely independent, life can be complex. The figure shows a couple of common ways that and-states can communicate and synchronize with each other. The first is via the use of guards. The evDataReady event is guarded by the condition "[IS_IN(Waiting)]." The IS_IN operator only returns TRUE when the other and-state is currently in the specified state.

Another common means for and-state synchronization is called "propagation of events," in which one and-state generates an event that is then processed by the other and-state. We see that the transition with the event trigger "evBad" generates an event "evAbort" that is used in the upper and-state. The way to think about event processing with and-states is to imagine that each active and-state receives its own individual copy of each event received by the object and is free to act on or discard that event as appropriate. It is common for multiple and-states to respond to the same event sent to the other, each independently.

As mentioned previously, there are special annotations or marks used in statecharts for specific purposes. These are collectively known as pseudostates. Psuedostates are most certainly *not* states because the object can't "rest" at a pseudostate as it can with a state. Nevertheless, pseudostates provide a broad set of capabilities to statecharts that are difficult to replicate with only states and transitions. The most common pseudostates are shown in Figure 1-12.

The UML defines a number of different pseudostates, as shown in Figure 1-12. We've already seen some of these, but others have not yet been introduced. Here are some brief descriptions.

- *Branch or Conditional*[2]
  The branch pseudostate indicates a set of possible target or-states, at most one of which will be selected on the basis of a guarding condition. The branch pseudostate is nothing more than a junction with guards on exiting transition segments. However, it was called out in previous versions of the UML with a special icon (either a © or a small diamond) and is still indicated using an independent icon by many modeling tools, so it is separately identified here.

- *Terminal or Final*
  The final state indicates that the enclosing composite state is terminated. If the final state appears in the outermost level of nesting, it

---

2. This pseudostate was removed in the 1.3 revision of the UML after it was noted to be just a kind of the junction pseudostate. However, since it is still widely used in tools, I have continued to use it here.

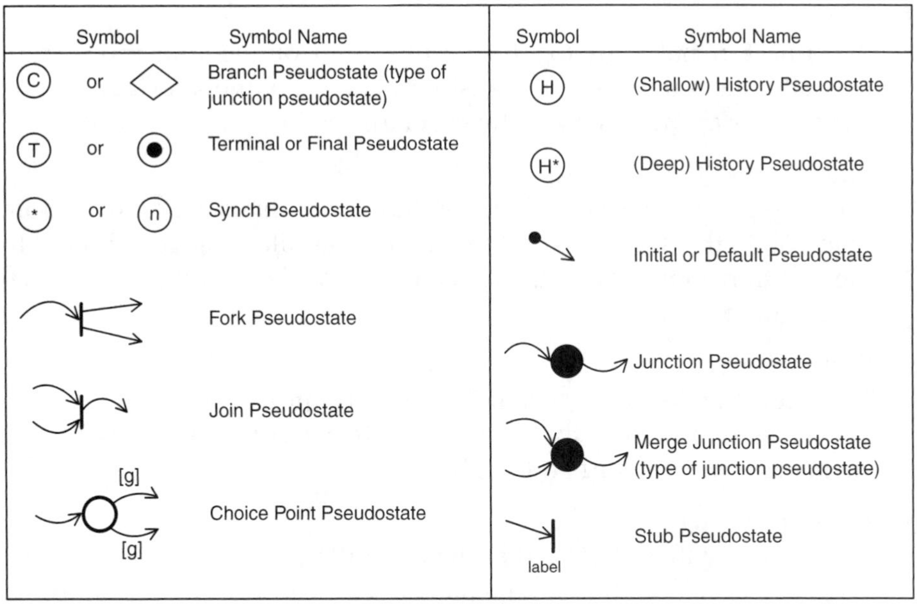

Symbol	Symbol Name	Symbol	Symbol Name
Ⓒ or ◇	Branch Pseudostate (type of junction pseudostate)	Ⓗ	(Shallow) History Pseudostate
Ⓣ or ⊙	Terminal or Final Pseudostate	Ⓗ*	(Deep) History Pseudostate
⊛ or ⓝ	Synch Pseudostate		Initial or Default Pseudostate
	Fork Pseudostate		Junction Pseudostate
	Join Pseudostate		Merge Junction Pseudostate (type of junction pseudostate)
[g] [g]	Choice Point Pseudostate	label	Stub Pseudostate

Figure 1-12: *Pseudostates*

indicates that the object no longer accepts any event, usually because it is about to be destroyed.

- *Synch*
  A synch pseudostate is a kind of queue holding logical (that is, "color-less") tokens and is used as a kind of guard between and-states. A transition may fork into one state and a synch pseudostate. When this transition is taken, it "deposits" a token into the synch pseudostate. In a transition from the synch, pseudostate terminates on a join in another and-state and acts like a guard on that transition. When the synch state contains one or more tokens, the guard is TRUE and the guarded transition can be taken, and when it does, one token is removed from the synch pseudostate.

- *Fork*
  A connector that branches into multiple transitions, each entering a different and-state from a single input transition. This is not the same as a branch because in a branch only a single transition activates; in a fork, all outgoing transition segments activate.

- *Join*
  A connector that joins together multiple incoming transitions from peer and-states into a single transition. This is not the same as a merge. (And-states are discussed in the previous section.)

- *Choice Point*
  A choice point is a kind of junction that executes its action list before going on to the next transition segment. This allows actions bound to the first transition segment to execute prior to the evaluation of subsequent guards.

- *Shallow History*
  This pseudostate indicates that the default state of a composite state is the last state visited of that composite state, but *not* including nested substates (their defaults still apply).

- *Deep History*
  This pseudostate indicates that the default state of a composite is the last state visited of that composite state, including substates nested arbitrarily deeply.

- *Initial or Default*
  Within a superstate context, the initial pseudostate indicates which substate is initially entered as a default. The initial substate may be overridden, either by transitioning directly to a substate or with the history pseudostate.

- *Junction*
  Vertices used to join together multiple transitions or to divide a transition into a set of sequential transition segments. Regardless of the number of transition segments connected, they all execute in a single run-to-completion step.

- *Merge Junction*[3]
  A junction in which multiple incoming transitions can be joined together to create a single transition entering an or-state. This is used as shorthand, particularly when multiple transitions, triggered by different events, share a common action list and/or guard and a common target state.

---

3. The merge pseudostate is also just a kind of junction and was removed from the UML metamodel.

- *Stub*

  A stub pseudostate is basically a "diagram connector" linking a state machine transition appearing on one diagram to one appearing on another. For example, when a transition enters a substate of a composite state, but the details of that composite state are shown on a different statechart, then the transition "enters" a stub state on the primary statechart and "leaves" the stub state on the submachine statechart.

For a more in-depth discussion of statecharts and pseudostates, see [2].

1.4.4 Activity Charts

Activity charts are a specialized form of statecharts in that they share a common underlying semantic metamodel, although this is likely to change in UML 2.0. The notation for activity charts is reminiscent of flowcharts (as seen in Figure 1-13), which is basically what an activity chart is: a concurrent flow chart. In usage, activity charts are used to model sequential and concurrent control flow, when control flows from state to state primarily on the basis of *completion* of the previous work rather than on the basis of the reception of external events. In the figure, you can see the states have entry and exit actions, as normal states do, but primarily control flows from one state when the actions in it are complete. While you can name the event transitions, just as you can in statecharts, you can also use special symbols, such as the event reception state and event transmission state to show the cases where event reception and transmission occur.

In practice, statecharts are used to model the reactive behavior of classes and use cases when they proceed via the reception of events. Activity charts are used to model control flow behavior of operations, use cases, and, less often, classes. For this reason, a common use of activity charts is to show computational algorithms.

1.4.5 Interactions

In the previous section, we saw how the behavior of individual classifiers, such as classes and use cases, can be modeled using statecharts and their close cousin, activity charts. In this section, we will see how the UML models the collaborative behavior of multiple entities working together. Collectively known as *interactions,* collective behavior concerns itself with the (partially) sequenced exchange of messages (which may be events,

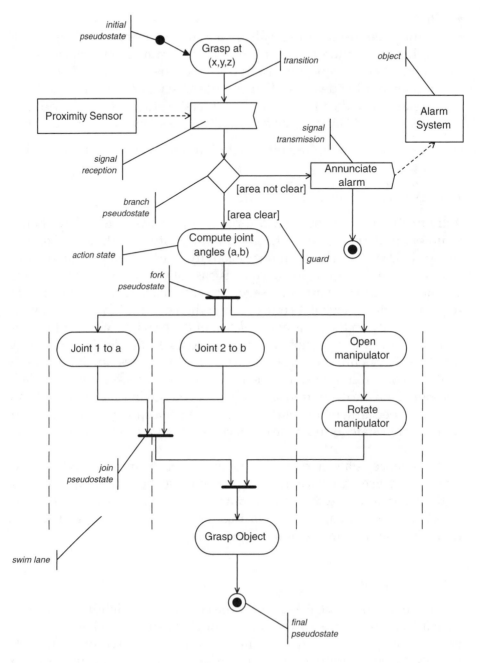

Figure 1-13: *Activity Chart*

operation calls, or instance creation/destruction actions), among a possibly large set of interacting objects.

There are two diagrammatic forms in the UML for depicting interactions: collaboration diagrams and sequence diagrams. Collaboration diagrams are basically object diagrams with messages shown with numbers. One such collaboration diagram, depicting a scenario for a Jolt Cola machine, is shown in Figure 1-14.

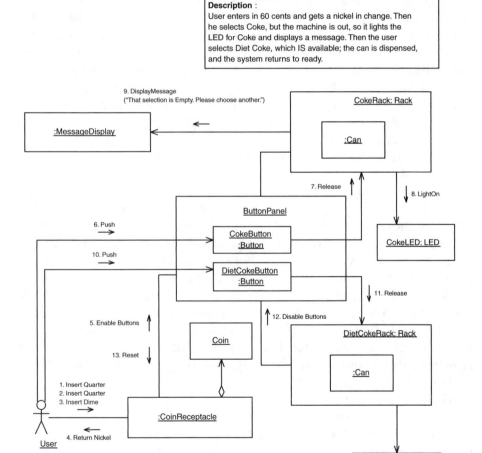

Figure 1-14: *Collaboration Diagram*

You can see that the collaboration diagram shows both the structure of the objects in the collaboration and the ordered set of messages in the scenario. The difficulty with collaboration diagrams is equally apparent: Because sequence is shown with numbers, finding the next message in the sequence involves some searching. For this reason, collaboration diagrams are used less than the other kind of interaction diagrams—sequence diagrams—which we describe next.

The next figure, Figure 1-15, shows the very same scenario, but instead as a sequence diagram. As previously mentioned, sequence diagrams are more commonly used than collaboration diagrams, even though they show basically the same information. The reason is that sequence diagrams emphasize sequence over structure, so it is very easy to find the "next" message—it is the message following the current one in the diagram. Time goes down the page but not usually linearly. That is, further down implies later in time, but 2 cm at one place in the diagram does not imply the same amount of time as 2 cm somewhere else on the diagram. Sequence diagrams *can* be made linear by attaching a time line "ruler" along one edge, but more commonly timing constraints are added. Two common forms for timing constraints are shown in Figure 1-15, as indicated by callouts.

The vertical lines, called "lifelines," represent the object (or object role). Objects (or object roles) can both send and receive messages. Messages are shown by the arrowed lines going from one lifeline to another.

There are many annotations that are commonly added to sequence diagrams to show various things, but they are beyond the scope of this book. Interested readers are referred to [1] or other books on the UML.

A note on ordering in interactions is appropriate here. Most UML users, even experienced ones, are surprised to learn that interactions are only partially ordered. They expect that if a message begins or terminates below another, then it comes *after* the other in absolute time. However, this is not quite true. Sequence diagrams have concurrency semantics.

For example, does message A precede B in Figure 1-16? The answer is, *We don't know.* If all of the objects are concurrently running, they may be running in different locations. The diagram does not give enough information to determine whether message A actually precedes B, which is the common interpretation. Most people using sequence diagrams conclude that A precedes B because they implicitly assume nonconcurrent semantics in the system. In the presence of concurrency, we don't know, *or care,* which comes first.

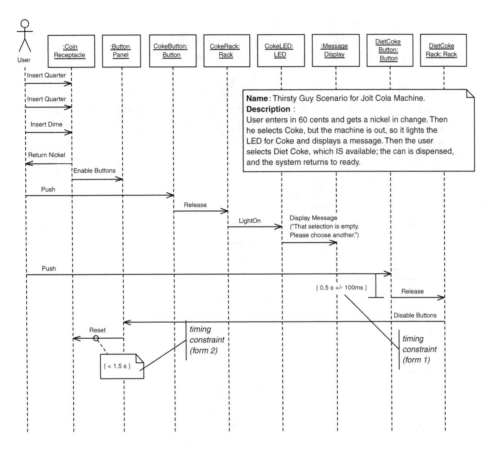

Figure 1-15: *Sequence Diagram*

The situation is even a bit more complex than that. Let us assume that two events are associated with each message: a send event and a receive event. On a single processor with objects in the same thread using a synchronous rendezvous, we can collapse the message into a single event, but in general we must assume the possibility of distributed objects running in different threads. We can assume that the send precedes the receive, which removes half of the possibilities. The remaining possible orderings are as follows.

    A.send -> A.receive -> B.send -> B.receive
    A.send -> B.send -> A.receive -> B.receive
    A.send -> B.send -> B.receive -> A.receive

B.send -> B.receive ->A.send -> A.receive
B.send -> A.send -> B.receive -> A.receive
B.send -> A.send -> A.receive -> B.receive

These are all equally valid interpretations of Figure 1-16.

Looking at the rest of the sequence diagram, what else can we say about it? Quite a bit, although not as much as might be intuitive. For example, we can say not only that C.send precedes C.receive but we can also say that C.receive precedes D.send because along a single lifeline,

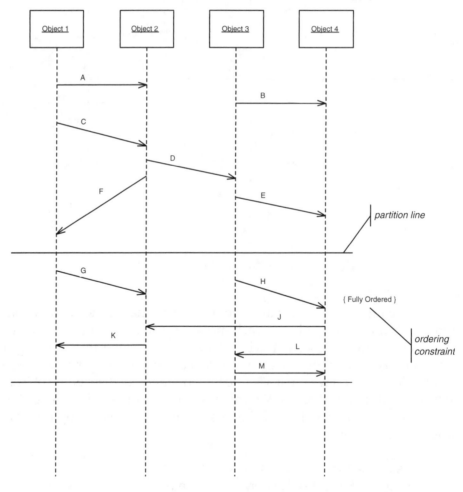

Figure 1-16: *Sequence Diagram*

events are fully ordered. So we know that the following orderings are determined.

> C.send -> C.receive -> D.send -> F.send -> F.receive
> D.send -> D.receive -> E.send -> E.receive

But we can say nothing about the orderings of [F.send, E.send] and [F.receive, E.receive]. When desirable, you can add a constraint {fully order} to a set of messages to indicate that the intuitive interpretation is in fact the correct one. This is shown in the bottom half of the figure. The constraint is applied between the set of partition lines, denoting that the proper interpretation of the ordering of those messages is as follows.

> G.send -> H.send -> G.receive -> H.receive -> J.send -> J.receive
> -> K.send -> K.receive -> L.send -> L.receive -> M.send
> -> M.receive

1.5 Use Case and Requirements Models

A use case is an explicitly named capability of a system or large-scale element of a system. It is a functional aspect of the system that must return a result to one or more actors, and it should not reveal or imply anything about the internal implementation of that functionality. A use case is a placeholder for potentially many specific detailed requirements. The use case may be thought of as a "bag" that in some sense "holds" or contains a coherent, cohesive set of detailed requirements around the capability. Use cases are commonly applied to systems, of course, but in large-scale applications, to subsystems and components as well.

There are two different kinds of requirements typically applied against a system or system element: functional requirements and so-called non-functional or Quality of Service (QoS) requirements. Functional requirements refer to what the system needs to do, as in "The system shall maintain the attitude of the spacecraft." QoS requirements refer to *how well* the functional aspects are to be achieved, as in "The system shall maintain the attitude of the spacecraft *within two degrees of roll, pitch, and yaw from the control settings.*"

Use cases are represented as ovals that associate with actors, indicating that the realizing collaborations interact in meaningful ways with those specified actors. In addition, use cases may relate to other use cases, although the novice modeler is cautioned against overuse of these relations.[4] The three relations among use cases are generalization (one use case is a more specialized form of another), includes (one use case includes another to achieve its functional purpose), and extends (one use case may optionally add functional aspects to another). An example use case diagram is shown in Figure 1-17.

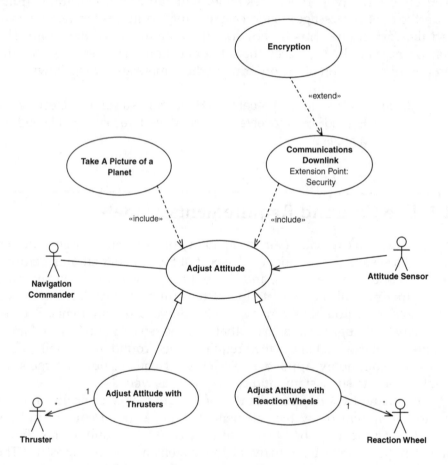

Figure 1-17: *Use Cases*

---

4. In my experience, it is all too easy to use the use case relations in a misguided attempt to functionally decompose the internals of the system, which is *not the point*. The purpose of use cases is to define the functional behavior of a system, subsystem, or other large-scale classifier in an implementation-free way.

Since a use case provides little more than a name and relations to actors and other use cases, the detailed requirements must be captured somewhere. The ROPES process refers to this as "detailing the use case." There are two complementary approaches to detailing use cases: by example and by specification. In both cases, however, the internals of the structure of the system cannot be referred to, since the requirements should be captured in an implementation-free manner.

The most common use of use cases is to capture requirements for systems, but it can be used on any nonprimitive piece of the system as well. It is common for complex large-scale systems, such as aircraft or automobiles, to also apply use cases to the subsystems as well. This is especially true when the subsystems are to be developed by independent teams and *especially* when they are geographically separated from the rest of the developers.

1.5.1 Capturing Black-Box Behavior Without Revealing Internal Structure

Use cases may be thought of as "bags" that contain related detailed requirements. These requirements, as mentioned previously, may be a combination of functional and QoS requirements. These details are captured in one or both of two ways: scenario modeling or specification.

Scenario modeling of use cases involves the creation of sequence diagrams that capture different scenarios of the use case. Each scenario captures a very specific system-actor interaction. These scenarios capture messages sent to the system from the actors and from the system to the actors, as well as the allowable set of sequences of such messages.

When doing scenario modeling, it is important to remember the purpose is to capture requirements, not to functionally decompose the internals of the system. Therefore, for requirements scenarios, the only classifiers that may appear are the system actors and the system or the use case, not pieces internal to the system. In the case of subsystem use cases, the peer subsystems are treated as actors to the subsystem of concern.

The other approach to requirements capture is via *specification*. The specification may be done via the "Victorian novel" approach—by entering "shall" textual statements in the description of the use case. The other approach is to use a formal behavioral specification language, such as statecharts or activity charts, to define all possible scenarios. When statecharts are used in this way, messages from the actors are represented as events on the statechart, while messages from the system to the actors are shown as actions on the statechart.

1.6 What Is a Design Pattern?

A design pattern is *a generalized solution to a commonly occurring problem.*
What problems do design patterns solve? Well, the ROPES process
defines *analysis* as identification of the essential properties of the system,
such that if the delivered system does not have those properties, it is incorrect or incomplete. Design, on the other hand, is all about *optimization.*
The hard part about design is that there are *so many things to optimize and
so little time.* A design model differs from an analysis model in that it contains aspects that are not required but are included to make the system
work better in some way. The following are some of the ways a design
may optimize an analysis model.

- Performance
  - Worst case
  - Average case
- Predictability
- Schedulability
- Minimize resource requirements
  - Memory
  - Heat
  - Weight
- Reusability
- Portability
- Maintainability
- Readability
- Extendability
- Development time/effort
- Safety
- Reliability
- Security

Now the *really hard part* of design is that you typically must optimize
against many or all of these aspects simultaneously. The system QoS
requirements ultimately drive the design because the QoS requirements
specifically state which of these aspects are most important and the specific acceptance criteria for what is "optimal enough." To optimize all of

these at once, we must rank them in order of importance to the success of the project and product. In some systems, safety and worst-case performance may be crucial, whereas reusability and security are relatively unimportant. In other systems, time to market and portability may be much more important than performance issues. Thus, a good design optimizes the analysis model with all of the important QoS aspects ranked in accordance to their importance to the success of the project or product.

Since design is all about optimization, design patterns are all about optimization, too. They optimize some aspect of the system in some way while deoptimizing it in some other ways. As designers, it is our job to determine which set of patterns form a "best fit" of all the possibly conflicting design optimization criteria.

A pattern consists of three important aspects. First, there is the *Problem*. This is a statement of the aspect of design that the pattern is meant to address—that is, the specific optimization or QoS aspect solved by the pattern. Next, there is the *Solution*. This is the pattern itself. The pattern is shown as a structural (class) diagram with the roles indicated. Finally, there are the *Consequences*. Since a pattern optimizes some aspects over others, it is important to understand the negative as well as the positive aspects of the pattern because optimizing one aspect almost universally means deoptimizing some other aspect. In addition, each pattern is presented with an *Example* to show how the pattern might be applied to a problem in the real-time and embedded domain.

Another way to look at a design pattern is as a parameterized collaboration. A collaboration is a set of classifier roles working together to achieve a higher-level purpose, such as the realization of a use case. A design pattern is parameterized in the sense that it defines a set of roles that will be ultimately played by objects that you create in the specific application. The pattern defines a structure and a set of supporting behaviors that optimizes how that structure collaborates.

Most design proceeds largely through the application of design patterns. Design patterns may be applied at different levels of scope. Architectural patterns affect most or all of the system—that is, architectural patterns are broadly and strategically applied to the system. This book concerns itself with architectural patterns of particular relevance to real-time and embedded systems. Architectural patterns are typified by patterns such as those to be found in [4]. There are also patterns more local in scope, such as those in the class GoF (Gang of Four) reference [5]. We call these *mechanistic design patterns* because they define mechanisms for object collaborations. Such patterns have a much more limited scope—a single collaboration. Mechanistic design patterns are not discussed in this book.

The ROPES process (see Chapter 3) identifies these five primary aspects of architecture.

- Large-scale organization
- Concurrency and resource management
- Distribution across multiple address spaces
- Safety and reliability aspects
- Mapping of the other aspects onto the underlying computing platform(s)

A system model embodies all of these aspects. It is possible to create diagrams that depict these aspects in isolation from the others. We refer to these as architectural views. This book is organized around those five architectural views and presents patterns that optimize different aspects of each of these views.

The first view is called the Subsystem and Component View. It consists of ways of organizing the system at a high level to optimize how these large-scale pieces work together, how they are constructed, or how they are managed. These patterns are discussed in Chapter 4.

The next view has to do with the management of task threads and finite resources. Because this is so important for real-time and embedded systems, three chapters are devoted to this topic. Chapter 5 discusses patterns for the identification and scheduling of task threads. Chapter 6 focuses on patterns that optimize the use of memory, including allocation and deallocation. Chapter 7 deals with policies for effective use and sharing of resources when contention is a serious concern.

The next aspect of design is how objects are distributed across multiple address spaces and possibly remote computers. This includes the policies and procedures for objects to find each other and collaborate. This aspect includes communications protocols. Chapter 8 provides a number of patterns useful for real-time and embedded systems. This chapter includes some different deployment patterns to optimize the allocation of software to the underlying computing hardware.

The last chapter focuses on the problems of safety-critical and high-reliability systems. There are a number of ways that different aspects of safety, reliability, and cost can be played against each other, and that is the topic of Chapter 9.

It is not only common but practically *required* that you will mix architectural patterns from most or all of these views. A particular system may not have any special concerns around—say, Safety or Distribution—but most systems will require optimization (and hence pattern application) in most or all of these aspects.

1.7 References

[1] *OMG Unified Modeling Language Specification Version 1.4*, Needham, MA: Object Management Group, 2001.

[2] Douglass, Bruce Powel. *Real-Time UML, 2nd Edition: Developing Efficient Objects for Embedded Systems*, Boston, MA: Addison-Wesley, 2000.

[3] Douglass, Bruce Powel. *Doing Hard Time: Developing Real-Time Systems with UML, Objects, Frameworks and Patterns*, Reading, MA: Addison-Wesley, 1999.

[4] Buschmann, F., R. Meunier, H. Rohnert, P. Sommerlad, and M. Stal. *A System of Patterns: Pattern-Oriented Software Architecture*, New York, NY: John Wiley and Sons, 1996.

[5] Gamma, E., R. Helm, R. Johnson, and J. Vlissides. *Design Patterns: Elements of Reusable Object-Oriented Software*, Reading, MA: Addison-Wesley, 1995.

Chapter 2

Architecture and the UML

This chapter discusses the following.

- The definition of *architecture*
- Logical architecture
- Physical architecture
- The Five Views of architecture
  - Subsystem and Component View
  - Concurrency and Resource View
  - Distribution View
  - Safety and Reliability View
  - Deployment View
- Implementing architectures
  - Model-driven architecture
  - Creating architectural elements

2.1 Architecture

There are many ways to define the term *architecture.* We will define it in a specific way here and use it as a basis for capturing patterns for the main part of this book. Architecture is defined as *the set of strategic design decisions that affect most or all of the system.* The differentiation from other (smaller-scale) design decisions has to do with the scope of the decision being made. Whether to make an association for one particular class a pointer or a reference is not, by this definition, an architectural decision. Architecture normally refers to the structural organization of systems and only implicitly refers to behavioral aspects. We are concerned with architecture in this book because we want to identify structural organizational patterns that have various properties that we find useful.

Architecture is a part of design. As we will see in the next chapter, design differs from analysis. Analysis is defined to be the specification of the *essential* aspects of a system—that is, those aspects without which the system is considered to be incorrect or incomplete. Analysis is driven by the functional requirements of the system or what the system needs to accomplish. Many different designs can be used to implement the same analysis model. The criteria that we use to select one design over another is *how well* the implementation works—how quickly, how predictably, how reliably, how safely, how reusably, and so on. These aspects are collectively referred to as *qualities of service* (QoS). In some systems, worst-case performance and safety are the most important aspects of a good design, and that drives the developer to certain design solutions. In other systems, distributability across many platforms and reusability are more important, driving that developer to different design solutions. Architecture is a part of design because there are many designs that could be used to implement an analysis model, so it is not, in that sense, *essential.* A good architecture is at least approximately optimal in terms of the various QoS properties of the system.

What makes design *hard* is that many of the desired or required QoS aspects may be conflicting. For example, you might strongly desire that the system be optimal in terms of worst-case performance. On the other hand, you may also need to make the system highly reusable. These properties are usually at odds with each other, and a good design strikes the right balance between opposing design concerns. In fact, a good design optimizes the importance-weighted sum of all the desired or required QoS aspects of the system. If you think of each QoS aspect as an independent feature with its relative importance as a weighting factor, then a good design finds a nonlinear optimal sum among all these independent aspects. In other words, a good design finds the minimum

$$\min[\sum QoSFeature_j * Weight_j],$$

where $Weight_j$ refers to the relative importance of the associated jth QoS-Feature.

The ROPES[1] process is discussed in more detail in Chapter 3. For now, just understand that it is an iterative approach to systems development in which architecture plays a crucial role. Figure 2-1 highlights the parts of the ROPES spiral model where architecture is of particular relevance.

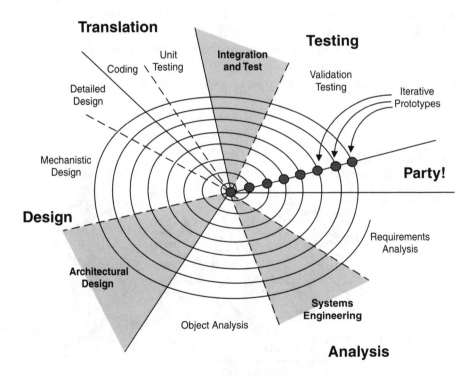

Figure 2-1: *ROPES and Architecture*

---

1. Rapid Object-oriented Process for Embedded Systems

2.2 Logical and Physical Architecture

The ROPES process defines two fundamental kinds of architecture: logical and physical. The logical architecture refers to the organization of things that exist only at design time—that is, the organization of classes and data types. Logical architecture is concerned with how models are themselves organized, and this organization can be simple or very complex, depending on the needs and structure of the team(s) using it. The logical architecture is unrelated to the organization of the system at runtime, although one of the logical architecture patterns is to mirror the physical architectural structure. Figure 2-2 shows the roles of logical and physical architectures.

Although Systems Engineering is in the analysis phase of the spiral, it really focuses on system *design.* Systems Engineering is an optional phase in the ROPES process and is included either when there is significant hardware/software codesign or when the system is complex enough to be broken across multiple teams. Systems Engineering is placed in the analysis phase because in complex systems, analysis often must take

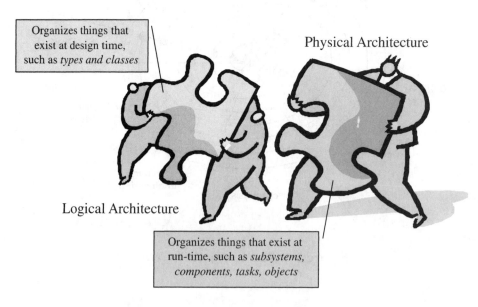

Organizes things that exist at design time, such as *types and classes*

Physical Architecture

Logical Architecture

Organizes things that exist at run-time, such as *subsystems, components, tasks, objects*

Figure 2-2: *Logical and Physical Architecture*

place at the subsystem level of abstraction as well as at the system level. However, to be effective, there must be an overall run-time structure into which those smaller analysis efforts will fit. A high-level subsystem model provides exactly that.

In the Systems Engineering phase, the primary work activities are as follows.

- Identification of the high-level subsystems and their relations
- Mapping the system-level requirements (captured as system level use cases) to subsystems (as subsystem-level use cases)
- Specification of subsystem interfaces
- Detailing of multidisciplinary algorithms—that is, algorithms met by a combination of hardware and software

Systems Engineering phases exist so the different teams can go off and work more or less independently within a well-defined framework into which their subsystem will ultimately fit. For this to occur, a high-level run-time architecture must be in place, with well-defined interfaces among those elements. That is the primary job for Systems Engineering.

Architectural design work primarily is done, naturally enough, in the architectural design part of the design phase. Here, strategic design decisions are made in each of the five views (or four views, if the subsystem architecture is already defined in the Systems Engineering part). These views will be detailed in the next section.

The last place where architecture is a primary concern is the integration and test phase. In this phase, pieces of the architecture are brought together in an incremental fashion to construct the system prototype. This is primarily a test of the architecture and the interfaces of the architectural pieces.

For the most part, architecture is done through the application of architectural design patterns, as we'll discuss in the next chapter. A design pattern, as we will see, is a generalized solution to a commonly occurring problem. Design patterns have three primary parts: a problem to be solved, the solution (the pattern), and a set of consequences. With architectural design patterns, the problem to be solved is always based in optimizing some small set of QoS properties at the expense of others. Certain patterns optimize safety but do so by increasing recurring cost or complexity. Other patterns enhance reusability but at the expense of average execution time. Still others optimize predictability of execution time at the expense of optimal worst-case execution time.

Patterns can be mixed and matched as necessary, although clearly some mixes won't make any sense. It is common, for example, to mix a pattern for primary subsystem organization with another pattern for allowing distributed objects to communication and another pattern for concurrency management and another pattern for fault management and still another pattern for mapping to the underlying hardware. This gives rise to the notion of different aspects of architecture. The complete architecture of the system is the melding together of all the architectural patterns used. In the ROPES process, we identify five different views of architecture. It is common to have at least one pattern from each (and in some cases, more than one pattern in each) mixed together to form the complete system architecture.

2.2.1 Logical Architecture

There are many possible logical architectures—that is, ways to organize your design model. The ROPES process recommends a logical architecture based on the concept of *domains.* A domain is an independent subject area that generally has its own vocabulary. The use of the term *domain* in this way is similar to its use in [1]. Domains provide a means by which your model can be organized—partitioned into its various subjects, such as user interface, hardware, alarm management, communications, operating system, data management, medical diagnostics, guidance and navigation, avionics, image reconstruction, task planning, and so on.

Used in this way, a domain is just a UML package. UML packages contain model elements, but other than providing a namespace, packages have no semantics and are not instantiable.[2] The UML does not provide a criterion for what should go in one package versus another, but domains do. For this reason, we represent domain as a «domain» stereotype package that includes a mission, specifically "hold classes and types around the common subject matter." The use of domains does not dictate how objects will be organized and deployed at run-time but what the physical architecture is all about.

Figure 2-3 shows a typical domain diagram—a package diagram that shows the relations of the domains themselves and the classes within the domains. In the figure, we see that the alarm domain contains classes around the concept of alarm management: a couple of types of alarms, an

---

2. In other words, you cannot create an instance of a package at run-time. Packages are a purely design-time organizational concept.

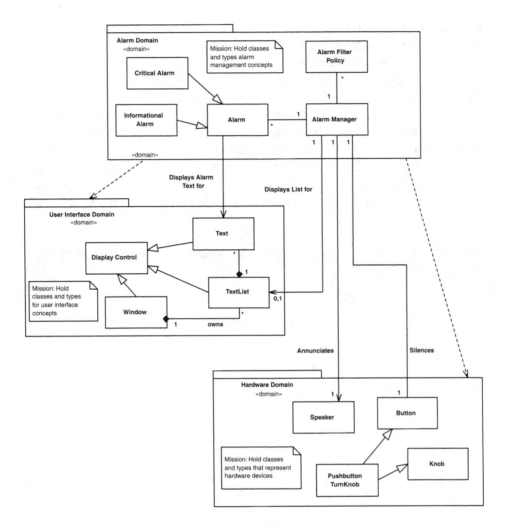

Figure 2-3: *Logical Domain Architecture*

alarm manager, and an alarm filter policy class. The alarms must be displayed in a list, so the alarm manager associates with a text list class that is a user interface element and so is found in the user interface domain. Alarms themselves are displayed as text, so the alarm class (in the alarm domain) associates with the text class in the user interface domain. Alarms must also be annunciated, so the alarm manager associates with the speaker class in the hardware domain. Also, the user needs to be able to acknowledge and silence the alarm, so the alarm manager associates with a button class from the hardware domain.

Domains are often arranged in one-way dependency hierarchies, as shown in Figure 2-4. The more abstract (closer to the problem space) domains depend on the more concrete (closer to the hardware) domains. This can be represented using dependencies from the more abstract to the more concrete domains. This manifests itself in primarily one-way associations from classes in the more abstract domains to classes in the more concrete domains. This is what we usually want: Most associations are ultimately one-way relationships anyway. A button, for example, need not know (and you don't want it to know!) that it is connected to an alarm

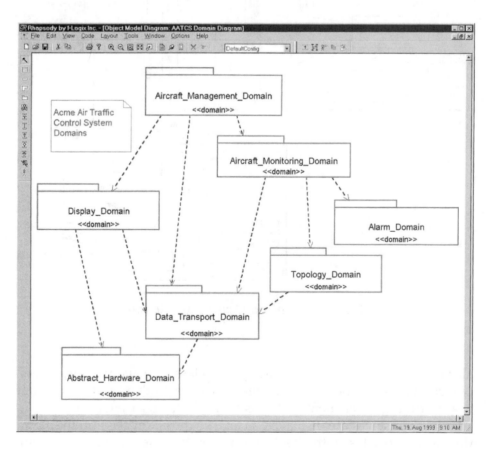

Figure 2-4: *Domain Hierarchy*

manager, or an elevator, or a microwave emitter. A button is a button is a button. In principle, you do not want the button to know anything about its usage context. Usually, the more concrete class does not know the specific client who wants to use its services, and this is inherent in the classic "client-server" model of relations. The astute reader will note that the relationship between the alarm manager and the button classes is a bidirectional association. How we would expect the relationship to work is that when an episodic event occurs with the button (for example, "Press event"), it notifies the alarm manager. To make this into a one-way relationship, the button might have a "subscribe(addr)" operation that enables the alarm manager to give the button enough information to contact it (for example, the address of an event acceptor function) when the button receives a push event.

Generalization relationships typically fall inside a single domain, and domains may be subdivided into smaller packages, either to represent smaller subject matters or simply to divide up the work into smaller pieces to distribute to development team members.

Physical architecture is concerned with the organization of things that exist at run-time. While packages (and therefore domains) don't exist at run-time (being solely design-time concepts), they provide a place for the definition of the classes that will be used via instantiation in the various subsystems.

Domain structure usually does not completely reflect the physical architecture. For example, the physical architecture may have the concept of a "power subsystem," which is constructed from instances of the classes defined in various domains. For example, the power subsystem may contain instances of many classes from a number of different domains, as shown in Figure 2-5. Using the standard name scoping operator "::," the name of the domain package precedes the name of the class. So, for example, hardware_domain::switch is the class switch in the hardware_domain package, whereas communications_domain::message_transaction is the message_transaction class in the communications_domain package.[3]

That being said, often there may be specialized domains containing classes only instantiated in one subsystem. For example, classes from a guidance and navigation domain will be likely instantiated solely in a navigation subsystem. Most domains are more general than that, however, and are represented in many, if not all, subsystems.

---

3. We could also have nested the package inside the subsystem as a notational alternative.

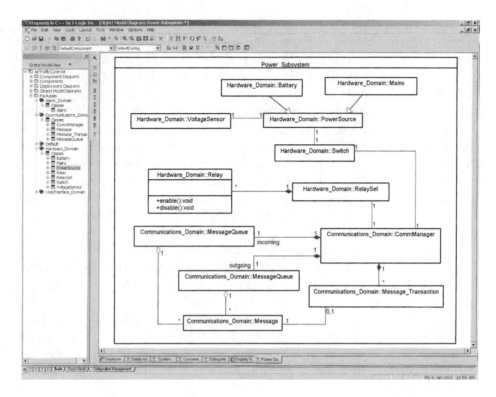

Figure 2-5: *Relating Logical and Physical Architecture*

2.2.2 Physical Architecture

Physical Architecture refers to the large-scale organization elements of the system at run-time, so these elements must be instantiable things. The typical elements are subsystems, components, and «active» objects, but other specialized forms, such as a channel (see Chapter 9) may be used. These large-scale organizational elements don't do much in and of themselves, but they organize the more primitive instances that do the real work and provide management oversight and delegation of requests and messages to the appropriate objects. They allow us to view and understand the system at different levels of abstraction. This is crucial for the construction and understanding of large, complex systems. We need to look at assemblies of parts and refer to them as a single, albeit more abstract, element. Figure 2-6 shows a common set of abstraction levels.

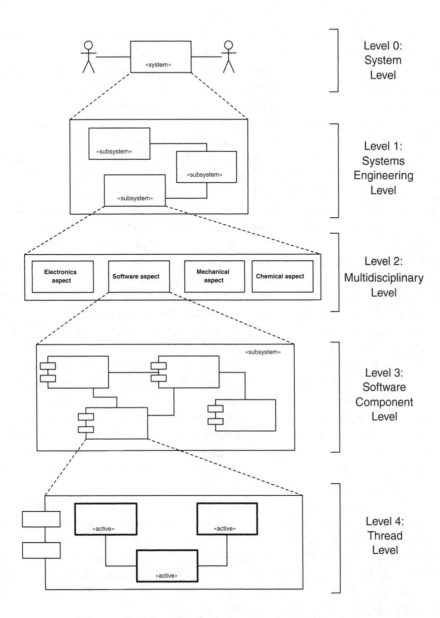

Figure 2-6: *Levels of Abstraction in Architecture*

The most abstract level in the figure is the complete System Level (Level 0)—for example, "Mars Sample Return Mission." The next level down is the Systems Engineering Level (Level 1), where subsystems are defined. In the Mars project example, subsystems might be "Deep Space Network," "Launch Vehicle," "Orbiter," "Lander," "Spacecraft," and "Ground System." There can be multiple sublevels at this level of abstraction before the system is further decomposed into hardware and software aspects. For example, the "Spacecraft" could be decomposed into subsubsystems such as "Guidance and Navigation," "Avionics," "Attitude Control," "Communications," and "Power Management."

Next, we've decomposed the system into the different disciplines (Level 2): Electronic, Mechanical, Chemical, and Software. If a system uses COTS (Commercial Off The Shelf) hardware, then this step is usually skipped, but if you are developing novel hardware, then it may be very important. Notice that hardware/software decomposition is done primarily at the subsystem level rather than at the system level. For example, the Attitude Control Subsystem can be thought of as being composed of electronic aspects (processors, relays, motors, valve controls, a variety of sensors and serial connections), mechanical parts (reaction wheels, thruster assemblies, fuel lines and mixers, and enclosures), chemicals (fuel mixture and oxygen), and, of course, software (the "smarts" to receive and interpret commands, control electronic parts that control mechanical parts that work with chemicals).

The software for the subsystem may then be decomposed into its major architectural units, often components (Level 3), although the notion of a software subsystem can be used here just as well. These are the major replaceable pieces of software that comprise the subsystem. For example, these components for the Attitude Control System might include a TCP/IP communications protocol stack, math library, PID control loops for reaction wheels and thrusters, fuel management component, reaction wheel control component, and so on.

Last, we see the Thread Level (Level 4). This is the level at which concurrency is managed. Some components may be "passive" in the sense that they execute in the thread of the caller. However, there will be at least one component (or software subsystem) that creates and executes at least one thread. These threads will be owned by design-level «active» objects that also aggregate, via composition, the so-called primitive objects that ultimately perform application services.

The next level down is the Object Level (not shown). These are the primitive objects that do the real work of the system. In any particular system, there may be either a greater or fewer number of these abstraction levels, depending on the complexity and scale of the system. For a cardiac pacemaker, you might represent only the System Level and the Thread

Level of architecture, while in our Mars project example, you might ultimately have as many as eight or ten levels. Not all of these levels need to be visible to all developers, of course.

The physical architecture may be constructed from virtually any model organization, and so is considered distinct from the organization of the model per se, although it is possible to organize your model around the physical architecture. The high-level physical architecture is usually constructed in with the Systems Engineering phase of the ROPES spiral, but it may be deferred to the architectural design phase if the Systems Engineering phase is omitted.

Physical architecture has five primary aspects, called the Five Views. These focus on more or less independent aspects of the large-scale runtime structure of the system. Of course, ultimately there is only one system, so we refer to them as views because they focus on a single aspect of the system at a time.

2.3 The Five Views of Architecture

The ROPES process identifies the Five Views of (physical) architecture. These aspects are not completely independent and certainly should not conflict with one another. The best way to think about this is to understand that there is a single model underlying the system that includes the architecture. The views just look at parts of that single model that are related to each other in specific ways. So these are not independent aspects but a filtered view that only shows certain aspects at a time.

The Five Views of architecture defined in the ROPES process are shown in Figure 2-7.

These views of architecture capture structure aspects and so are typically captured with UML structural diagrams. A concurrency "Task Diagram," for example, is nothing more than a class diagram showing the structural elements related to the concurrency view—things like «active» objects, message queues, semaphores, and the like. To show architectural behavior, it is usually the interaction of the architectural elements that is of primary concern, so mostly sequence diagrams are shown. To show the behavior of the architectural element in isolation, usually the functionality is divided up into use cases for the element, and then each of these may be detailed with a statechart or activity chart.

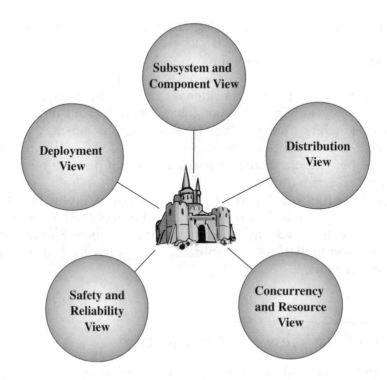

Figure 2-7: *The Five Views of Architecture*

Figure 2-8 shows a system view for an air traffic control system, using Rhapsody from I-Logix,[4] a common tool used in the real-time and embedded development environment. We will provide an example using Rhapsody for the various aspects that might be used in such a hypothetical air traffic control system. We see in Figure 2-8 the System object *ACME_AirTrafficControlSystem* and its environmental context. This consists of the actors[5] with which the system interacts.

2.3.1 Subsystem and Component View

The Subsystem and Component View (or Subsystem View for short) identifies the large-scale pieces of the system and how they fit together. As

---

4. Interested readers should see I-Logix's Web page: *www.ilogix.com.*
5. An actor is an object outside the scope of the system that has interactions of interest with the system as the system executes.

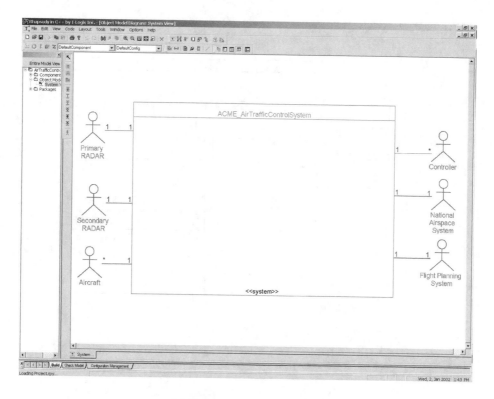

Figure 2-8: *System View*

previously mentioned, this is usually done during the Systems Engineering phase, but it may also be done later in the architectural design phase for projects not using a Systems Engineering phase. Subsystem architecture is captured using a subsystem diagram (see Figure 2-9), which is really a class diagram that shows primarily the subsystems.

In a software-only development in which one is not concerned about the underlying hardware (or at least not very concerned), a subsystem is a run-time organization of software. It is a "large-scale" object that contains, via composition, "part objects" that do the real work of the subsystem. The criteria for inclusion in the subsystem is "common behavioral purpose"—that is, the objects included in the subsystem are there because they contribute to the subsystem's use case realization. Software subsystems provide a means for thinking about systems at different levels of decomposition rather than just as a flat sea of relatively undifferentiated objects.

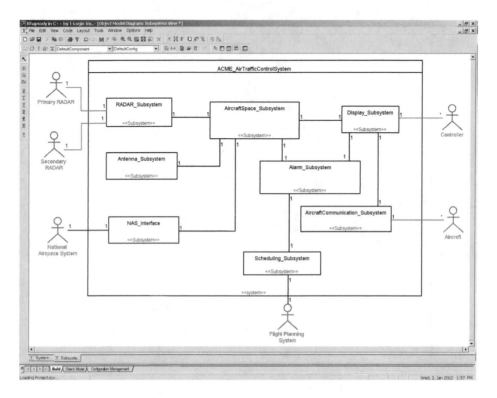

Figure 2-9: *Subsystem View*

The subsystem concept can be used in a couple of different ways. Subsystems can be used to reason about systems before they are broken down into hardware and software parts, as discussed in the previous section. You may also use subsystems as a software-only concept. In either case, a subsystem is a really big object that provides well-defined interfaces and delegates service requests to internal hidden parts. How you use these UML building blocks is up to you. UML provides the vocabulary, but it's up to you to write the story.

If a component-based development approach is used, then components are also architectural elements. The UML has a different icon for components, although UML 1.x is not prescriptive about the differences between a component and a subsystem. In the UML, a subsystem is basically a big object that contains "part" objects that do the real work of the subsystem. A component, on the other hand, is a replaceable part of the system. Typically, components use a component framework for loading and unloading components, component identification, and so on. Nevertheless, the distinction between subsystem and component isn't clear. Is a component bigger or smaller than a subsystem? How should they be mixed and matched? The UML does not say anything about these issues. As a general rule, I recommend that subsystems are the largest-scale parts of a system, and these may be internally decomposed into components as desired. An example of that perspective was provided in Figure 2-6.

The UML component diagram is just another structural diagram—this time emphasizing the component aspects of the system. An example of a component diagram is given in Figure 2-10. It shows the components for the Display_Subsystem of the *ACME_AirTrafficControlSystem.*

There are patterns around how to effectively use these elements to architecturally structure your system. Chapter 4 discusses those that have particular relevance to real-time and embedded systems.

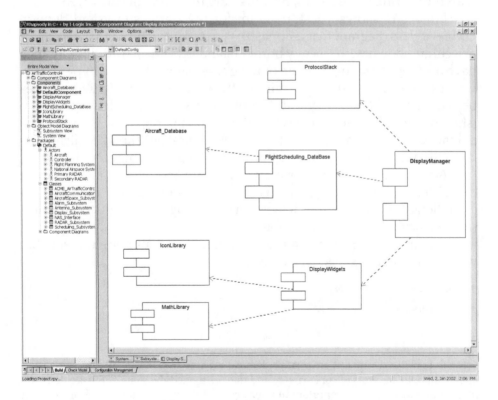

Figure 2-10: *Component View*

2.3.2 Concurrency and Resource View

This view of the system architecture focuses on the management of resources and the concurrent aspects of system execution. Because of the importance of this aspect, it is the subject of Chapters 5, 6, and 7. By *concurrent*, we mean that objects may execute in parallel rather than sequentially. We are stating that we neither know nor *care* about the relative order of execution of actions between the threads,[6] except where specifically mentioned. These points of synchronization are often called *rendezvous* and are the hard parts of concurrency modeling. Sharing data and information is a common reason for threads to rendezvous and synchronize. Another is the need to control and coordinate asynchronously operating system elements.

A *resource* is an element that has a finite and quantifiable aspect to its provided service. For example, it may only allow a single accessor at a time to its internal data. Since the hard parts of concurrency have to do with the sharing of resources, resources are treated with concurrency.

Figure 2-11 shows a task diagram for the alarm_subsystem done in UML—a class diagram that emphasizes the task structure. All the «active» objects are shown with a heavy border (standard UML). Additionally, they have a «Task» stereotype. Some of the classes show the stereotype as text, whereas others use an icon. Similarly, the figure contains two «resource» objects: *AlarmList* and *ListView*. The first is associated with a semaphore (shown to its left) that manages the serialization of requests. The second is managed by its owning thread *Alarm_Annunciation_Thread*, which, incidentally, has a «MessageQueue» object to manage information sharing.

«Active» objects are the primary means for modeling concurrency in the UML. An «active» object owns the root of a thread and manages the execution of the thread and delegation of messages from the thread message queue to the appropriate objects.

There are a number of common strategies for identifying threads that will be later reified as «active» objects.

- Single-event groups
- Event source

---

6. In this book *thread* and *task* are treated identically. There are some detailed design differences, but both are units of concurrency and may be treated the same at the architectural level. If that distinction is important in your design, then you can make it clear by using appropriate stereotypes.

- Related information
- Interface device
- Recurrence properties
- Target object
- Safety level

The single-event groups strategy creates a separate thread for every event, and that event pends on its occurrence. This strategy is useful for simple systems, but it doesn't scale up to large complex systems well.

The event source strategy creates a thread for each source of an event and pends on any event from that source. It is useful when you have a small number of event sources and relatively simple designs.

The related information strategy creates a thread that manages all data within a topic or subject matter, such as all information related to cardiac health. In an anesthesia machine, this information might include pulse

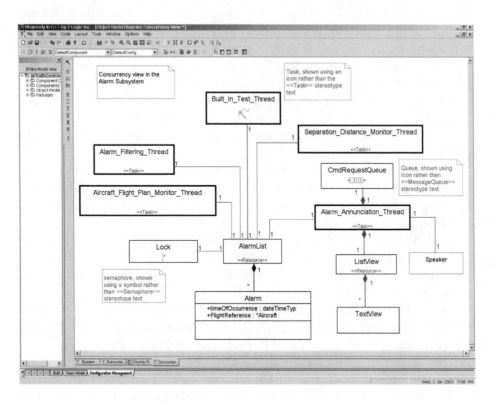

Figure 2-11: *Concurrency and Resource View*

rate (from a blood pressure monitor), heart rate (from an ECG monitor), preventricular contraction count, cardiac output, stroke volume, temperature of the blood coming from the Superior Vena Cava and emptying in the right atrium, and so on. This information comes from a variety of sources, and a single thread could manage it. This strategy is effective for "sensor fusion" applications that require significant processing of data from disparate sources. Further, this strategy tends to reduce the number of thread rendezvous, which can be a source of significant overhead.

The interface device strategy is a specialized form of the event source strategy that is used for systems with multiple data and command buses. One or more threads are spawned to manage the bus traffic and related processing.

The recurrence properties strategy is a demonstrably optimal strategy for thread selection when schedulability of the threads is an important concern. The recurrence properties include whether the event set processed by the thread is periodic (time-based) or aperiodic (event-based). Periodic tasks execute and do work every so often with a defined frequency of execution. It is common to have several periodic tasks, each handling events that occur in a common time frame—for example, one for the 10-ms-based events, one for the 100-ms-based events, and another for the 250-ms-based events. Aperiodic events can either be handled by a general aperiodic event handler, or you can introduce a separate thread for each aperiodic event (the same as in a single event group strategy). Most systems must process a combination of periodic and aperiodic events.

The target object strategy creates a thread for a few special objects that are the target of events from disparate sources. For example, database or data manager objects sometimes have threads assigned to them so they can do appropriate processing.

The safety level strategy creates threads for managing safety and reliability functionality, such as the execution of periodic built-in tests (BITs), stroking watchdogs, monitoring actuation to ensure that it is proceeding correctly, and so on.

However you finally decide which set of threads you want to use, the common development approach is to first construct the *collaborations*—sets of objects working together to realize a use case—and then identify the set of threads and create an «active» object for each thread. Each "primitive" object from the collaboration is aggregated via composition by the appropriate «active» object, allowing it to execute in the appropriate thread.

2.3.3 Distribution View

The Distribution View deals with how objects that may be in different address spaces find and collaborate with each other. The Distribution View includes policies for how the objects communicate, including the selection and use of communication protocols. In asymmetric architectures, an object is dedicated to a particular address space at design time. This makes finding that object during run-time easy, since the other objects can be granted a priori knowledge about how to locate and contact the object in question. In symmetric architectures, the location of an object isn't decided until run-time. Symmetric architectures are useful for complex system that must dynamically balance processing load over multiple processors. When objects become ready to run, the distributed OS runs the object in an optimal locale, based on the current loadings on the various processors. This improves overall performance but at a cost: increased complexity. How, for example, can objects find each other during run-time? This is the subject of the distribution patterns in Chapter 8. Figure 2-12 shows an example of using a broker architecture to mediate communication among distributed objects.

Selecting a distribution architecture is highly driven by the quality of service of the collaboration. The most relevant qualities of services to drive the distribution architecture include the following.

- Performance
  — Worst case
  — Average case
  — Predictability
- Throughput
  — Average
  — Burst
- Reliability
  — Of message delivery
  — Of message integrity
- Recurring (hardware) cost

Of course, in real-time and embedded systems, performance can be crucial to system success. In hard real-time and safety critical systems, worst-case delivery time is the most important concern. For example, control loops are notoriously sensitive to time delays. To implement distributed closed-loop control systems, you want an architecture with a protocol, such as a UDP transport protocol on top of an Ethernet network protocol, will serve this purpose well if the average load is low. CDMA stands for Collision Detect Multiple Access and allows multimastering of the bus. When collisions occur, the senders back off and retry later, usually at random times. When loading is low, the overhead of such a protocol is low, resulting in good (average) performance. Once loading reaches about 30 percent, however, the bus spends a disproportionate amount of time arbitrating collisions, and performance drops drastically. For systems in which peak loads are few and far between, and individual message delivery times are not crucial, CDMA can be a good choice. Interestingly, many systems are built on CDMA when it is demonstrably a poor choice given the quality of service requirements for the system.

TDMA, or Time Division Multiple Access, protocols work by dividing up time available to communicate among the devices on the bus. Each device gets to transmit for a certain period of time and then passes along a "master token" to the next device on the bus. TDMA protocols have low communication arbitration overhead but don't scale up to large numbers of devices well. Further, like a round robin approach to task scheduling, such a system is not responsive in an event-driven application, since an event requiring transmission must wait until the owning device has the master token.

Priority-based protocols typically have more overhead on a per-message basis but allow higher-priority messages through first at the expense of lower-priority messages, making it a natural fit for systems in which scheduling is primarily priority driven. Bit-dominance protocols are a common way to achieve priority-based messaging. In a bit-dominance protocol, each sender listens to what appears on the bus while it's transmitting. If a higher-priority bit occurs in the bus when it sent out a lower-priority bit, then it assumes that it is in conflict with a device trying to send out a higher-priority message, and so it drops out to retry later. The device sending out the higher-priority message "wins" and keeps transmitting. For example, this is how the CAN bus protocol works. Each message contains a priority sequence called a message identifier, followed by the message contents. If each message has a unique identifier, then it has a unique position in the priority scheme. An issue with the CAN bus protocol is that it allows only 8 bytes of data per message, requiring larger messages to be fragmented into multiple bus messages during transmission and reassembled at the receiver end. The SCSI bus is another example of a priority-based transmission protocol, but the SCSI bus is also a parallel bus, meaning that it can achieve greater bandwidth.

Complicating its use as a general message passing bus, however, is the fact that the priority is not based on the message but on the device transmitting the message.

Reliability for distribution means the reliability of correct message delivery. There are many reasons why messages might not be properly delivered, such as attenuation due to distance, interference from electrical noise, temporary or permanent failure of the media, or associated device and software or hardware design flaws. These things may be handled by adding complexity into the communications protocol to check the integrity of messages and to retry transmission if the message is either corrupted or not delivered. Of course, redundant buses are a solution as well, with the advantage of improved reliable and timeliness in the presence of errors but at a higher recurring cost.

Software solutions for message integrity usually require the addition of some level of redundancy, such as a parity bit (very lightweight), checksum (lightweight), or cyclic redundancy check (CRC). Of these, the best is the CRC because it will identify all single and x-bit errors as well as a very high percentage of multiple-bit errors. CRCs are somewhat more complex to compute than a checksum, but a table-driven CRC computation can be very fast, and hardware chips are available that can compute a CRC from a serial bit stream.

Another approach is using Hamming codes, which are codes that are differentiated by what is called a Hamming distance—the minimum number of bit errors necessary to come up with an incorrect but valid code. For example, in an 8-bit byte, the following codes have a Hamming distance of 2 because they require two bits to be modified before you can come up with another valid code.

Binary	Decimal	Hexadecimal
00000000	0	0H
00000011	3	3H
00010100	20	14
10001000	136	88

The use of Hamming codes provides some protection against bit errors because it requires multiple bit errors to construct another valid possibility. It is even possible to send the message multiple times (usually twice, if error detection is required, and thrice, if error correction is needed). If the message data is sent twice, then the second copy can be sent as a ones-complement of the original so that stuck-at bit errors can be detected.

2.3.4 Safety and Reliability View

The Safety and Reliability View examines how system redundancy is defined and managed to raise system reliability and safety. The safety and reliability architecture is concerned with correct functioning in the presence of faults and errors. Redundancy may be used in many ways to get different degrees and types of safety and reliability. Chapter 9 provides a number of patterns in common use in highly reliable and safety-critical systems.

In Figure 2-13, *heterogeneous redundancy* (also known as *diverse redundancy*) is used to provide protections from failures and errors. The primary radar channel processes surface reflection RADAR information, producing three-dimensional position data (in terms of direction, range, and azimuth) as well as velocity data using the Doppler effect. The secondary channel uses the beacon return codes to get a transponder code from the aircraft and the aircraft's position and velocity information.

Reliability is a measure of the "up-time" or availability of a system—specifically, it is the probability that a computation will successfully complete before the system fails. It is normally estimated with mean time between failure, or MTBF. MTBF is a statistical estimate of the probability of failure and applies to stochastic failure modes.

Reducing the system down time increases reliability by increasing the MTBF. Redundancy is one design approach that increases availability because if one component fails, another takes its place. Of course, redundancy only improves reliability when the failures of the redundant components are independent.[7] The reliability of a component does not depend on what happens after the component fails. The reliability of the system remains the same whether the system fails safely or not. Clearly

---

7. Strict independence isn't required to have a beneficial effect. Weakly correlated failure modes still offer improved tolerance to faults over tightly correlated failure modes.

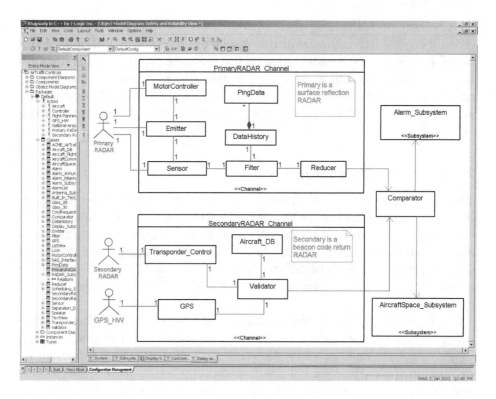

Figure 2-13: *Safety and Reliability View*

the primary concern relative to the reliability of a system is the availability of its functions to the user.

Safety is distinct from reliability. A safe system is one that does not incur too much risk to people or equipment (see [2] and [3]). A *risk* is an event or condition that can occur but is undesirable. Risk is the product of the severity of the incident and its probability. The failure of a jet engine is unlikely, but the consequences can be very high. Thus, the risk of flying in a plane is tolerable, even though it is unlikely that you would survive a crash from 30,000 feet. At the other end of the spectrum, there are events that are common but are of lesser concern. There is a risk that you can get an electric shock from putting a 9-volt battery in an MP3 player. It could easily occur, but the consequences are small. Again, this is a tolerable risk.

The key to both safety and reliability is *redundancy*. For improving reliability, redundancy allows the system to continue to work in the presence of faults because other system elements can take up the work of the broken one. For improving safety, additional elements are needed to monitor the system to ensure that it is operating properly and possible other elements are needed to either shut down the system in a safe way or take over the required functionality.

2.3.5 Deployment View

The deployment view focuses on how the software architecture maps onto the physical devices such as processors, disk drives, displays, and so on. The UML uses the concept of a *node* to represent physical devices. These are often stereotyped to indicate the kind of hardware the node represents. Some models only differentiate between processors (devices that execute code that you write) and devices (ones that don't), while other models identify more detail such as whether a device is a stepper motor, DC motor, thermometer, IR sensor, and so on.

Figure 2-14 is a typical UML deployment diagram; most stereotypes are shown using icons, but text in guillemets («Bus») can be used as easily and is a matter of personal preference. This deployment diagram shows two «Bus» devices, several different processors, redundant flight recorder devices, and redundant display controllers. The diagram also indicates some of the components executing on selected processors.

The primary use for the Deployment View is to represent asymmetric deployment architectures. Then the hardware platform can be schematically represented, and the mapping of software subsystems and components can be detailed. For asymmetric systems this is particularly important to understand how the software on the different processors will collaborate, and it permits performance analysis. You can either nest the software components inside the system or use a dependency from the component or software subsystem to indicate that the node supports or executes that software element. Figure 2-14 shows a couple of nodes with components nested inside them. Any software element can be shown in this way, but usually components and subsystems make the most sense.

For symmetric architectures, the deployment diagram is perhaps less interesting but only marginally so. The underlying hardware is even then a mixture of symmetric and asymmetric aspects. The "interesting"

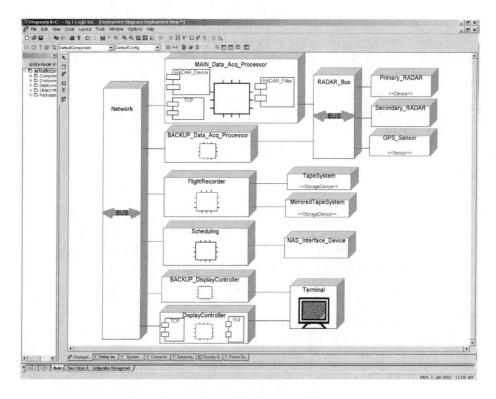

Figure 2-14: *Deployment View*

part—the execution of software elements on the nodes—is in principle not known when the deployment diagram is drawn at design time. In some cases, a software element might even migrate from one node to another. The UML provides the «becomes» stereotype of the dependency relation to indicate that an element might move from one node to another, such as might happen in the event of a fault on the original processor.

2.4 Implementing Architectures

In 2000, the Object Management Group (OMG), owners of the UML standard, launched the Model-Driven Architecture (MDA) initiative [4], [5].

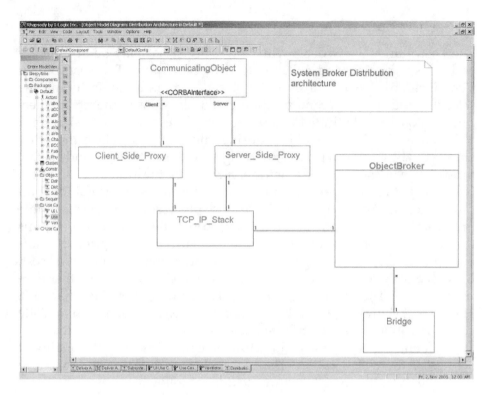

Figure 2-12: *Distribution View*

short worst-case delivery time for certain messages, implying that a priority-based message delivery scheme might be the most appropriate. In such a case, using an asymmetric architecture (or some variant of the observer pattern) with a predictable priority-based transport protocol might fit the system performance needs—for example, an asymmetric distribution on top of a bit-dominance protocol, such as the CAN bus protocol.

In so-called "soft" real-time systems, the average performance is a more important criterion than worst-case performance. Average performance may be measured in terms of average length of time for message delivery or in "mean-lateness" of the messages. Such systems usually don't care if a small set of the messages is late when the system is under load, as long as the average response is sufficient. In some cases, it may even be permissible to drop some messages altogether when the system is under stress. For example, a broker pattern with a CDMA transport

MDA is an attempt by the Object Management Group to unify the two primary independent technologies owned by the OMG: CORBA and the UML. The OMG has always been primarily concerned with interoperability of systems—both in terms of running on distributed heterogeneous hardware (the CORBA part) and of models (the UML part). This interoperability has been both in terms of integration with legacy systems and with systems you plan to construct or integrate with in the future even though they haven't yet been planned. The primary advantage of the MDA is a unified approach to the design and development of platform-independent systems that can be easily ported from one environment to another and can be hosted on heterogeneous environments easily.

2.4.1 Alphabet Soup: CORBA, UML, and MDA Basics

CORBA (Common Object Request Broker Architecture) is a powerful, mature technology for constructing systems that are distributed across many, usually heterogeneous, computing environments. This is accomplished through the application of the *Broker Design Pattern* (see Chapter 8). This is an architectural design pattern in which the centerpiece is the underlying CORBA infrastructure: the Object Broker. One of the difficulties in large-scale distributed systems design is designing so-called *symmetric architectures*—architectures in which you don't know at design time where objects and services will run. Many complex systems must perform dynamic load balancing, executing objects and services from currently lightly loaded processors in your system. Since you cannot predict at design time where these services will execute, how do you invoke them?

That's where the Object Broker comes in. The Object Broker serves as a repository so that at run-time when one object is ready to provide services, it registers with the Broker. Later, when another object needs to invoke the services of the former, it locates the desired object by asking the Broker. The Broker serves as dynamic glue to bind together objects that need to collaborate but lack the a priori knowledge of how to find each other—sort of the computational equivalent of a dating service.

The entire infrastructure must also include bindings to different communications protocols—the most common being TCP/IP—and bindings to different source-level languages—such as C, C++, and Java, to name but a few. Because hand-coding all the relevant calls into the Broker when all you really want to say is "Send a message to Object X" would be tremendously onerous, CORBA implementations use what is called IDL—Interface Description Language (which happens to look a lot like C++). You write your object requests in IDL, ignoring for the most part the fact that you're using CORBA. But since you are writing service requests in IDL, the IDL compiler takes your relatively high-level program and generates your selected source-level language statements that make the calls into the CORBA infrastructure, effectively removing your need to be overly concerned with how it all happens.

CORBA is an infrastructure ("middleware") standard (a simplification—it's actually a set of *many* interrelated standards), and so there are many CORBA-compliant implementations that run on many different hardware platforms. The standard was constructed so that in principle, the same program runs *no matter what the underlying platform looks like.* This greatly simplifies integration and portability, as you can imagine.

Of course, to complicate the issue, there are a great many middleware standards: COM+, .NET, Enterprise Java beans, XML/SOAP, CORBA Component Model (CCM), to name a few. So the problems of integrating across multiple middleware infrastructure platforms exist as well.

The UML, on the other hand, is a *modeling standard.* The UML is a standardized language for specifying and describing system requirements and designs. In many respects, the UML is more general than CORBA because it can be used to create non-CORBA models as easily as CORBA-compliant models. It provides notation and semantics for specifying structure (in terms of object and class structure, component structure, deployment structure, and model structure), behavior (both in terms of individual objects and classes and in terms of collaborations of objects), and functionality (implementation-free requirements).

Because the UML is a modeling standard, it too is independent of the underlying hardware platform, although being essentially a very high-level programming language, you can specify OS and hardware-dependent aspects if desired. But for the most part, the hardware-dependent aspects of your application are added during the implementation of the model—whether that model is hand-coded or the code is generated automatically by your UML design automation tool.

One of the strengths of the UML is its ability to be adapted to specific vertical markets with specific concepts and needs. In the UML standard, these are called *profiles.* One such profile, the *UML Profile for Schedulability, Performance and Time* [6], the so-called *Real-Time UML Profile*, was recently adopted by the OMG. A profile is a subset of the UML, with semantics consistent with the UML standard but with some small extensions, including stereotyped elements, tagged values, constraints, and possibly some special notations. There are many UML profiles today, and that number is expected to grow significantly in the next couple of years.

There are other modeling standards within the OMG as well—Metamodel Object Facility (MOF) and Common Warehouse Model (CWM)—with which your UML-designed applications must somehow interact.

2.4.2 MDA to the Rescue

So you can see the problem. We have a proliferation of component and distribution infrastructure environments, an ongoing evolution to new source-level programming languages, and different modeling standards. How does one build a system today that integrates these disparate technologies? How does one build a system today that will be robust and stable in the years to come as even more new technology comes into use?

MDA exists to bring the whole shebang together via the application of modeling technology. The MDA is a development approach to develop applications that integrate today and in the future. In MDA, you develop a UML model of your application that is *platform-independent*. This platform independent model (PIM) is then mapped into one or a set of appropriate infrastructure and implementation environments, such as CORBA and C++, or .NET and Java. The MDA will provide standard mappings to help tools automate this process to ease the programmer burden inherent in developing PIMs.

Once the PIM is constructed, the next step is to create the application itself. This can be done in a number of different ways, such as constructing layered models (the PIM being the upper layer and the technology-specific infrastructure specified in lower layers) or through the use of translation tools that automatically perform the mapping of the PIM to a specific target platform. The more general application PIM semantics are then carried through into the more detailed platform-dependent application (PDA).

The most robust, and programmer-efficient, means to do this is to automatically generate the PDA from the PIM and a UML-compiler to apply the mapping rules from the PIM to the specific infrastructure technology.

Because MDA is inherently platform-independent, adding new platforms, such as operating systems, source-level languages, and distribution and component middleware infrastructures, is comparatively simple because it is a matter of defining the appropriate mapping rules and then constructing a compiler to apply the mapping. This allows the developer a greatly enhanced ability to reuse existing designs as the implementation technology evolves, as well as integrating diverse platforms together into well-coordinated systems.

The application of MDA does not mean that we need to throw away all previously constructed legacy systems. These legacy systems can be reused by wrapping them with MDA-compliant interfaces, constructed with the same modeling tools, so that they can work with the new and evolving MDA systems. Of course, as the legacy systems themselves are maintained, they may be redesigned incrementally over a relatively long period of time to make them internally MDA compliant. This provides a smooth migration path from noncompliant applications to fully MDA-compliant systems in the future.

The big win is a huge ROI on your intellectual investment, your application-specific intellectual property that is now captured in platform-specific models. By moving to MDA compliance, the investment in this corporate IP can be retained and enhanced without requiring the traditional throw-away-and-redesign.

2.4.3 Creating Architectural Elements—the Model Level

Okay, so at this point we have a fair idea of what architecture means, the (five) important architectural aspects, and the advantage of the MDA approach. So how do we go about actually creating architectural elements?

2.4.3.1 Basic Elements

In the "small," the fundamental concepts to consider are class and interface. Implementation of classes in C++ and Java is straightforward because in both cases classes are a native concept. In C-based object-oriented programming, structs are used (in C++, struct and class are basically identical) [7]. The difference between C and C++ is that in C++ struct can contain member functions, whereas in C, structs contain only data. The common solution for this in the C world is to define the member functions separately and embed pointers to those functions into the C struct. In this way the member function can be invoked by dereferencing the pointer. There is a difficulty in identifying which instance of the struct should be referenced by the member function. After all, struct is a type, and there may be any number of instances, each with independent data values at run-time. C++ compilers solve this problem by invisibly embedding a *this* pointer as the first argument to all nonstatic member functions. In C, the *this* pointer must be made explicit. For example, if a class in C++ is defined to be

```c
class Foo
private:
      int data;
public:
      int getFoo(void) { return data; };
      void setFoo(int d) { data = d; };
}; // end Foo
```

an equivalent class in C would be

```c
typedef struct Foo Foo;
struct Foo {
      int data;
      int (*getFoo)(Foo* const this);
      void (*setFoo)(Foo* const this, int d);
};

int getFoo(Foo *this) { return this->data; };

void setFoo(Foo *this, int d) { this->data = d; };
```

or alternatively, the member functions don't have to be a part of the struct declaration.

```c
typedef struct Foo Foo;
struct Foo {
      int data;          /*## attribute data */
};

int Foo_getFoo(Foo* const this) {
        return this->data
};

void Foo_setFoo(Foo* const this, int d) {
        this->data = d
};
```

Interfaces are a native concept in Java, and the UML interface maps directly to the Java interface. C and C++ don't have interfaces per se, and so interfaces in your model must be mapped somehow to concepts that *are* supported. There are two common approaches: the use of interface classes to represent the interface and inheritance from abstract classes. An interface class can be a substitute for an interface. Its implementation just delegates the implementation off to the concrete (implementation) class. It differs from true interfaces in that interface classes can have attributes and must have methods, whereas true interfaces cannot have attributes or methods, only operations. Interface classes are a bit more general than interfaces because while the name and parameter list of a class method must exactly match the name and parameter list of its matching operation, an interface class can massage the information where necessary. This means that the interface class is somewhat more powerful because it can perform "impedance matching" from one form to another, possibly invoking multiple different operations with different classes. This is also known as the Adapter Pattern [8].

Generalization from abstract classes and the use of interfaces serve the same purpose: to enforce interface compliance. Interfaces have no data and declare operations but do not provide the implementation—easily represented by data-free abstract classes.[8] So when you use an explicit interface in a model that is being translated to C++, one solution is to just create an abstract class with the required operations declared as *virtual* and then subclass it and define those methods in the concrete (implementation) subclass. This solution works in C as well, but the implementation of generalization requires some elaboration.

C++ supports the notion of polymorphism. A more general class can define an operation and it can be redefined in the subclass. When you call the method of an object, the most specific method appropriate for the object will be invoked. Further, the operations may even have different parameter lists, and the function to invoke is distinguished by the compiler at compile time on the basis of the name of the class, the name of the operation, and the list of parameters and their types.

Internally, C++ compilers do this through the introduction of "name mangling." Really, as far as the computer is concerned, the fact that one operation has the same name as another is incidental—they are distinctly different methods to invoke. So the original AT&T Cfront translator added the name of the class to the name of the operation to keep them straight.

---

8. An abstract class is one that is not instantiable because it declares an operation but does not provide an implementation method for it.

For example, the function Foo::setFoo(int d) might be mangled to be __Foo_setFoo_FSi, where Foo is the name of the class, setFoo is the name of the function per se, the following F indicates that it is a function, and Si indicates that the parameter is a signed int. If you are hand-writing your own C code from UML models, then you will have to mangle your own names if you want to support generalization and operator overloading. While it isn't difficult to do, it does make it more interesting to debug your program at the C level—especially when the function has a long parameter list.

For operator overloading to work well, the methods of a class should be *virtual*. In C++, this means that the function calls are dynamically dispatched using a virtual function table, or VTBL for short. This adds a very small amount of overhead but provides the significant benefit of making generalization work effectively. In C++, with its "you only pay for what you use" philosophy, you must include the virtual keyword. In Java, functions are virtual unless you go out of your way to make them *final*, *static*, or *private*. To use dynamic dispatching in C, you'll have to explicitly construct the VTBL yourself. This is nothing more than an index array of function pointers. When the virtual method is called, the call provides the index of the appropriate function in the appropriate class, using indexed offset addressing rather than direct addressing.

Implementing unary or optional (0,1) associations is straightforward: In C and C++, you will primarily use pointers, and in Java, you must use references. The various kinds of associations—normal association, aggregation, and composition—can all be implemented in this way. The primary distinction is that with composition, only the composite is responsible for the creation and the destruction of the part object, but this needn't change the implementation of the association itself.

When the association is "many" (*), then the most common implementation approach is to use a container class. In this case, a 1-* association between a class and a multiple becomes a 1-1 association from a class to the container, and then the container manages a 1-* association with the multiples (that is, after all, what containers do). Figure 2-15 shows how this works. The *ButtonPanel* class aggregates a collection of buttons. Rather than write in the *ButtonPanel* class itself all the logic to add, remove, find buttons, we delegate this to a *ButtonList* class. In this case, it is a parametric instantiation of the general template class *List*. The instiantiation process is done with the «bind» stereotype of dependency, binding the actual parameter (class *Button*) with the formal parameter (*T*).

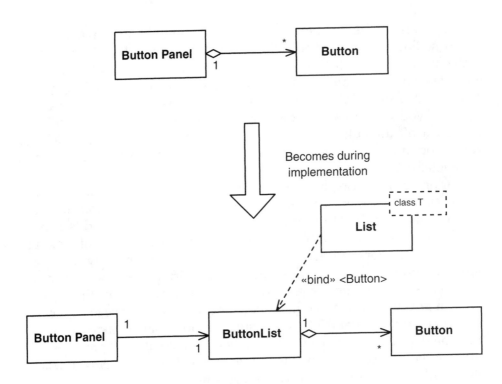

Figure 2-15: *Container Pattern*

Some UML-compiler tools, such as Rhapsody from I-Logix, apply the Container Pattern for you automatically when you generate the code from the model. However, if you manually code your model, then you will have to manually insert the containers. The C++ standard includes the Standard Template Library, a large set of different kinds of templatized[9] containers such as vector, stack, queue, list, map, and so on. Of course, there's no reason why you can't just write your own container and not use the standard containers, but there is little reason not to take advantage of them if you can. Java does not currently support parameterization, but containers are also available because in Java all objects are ultimately children of class *Object*. You can simply create a container class

---

9. A "template class" is C++-speak for *parameterized class* in the UML. Parameterized classes were introduced in Chapter 1.

that can contain objects and then use it to contain objects of any type. You can also use the containers defined in the standard library java.util.

In C, you'll have to either hand-code your containers, buy commercial off-the-shelf container libraries, or use macros to emulate parameterized classes.[10]

2.4.3.2 Logical Model

For the larger-scale organization of the model, the primary organizational element is the package and the particular stereotype «domain». This maps directly to C++ namespace and to Java packages. C has no namespace concept, and traditionally files are used to limit visibility and name scope.

2.4.3.3 Physical Model

The physical model implementation is rather straightforward in virtually all cases. When in doubt for how to implement an architectural element, you can almost always do it as a class (in C++ or Java) or struct (in C).

2.4.4 Subsystem and Component View

The primary elements in this view are components and subsystems. These are basically just classes that contain others via the composition relation. These larger-scale classes may have use cases (while packages such as domains do not), and particular emphasis is placed on getting the interfaces well specified. The interfaces are collections of operations of these large-scale classes that are exposed to other subsystems (and potentially their parts as well), and so may be invoked. Internally, these operations delegate the actual work to the contained part objects. There need not be a one-to-one mapping between a subsystem interface operation and a part object method. In general, the subsystem must create and destroy the part objects and orchestrate their collaboration. This may involve delegation of portions of the requested service to many different part objects.

Components may be implemented in exactly the same fashion. If the system uses a commercial component framework, such as COM+, .NET,

---

10. In the original implementation of C++, templates were implemented using macros, so it *can* be done.

or CCM, then those frameworks will impose specific structural and behavioral requirements on the component classes as well. In COM+, for example, it is common to have a one-to-one mapping to the underlying part COM+ enabled class. For specifics, see references on the particular component framework of interest.

2.4.5 Concurrency and Resource View

The basic UML element of concurrency is the «active» object. This is nothing more than a class that, in its constructor, creates a thread to run in and its destructor removes it. How to create and destroy threads is very OS-dependent. For example, VxWorks from Wind River uses taskSpawn() to create a task and taskDelete() to remove one. The other task control functions, such as creating and deleting semaphores, pending on event queues, and so on, are likewise OS-specific.

Generally, it is recommended that «active» classes not be application-domain classes but exist instead in a separate OS domain. The «active» class works best as a superclass from which you subclass when you make the subclass active. The application objects can then be aggregated into the «active» class via composition to do the real work.

The «active» object also must usually handle asynchronous rendezvous. This is usually done with message queues (also available from most operating systems—see the Message Queue Pattern in Chapter 5). When it runs, it reads the posted messages and then delegates it to the appropriate target object(s). For synchronous rendezvous, that means that an object that nominally runs in the thread of one «active» object is invoked using a direct call across the thread boundary. Serialization of access is almost always required in this case. This is most effectively accomplished by allocating a semaphore from the OS and invoking it from all public operations that are potentially in conflict (see the Guarded Call Pattern in Chapter 5). Resource objects are also implemented with some protection mechanism, and by far, semaphores are the most common solution used.

2.4.6 Distribution View

There are a great many approaches to make systems distributable (see Chapter 8 for a number of distribution patterns). In asymmetric distribution architectures, you usually want to have a communications component that understands how to transmit and receive messages with the necessary qualities of service. There is still the issue of how the messages are constructed. A "makeAmessage()" method for the communications component is one possibility. Another is that each object that needs to communicate across the bus knows how to make and interpret messages: This can be accomplished by subclassing a CommunicatingObject class. The communications component needs to be able to locate the objects targeted by messages, and one way to achieve that is through registration of a global object ID and a receptor function address. Symmetric architectures usually use some form of middleware, such as a CORBA ORB.

2.4.7 Safety and Reliability View

Safety and reliability also use large-scale objects to manage the redundancy. Subsystems are often used for this purpose. Channels are a kind of subsystem, presented in Chapter 9. Of course, just *having* the redundancy doesn't solve the problem. How to use the redundancy is the point of the patterns presented in Chapter 9.

It is usually technically much easier to improve safety and reliability by running the redundant elements on separate processors, avoiding "common mode failures" in which a single point failure brings down all redundant copies of an element. A variant on this is to separate the safety-critical aspects onto a separate processor from the nonsafety-critical elements. Since it is much harder and more expensive to make an element safe, reducing the size of that element by isolating it away from aspects that needn't be safety-critical can simplify the development effort a great deal.

2.4.8 Deployment View

The deployment view identifies how the software units, particularly the subsystems and components, map onto the hardware processors in the system. The most common solution for this is to create a separate executable for each separate processor, each executable consisting of a set of subsystems and/or components. It is equally reasonable to write multiple application executables for each processor as well. If your underlying OS provides different levels of protection of threads, then usually different applications are more protected from each other, but the overhead for task rendezvous is relatively high. Running a single application with multiple subsystems with their own threads allows for potentially lighter-weight rendezvous but may provide less protection from other misbehaving threads.

2.5 References

[1] Shlaer, Sally, and Steve Mellor. *Object Lifecycles: Modeling the World in States,* Englewood Cliffs, NJ: Prentice-Hall, 1992.

[2] Leveson, Nancy. *Safeware,* Reading, MA: Addison-Wesley, 1995.

[3] Douglass, Bruce Powel. *Doing Hard Time: Developing Real-Time Systems with UML, Objects, Frameworks and Patterns,* Reading, MA: Addison-Wesley, 1999.

[4] Richard Soley and the OMG Staff Strategy Group. *The Architecture of Choice for a Changing World, Document 00-11-05.PDF,* Needham, MA: OMG, 2000. *www.omg.org.*

[5] OMG Architecture Board (ORMSC). *Model-Driven Architecture (MDA), Document ormsc/01-07-01,* Needham, MA: OMG, 2001. *www.omg.org.*

[6] *Response to the OMG RFP for Schedulability, Performance, and Time, Document ad/2001-06-14,* Needham, MA: OMG, 2001. *www.omg.org.*

[7] Holub, Allen. *C + C++: Programming with Objects in C and C++,* New York: McGraw-Hill, 1992.

[8] Gamma, E., R. Helm, R. Johnson, and J. Vlissides. *Design Patterns: Elements of Reusable Object-Oriented Software,* Reading, MA: Addison-Wesley, 1995.

Chapter 3

The Role of
Design Patterns

This chapter discusses the following.

- The ROPES development process
- Why process?
  - ROPES process overview
    - Key enabling technologies
    - Process timescales
  - ROPES microcycle in detail
    - Party!
    - Analysis
    - Design
    - Translation
    - Test
- Design pattern basics
  - What is a design pattern?

- • Basic structure of design patterns
- • How to read design patterns in this book
- • Using design patterns in development
  - • Pattern hatching
  - • Pattern mining
  - • Pattern instantiation

3.1 Introduction

In this chapter, we define design patterns and discuss why they are useful and how to apply them in the design of systems. Before we go into patterns per se, however, it will be useful to review software development process. Development processes govern what activities you do, how you do them, and when you do them. The question "How do I use design patterns?" is fundamentally a *process* question.

There is a very broad range of development processes in use today, from "We don't need no stinking process" to very formal rigorous processes. In order to frame our discussion of how and when to apply design patterns, we must do so in the context of a reference process. For this purpose, this chapter begins with a short discussion of the ROPES[1] process—a process used in a great many real-time and embedded development environments. Once that is done, we will discuss the application of patterns, using the ROPES process as an example. If you use a different process, then you may need to adapt the rules for pattern usage accordingly.

3.2 The ROPES Development Process

Most software projects run late, miss functionality goals, have numerous and *serious* defects, and generally cost much more to produce and main-

---

1. Rapid Object-oriented Process for Embedded Systems

tain than estimated—*every* time. Why is that? I believe it's because software is just plain *hard*. It is hard in principle because it involves the most complex parts of the entire system coded up into inflexible rules of logic, implemented in formal and unforgiving languages. Either that, or it's because we're all stupid. I prefer to believe it's hard. (That's my story, and I'm sticking to it!)

Software is among the most complex artifacts created by humans today, rivaling the most complex physical structures ever created by man. It is not bound by physical constraints. Instead, we must not only make up the rules for what the system has to do, we also have to create the environment in which those rules make sense, the terms and concepts we want to use, and the semantic laws that govern how those concepts interact.

It is as if we wanted to construct a bridge, but first we had to decide how to make a rock from which to make concrete, from which we made structural members. And not only *make* the rock but also define all of its physical properties, such as weight, density, tensile strength, shear strength, porosity, and so on. *And* we would have to define what these concepts mean—for example, what do we mean by *weight,* and how does it relate to the gravitational field of the earth? Further, we would have to define whether we started to construct the structural members first or part of the span. Then we have to determine how to connect the parts—because, after all, we can use cables, chemical bonding, welding, and so on. And what do *those* things mean? If this sounds daunting with respect to the job of building a bridge, then it should also sound difficult with respect to constructing software systems because we do the analogue of these things on a daily basis when we construct software systems.

In order to actually get things built, we try to simplify the overall problem. We construct logic systems with relatively simple and unambiguous rules, such as programming languages, that allows us to reason about the rules that we want our system to implement. We also simplify how we construct and put together the pieces of the system and decide that it's correct. To simplify our problem, we define a simple set of rules and guidelines that control what we do and when we do it, and the structure and content of what we produce. We call rules that govern how we work *process*.

3.2.1 Why Process?

The basic reason why we as software and system developers should be concerned about and use a good process is to improve our lives and our products. Specifically, a good process does the following.

- Provides a project template to guide workers through the development and delivery of a product
- Improves product quality in terms of
  — Decreased number of defects
  — Lowered severity of defects
  — Improved reusability
  — Improved stability and maintainability
- Improves project predictability in terms of
  — Total amount of effort
  — Length of calendar time required for completion
- Communicates project information appropriate to different stakeholders in ways that they can use effectively

If your process doesn't achieve these goals, then you have a *bad* process, and you should think about changing it for the better. These goals can be achieved with a good process, or they can be inhibited by a bad process.

So what's a process? In ROPES, we define a process as follows.

> A **process** is the specification of a sequenced set of activities performed by a collaborating set of workers resulting in a coherent set of project artifacts, one of which is the desired system.

A process consists of *worker roles*, the "hats" worn by workers while they do various project activities. Each activity results in the creation or modification of one or more *artifacts*. For example, most processes have requirements capture (activity) somewhere early on before design occurs. This is performed by someone (worker) acting as a requirements specifier (worker role), and it might result in a requirements specification, a set of use cases and elaborated sequence diagrams (artifacts). A high-level view of the basic elements of a development process is shown in Figure 3-1.

The activities are the tasks the worker does in performing his or her duty. At the high level, these activities are modeled as the development phases, such as "requirements analysis" or "integration and test." Activities are typically subdivided into subactivities, possibly at several different levels of abstraction. At a more detailed level, activities may be, for example, creating a single (or several) sequence diagrams, writing code for a class method body, unit testing a class, or reviewing a document.

Artifacts are what is created or modified during activities. The single most important artifact is the "system" being produced, but there are many others that may be produced. Generally speaking, every activity

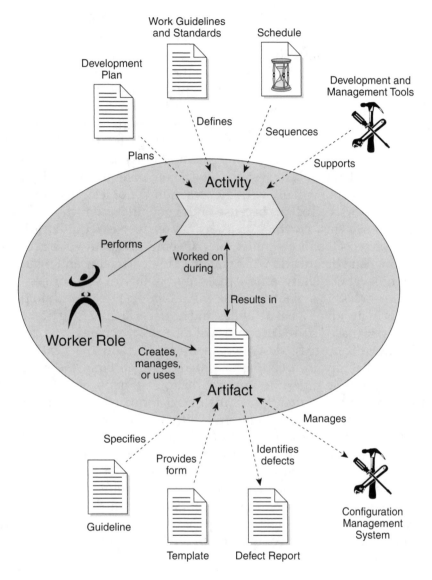

Figure 3-1: *Basic Elements of Process*

results in the creation or modification of at least one artifact. Some common artifacts are requirements specifications, use case diagrams, system prototypes, class diagrams, source code, test plans, test vectors, reuse plan, and meeting minutes.

One of the desirable properties for a process is *scalability.* This means that the process works well for a small project and is not too onerous in terms of effort and yet also works well for large projects, providing all of the communication and artifacts needed there as well. In general, scalability means that if x effort is required for a project of size y, then an effort of *100xc* (where c is a constant) is required if the size of the project is *100y*. Process scalability must take into account the fact that the larger the project, the more ritual required. As the project scale grows, teams become less colocated and more global; systems gain additional levels of abstractions such as subsystems, subsubsystems, and so on; potential lines of communication grow exponentially with the total number of team members; and the cost of errors skyrockets because of the potential interaction of effects in complex systems. For these reasons, more rigor is required for more complex projects than for simpler ones. Overall, scalability of a process is achieved when you only do what you need to do to create and maintain a consistent level of quality, effort, and predictability of your project—neither more nor less. A scalable process will provide guidelines to aid project managers in deciding what activities and artifacts are necessary and what is appropriate based on the properties of the project at hand.

The ROPES process, described in more detail in the next section, achieves scalability in a couple of different ways. First, the process is viewed at multiple timescales: macro, micro, and nano. Smaller projects will give much more attention to the micro and nano cycles, but as the projects grow in size, more attention is shifted to the macro scale to organize and orchestrate the entire development process. Second, a number of artifacts are optional and created during the process only if necessary. Hazard analysis, for example, is only used for safety-critical applications. The subsystem architecture view, for another example, is only created when systems are large enough to profit from such decomposition. In fact, the entire systems engineering phase is optional and is used only when the system is either complex or when there is significant hardware-software codesign.

3.2.2 ROPES Process Overview

The ROPES process is a general systems development process that, while emphasizing the software development aspects, includes systems engineering and systems integration and test as well. It is, and continues to be, a work in progress that has evolved over the last 25 years. New concepts and methods are added and adapted as they become proven, and older ones are discarded when they no longer serve the need. The ROPES process has been used effectively on very small one- to three-person projects as well as large teams consisting of hundreds of members. ROPES is a highly scalable, "medium-weight" process, striking a balance between static heavyweight processes and lightweight, so-called "agile methods," such as Extreme Programming (XP) [1], while incorporating aspects of both.

ROPES has but a single mission: "to produce systems with less effort, fewer defects, and greater project predictability." Although it emphasizes aspects that are of particular importance to real-time and embedded systems developers, ROPES is certainly more general than that—being applicable to all kinds of software-intensive systems development efforts [2]. It is constructed to optimize technology to achieve its mission, and it focuses special attention on six key technologies.

3.2.2.1 Key Enabling Technologies

Developers using the ROPES, or any other modern process, will employ a great many technologies from compilers to configuration management to the Internet. However, there is a small number of technologies that provide key advantages that the ROPES process attempts to optimize (see Figure 3-2).

3.2.2.1.1 Visual Modeling   Visual modeling brings two primary things to the table for the development of systems and software: the ability to look at and focus on different aspects of the system and the ability to look at an aspect of the system at different levels of abstraction. Just as when we construct an office building, we need to look at floor plans, structural members, heat exchange, water flow, and vibration resistance, when we build software, we must be able to focus on the structural aspects, the behavioral aspects, and the functional aspects.[2] Further, we must be able to look at these aspects at many different levels of abstraction from a very high-level system view to a very low-level "transistor" view. Only having the source code makes it extremely difficult to focus on different aspects or at any level of abstraction different from the code itself.

3.2.2.1.2 Model Execution   It has been said that the best way to have no defects in a product is to *not put them there*. Okay, but since we are fallible,

---

2. *Functional* in this context means "implementation-free required functionality."

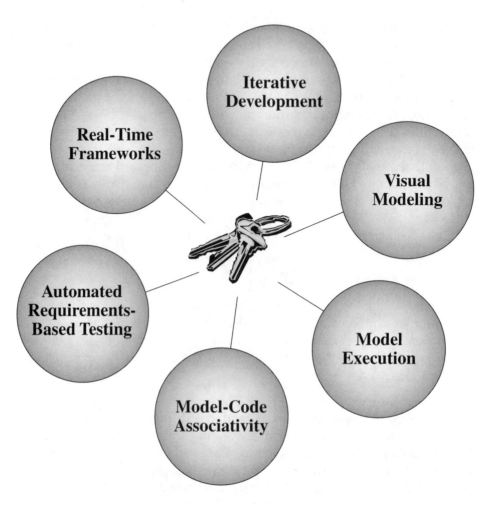

Figure 3-2: *Key Enabling Technologies*

what does that mean in practice? What I think it means is that we can identify defects as soon as we introduce them. If we're constructing a class diagram of 50 collaborating objects, and we make an error in the statechart of the second object, we want to be able to look at that second object *as soon as we insert the defect* and see that it is obviously in error. How can we do that?

The answer is *model execution.* The use of executable models allows us to execute and test even partial models as soon as we capture them in our design tool. This means that testing doesn't just come at the end but is an integral part of identifying each of the 50 objects in our collaboration. With modern tools, a partially completed collaboration can be ready for execution literally at the press of a button and can be debugged and tested at the model level (as opposed to code level) using model-level debuggers. Rhapsody, a UML-compliant executable modeling tool from I-Logix,[3] is a prime example of this and will be referenced in this discussion.

This is a new way of developing systems. The traditional way of developing systems, even with visual modeling tools, is to create huge models and then set about getting them to work. This "test at the end" philosophy is very difficult and error-prone, and by the time it does identify errors, they have often spread throughout much of the system. This makes tracking down and stamping out all the defects an arduous task, consisting of writing possibly thousands of lines of code and getting them to not only compile but be correct.

With the test-as-you-design approach, you might put down two or three related objects and demonstrate that within that context, these objects work properly. This is generally very easy because the scope of the testing problem is small. Once you have that small set of objects working, you add the next few and get them to work. The idea is to *always construct your design using pieces known to work properly.* Then, as you add more functionality to your collaboration, you introduce only small changes before reexecuting and retesting your model.

The primary reason this hasn't been done traditionally is the difficulty in getting the models to execute. It involved closing down the modeling tool, getting out the source code editor, pounding out some source code, compiling it, fixing the compilation errors until you have a clean build and then debugging it with a source-level debugger, identifying the coding (translation) errors and fixing them in the source editor and repeating the process, and finally (!) identifying the modeling errors, closing down your debugging environment, and reopening the modeling tools and making an "equivalent fix" in your model. This is such a pain that developers put it off as long as possible.

However, with the use of executable models, it is a simple matter to construct the parts of the model you want to execute, *push a button* to generate the code, and then debug and test it using the *visual debugger* (rather than the source-level debugger). This tests and debugs your model using

---

3. I-Logix Inc., 3 Riverside Drive, Andover, MA 01810. Tel: 978-682-2100. Fax: 978-682-5995. *http://www.ilogix.com.*

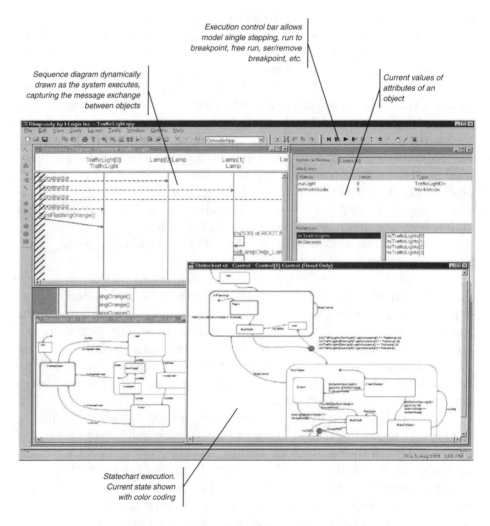

Execution control bar allows
model single stepping, run to
breakpoint, free run, ser/remove
breakpoint, etc.

Sequence diagram dynamically
drawn as the system executes,
capturing the message exchange
between objects

Current values of
attributes of an
object

Statechart execution.
Current state shown
with color coding

Figure 3-3: *Visual Model Execution and Test*

modeling concepts, not source-level concepts. A screen snapshot of Rhapsody executing a model is shown in Figure 3-3.

In Figure 3-3, the statecharts for two objects are shown with color-coding,[4] indicating their current state. The sequence diagram is dynamically drawn as the objects run, providing a visual history of their collaboration.

---

4. Hard to see on a black-and-white page, though!

You can also view the current attribute values of the objects, look at the call stack and event queues, and so on. In effect, this is the model analogue to the source-level debugger. The model can be executing on your desktop or on the actual target hardware and in either case send the execution information back to Rhapsody for display and control.

Using this kind of tool greatly facilitates the running of the model because creating a running application from the selected portion of your model is literally no more difficult than clicking the mouse, and it generally requires only a few seconds. Execution is tightly integrated with your model, and you can test and debug with the same concepts that you used to design the model. Finally, because it is so simple and fast, there is no reason not to do this *all the time*. We will see how we use this later in the "nanocycle" for software design and construction.

3.2.2.1.3 Model-Code Associativity

One of the painful aspects of using visual models comes from the fact that generally there is no rigorous connection between the visual model of the system design and the source code that is compiled to construct the running system. In fact, many people think their task is to maintain two very different views of the model—the graphical diagrams and the source code—in synch. What happens inevitably is that eventually the graphical diagrams and the source code gradually begin to deviate from each other until finally the graphical representation is abandoned altogether and all work is shifted to the source code. As we've seen, there are some real benefits to using graphical languages such as the UML to represent your system, so abandoning it to leave an entirely code-based system is a *bad thing*.

The issue, I believe, is that the metaphor is flawed. The problem is not to maintain two separate models in synch but to maintain a single model of which graphical representation and source code are merely two dynamically linked views. A model can be thought of as a coherent set of semantic entities and their relationships. A class diagram represents some of those, and so is a view of that underlying semantic model. As is a statechart. As is a sequence diagram. As is source code. Make changes in one view, and because that view is dynamically linked to the underlying semantic model, all the other views change automatically to reflect the changed semantics. We call this *dynamic model-code associativity*.

Modeling tool support is required for this to become a reality, but fortunately, there are tools on the market that do a good job at this. Some "executable modeling" tools achieve this by generating code automatically from the model and not allowing the developers to modify it. While it is true that most fundamental changes to the model should probably be done in graphical views, most developers consider unacceptable the restriction that they cannot modify the code at all without breaking the linkage to the semantic model. There are times when they want to modify the code, such as when they're doing a rapid coding/debugging nanocycle. What you want in principle is to be able to work in any model view, including source code, and have the changes applied to the underlying semantic model automatically. Fortunately, such tools exist, of which Rhapsody is one example.

3.2.2.1.4 *Automated Requirements-Based Testing* If we think of debugging as "playing around with the model to make sure that it is relatively defect-free," then testing is a more rigorous process to ferret out and remove defects from a system. In high-reliability systems development, testing is often 50 percent or more of the entire development effort, even though it is widely acknowledged that it is impossible to exhaustively test modern systems. Any good development process should reduce the tremendous cost of testing while at the same time improving its effectiveness.

One of the reasons that testing is so expensive is that it usually takes place only at the end. This is the most expensive place to identify defects. The ROPES process attempts to place the identification and removal of defects much earlier in the process.

The reason that testing at the end is so expensive has to do with the nature of the really expensive defects. The really expensive defects are called *strategic defects*—requirements and architectural defects. The reason these defects can cost as much as 10,000 times the cost of simple coding errors is twofold. First, they are broad-sweeping in their scope, affecting many parts of the system. Second, they tend to be introduced very early and caught very late. This means that as other pieces of the system are added, these new parts depend on these basic flaws. Thus, fixing the original defect means that all of the potentially subtle dependencies must be tracked down and repaired as well.

ROPES provides a evolutionary requirements-based testing strategy that continuously tests the system against what it is supposed to do. This results in much earlier identification and removal of defects at a much lower cost. Automated support for early testing that can evolve with the system design greatly enhances the efficacy of this approach.

Testing in ROPES is done in a small scale during what is called the nanocycle (more on this later) and in a larger scale during the microcycle (spiral) via incremental construction of the system. The primary artifact produced during each microcycle is an executable, tested version of the system called a *prototype*. A prototype builds on previous prototypes by adding more functionality. Each prototype has a *mission*—the purpose of the prototype—that is explicitly tested during the test phase of the microcycle. Usually, a prototype's mission is a small set of use cases and/or the reduction of some small set of risks. The prototype produced is a high-quality artifact containing code that will actually be shipped to the customer when the system is released. However, early prototypes do not contain all of the system functionality, and so they are incomplete. Whenever possible, prototype functionality is introduced in a high-risk-earliest fashion with the explicit purpose of reducing the largest risks as early as possible.

Figure 3-4 shows schematically the evolution of prototypes. In this example, the first prototype is called "Hello World" and has a precisely defined mission: create the basic subsystem architecture, perform low-level data acquisition, and display those data values in a basic user interface. This prototype is produced during the first microcycle and is tested against that mission. Defects identified during testing are either repaired then (if they are serious) or noted for fixing in the next microcycle. Note that the basic high-level architecture is in place already in this early prototype. If it has a fundamental error, it will likely be found in the testing of this prototype. Fixing any such errors now will be much cheaper than if we wait until the entire system is constructed and *then* find and repair the flaw.

The next prototype contains all the elements of the first but adds several new ones. It also has a well-defined mission: integrate a transport protocol so that objects can collaborate across different address spaces, display the data as a waveform on the user interface, permit the user to control the setting of the control variables, and perform data logging. The architecture is tested *again* during the test of this prototype. Architectural flaws that passed through the first prototype validation test will likely be uncovered during this prototype's testing. This is *still* much earlier than if the error is caught at the end of the project.

The last prototype in the figure adds even more to its predecessor. It adds reliable communications and sockets for long-duration dialogs among the distributed processors, adds the facility to do closed-loop control of actuation, and adds in the built-in test functionality.

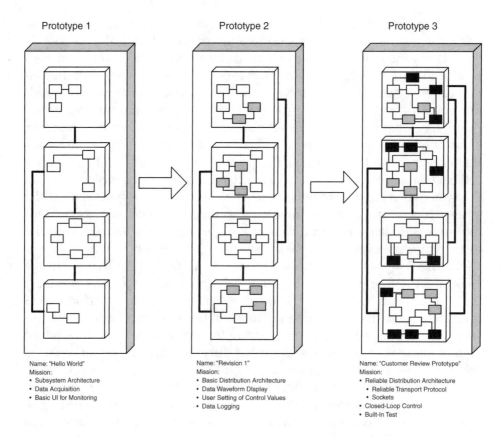

Figure 3-4: *Incremental Development with Prototypes*

In reality, as we'll see, a prototype is usually completed and tested every four to six weeks. Some projects may create prototypes in a longer or shorter period. However, longer periods between prototypes raises the risk that repair of defects may require more effort than if those defects were identified earlier. The benefit of building and testing incremental prototypes is that the high-risk features are tested as early as possible and potentially serious defects can be repaired while it is still easy to do.

Using automated tools to convert the requirements for the prototype into test vectors that can be applied against the prototype can provide a tremendous time and effort savings. And when the tools can partially or completely automate the testing process, then the savings are improved even more.

3.2.2.1.5 *Frameworks*   In my experience, 60 to 90 percent of every application you construct is very similar to previous applications. Every system you construct requires a common set of functions—like manage the creation and destruction of objects, manage memory, schedule tasks, handle interrupts, queue events for asynchronous task rendezvous, serial access with semaphores for synchronous task rendezvous, execute state machines, and so on. And yet, we create code to do these things as if it were novel each and every time we build a new system. Wouldn't it be nice to start your next project with a partially completed application that already knew how to do all those things so all you had to do was add that 10 to 40 percent application-specific code?

That's the power of frameworks. A framework is a "partially completed application that you customize or specialize for your specific application." A framework differs from a library in that a library is a passive thing that you call to invoke a service. A framework is your application that invokes the problem-specific services that you want performed.

The creation of frameworks is much more difficult than the creation of applications. Fortunately commercial frameworks are available. Microsoft's MFC (Microsoft Foundation Classes) and Borland's OWL (Object Windows Library) are examples of commercial frameworks that have improved developer productivity within those environments by an order of magnitude. Some executable tools provide frameworks for your applications as well. Some companies are investing in the construction of domain-specific frameworks for automotive, aerospace, and other application domains. The initial cost of development for frameworks is high, but the long-term benefits are potentially tremendous.

3.2.2.1.6 *Iterative Development*   The last key technology is the improvement in productivity and predictability we gain by employing iterative, incremental development to the creation of software-intensive systems. There has been a great deal published about the effective use of the spiral development lifecycle and its advantages. The primary advantage, in my experience, is the early testing of systems. Far too many people throw a system together with low-quality software parts and then beat on it with testing until it (more or less) works. The essence of the spiral lifecycle is that it is *incremental*—building small pieces of the system and proving that they work and then adding more pieces and proving that *they* work, and so on. The results are higher-quality software done with much less rework and in less calendar time and less effort. The iterative spiral is the centerpiece of the ROPES process, but it is really only one of three differ-ent time-based views of the project.

3.2.2.2 Process Timescales

Even though the waterfall lifecycle has been pretty resoundingly denounced over the last 20 years, it is still by far the most common way of scheduling and managing projects. The reason is that is it easy to plan and understand. The problem that no project actually follows such a lifecycle leads to any number of problems in the development process. The most fundamental difficulty with the waterfall lifecycle is that defects intro-duced early in the process are not identified or fixed until late in the process. By far, the most expensive defects are specification and architec-tural defects. The reason that these defects are so expensive is that their scope is far reaching and because many other system aspects end up depending on them. In order to fix such defects, it is necessary to also fix all the aspects of the system that depend on those flaws. This is inherent in the waterfall lifecycle because *testing comes at the end.* The longer you wait to identify and repair defects, the more they have become entrenched, and the greater the number of dependencies on the flawed aspects.

To reduce or remove the problems associated with the simplistic waterfall lifecycle, the spiral or iterative lifecycle has become popular. The basic advantage of the spiral lifecycle is that the system is tested, early and often, so that fundamental flaws can be caught early when there is less rework to do. This is done by breaking up the development project into a set of smaller projects and scheduling them so that one such sub-project builds on and uses those that come before and provides a building block for those that come after. This is the "spiral." Each subproject is more limited in scope, is produced with much greater ease, and has a much more targeted focus than the entire system. The result of each sub-project or spiral is an *iterative prototype*—a functional, high-quality system that is not as complete (or perhaps not done in as high fidelity) as the final system. Nevertheless, the prototype does correctly implement and exe-cute some portion of the requirements and/or reduce some set of risks.

The ROPES process can be conceptualized as occurring simultane-ously in three different scales or time frames (see Figure 3-5). The *macro-cycle process* occurs over the course of many months to years and guides the overall development from concept to final delivery. The ROPES macro process has four primary, but overlapping, phases. Each macrophase

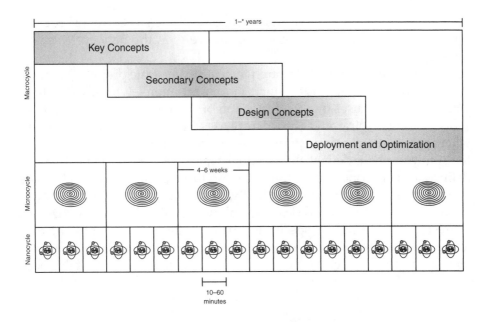

Figure 3-5: *ROPES Spiral Macrocycle*

actually contains multiple microcycles, as we will see shortly, and the result of each microcycle is the production of an iterative prototype.

The macrophases are a way of showing that the missions of the prototypes evolve over time. The early prototypes tend to focus on key concepts, such as requirements, architecture, or technology. The next several prototypes introduce and focus on the secondary concepts of requirements, architecture, and technology. After that, the focus shifts to design and implementation concerns. The last set of prototypes emphasizes optimization and deployment (in the target hardware and in the customer's environment). The shift in focus of the prototypes tends to be gradual, hence the overlapping nature of the macrophases.

The microcycle has a much more limited scope than the macrophase. It is usually completed within four to six weeks, whereas a macrophase may last many months or years. The microcycle is focused around the production and delivery of a single prototype with limited but high-quality functionality. This is most commonly focused around one or a small number of use cases, but it may also include specific risk-reduction activities.

The nanocycle is the most limited scope of all—on the order of a few minutes to hours. In the nanocycle, ideas are modeled/executed/fixed at a very high rate. The so-called "agile processes," such as Extreme Programming (XP) approach, focus almost exclusively on the nanocycle scale of development.

The macrocycle extends through the entire life of the project. The microcycle, on the other hand, is of much shorter duration—typically four to six weeks—and it focuses on the production of a single prototype.[5] Figure 3-6 shows a single spiral and the microphases involved. The Party phase is where project planning and periodic assessment takes place. Following that, the Analysis phase defines the essential aspects of the prototype; these are defined to be the aspects such that if the produced prototype doesn't possess them, it must be considered to be faulty. The Analysis model may be implemented by any number of designs. Following this, Design optimizes the analysis model by making specific technology selections and applying them to the analysis model. The Design phase, incidentally, is where design patterns are applied, which is, of course, the focus of the main part of this book.

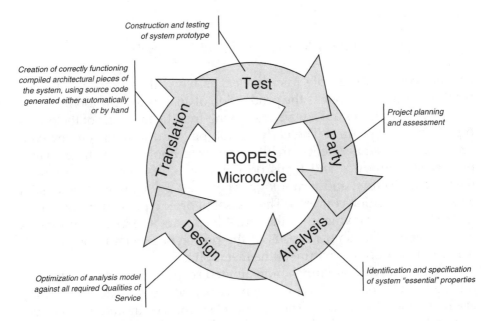

Figure 3-6: *ROPES Microcycle (Overview)*

---

5. In large projects with disparate teams, it is possible to run prototypes in parallel and merge them together in a future prototype.

Following the Design phase, the Translation phase produces the compiled and linked architectural pieces of the system. Finally, the Test phase integrates these architectural pieces together and tests that they correctly implement the architecture as well as satisfy the prototype's mission.

The next timescale down is called the *nanocycle*. The premise is that as you construct the model you are constantly testing to be sure that you've got it right so far. Thus, you continuously test, on your desktop or on the target hardware, as you modify code, add objects, change relationships, and so on. Your goal in the nanocycle is to never be more than a few minutes away from being able to execute and test your model. Figure 3-7 shows the basic work activities of the nanocycle. The entire nanocycle usually lasts only a few minutes, and with the use of modern UML compiler tools, the generation and compilation of code should normally take less than a minute.

3.2.2.2.1 Semispiral Lifecycle Model Some managers, developers, and organizations are very uncomfortable with a fully iterative approach

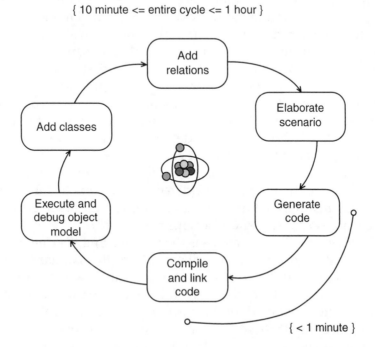

Figure 3-7: *ROPES Nanocycle*

because it's different and it entails deferment of the identification of requirements and architectural details later than the waterfall lifecycle. These concerns are not entirely groundless. In some situations, the system development involves significant hardware development with very long hardware production times. This means that the hardware development must precede the software development by a significant period of time, and all the requirements for the hardware must be understood prior to the production run. In this case, a fully iterative solution, which doesn't uncover detailed requirements until the spiral during which they will be designed and implemented, may not be appropriate. In other cases, an organization may be funded just to develop a requirements model. This happens in some DoD projects, for example. In this case, a fully spiral approach is also inappropriate.

To address these other projects to which a fully incremental spiral approach doesn't apply well, the ROPES process provides the *semispiral lifecycle*—a combination of waterfall and spiral models that is tailored to address projects in which a more complete requirements and/or systems engineering effort is required up front.

Figure 3-8 shows the dual aspects of the semispiral lifecycle. The first two phases, Requirements Analysis and Systems Engineering, are done outside of the iteration, just as they are done in a waterfall lifecycle. That is, they are done just once but more completely than in a single spiral of the spiral lifecycle. In the spiral lifecycle, the first iteration will identify the "lay of the land" of the requirements—the primary capabilities of the system—but won't identify and define the detailed requirements for those capabilities until they are to be implemented in the current proto-type. The detailed requirements definition is deferred until later so that the more critical or higher-risk aspects of the system can be specified and designed earlier. In the semispiral model, *all* requirements are fully detailed before the phase is considered to be complete. Of course, just as in the classic waterfall lifecycle, if the requirements are in error, then they will be more expensive and laborious to correct.

Following the Requirements is the Systems Engineering phase. This is similar to the Systems Engineering phase in the standard spiral micro-cycle (described in the next section), but again, it will be more complete than in a full spiral lifecycle. In the full spiral approach, only the parts of the architecture required for the current prototype are defined in the System Engineering phase so that the architecture grows over time. Not true with the semispiral lifecycle! In this latter case, the entire (high-level) architecture is defined first, and then the subsystems of the architecture

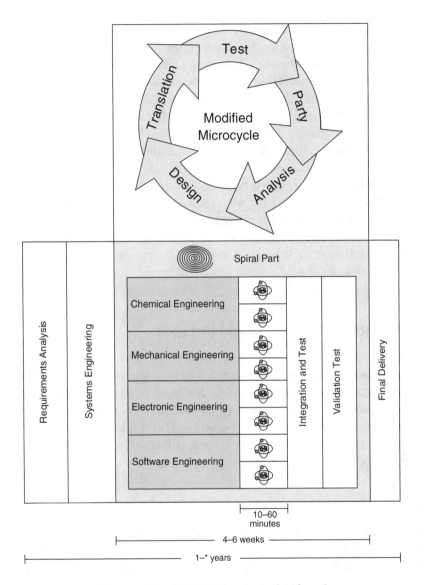

Figure 3-8: *ROPES Semispiral Lifecycle*

are decomposed into software and hardware aspects before turning loose the engineers in the various disciplines to work on the design.

The primary difference between the waterfall and the semispiral lifecycles is the Spiral Part, in which a series of prototypes are created from elements created by the different engineering disciplines working in parallel. They are brought together during the Integration and Test phase, and the prototype is validated during the Validation Test phase. While in the spiral model, the detailed requirements are *defined and realized* in the spirals. In the semispiral model, they are only *realized* in different spirals. So early on, in the first Party phase of the Spiral Part, the set of prototypes and their properties are defined in terms of when requirements will be realized via design, which prototypes will integrate which hardware and software elements and their level of maturity, and so on. For example, the breadboarded hardware may be integrated with the software in prototype 3, while in prototype 7 the mechanical enclosures are integrated with the fuel valves and chemical mixing, electronic motors, and software control of the valves and motors. Then in prototype 10, the actual production electronic hardware will be integrated with the production mechanical parts. These prototypes, just as in the full spiral model, are the primary scheduling points against which progress is tracked and measured.

3.2.3 The ROPES Microcycle in Detail

The ROPES microcycle has been discussed from an overview perspective, but to understand how to use the process, it is necessary to understand in more detail the work activities and artifacts produced. The full spiral ROPES microcycle is shown in Figure 3-9.[6] We see that each of the primary phases in the spiral has subphases. The work activities are almost identical in the semispiral lifecycle, and differences will be noted in the relevant subphase description.

3.2.4 Party!

The spiral starts in the so-called Party phase,[7] which is the location of the primary project planning and ongoing assessment activities. During the first spiral's Party phase, the general schedule, software development

---

6. It should be noted that some authors show the spiral spiraling outwards rather than inwards, as it is here. It is shown spiraling inwards to emphasize the convergence of the prototype to the final delivered system.

7. The Party phase corresponds to both Initial Concept and Postmortem Assessment phases in some other development process models. The use of the term *party* is to reinforce the notion of "celebration of ongoing success" rather than "figure out what went wrong."

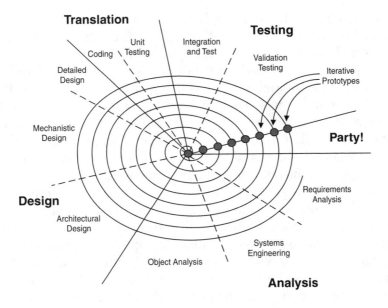

Figure 3-9: *ROPES Spiral Microcycle (Detail)*

plan, configuration management plan, reuse plan (if any), project scope, initial primary use case set, and engineering approach are selected and defined. On subsequent spirals, the project and system are assessed against those plans and modified as necessary. The Party phase includes the following areas.

- Schedule
- Architecture
- Process
- Next prototype mission

One of the more serious project management mistakes is inadequate assessment and adjustment of projects during their execution. As DeMarco and Lister note, "You cannot control what you do not measure" [3]. It is equally important, however, that if you *do* measure, you must apply the information to make adjustments. In terms of schedule, such adjustments may be reassignment of resources, reordering activities, deletion of activities, reductions (or enhancements) of scope and/or quality, rescheduling subsequent activities, and so on.

Because the selection and implementation of a good architecture are crucial to the long-term success of a project and product, the Party phase evaluates architecture on two primary criteria. First, is the architecture adequately meeting the needs of the qualities of services that are driving the architectural selection? Second, is that architecture scaling well as the system evolves and grows? The process of reorganizing the architecture is called *refactoring* the system. If the project team finds that the architecture must be significantly refactored on each prototype, then this is an indication that the architecture is not scaling well, and some additional effort should be given to the definition of a better architecture.

Early on in the project, selections are made about how to manage the project—what tools will be used, where they and their data are located and how they are accessed, security procedures, artifact review and quality assessment procedures, work and artifact guidelines, and so forth. It is likely that at least *some* of these decisions will prove to be suboptimal as the project proceeds. Rather than live with a suboptimal process, the Party phase seeks to improve the process during the course of the project rather than waiting until the *next* project. For example, it might be that the decision was made to run the configuration management repository on a remote server so that the distributed team could access it. However, during the first prototype, it is discovered that the low speed and poor reliability of the particular network server used are significantly hampering the team's ability to access the configuration items. The Party phase Process Assessment activity provides an opportunity to identify and remedy that problem.

Last, although the plan for the prototype mission is decided early on (and scheduled against), this plan is reviewed and possibly adjusted at each iteration. It is common to make minor adjustments about the mission scope, but if nothing else, explicitly reviewing the plan ensures that everyone knows what to do over the next four to six weeks it takes to complete the microcycle.

3.2.5 Analysis with the ROPES Process

The purpose of analysis is to define the essential properties of the system to be developed. *Essential* refers to properties whose absence makes a system *wrong* or *incomplete*. Whether the system internally contains a serial port is not an *essential* property, but the fact that it can control the internal actuators *is*. True enough, there are times when this distinction becomes fuzzy, but many embedded systems developers have difficulty distinguishing between analysis and design concerns. Analysis is typically a black-box view, and any design that provides the required functionality within the specified QoS is sufficient. In the ROPES process, a strong distinction is made between decisions that are essential (analysis) and decisions that are for optimization (design).

3.2.5.1 Requirements Analysis Phase

In the Requirements phase, the requirements of the current prototype are identified and captured in detail. The use cases for the prototype have already been selected, but the detailed specification of what the use cases contain has not. An exception is in the semispiral lifecycle, where the details have already been fully elaborated prior to starting the spirals. In the semispiral case, the Requirements phase in the spiral is superfluous except for selecting which detailed requirements are to be implemented in the current prototype.

There are two primary ways to detail a use case: by example and by specification. *By example* means that a (possibly large) set of scenarios is created that illustrates typical and exceptional uses of the system for the use case in question. The advantages of scenarios are that they are easy for nontechnical stakeholders to understand and they can serve as a basis for the set of test vectors to be applied later to the completed prototype. The disadvantages of scenarios are that requirements of a use case are spread out over possibly dozens of different sequence diagrams rather than being in a single place, and the requirements may be difficult to represent concisely. Additionally, some things, such as negative requirements (for example, "The elevator shall not leave the floor with the door open") are very difficult to state. Scenarios are most commonly captured using UML sequence diagrams.

The other approach to detailing use cases is by specification. This specification may be informal, using text to describe the requirements of the use case or a formal behavioral language such as Z, temporal logic, UML statecharts or UML activity diagrams. The advantages of detailing use cases by specification are that it is concise, it is more precise than scenarios, and it is easy to represent requirements that are difficult to show in scenarios. The disadvantages are that it is more difficult to understand, particularly for nontechnical personnel, and directly relating the requirements to the design may be more difficult as well. For continuous and piecewise continuous behavior requirements, we recommend using control law diagrams and binding these to individual use cases.

Both of these approaches are useful, and in fact, the ROPES process recommends that *both* are used. A formal specification using statecharts or activity diagrams captures the requirements concisely, whereas scenarios derived from the formal specification can help nontechnical stakeholders to understand the system. Further, the scenarios derived from the formal specification may be used to generate the test vectors for validation at the end of the microcycle.

Requirements are detailed using a combination of the following.

- Sequence diagrams
- Statecharts
- Activity diagrams
- Control law diagrams (non-UML)
- Textual descriptions
- Constraints

3.2.5.2 Systems Engineering Phase

The Systems Engineering phase is actually high-level architectural design. It is an optional part of the microcycle, used when the project has a significant amount of hardware-software codesign or the project is complex enough to require a number of separate teams. The purpose of constructing a high-level design at this point is so the teams can work on their pieces of the architecture and have a framework into which to plug their architectural elements. These are the primary activities of the Systems Engineering phase.

- Define subsystem architecture
- Define subsystem interfaces and interaction protocols (the set of allowable message sequences)
- Define how the subsystems collaborated together to realize the system use cases, specifying the role of each subsystem in the collaboration but not the detailed internal structure of that subsystem
- Decompose system use cases and requirements into subsystem use cases and requirements and allocate them to the appropriate subsystems
- Algorithmic analysis and control law specification for systems that exhibit continuous and piecewise continuous behavior
- Break down the subsystems into their technical disciplines: electronic, mechanical, chemical, and software

The primary representation used in Systems Engineering is the subsystem diagram. This is nothing more than a class diagram that shows primarily the elements of the subsystem view: subsystems, actors, interfaces, and associations. The collaborative behavior of the subsystems is shown using primarily sequence diagrams. The specification of the individual subsystem requirements uses all the same techniques as in the Requirements phase but now at the subsystem level. The hardware-software decomposition is shown using deployment diagrams. Interfaces can be shown using class diagrams that explicitly show the interfaces and their properties or using a textual specification of the interfaces. In any case, it is important to capture the messages accepted (and possibly emitted as well), their parameter lists, and limitations on their use via constraints or statecharts.

Representing algorithmic and continuous behavior is problematic, since UML is a discrete modeling language. The most common approaches are to use UML activity diagrams (see [7] for an example) or to use control law diagrams to represent this aspect and bind them to individual use cases at the subsystem level.

3.2.5.3 Object Analysis Phase

A use case can be thought of as a bag that contains a set of detailed requirements relating to a single system capability. The realization (implementation in UML-speak) of a use case is a collaboration—a set of objects working together to achieve this coherent set of requirements. Object analysis in the ROPES process is primarily done to construct this collaboration of objects and is performed one use case at a time. This means that for the current prototype, one collaboration is constructed for each use case implemented by the prototype. If the systems engineering step is present, this is done at the subsystem level by each separate subsystem team; otherwise the collaboration is constructed at the system level. Using an appropriate logical architecture (see Chapter 2) to organize the system model allows the subsystems to share common objects, classes, and types by placing them in shared domains. Typically, each domain has a "domain owner" in charge of the contents of the domain. If a subsystem team member wants to put a class in that domain, it goes through the domain owner to ensure a consistent, clean set of classes.

Care should be taken to minimize the introduction of design elements during analysis. Limit the collaboration at this point to elements that clearly must be present in the object analysis model. For example, if the collaboration is to model the use case "Manage Account" for a banking system, then if the collaboration does not contain an object such as *customer, account, debit transaction,* and *credit transaction,* then you'd say it was *wrong.* In a navigation system, you would expect to see concepts represented by objects or their attributes, such as *position, direction, thrust, velocity, altitude, waypoint,* and *trajectory.* The goal is to include only the objects and relations that are crucial for correctness and to omit design optimizations. The objects and attributes are named using the proper problem domain vocabulary for the concepts they represent.

A key question arises during the construction of the object collaboration: "Is this right?" Are the concepts properly represented? Are the relationships among those concepts correct? Do they behave appropriately? The answer to these questions is answered rapidly during the nanocycle. You can really only evaluate the correctness of an object model via *execution and test.* This is done by generating and executing the code of the object analysis model while it is in various stages of completion, rather than waiting until the end. Take the sequence diagrams used to show scenarios that captured the requirements in a black-box way and *elaborate* them with the objects just created and demonstrate, via execution, that they fulfill the expected roles within that scenario realization. Tools such as Rhapsody allow you to execute your model and dynamically construct a sequence diagram of the collaboration as the system executes. During this process, it is not uncommon that hidden requirements may be uncovered during object analysis.

The collaborations are captured as class diagrams—no surprise there. Individual object behavioral specifications are usually captured as a statechart (if the objects react to events in a discrete way) or activity diagrams (if not). The behavior of the collaboration as a whole is captured primarily with sequence diagrams.

3.2.6 Design with the ROPES Process

An analysis model defines a coherent set of required properties of the system under development. A design model is a more concrete blueprint for exactly *how* those properties will be realized. An analysis model may be implemented by many different designs with different optimization characteristics. A design is a particular solution to the problem. Design is always an optimization of an analysis model. The set of optimization criteria is the required qualities of service of the system. The difficult part of design is that many different QoS properties must be simultaneously optimized, some of which may be in conflict with others. Design decisions are made at three levels of abstraction: architectural (system scope), mechanistic (collaboration scope), and detailed (object scope).

3.2.6.1 Architectural Design Phase

As discussed in some detail in Chapter 2, the ROPES process recognizes these five important views of architecture.

- Subsystem and Component View
- Concurrency and Resource View
- Distribution View
- Safety and Reliability View
- Deployment View

In the Architecture Design phase, one or more of these views is elaborated, depending on the needs of the current prototype. This is done primarily via the application of architectural design patterns (see Section 3.4). These patterns are large in scope, affecting most or all of the system, similar to many of the patterns presented in [4, 8].

Architectural design representation uses the same views as in Systems Engineering and Object Analysis: class diagrams to represent the structure and sequence diagrams to represent collaborative behavior. Components are similar to subsystems and may be mixed on the subsystem diagrams or put into separate component diagrams. Since subsystem, component, and class diagrams are all structural, you can mix elements on the structural diagram as appropriate. The concurrency and resource view will emphasize «active» objects and other objects that are important in this view—features such as event queues and semaphores, for example. The deployment view uses primarily deployment diagrams.

3.2.6.2 Mechanistic Design Phase

The Mechanistic Design phase is concerned with the optimization of individual collaborations so the scope of mechanistic design decisions is generally an order of magnitude smaller than those found in architectural design. Similar to architectural design, mechanistic design largely proceeds via the application of design patterns, although the scope of the patterns is much smaller than those found in architectural design. This is where the classic Gang of Four patterns [5] and other more fine-grained patterns are applied.

The mechanistic design view is an elaboration of the object analysis view and uses the same graphical representation: class and sequence diagrams for collaborations structure and sequence, activity, and statechart diagrams for behavior.

3.2.6.3 Detailed Design Phase

The Detailed Design phase elaborates the internals of objects and classes, and it has a highly limited scope: the individual object or class. Most of the optimization in detailed design focuses on these issues.

- Data structuring
- Algorithmic decomposition
- Optimization of an object's state machine
- Object implementation strategies
- Association implementation
- Visibility and encapsulation concerns
- Ensuring compliance at run-time with preconditional invariants (such as ranges on method parameters)

There are many rules of thumb, guidelines, and practices for detail design, although these commonly fall under the title of "idioms" rather than "patterns." For most objects, detailed design is little more than a trivial detail, but there is usually a small (5 to 10 percent), but important, set of objects that requires special attention during detailed design.

Generally, it is considered "good form" for object attributes to be "primitive"—things like integers, floating point numbers, and strings. Sometimes, for optimization reasons, the structure is not primitive, in which case its organization may be a concern. Algorithmic decomposition is usually shown with activity diagrams, whereas statecharts represent the state machines. Most of the rest of the object details are stored internally inside your design tool, since it is normally not helpful to show them graphically. For a more detailed discussion of what goes on in the Detailed Design phase see [6, 7].

3.2.7 Translation

The Translation phase is concerned with the correct construction of the properly working architectural elements. This phase includes the generation of code (whether it is automatically generated from your model, written by hand, or a combination of the two), unit level testing of that source code and the associated model elements, integration with legacy source code, the linking together of the pieces of the architectural element (including, possibly, legacy components), and the unit testing of the architectural element itself.

The following are the primary artifacts for the Translation phase.

- Source code generated from the model elements
- Unit test plan, procedures, and results (textual documents)
- Inspection report for the source code (textual document)
- Compiled and tested software components

3.2.8 Test

The Test phase constructs the prototype from the architectural elements and ensures that they fit together (Integration and Test) and that the prototype as a black box meets its mission statement (Validation Test). The first of these, Integration and Test, is concerned with architecture. The tests are "gray box" and are limited to demonstrating that the interfaces of the architectural elements are used properly and that none of the constraints are violated. This normally proceeds in a stepwise fashion, according to an integration plan, that adds the architectural elements one at a time, testing to ensure that the partially integrated prototype works as expected so far. It is in this phase that hardware elements are formally integrated with the software elements for prototypes that have hardware-software integration as part of their mission. The integration test plan and procedures may be developed once the subsystem and component architecture of the prototype is specified—that is, either at the end of Systems Engineering or Architectural Design (if the Systems Engineering phase is skipped).

The Validation phase tests the assembled prototype against its mission. The mission for a prototype is normally a small set of use cases and/or the reduction of a small number of risks. The validation test plan and procedures may be written as soon as the requirements for the prototype are understood—that is, at the end of the microcycle's Requirements Analysis phase.

If defects are found during testing, they may be either fixed then (required if the defect is severe enough to stop the continuation of testing) or deferred until the next prototype.

These are the primary artifacts for the Test phase.

- Integration test plan, procedures, and results
- Validation test plan, procedures, and results

- Tested, executable prototype
- Defect report

3.3 Design Pattern Basics

Experienced developers find that when they are trying to solve a new problem, the situation usually has something in common with a solution they have already either created or seen. The problems may not be identical, and an identical solution will rarely solve a new problem, but the problems are *similar,* so a similar solution should work. This *similar* solution generalized and formalized, is called a design pattern. Creating design patterns is a problem of abstracting the similarities of the two problems and the solution so that the generic aspects of the original solution can be applied to the new problem.

Of the two fundamental concerns associated with patterns, the first has to do with the application of patterns. The problem of identifying the nature of the problem and examining the patterns "library" for the best ones to apply is called *pattern hatching* [9]. And, as John Vlissides, author of that excellent book, points out, this name implies that we're not creating something new but "developing from preexisting rudiments." These preexisting rudiments are our captured design patterns that we can use to construct solutions that work in novel circumstances.

The other issue, of course, is the identification and capture of new patterns to add to the library. I call this process *pattern mining.* It involves the abstraction of the problem to its essential properties, creating a generic solution and then understanding the consequences of that solution in the problem context in which the pattern applies.

Patterns are not just software reuse but rather a kind of *concept reuse.* Most patterns, such as those presented in this book, are design patterns. Design is always an optimization of an analysis model, and design patterns are always a general concept for how to optimize an analysis model in a particular way with particular effects.

Optimization is a fickle partner. Optimization always entails improving some aspect of the system at the expense of others. For example, some patterns will optimize reusability at the expense of worst-case performance. Other patterns will optimize safety at the expense of system recurring cost (cost per shipped item). Whenever you optimize one set of aspects you *deoptimize* others. This is just a fact of life, or else we would all be driving at the speed of sound with no need for gasoline and at zero risk and cost.

3.3.1 What Is a Design Pattern?

A design pattern is "a generalized solution to a commonly occurring problem." To be a pattern, the problem must recur often enough to be usefully generalizable. The solution must also be general enough to be applied in a wide set of application domains. If it only applies to a single application domain, then it is probably an *analysis pattern*. An analysis pattern is similar to a design pattern, but it applies to a specific application domain, such as finance or aerospace. Analysis patterns define ways for organizing problem-specific object analysis models within a single application domain. See [12] for some examples of domain-specific analysis patterns.

Analysis is driven by *what* the system must do, whereas design is driven by *how well* the system must achieve its requirements. A design pattern is a way of organizing a design that improves the optimality of a design with respect to one or a small set of qualities of service. Here are some of them.

- Performance
  - Worst case
  - Average case
- Predictability
- Schedulability
- Throughput
  - Average
  - Sustained
  - Burst
- Reliability
  - With respect to errors
  - With respect to failures
- Safety
- Reusability
- Distributability
- Portability
- Maintainability
- Scalability

- Complexity
- Resource usage—for example, memory
- Energy consumption
- Recurring cost—for example, hardware
- Development effort and cost

Of course, as we discussed in the previous chapter, many of these QoS properties are to some degree conflicting. A design pattern always has a focused purpose: to take one or a small set of these QoS properties and optimize them at the expense of the others.

Patterns may be applied at the different levels of design abstraction. Architectural patterns, the focus of this book, have systemic scope and apply mostly to only one of the Five Views of architecture. At the next level down in design abstraction, mechanistic design patterns apply to individual collaborations, optimizing the same QoS properties but in a more narrow arena. Patterns usually do not apply to detailed design, but idioms and practices do.

The patterns presented in this book are primarily *structural design patterns.* That is, they call for organizing systems or parts of systems in certain ways so that behavioral strategies can be applied to optimize the desired QoS. Patterns need not be structural. The book *Doing Hard Time* [6], for example, provides a set of *behavioral* design patterns for ways in which state machines may be "behaviorally structured" to optimize how the state machine works.

Sets of interrelated patterns tailored specifically to work well together are called *frameworks.* In a framework-based development effort, the majority of the application is provided by the instantiated framework. This includes the "meat and potatoes" of the application, offering services to construct GUI elements, manage devices, manage concurrency, execute state machines, and so on. The developer need only then build the elements of the system that are peculiar to that *particular* system, relying on the framework to support those application services.

Frameworks provide four primary usage strategies—instantiation, generalization, parameterization, and extension—and many frameworks use all four. The instantiation usage strategy uses some aspect of the framework, such as scheduling threads or executing state machines, directly with no change. The generalization strategy takes an abstract framework element and specializes it, adding new functionality. A real-time framework might provide a *Sensor* class that fits into a Model-View-

Controller style pattern, with the expectation that you will subclass this *Sensor* class for your particular device and overwrite the inherited methods. This is a very common way of using patterns. Parameterization is applied when the Framework provides parameterized classes—such as containers in C++'s STL—with the intention that you will provide the actual parameters when you instantiate that portion of the framework. Finally, most frameworks have special places were you can plug in pieces and extend the framework. An example of this would be plugging in a CAN bus communications protocol or an HDLC (High-level Data Link Communications) protocol. The disadvantages of frameworks are that they limit the ways in which you do things and frameworks are *much* more difficult to design and construct than applications, even though they greatly simplify application development. Nevertheless, frameworks are prime examples of effective use of patterns.

3.3.2 Basic Structure of Design Patterns

According to Gamma et al. [5], a pattern has these four important aspects.

1. *Name*
   The name provides a "handle" or means to reference the pattern.

2. *Purpose*
   The purpose provides the problem context and the QoS aspects the pattern seeks to optimize. The purpose identifies the kinds of problem contexts where the pattern might be particularly appropriate.

3. *Solution*
   The solution is the pattern itself.

4. *Consequences*
   The consequences are the set of pros and cons of the use of the pattern.

The pattern *name* brings us two things. First, it allows us to reference the pattern in a clear, unambiguous way, with the details present but unstated. Second, it gives us a more abstract vocabulary to speak about our designs. The statement "The system uses a layered structural architecture with messages queuing concurrency distributed across a symmetric deployment with a broker pattern" has a lot of information about the overall structure of the system because we can discuss the architecture in terms of these patterns.

The *purpose* of the pattern brings into focus the essential problem contexts required for the pattern to be applicable and what qualities of service the pattern is attempting to optimize. This section specifies under which situations the pattern is appropriate and under which situations it should be avoided.

The *solution*, of course, is the most important aspect. It identifies the elements of the pattern and their roles in relation to each other. As we'll see in the next section, these elements are replaced by, or subclassed by, your application objects to instantiate the pattern.

The *consequences* are important because we always make tradeoffs when we select one pattern over another. We must understand the pros and cons of the pattern to apply it effectively. The pros and cons are usually couched in terms of improvement or degradation of some qualities of service, as well as a possible elaboration of problem contexts in which these consequences apply.

3.3.3 How to Read Design Patterns in this Book

All the patterns of this book are organized in the same fashion to improve the usability of the patterns.

- *Abstract*
  The abstract gives a brief description of the pattern use or justification. This is meant as an overview of the problem, solution, and consequences.
- *Problem*
  The problem section gives a statement of the problem context and the qualities of service addressed by the pattern.
- *Pattern Structure*
  This section provides a structural UML diagram of the pattern, showing the important elements of the pattern. These elements are the places into which you will substitute your own specific application elements to instantiate the pattern. Relations among elements of the pattern are shown as well.
- *Collaboration Roles*
  This section elaborates the properties of the individual elements in the pattern collaboration.
- *Consequences*
  The consequences section describes the tradeoffs made when the pattern is used.

- *Implementation Strategies*
  This section discusses issues around the implementation of the pattern on different computing platforms or in different source-level languages.

- *Related Patterns*
  The related patterns section references other patterns in this book that may be used instead of this pattern (with different optimization criteria, of course) or are often used in conjunction with this pattern.

- *Example Model*
  Each pattern is shown in an example that illustrates how the pattern is applied in some particular case. This usually involves the presentation of a UML structural diagram showing particular application elements fulfilling the pattern collaboration roles and a sequence diagram showing one trace through the execution of that collaboration.

The notation used throughout this book is generic, standard UML. The UML represents a collaboration using a dashed oval. A pattern as a *parameterized collaboration* uses a dashed oval as well. The dashed oval itself adds little information to the structural diagram, so it is omitted in this book. Chapter 1 introduced the UML basics, and Appendix A gives a UML notational summary. For a more detailed understanding of the UML itself, see [6, 7, 10, 11].

There is very little source-level code in this book because the book concerns itself with architecture. Code examples to illustrate these points would either be too simplified to be useful or would be too lengthy. Using UML models as examples, we believe, suits the purpose and focus of the book better.

3.4 Using Design Patterns in Development

By this point, you should have a reasonably good understanding of what a pattern is and how one is organized. You should also have a fair grasp of the ROPES process and our view of where design fits into the overall scheme of things. From the previous chapter, you got a foundation in what we mean by the term *architecture* and the Five Views of architecture. In the first chapter, you read about the basic building blocks of the UML. At this point, you are almost ready to examine the patterns in this book and apply them to your applications development. But first, let's briefly discuss how we might use patterns in our daily work lives.

3.4.1 Pattern Hatching—Locating the Right Patterns

You're facing a design problem. How do you find the patterns that can be applied to solve your particular design issues? We recommend a multi-step approach, as shown in Figure 3-10.

1. First, before starting your design, familiarize yourself with the patterns literature.[8] There are a number of books, papers, and Web sites devoted to patterns in many application domains. Some of those patterns are given here, and others are given in the references. Once you

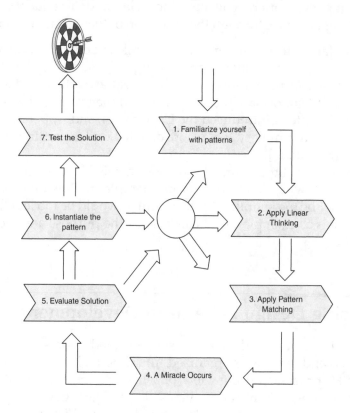

Figure 3-10: *Pattern Hatching*

---

8. That means "Read the book!"

have increased your vocabulary to include patterns likely to be relevant to your application domain, you have more intellectual ammunition to face your design challenges.

2. Apply "linear thinking." Characterize the nature of the design problem you face. What is the scope of the problem—architectural, mechanistic, or detailed? What are the relevant quality of service issues—worst-case performance? Reusability? Safety? Portability? Memory usage? Rank them according to criticality. Sometimes once you've done this, a design solution will suggest itself.

3. Apply pattern matching. This is the fun part. Your cerebral cortex is a wonderful pattern-matching machine. It operates autonomously from your linear thought processing. This is why you have the "Eureka!" experience when you're in the shower, getting ready for bed, or eating dinner.[9] Once you've applied the linear thinking step, your unconscious pattern-matching machinery has enough information to go to work.

4. "A miracle occurs." The pattern-matching machinery identifies a potential solution, usually the application of a pattern, whether that pattern was explicitly formulated as a general solution or not. This doesn't mean that the proposed solution is a good one, just that it matches the desired properties closely enough for further evaluation.

5. Evaluate the proposed solution. This is another application of linear reasoning in which you logically analyze and evaluate the pattern suggested. If the solution is good, then you apply it (step 6); if not, you clearly go back to step 3, or perhaps even step 2.

6. Instantiate the pattern. Organize your structural elements to be consistent with the pattern. This may involve breaking objects apart, merging them together, reassigning collaboration responsibilities, or introducing new elements altogether.

7. Test the solution. Elaborate your analysis scenarios with the elements of the collaboration, and demonstrate that they meet the functional and behavioral requirements. Once you're satisfied that the collaboration is doing the right thing, measure the desired qualities of service, if necessary, to ensure that the pattern is achieving your quality of service goals. This is especially true for performance and resource usage goals.

---

9. For me, it occurs mostly when I run. In fact, I measure problem difficulty in *miles*—how far I have to run to solve the problem. The downside is that it can be a hard sell to managers when you tell them, "I have to solve this design problem, so I'm going to run ten miles. See you in an hour and a half. It's work—*honest!*"

3.4.2 Pattern Mining—Rolling Your Own Patterns

Creating your own pattern is useful, especially when you have a depth of experience to understand the optimization issues in a particular area and sufficient breadth to understand the general properties of the solutions enough to abstract them into a generalized solution. We call this *pattern mining* (see Figure 3-11). Pattern mining isn't so much a matter of invention as it is discovery—seeing that this solution in some context is similar to that solution in another context and abstracting away the specifics of the solutions. Keep in mind that to be a useful pattern, it must occur in different contexts and perform a useful optimization of one or more qualities of service.

3.4.3 Pattern Instantiation—Applying Patterns in Your Designs

Pattern instantiation is the opposite of pattern mining. It is applying the pattern to a particular collaboration to gain the benefits of the pattern (see

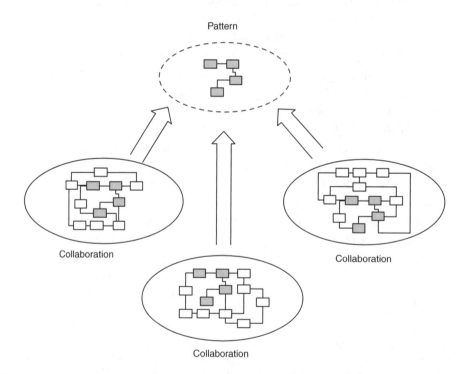

Figure 3-11: *Pattern Mining*

Figure 3-12). Patterns are normally applied to an object collaboration. A collaboration is a set of objects (at some scope these may be small, low-level objects, whereas at others they may be large-grained objects such as subsystems and components). The purpose is to organize, and possibly elaborate, this already existing collaboration with the pattern.

The application or instantiation of a pattern in your design is a matter of defining the elements that will fulfill the collaboration roles in the application. For some of the patterns you may create the role as a superclass from which you subclass to instantiate that pattern. In other patterns, you may simply replace the pattern element with one from your application domain, adding in the required operations and behavior. Or you may choose to create objects just as they exist in the pattern itself.

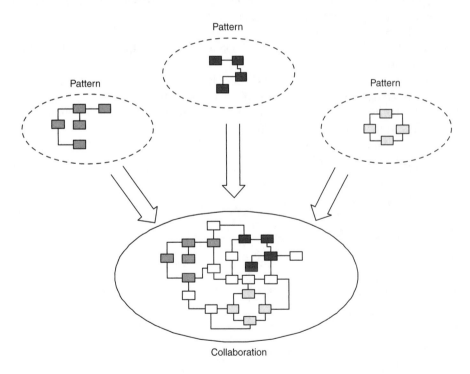

Figure 3-12: *Pattern Instantiation*

3.5 References

[1] Beck, Kent. *Extreme Programming Explained*, Boston, MA: Addison-Wesley, 2000.

[2] Douglass, Bruce Powel. "On the ROPES," *Embedded Systems Programming*, December 2000.

[3] DeMarco, Tom, and Timothy Lister. *Peopleware: Productive Projects and Teams*, New York: Dorset House Publishing Company, 1987.

[4] Buschmann, F., R. Meunier, H. Rohnert, P. Sommerlad, and M. Stal. *A System of Patterns: Pattern-Oriented Software Architecture*, New York: Wiley and Sons, 1996.

[5] Gamma, E., R. Helm, R. Johnson, and J. Vlissides. *Design Patterns: Elements of Reusable Object-Oriented Software*, Reading, MA: Addison-Wesley, 1995.

[6] Douglass, Bruce Powel. *Real-Time UML, 2nd Edition: Developing Efficient Objects for Embedded Systems*, Boston, MA: Addison-Wesley, 2000.

[7] Douglass, Bruce Powel. *Doing Hard Time: Developing Real-Time Systems with UML, Objects, Frameworks and Patterns*, Reading, MA: Addison-Wesley, 1999.

[8] Zalewski, Janusz. *Real-Time Software Architecture and Design Patterns: Fundamental Concepts and Their Consequences*. Annual Reviews in Control, Vol. 25, No. 1, pp. 133–146, July 2001.

[9] Vlissides, John. *Pattern Hatching: Design Patterns Applied*, Reading, MA: Addison-Wesley, 1998.

[10] Rumbaugh, J., I. Jacobson, and G. Booch. *The Unified Modeling Language Reference Manual*, Reading, MA: Addison-Wesley, 1999.

[11] *OMG Unified Modeling Language Specification Version 1.4*, Needham, MA: Object Management Group, 2001.

[12] Fowler, Martin. *Analysis Patterns: Reusable Object Models*, Reading, MA: Addison-Wesley, 1997.

Part  II

Architectural Design Patterns

Introduction

Analysis identifies the essential, or required, properties of a system under development. Design adds specific details meant to optimize the design in order to "best" meet system needs. As discussed in Chapter 3, the ROPES process breaks down design into three abstraction levels, based on the scope of the decisions made. This part focuses on design patterns that address the largest-scale system design concerns: *architectural design.* The design choices made in architectural design affect most or all of the systems under development. Most of these choices can be grouped into one of the following areas.

- Domain view
- Subsystem or component view
- Concurrency view
- Distribution view

- Safety and reliability view
- Deployment view

The first two deal with what some developers call the *logical-physical dichotomy*. A *domain* is an area of subject matter, usually with its own specific vocabulary, and often it requires a specific area of expertise. Domains are modeled as a stereotype of package «domain». The set of domains decompose what Grady Booch calls the "sea of classes" [1] into relatively small, manageable subject matters that may undergo some level of independent analysis. Virtually *all* classes will be defined in the domains. In fact, virtually each generalization taxonomy is located within a *single* domain. Domains themselves may be divided up into small subpackages for parceling out to different developers or teams of developers. The set of domains comprises the *logical* or *essential* model of the system. This logical model does not concern itself with how it will be structured into run-time artifacts (the job for the subsystem and component model) but instead focuses on the classes and relationships required for logical correctness. To be sure, object collaborations normally span multiple domains in order to achieve the required use cases. Nevertheless, each class is defined within a single domain, and the classes are grouped together into a domain when they fall within the same subject matter. Example domains typically found in embedded systems include user interface, hardware abstraction, data management, data communication, and alarm management. Application areas will add their own more specific domains such as guidance and navigation, attitude control, anesthesia delivery, patient monitoring, aircraft targeting, and so on. It is common for a domain to define classes that instantiate in many or all subsystems. For example, all subsystems may need to communicate across a bus. The classes that define the means to marshal, send, and receive messages across a bus are defined in a communications domain, but they may be instantiated in all subsystems. It is also common for classes defined with a domain to be instantiated only within a single subsystem. For example, while a spacecraft attitude control subsystem will contain instances of classes from multiple domains, classes defined within an attitude control domain will likely only be instantiated within the attitude control subsystem.

A *subsystem*, unlike a domain, is not a logical structure but a *run-time artifact*. It is an organization composed of objects, rather than classes, based on common run-time behavioral purpose rather than subject matter. A subsystem contains objects instantiated from classes from many or all domains defined within a system. In the UML, a subsystem is a meta-subclass of both *Classifier* and *Package,* making it both a structural executable entity and a container for instances. Subsystems do not define the classes they instantiate (those classes are defined in the relevant domains),[1] but they *do* contain instances. Subsystems are rather large things and may be composed of *components* rather than directly of class instances. In the UML, a component is a run-time artifact that represents a replaceable piece of a system or subsystem. Components, in turn, contain object instances of various kinds, including, for example, «active» classes that serve as the roots of threads. The subsystem and component model is one aspect of what is called the *physical model.* Another aspect is the deployment view, which is where these run-time artifacts actually get mapped to the underlying hardware. The only classes actually defined within a subsystem are those responsible for organizing the execution of instances of the domain classes. These will include composite objects (see the *Recursive Containment* pattern, for example) and interface classes for these composites.

One of the advantages of separating the logical and physical models is that they may vary independently. A logical model may be "repackaged" into a different set of subsystems and components to efficiently map to different hardware configurations. Similarly, a common subsystem organizational model (especially when built up around teams with specific expertise) may be reused to package different logical elements. Chapter 4 provides structural patterns for both the logical and subsystem models.

The concurrency view is also part of the physical model; it represents the mapping of instances to threads of control. In the UML, a thread is managed by an «active» object and is part of a component or subsystem. Passive objects are aggregated by the active object (normally using the strong form of aggregation, called *composition*) and execute in the thread of their composite «active» object. The concurrency view concerns itself with the identification of threads, the mapping of objects to threads, and the rules for managing thread execution and the sharing of common resources.

The distribution view is about principles and means by which objects distributed among different address spaces will communicate. Objects may be distributed among different threads of a single processor, among

---

1. There are exceptions to this rule. Specifically, classes solely used to organize and deploy the instances of the domain classes (e.g., the subsystems themselves) and provide interfaces to these organizational classes are normally defined by the subsystem itself. The real work, though, is done by instances of the classes defined in the domains.

multiple processors, or among different remote systems. Concurrency and distribution patterns are presented in Chapters 5, 6, 7, and 8.

The safety and reliability view focuses on organizational principles necessary to meet system safety and reliability requirements. *Safety* refers to "freedom from accidents or losses," while reliability refers to "probability that a system will continue to achieve its behavioral function." These are significantly different concerns. In some systems, improving reliability decreases safety and vice versa. See [2] for more information on the relevant concepts of safety and reliability as they apply to embedded and real-time software. Safety and reliability patterns are presented in Chapter 9.

We present patterns organized into these different aspects of architectural design. As an aside, many of these patterns are structural in nature, and code-based examples fail to properly illustrate their character. For this reason, many of the architectural patterns will provide C and C++ implementation guidelines rather than actual code. Where actual source code is useful to illustrate the pattern, source code will be provided preferentially.

References

[1] Booch, Grady. "Software as a Strategic Weapon" in *Best of Booch*, New York: SIGS Books and Multimedia, 1996.

[2] Douglass, Bruce Powel. *Doing Hard Time: Developing Real-Time Systems with UML, Objects, Frameworks, and Patterns*, Reading, MA: Addison-Wesley, 1999.

[3] Rumbaugh, J., M. Blaha, W. Premerlani, F. Eddy, and W. Lorenson. *Object-Oriented Modeling and Design*, Englewood Cliffs, NJ: Prentice Hall, 1991.

[4] Buschmann, F., R. Meunier, H. Rohnert, P. Sommerlad, and M. Stal. *A System of Patterns: Pattern-Oriented Architecture*, New York: John Wiley & Sons, 1996.

Chapter 4

Subsystem and Component Architecture Patterns

The following patterns are presented in this chapter.

- Layered Pattern: Organizes domains into layers of abstraction
- Five-Layer Pattern: A specific set of layered domains for small to medium systems
- Microkernel Architecture Pattern: Organizes system into a set of core services with optional services that may be linked to it
- Channel Architecture Pattern: Organizes system into sets of sequential transformational elements
- Recursive Containment Pattern: Organizes the system into several layers of abstraction
- Hierarchical Control Pattern: Distributes complex control algorithms at different levels of abstraction
- Virtual Machine Pattern: Enhances portability by constructing the system in terms of an abstract machine

- Component-Based Architecture Pattern: Organizes system into replaceable units with opaque interfaces
- ROOM Pattern: Organizes system using a set of heavyweight abstractions with strong encapsulation

High-level structural patterns are those that refer to the organization of the domains of the logical model, subsystems and components of the subsystem, and component view, and nodes (and the mapping subsystems and components to nodes) of the deployment view. In this chapter we examine all of these types of patterns as a group, and we define which pattern applies to which view.

Note: As with all architectural patterns, we do not provide coding examples of the patterns. Because of the scale of architectural patterns, the number of lines of code would be cumbersome and not particularly helpful for understanding the pattern. Instead, we have provided specific application models that illustrate the application of the pattern.

4.1 LAYERED PATTERN

The *Layered Pattern* organizes domains into a hierarchical organization based on their level of abstraction.

4.1.1 Abstract

Many systems domains may be thought of as comprising a set of semantic concepts at a particular level of abstraction. The more abstract concepts in one domain are realized in terms of more concrete concepts in others. For example, Figure 4-1 shows how the concepts useful to a cardiologist can be expressed in less abstract terms. Cardiologists think in terms of concepts such as *heart block, preventricular contraction,* and *heart rate.* These may be expressed in terms of myoneurobiology. Myo-neurobiology can be expressed in terms of cell

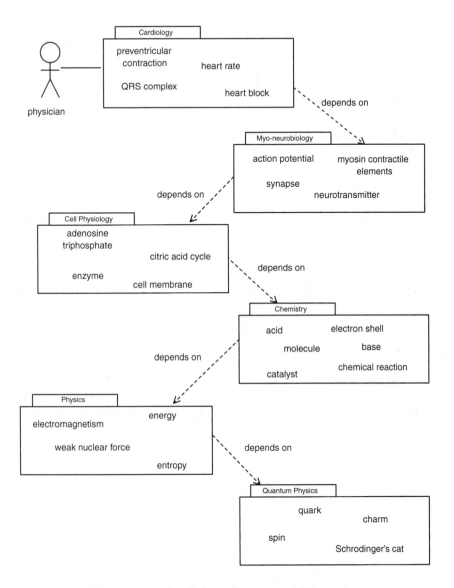

Figure 4-1: *Cardiology Conceptual Hierarchy*

physiology. The functioning of cells can be explained in terms of chemical reactions of complex molecules including enzymes, neurotransmitters, and energy substrates such as adenosine triphosphate (ATP). Chemistry can be explained in terms of the underlying physics of electron shell interactions. Ultimately, atomic physics can be explained (although often with some difficulty, as I recall ☺) in terms of quantum physics. However, the cardiologist would find it difficult to focus on his immediate concerns if he was required to always think in terms of chemistry (let alone the underlying physics) rather than the more suitable abstract concepts of cardiology. By constructing a set of abstractions that makes sense to the cardiologist but ultimately depend on less abstract concepts, he or she can work more effectively. So it is with software developers.

4.1.2 Problem

In a system in which abstract domains must be implemented in terms of more concrete (less abstract) domains, we need a simple organizational pattern. Additionally, in many systems we need portability of the application to other platforms, or we want to provide an abstract platform or execution environment for which applications may be easily adapted.

4.1.3 Pattern Structure

Figure 4-2 shows the organization of the layered pattern. Note that it only contains a single primary element (the domain package) and its interface; the constraint elucidates the structure of the pattern.

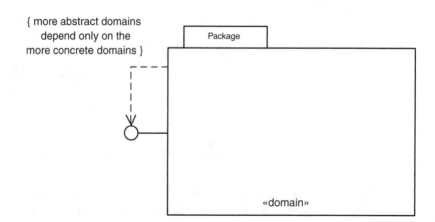

Figure 4-2: *Layered Pattern Structure*

4.1.4 Collaboration Roles

This is a very simple pattern with a single role used recursively.

• *Domain*
The *domain* role is an idiomatic use of the UML concept of a package. A package in the UML may be thought of as a bag that contains model elements. No guidance is provided by the UML *per se* on suitable criteria for selection of which elements should be put in which packages. One criteria is to group model elements by common subject matter. All of the concepts of a single subject matter normally share a common vocabulary. This subject matter is called a *domain*. For example, a common domain is *user interface*. In such a domain, one would expect to find classes such as *window, scroll bar, font, image, dialog box, cursor*, and so on.

4.1.5 Consequences

The Layered Pattern allows the system to provide highly abstract concepts, closely relevant to the application's needs and vocabulary, even when those services will ultimately be provided by a set of simpler services provided by more concrete classes. In a *closed layered architecture*, the classes in one layer can only invoke operations of classes in the same layer or in the next layer down [3]. In an *open layered architecture*, classes in one layer may invoke operations of classes in the same or any layer below it. There may be some loss of performance by providing a model with many abstraction levels with a closed layered architecture. On the other hand, a closed layered architecture offers significantly better encapsulation, and it is generally much easier to correctly modify the classes in one layer because you can be assured that only classes in that layer or the one immediately above it will be affected.

Layered logical architectures tend to be very portable. The upper layers are more application-specific, while the lower layers are more platform-specific. A layered architecture allows portability in both directions. Applications are more portable because the lower layers can be easily replaced with similar lower layers specific to other platforms. On the other hand, the upper layers can be easily replaced to allow other applications to be deployed on the same platform.

4.1.6 Implementation Strategies

Implementation of a layered architecture is quite straightforward. Although the dependency relationships among the layers are present, the important relationships are ultimately the one-way client-server associations among the classes in one layer and the classes in the lower layer(s) invoked. It is crucial that these associations between layers are one way, allowing messages to be sent to the lower layers but not the other way. The lower-level abstractions cannot depend on the higher-level abstractions that use them.

4.1.7 Related Patterns

The Five-Layer Architecture Pattern, also in this chapter, is a particular adaptation of this pattern common to real-time and embedded systems. The Recursive Containment Pattern is to physical architecture what the layered pattern is to logical architecture.

4.1.8 Sample Model

A simplified model is shown in Figure 4-3. In this example, the logical model of an ECG monitor is divided up into four domains: an *ECG_Domain* containing medical-related classes; a *Trend_Domain* containing classes related to managing histories of data streams; an *Alarm_Domain* that provides classes necessary to manage and annunciate alarms; a *UserInterface_Domain* whose classes provide views of data; and a *Transport_Domain* containing classes to manage communication among distributed elements of the system.

Collaborations almost always span domain (and frequently subsystem) boundaries. Figure 4-4 shows an example collaboration of objects spanning domain boundaries in the set of layers. Note that, as is also common, the associations among the classes between domains are unidirectional, from the classes in the more abstract domains to the classes in the more concrete domains. As a general policy in the layered pattern, classes "know about" classes in the more concrete domains so that they can invoke their operations, but classes in the concrete domains don't know about their more abstract clients.

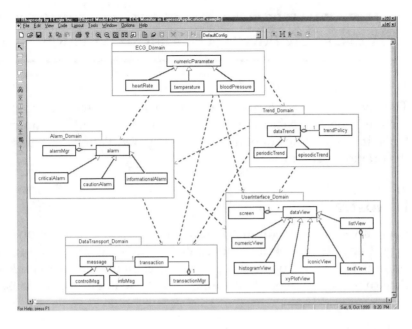

Figure 4-3: *ECG Domain Model*

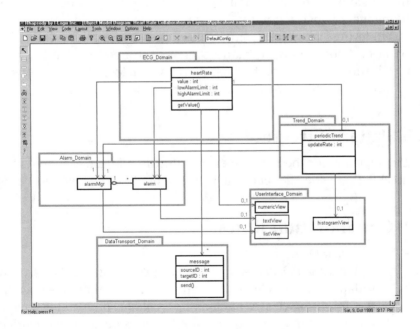

Figure 4-4: *ECG Collaboration*

4.2 FIVE-LAYER ARCHITECTURE PATTERN

The Five-Layer Architecture Pattern is a specific architecture useful for the general structuring of many embedded and real-time systems. It is a specific adaptation of the Layered Pattern, discussed in the previous section.

4.2.1 Abstract

For many small- to medium-scale systems, a similar organization of the logical architecture permits developers to quickly and easily understand the organization of a new system. The Five-Layer Architecture Pattern is a common one that applies broadly to many applications.

4.2.2 Problem

In a system in which domains can be thought of as being in a common layer of abstraction that must be implemented in terms of more concrete (less abstract) domains, we need a simple organizational pattern. Additionally, in many systems we need portability of the application to other platforms, or we want to provide an abstract platform for which applications may be easily adapted.

4.2.3 Pattern Structure

The structure for the Five-Layer Architecture Pattern is shown in Figure 4-5. It is a specific set of the layers defined in the Layered Pattern.

4.2.4 Collaboration Roles

- *Application Domain*
  The *Application Domain* contains the application-level classes. In a ventilator system, classes specific to that domain are specified. These might be classes such as *tidal volume, lung volume, respiration rate, inspiration to expiration ratio, pressure,* and *expiratory end pressure.*

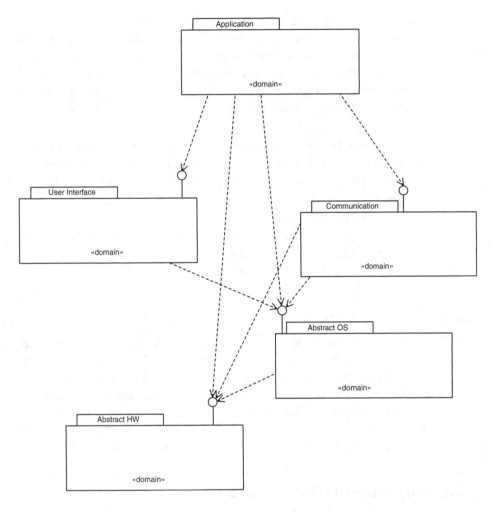

Figure 4-5: *Five-Layer Architecture Pattern Structure*

- *User Interface Domain*
  The *User Interface Domain* contains classes specific to the user interface: *window, scroll bar, font, image, dialog box, cursor,* and so on.

- *Communication Domain*
  The *Communication Domain* contains classes necessary to transport data, commands, and events among the objects. This domain is often subdivided into two subdomains: *middleware* and *data transport* (also known as *transport protocol*). The *middleware domain*

contains classes such as those found in CORBA, such as *CORBA message, broker, proxy,* and various transportable data types. The *data transport* domain contains classes necessary to marshal and unmarshal messages, convert to network format, fragment and defragment messages, perform reliable and unreliable transport, create sessions, maintain communication links, and so on.

- *Abstract OS Domain*
  The *Abstract OS Domain* focuses on adapters that isolate the system from the specific syntax and structure of the underlying OS. These will include classes to manage threads and memory as well as other typical OS services.

- *Abstract Hardware Domain*
  This domain provides classes that represent devices and their interfaces. Classes will include things like sensors, actuators, bus interfaces, and device drivers.

4.2.5 Consequences

The consequences of this pattern are largely the same as for the Layered Pattern. This pattern is usually open in the sense that the user interface domain may require the use of communications, but application communications are not mediated by classes in the user interface domain.

A small number of layers means that this pattern is likely to be highly efficient. However, because of the few layers, it may not provide an adequate set of domains to decompose complex systems.

4.2.6 Implementation Strategies

See Section 4.1, Layered Pattern.

4.2.7 Related Patterns

See Section 4.1, Layered Pattern.

4.2.8 Sample Model

The example provided here is a simple ventilator model shown in Figure 4-6. To keep the example tractable in the scope of a pattern example, only the most visible classes and relations are shown.

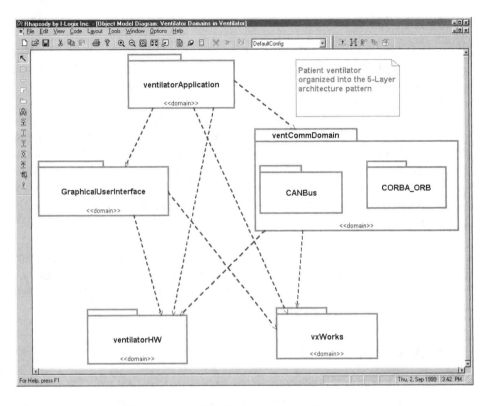

Figure 4-6: *Ventilator Example Domains*

The same implementation guidelines presented in Section 4.1.8 also apply to this architectural pattern.

4.3 MICROKERNEL ARCHITECTURE PATTERN

The Microkernel Architecture Pattern is a useful pattern when a system consists of a core set of services that may be augmented at build-time with a variety of additional services.

4.3.1 Abstract

It is possible to construct a subsystem from a core service set in such a way that the developer can choose the set of services needed in an application. Such a structure makes the subsystem much more reusable by providing build-time configurability. A common subsystem example is a real-time operating system (RTOS). Many, if not most, such subsystems contain a core set of services (such as create a task, delete a task, allocate and deallocate memory, provide task event and message queues, and schedule/execute a task set). On top of those services, the developer can link in additional components to provide more services. Common service components for RTOS include bus communications, file services, networking services, and middleware services (see the Broker Pattern in Chapter 8, Distribution Patterns). With this configurability, an RTOS becomes usable in a much wider set of application problems from tiny, highly memory-constrained systems to systems consisting of sets of high-powered networked CPUs.

4.3.2 Problem

Some subsystems provide a set of basic services that may be optionally augmented at build-time and must be reusable in a variety of contexts.

4.3.3 Pattern Structure

Figure 4-7 shows the organization of the Microkernel Architecture Pattern. The subsystem *Platform* is named thusly because the subsystem normally provides an executable infrastructure on which the application depends. All the components inside the platform provide opaque interfaces, the sum of which form the *API*. The order of dependency is that *Internal Components* depend only on the *Microkernel* and its interfaces (although sometimes special visibility is provided to interfaces that should remain hidden from the *Client*). *External Components* may use *Internal Components* or may use the *Microkernel* directly. The *Client* has access to all components, although, as mentioned before, certain internal interfaces may be hidden from the *Client*.

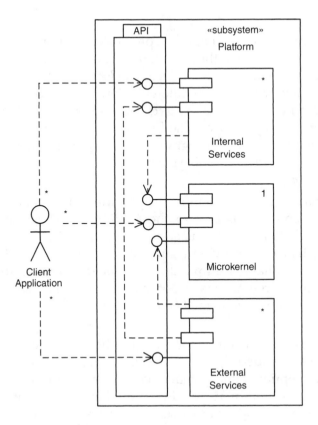

Figure 4-7: *Microkernel Architecture Pattern Structure*

4.3.4 Collaboration Roles

- *API*
  The *API (application program interface)* has the set of subsystem interfaces from the Microkernel, Internal Services, and External Services components. There may be more than one interface per subsystem.

- *Client*
  The *Client* is an actor outside the scope of the subsystem that uses the services provided by the subsystem. The *Client* is typically the user-designed portion of the overall system.

- *External Services*
  An *External Services* component provides an optional set of services commonly bound to the *Microkernel*. These services are accessible to the *Client* via a set of interfaces. An *External Services* component may provide a number of different interfaces. It is common to have many different *External Services* subsystems providing different sets of optional services. The *External Services* component is often written by a systems programmer to augment the features provided by the *Platform* subsystem vendor.

- *Internal Services*
  An *Internal Services* component provides an optional set of services commonly bound to the *Microkernel*. These services are accessible to the *Client* via a set of interfaces. An *Internal Services* subsystem may provide a number of different interfaces. It is common to have multiple different *Internal Services* subsystems providing different sets of optional services. *Internal Services* are typically provided by the *Platform* vendor.

- *Microkernel*
  The *Microkernel* component provides the core or minimum set of services provided by the subsystem. It is accessible to the *Client* and the optional subsystems via a set of interfaces. The *Microkernel* subsystem may provide a number of different interfaces. Both internal and external service subsystems typically use the services of the *Microkernel*.

- *Platform*
  The *Platform* is the reusable subsystem constructed of the various components and providing a set of interfaces through its API.

4.3.5 Consequences

The Microkernel Architecture Pattern provides a scalable system in which optional sets of services may be added to the system during system builds. This allows the subsystem to be configured optimally for the specific application environment. There is nothing in this pattern that specifically prohibits the run-time addition of components, but the *Component Architecture* pattern is more commonly used for this.

4.3.6 Implementation Strategies

The *Microkernel* provides the core services of the subsystem, on which the more elaborate services provided by the other components are based. In an RTOS application, this will include memory allocation, task scheduling, and a means for hooking in device drivers. The performance of the *Microkernel* component is usually the most critical, and for this reason, it is common that at least some of this component is implemented in assembly language (at least in the RTOS application domain). The other components are all implemented in a higher-level language such as C or C++. Thus, porting the subsystem to another processor is usually just a matter of rewriting the core services in the new processor's native assembly language and recompiling the other components.

Internal components contain a cohesive set of services that use the more primitive *Microkernel* services. The set of services provided within an internal or external component are determined by trading off the richness of the set of services with the fidelity of control desired for the complexity and size of the *Platform* subsystem. If a component contains a smaller set of services, but there are more of them, then a greater granularity is provided to the system builder. On the other hand, providing too many adds to the complexity of system builds and increases the depth of understanding required on the part of the system builder.

For example, it is common to provide an internal component for an RTOS, which provides basic file system services, such as directory maintenance, and the ability to create and destroy files. Without the ability to write and read files, however, such a component is, by itself, useless. So it makes sense to include some basic file I/O services as well within the same component. On the other hand, not all applications that need a file system may need random access file I/O. Sequential I/O may be adequate for their needs. In this case, the RTOS designer may well opt to create an enhanced file I/O component that uses the basic file I/O services but adds random access, as well as move, copy and append services.

4.3.7 Related Patterns

The Component-Based Architecture Pattern is a more general pattern that permits the addition of components at run-time. It is also less structured than the Microkernel Architecture Pattern.

The Layered Pattern is more general still, since it provides little more than a structuring strategy.

4.3.8 Sample Model

The model illustrating the Microkernel Architecture Pattern is shown in Figure 4-8. Not all dependencies are shown. It is assumed, for example, that the internal and external services all access the *Microkernel* for memory, tasking, and hardware abstraction as necessary.

In this model, three core *Microkernel* service components are provided. The *Task Management Component* provides task creation, deletion, and scheduling services. The *Memory Management Compo-*

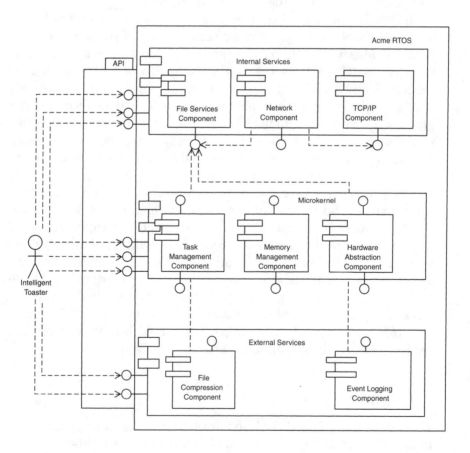

Figure 4-8: *nanoOS Model*

nent provides services such as a dynamic-sized heap and a set of fixed-sized heaps, including memory allocation, deallocation, and possibly garbage collection. The *Hardware Abstraction Component* provides hooks for linking in device drivers.

The set of three internal components use the facilities of the *Microkernel*. The *File Services* component provides services such as file creation, deletion, reading, and writing. The *TCP/IP Component* provides a communications protocol to organize messages among networked nodes. The *Network Services* uses the *TCP/IP* Component as a high-level protocol on top of the services that it provides (perhaps a low-level Ethernet CSMA/CD protocol) to provide a more abstract protocol for easier network communication. The *Network Component* itself offers the ability to send messages among network nodes and uses the *File Services Component* to provide remote file manipulation.

Two external components are shown in Figure 4-8. A *File Compression Component* provides services for lossy and non-lossy compression. Such services allow efficient use of finite resources such as communications bandwidth, memory, or disk space. The *Event Logging Component* monitors and logs system activity, such as might be required to debug run-time failures in the field. It uses the services of the *File System Component* to provide persistent storage.

4.4 CHANNEL ARCHITECTURE PATTERN

The Channel Architecture Pattern is useful in two different circumstances. First, it is useful when data within a data stream is sequentially transformed in a series of steps. Second, at the large scale, the Channel Architecture Pattern offers architectural redundancy for high-reliability and safety-critical applications.

4.4.1 Abstract

A *channel* can be thought of as a pipe[1] that sequentially transforms data from an input value to an output value. The internal elements of

---

1. In fact, this pattern is sometimes called the "pipe and filter" pattern, as it is in [4].

the channel work on the data stream in a kind of factory automation process. Each of the internal elements performs a relatively simple operation of the data: a single operational step in a larger sequential algorithm. It is common for multiple elements of the data stream to be in different parts of the channel at the same time. It is also common to increase throughput capacity to the system by adding multiple homogeneous (identical) channels. In high-reliability systems, multiple channels can operate in a variety of ways to achieve fault tolerance. Similarly, in safety-critical systems, multiple channels can improve safety by adding fault identification and safety measures. The details of the various reliability and safety subpatterns are discussed later in Chapter 9.

4.4.2 Problem

Many algorithms process data streams, applying the same set of operational transformations to each datum in turn, such as waveform scaling or application of a moving average digital filter. We would like an architectural structure that improves throughput capacity with the replication of architectural units allowing efficient processing of multiple data in different stages of processing. We also would like an architecture that improves reliability and safety through the simple addition of redundant processing.

4.4.3 Pattern Structure

Figure 4-9 shows the basic structure of the Channel Architecture Pattern. The data flows in a sequential manner from the *Input Source* actor, through the *Input Filtering* stage, through multiple *Transformational Processing* stages, through the *Output Filtering* stage, and finally to the *Output Sink* actor. Each of the stages represents an object with a set of services and internal attributes.

The datum itself is an object that undergoes a change of state at each transformation. It starts in the "Raw" state and is gradually roasted over time (not to stretch the metaphor too far, of course), resulting in the datum in its "cooked" state. The figure uses the UML "Object in State" notation, in which the state of the object is shown in square brackets.

The basic idea is that the datum is passed from object to object, undergoing some relatively small transformation at each step. The

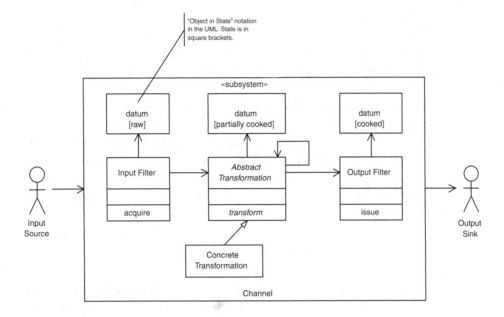

Figure 4-9: *Channel Architecture Pattern Structure*

transformational object may work on a single datum from start to end before handling the next, but in high-performance systems it is common for multiple data objects to be "in the pipe" at different stages simultaneously.

4.4.4 Collaboration Roles

- *Abstract Transformation*
  The *Abstract Transformation* class provides a common interface and operations within the channel pattern.

- *Channel*
  The *Channel* is an architectural subsystem. It includes (via composition relations) the other elements of the pattern. The advantage of using the *Channel* as a large composite object allows us to treat it as a single entity and replicate it to provide redundant processing or improved throughput.

- *Concrete Transformation*
  The *Concrete Transformation* class is a concrete (instantiable) sub-class of the *Abstract Transformation* class. Its *transform* operation is specialized for the particular stage in the algorithm.
- *Datum*
  The *Datum* is the information undergoing transformation. It is normally a behaviorally simple object with get and set operations. In the behavioral classification scheme of [1], it may be simple (its behavior is not dependent on its history), reactive (its behavior depends on a finite set of states), or continuous (its behavior depends on its history but in a continuous way).
- *Input Filter*
  The *Input Filter* class provides data acquisition and initial filtering of data from the sensor or input device.
- *Output Filter*
  The *Output Filter* class provides the means to send the data to the *Output Sink* in the proper format. It normally provides final filtering, data formatting, and output operations.

4.4.5 Consequences

The Channel Architecture Pattern is well suited to the sequential transformation of data from one state or form to another. It simplifies algorithms that can easily be decomposed into a series of steps operating on isolate elements from a data stream. Instances of channel subsystems can be added to improve throughput. The architecture is easily adaptable to handle multiple elements of the data stream in parallel, even when they are at different stages of processing.

4.4.6 Implementation Strategies

In the simple case, processing of a data stream takes place one datum at a time. It is acquired and preprocessed by the *Input Filter,* sent along the transformation chain, until it is emitted out of the *Output Filter* to the *Output Sink.* Then the next piece of information is processed, and so on.

This approach works well for non-real-time processing of data. However, it is often necessary to applying operational transformations to data streams in real-time, such as in such real-time applications as online autocorrelators, data trend analysis, imaging systems (such as SONAR and PET scanners), and waveform display systems. In these systems, a more time-efficient approach must be taken, and the transformation stages must keep up with the rate of incoming data. Such rates can be quite high—sometimes thousands or millions of data per second.

When there are real-time constraints that must be met, a common implementation approach is to allow all transformation steps to operate in parallel, albeit on different elements of the data stream. The handoffs can be either synchronous (normally when a single thread is used) or asynchronous (when each transformation stage executes in a different thread).

Further improvement in data throughput can be achieved by adding multiple channels, especially when the channels can execute on redundant hardware. To improve the throughput handling of a single channel, a channel multiplexer object is put in front of the set of channels—whose responsibility it is to feed the *Input Filter* of each channel in a fair way. A channel demultiplexer is put at the other end of the set of channels to take the data coming from the set of channels and send out a single processed data stream in the correct sequence to the *Output Sink.*

4.4.7 Related Patterns

There are a variety of variants of this pattern relevant to reliability and safety, provided in Chapter 9. For example, the Triple Modular Redundancy Pattern provides a three-channel system in which a comparator provides a winner-take-all approach to improving reliability. The Monitor-Actuator Pattern improves safety in the presence of faults by separating the actuation (data transformation) channel from a separate channel whose job it is to monitor the first channel.

4.4.8 Sample Model

Figure 4-10 shows an ECG monitor system structured using the Channel Architecture Pattern. This system processes an incoming data stream, from the ECG acquisition module. The top channel is concerned with processing the waveform into an intermediate form (indicated by the waveform data object in the *reduced* state), as well as scaling of that waveform in time and height for display. After the

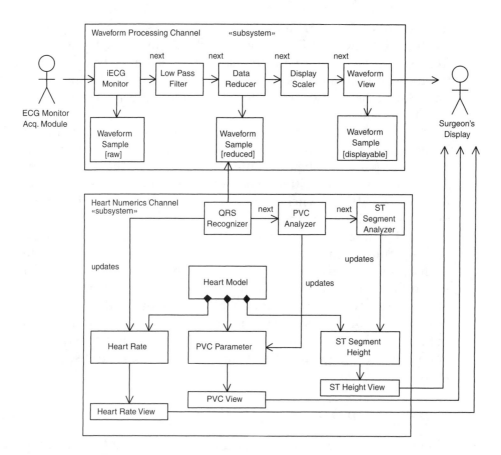

Figure 4-10: *ECG Monitor Channel Pattern Example*

initial processing, another channel also uses the waveform data stream in its *reduced* state and scans it, looking for specific artifacts that indicate QRS complexes (the heart beat), preventricular contractions (PVCs), and the elevation above baseline of the segment between the QRS complex and the T wave (the ST segment height).

The low pass filter transformation object attempts to remove high-frequency artifacts that are outside of the range of interest to the cardiologist. The next stage performs a data reduction from an incoming rate of perhaps 500 Hz to a more compressed stream at 125 Hz. This compression is done without loss of information because artifacts within the proper frequency range are carried over by the reduction algorithm. The display scaler object takes this reduced waveform and scales it to pixels, according to the current display sweep speed (common sweep speeds are 12.5, 25, and 50 mm/sec) and display resolution along both the x- and y-axes. Finally, the waveform view displays this *displayable* waveform in the proper window on the screen, erasing old data and drawing in the new data.

This waveform processing is time-critical because it is unacceptable to the user if the waveform is either jerky or if the delay between the occurrence and the display of cardiac information (normally less than 200 ms delay is perfectly fine for display purposes). It is likely, then, that a more detailed design of this model would break the waveform processing channel into three threads: one that runs at the rate of data acquisition (say, 500 Hz), one that runs at the display update rate (50 Hertz), and a third that is running when the other two are not, where most of the filtering occurs. No doubt FIFO queues would be used to buffer the timing between the threads, but if the queues are relatively small, then the processing delay will not be too large.

The Heart Numerics Channel begins work once the data is in the reduced state. Three different parsers scan over the reduced waveform, looking for different information. The QRS Recognizer looks for a specific wave shape that indicates a ventricular contraction (and delivery of blood to the arteries). The PVC Analyzer looks for extra ventricular contractions where they are not expected. The ST Segment Analyzer looks at the elevation of the electrical signal between certain aspects (specifically, the S and T waves) of the waveform. Heart parameters are updated on a regular basis, and every so often, this information is displayed on the screen. The numerics analyzers incorporate some form of digital filter so that the value they are monitoring is smoothed and does not change too rapidly.

4.5 RECURSIVE CONTAINMENT PATTERN

The Recursive Containment Pattern is a valuable pattern for very complex systems that realize thousands of requirements.

4.5.1 Abstract

The basic concept of the Recursive Containment Pattern is that the way to construct a very complex system is to think of it as a set of interrelated parts at a number of levels of successive detail, something like a microscope with multiple levels of magnification. At a given level of abstraction, an object provides opaque interfaces to its peers and collaborates with them to provide behavior larger than itself. This object internally implements its own behavior (invisibly to its peers) by delegation to smaller "part" objects that the object owns via composition relations. Each part object then implements its own opaque interface in terms of even smaller parts. This approach is applied recursively, creating smaller and smaller parts until each (leaf) part achieves a focused and simple responsibility that is easy to code.

4.5.2 Problem

A strategy is needed to decompose very large and complex systems in a manner that is straightforward but scalable and allows mapping of large abstract use cases in a way that is verifiable at each stage in the decomposition process.

4.5.3 Pattern Structure

Figure 4-11 shows the simple structure of the Recursive Containment Pattern. The system may be thought of as a (very) large object that contains (via composition relations) part objects. These part objects may be subsystems that are themselves composed of even smaller objects, and so on. This decomposition continues until the leaf objects have simple structures and provide simple services. The figure simply shows the pattern as a single object role with two association roles: a *Container* association role and a *Subordinate* association role.

4.5.4 Collaboration Roles

- *Element*
  The *Element* in the pattern has two basic features. First, it provides a set of services through one or more opaque interfaces. Second, internally, it provides these services largely by delegation and coordination of smaller parts.

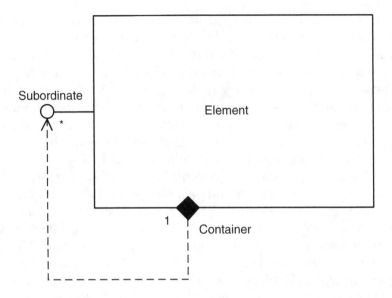

Figure 4-11: *Recursive Containment Pattern Structure*

4.5.5 Consequences

The significance of this simple pattern lies in the fact that collaborations may be viewed at multiple levels of abstraction. For very large and complex systems, this means that the system behavior may be viewed at several different levels of detail. At each detail, the *Element* can provide a number of use cases.

4.5.6 Implementation Strategies

Implementation of this pattern involves the repeated application of the simple containment pattern. Two opposite work flows are often used to create instances of this pattern. The top-down workflow starts at the system level and identifies structural objects that provide the services required to realize the collaboration. In real-time and embedded systems, many times there is a standard way of organizing the system into subsystems. This standard organization, even if previous systems were not object-oriented, may be incorporated using this approach. This can take advantage of the specialized skills often found in the subsystem specialists.

An additional advantage of this approach is ease of ensuring that as the developer moves down levels of abstraction, they are continuing to realize the use cases (that is, meet the system requirements). By creating scenarios at the highest level, one identifies the required system-actor interactions. By replacing the system object with its pieces, we can then test to ensure that we can still meet the same scenarios. These pieces can then be replaced by *their* pieces and the scenario reexecuted. This allows the developer to ensure that at every step of decomposition he or she is doing the right thing.

The other approach is to concentrate on domain construction—identifying the key classes and relations within the domains. Because of extensive previous experience, it may be possible to identify cross-domain collaborations that have worked well in the past and construct these into relatively larger building block objects. This can proceed until we get to the subsystem level. This approach is a natural one for many developers who specialize in one or a small set of domains, but it can be problematic because it isn't clear that the *right* parts are being built until enough of the building blocks are constructed to realize a known use case.

On a more detailed note, the composition relations used in the objects may be implemented via pointers in C and C++ (most common), so-called "automatic" classes, or references (when the part must always exist when the parent exists). When there are collections of parts, the Container Pattern is typically used to provide appropriate containers that can be iterated over. The container pattern is discussed in more detail in [2].

4.5.7 Related Patterns

This pattern is similar to the Composite Pattern of [2] and the Whole-Part Pattern of [3]. The Composite Pattern provides behavior only in the smallest level of decomposition (the "Leaf" objects). The Whole-Part Pattern provides services at every layer of decomposition, but it does not apply this structure at the highest levels of the architecture as we do here. Further, since these works predate the release of the UML, they do not integrate the concept of use cases and their realization in their discussions.

As noted above, [2] discusses the Container Pattern, which can be applied when the multiplicity of parts objects is potentially greater than one.

4.5.8 Sample Model

At the highest level, the use cases will be behavior-provided by the system as a whole rather than by individual pieces. A spacecraft might provide a use case such as "Take a picture of a surface feature on a planet." This use case is shown in Figure 4-12.

We can then decompose the spacecraft into subsystems that collaborate together to realize this system-level use case, as shown in Figure 4-13.

These subsystems are large objects (strictly speaking, subsystems in UML are both classifiers and packages, and as classifiers, they may have instances) that will realize their behavior via the many smaller objects they themselves contain. Nevertheless, the system-level use case will be realized by these subsystems collaborating together. This can be shown by elaborating the scenarios of the use case to include the subsystem level of detail.

The system level use case can be further decomposed into smaller use cases via the «includes» and «extends» use case relations, as shown in Figure 4-14. These use cases are normally decomposed down to the point where they are realized by a single object in

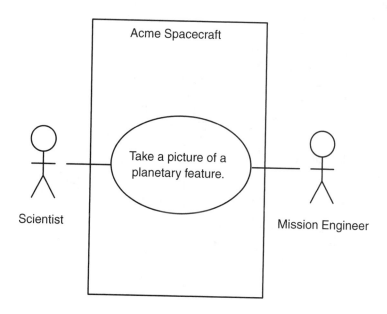

Figure 4-12: *High Level Use Case*

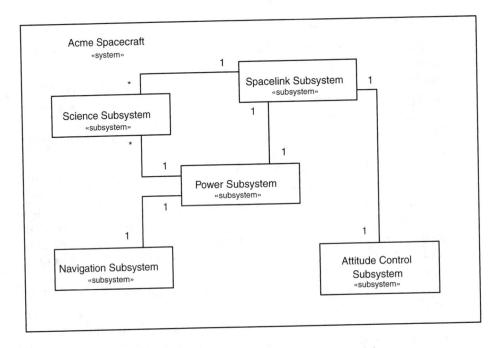

Figure 4-13: *Spacecraft Subsystem Model*

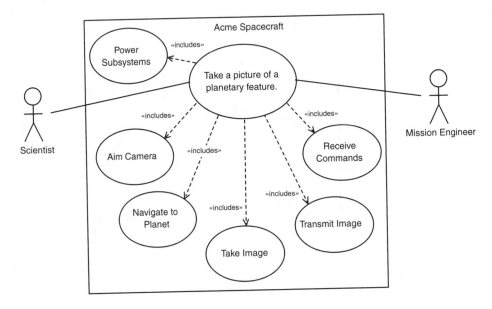

Figure 4-14: *Decomposed Use Cases*

the next layer down in the object model—in this case, the subsystems. The mapping of these use cases onto the subsystems is shown in Figure 4-15.

The subsystems in Figure 4-15 are themselves composite objects composed of smaller pieces. For example, the *Science Subsystem* will no doubt contain one or more cameras, lenses, filters, and so on. These objects will collaborate to realize the *Take Image* use case of that subsystem. Similarly, the *Power Subsystem* will contain things like batteries, solar cells, switches, relays, power budgets, and so on. The *Navigation Subsystem* will contain flight plans (consisting of smaller parts, such as waypoints and trajectories), a multidimensional map of the solar system, thrusters, and so on. Figure 4-16 shows some details of the subsystems. The take-home point here is that this approach can be recursively applied to provide as many levels of abstraction as necessary to detail with the system complexity.

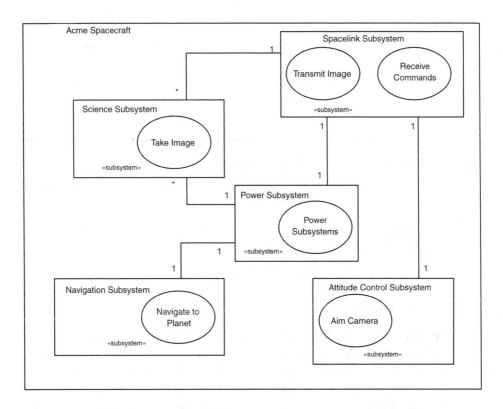

Figure 4-15: *Mapping Decomposed Use Cases to Subsystems*

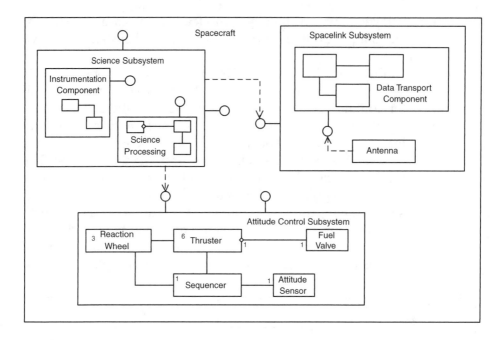

Figure 4-16: *Spacecraft Subsystem Details*

4.6 HIERARCHICAL CONTROL PATTERN

The Hierarchical Control Pattern is a specialized form of the Recursive Containment Pattern that distributes complex control algorithms among its various pieces.

4.6.1 Abstract

The Hierarchical Control Pattern uses two types of interfaces: control interfaces that monitor and control how the behaviors are achieved and functional interfaces, which provide the services controlled by the other set of interfaces. The control interfaces set the quality of service, such as fidelity, accuracy, and so on, as well as select policies that govern how the execution proceeds. The functional interfaces execute the desired behavior using the quality of service and policies set via the control interface.

Although there are many ways that the control interfaces can work, it is common to use a statechart to realize the control interfaces as well as coordinate the subordinate parts. Also, at each level, the class is typically reactive—using a statechart to control and manipulate the subordinate part objects.

Finally, similar to the Recursive Containment Pattern, the part objects are aggregated to the controller object via composition, and they may themselves be controllers at a more detailed level of abstraction, themselves containing even smaller objects, and so on.

4.6.2 Problem

A solution is needed for when it is desired to use a Recursive Containment Pattern but the objects must be configurable or their quality of service or execution policies must be controllable. Further, it is often desirable to separate the interfaces for this level of control and the actual functionality provided by the object.

4.6.3 Pattern Structure

Like the Recursive Containment Pattern, the Hierarchical Control Pattern is organized into hierarchies based on composition relations, as shown in Figure 4-17. The *Controller* orchestrates the implementation of its services via delegation and control of its subordinate parts. Subordinate parts may be either *Leaf Elements* or *Controllers*. *Leaf Elements* break the hierarchy and have no subordinate parts themselves (although they may have associations and participate in generalization taxonomies). *Controllers,* on the other hand have subordinate parts and provide two different kinds of interfaces (shown via shading in Figure 4-17): control interfaces and functional interfaces.

Control interfaces, as mentioned previously, are used to control and configure the implementation of services but not provide the application-level services themselves. The functional interfaces merely request that the application-level services be performed.

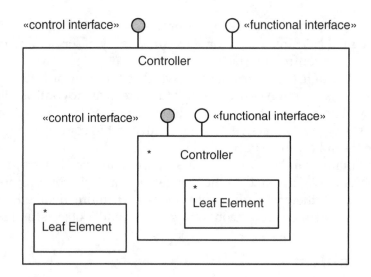

Figure 4-17: *Hierarchical Control Pattern Structure*

4.6.4 Collaboration Roles

- *Control Interface*
  The *Control Interface* provides services to manage how the functional services are performed—for example, switching to a different algorithm or providing a different quality of service. These services are not typically invoked by the same clients as the functional services.

- *Controller*
  The *Controller* role provides two kinds of opaque interfaces to its clients: control interface and functional interfaces. It implements these interfaces through delegation to its subordinate parts, which may be either *Controllers* or *Leaf Elements*.

- *Functional Interface*
  The *Functional Interface* provides the normal semantic services of the *Controller*. These services are delivered using the policies, algorithms, and qualities of service specified in using the *Control Interface*.

- *Leaf Element*
  A *Leaf Element* is a class of any kind other than a *Controller*. Typically, *Leaf Elements* are primitive and do not have composition

relations with still more primitive classes. However, they may have normal (and, less often, aggregation) relations with other classes and may participate in generalization taxonomies.

4.6.5 Consequences

Similar to the Recursive Containment Pattern, the primary advantage of this pattern is that it allows complex systems to be viewed at many levels of abstraction. In addition to that advantage, though, the use of separate control and functional interfaces provides a simple, scalable approach that can be used when the system must be highly configurable.

Since the *Leaf Elements* do most of the "real work" (for this reason, they are often called *semantic classes*), the job of the *Controller* is to coordinate and delegate pieces of service requests to the appropriate *Leaf Elements*. If the control is modal, which is a common application of this pattern, then the *Controller* will have a statechart that represents the configuration states of the subordinate parts. This is usually implemented as one peer and-state per *Leaf Element* in the statechart of the controller. Such a representation is very useful, particularly when the states of the various subordinate parts are not completely independent. The use of and-states makes it much easier to ensure that the subordinate parts are always in mutually compatible states. When the control or configuration behavior of the subordinate parts is *not* modal, then other means must be employed to track the behavior of the subordinate parts.

4.6.6 Implementation Strategies

This pattern is often implemented bottom-up. A set of *Leaf Elements* in a tightly coupled collaboration are found to be jointly configurable (their control states are not entirely independent), and it seems useful to have a superordinate controller manipulate them as a unit, so a *Controller* is added. As the modal control or configuration states of the *Leaf Elements* are discovered, a representation of these modal states, and their relations to the modal states of its peer *Leaf Elements* is added to the statechart of the *Controller*.

When a top-down approach is used, the pattern often starts as a more general Recursive Containment Pattern, using a composition-based decomposition of highly abstract elements into less abstract (more primitive) elements. Along the way, it becomes apparent that the collaboration of peer elements must be manipulated via a control interface (besides the opaque functional interface that was already available from the Recursive Containment Pattern), and so it is added. Then, a statechart for the control of the implementation of the interfaces is added to ensure that they remain compatible.

Regardless of which general implementation approach is used, the key implementation issues are the representation of the interfaces, the statechart for the *Controller,* and the use of the composition relation to glue together the levels of abstraction. Interfaces may be defined directly in source-level languages, such as Java, that directly support interfaces. In object-oriented languages that do not, such as C++, interface classes may be used. Interface classes are classes that do no real work, but they adapt a class with one set of operations to look like it has a different set. This is why it is sometimes called the Adapter Pattern. Interface classes may contain attributes and methods, whereas interfaces do not, so interface classes are somewhat more flexible than interfaces.

Because the *Controller* must coordinate the configuration and control states of the subordinate parts, it is important to ensure that the set of subordinate elements remains in consistent states. This is easy to do with a statechart for the *Controller,* especially if and-states are employed.

Finally, composition relations are most commonly implemented via pointers, although references and nested class instantiations can be used as well. With composition, the superordinate element has the explicit responsibility for both the creation and the destruction of the subordinate elements. If the subordinate has a fixed multiplicity, then the creation of those elements is normally done in the constructor. If it is a variable multiplicity, then the subordinate elements will be created (and destroyed) as needed.

4.6.7 Related Patterns

This pattern is a specialized form of the Recursive Containment Pattern discussed earlier. That pattern, in turn, is based on the Composite Pattern of [2] and the Whole-Part Pattern of [3].

As noted above, [2] also has a discussion of the Container Pattern, which can be applied when the multiplicity of parts objects is potentially greater than one.

4.6.8 Sample Model

Figure 4-18 shows an example of the Hierarchical Control Pattern. The functional services for the *Guidance Controller* object might be to ComputeTrajectory(), makeCourseCorrection(), scheduleCourse-Correction(), and so on. These functions could be performed using different algorithms if the spacecraft is currently launching, achieving orbital insertion, currently in orbit, or cruising between planets. They might differ, too, depending on whether the software is executing on a lander versus an orbiter versus a launch vehicle. They may change while the spacecraft loses mass (such as during launch

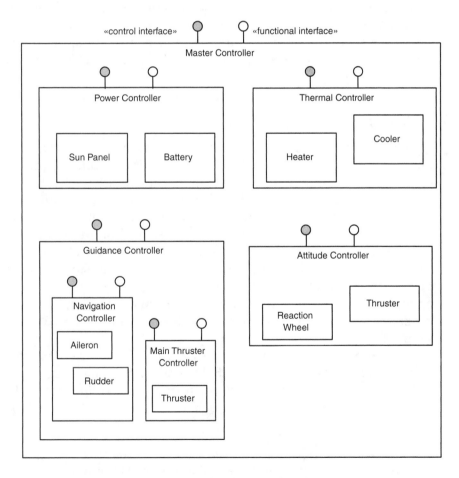

Figure 4-18: *Hierarchical Control Pattern Structure*

separation or due to the consumption of fuel). The separate control interface allows the algorithm and quality of service of these functional services to be changed on the fly while the system is running.

4.7 VIRTUAL MACHINE PATTERN

The Virtual Machine Pattern optimizes application portability at the expense of run-time efficiency. In applications where absolute raw performance is not a significant issue but being able to run the application on many different platforms *is*, or when many applications must run on many different platforms, the Virtual Machine Pattern is a good choice.

4.7.1 Abstract

Applications written to use a virtual machine are written to execute on an abstract machine. In fact, this abstract machine normally doesn't exist in hardware, so a virtual machine, written in software, interprets the instructions of the abstract machine by execution of instructions of a machine that *does* exist. Thus, a set of applications can be written for this virtual machine—possibly hundreds of applications—and this set of applications will run on *all* physical machines for which there is an appropriate virtual machine. This simplifies the porting of suites of applications to novel environments, since the applications themselves don't need to be rewritten. Only a single program (the virtual machine) must be developed for the actual target platform.[2]

This approach has been used successfully for a variety of programming languages, such as UCSD Pascal, BASIC, and Java. Typically, these applications execute much more slowly than natively compiled applications (often as much as 1/20 or 1/40 the speed of

---

2. I use the term *platform* because it may include not only the target CPU and physical devices but also device drivers for those devices and an operating system that orchestrates the use and collaboration of those devices.

compiled C or C++, for example), but if the applications are not time-
or performance-critical, this loss in performance may be more than
compensated for by the ease of porting.

4.7.2 Problem

The problem addressed by the Virtual Machine Pattern is to construct an infrastructure for application execution that is highly
portable for a large class of applications.

4.7.3 Pattern Structure

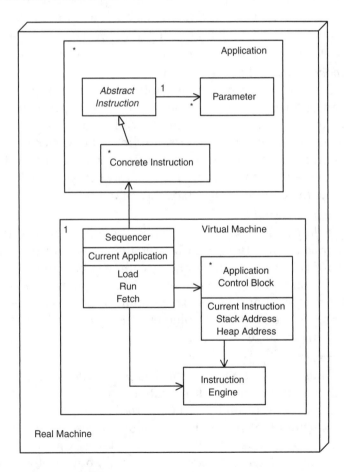

Figure 4-19: *Virtual Machine Pattern Structure*

4.7.4 Collaboration Roles

- *Abstract Instruction*
  An *Abstract Instruction* is an abstract base class of *Concrete Instruction*. Each *Abstract Instruction* may have zero or more *Parameters* associated with it. The use of the *Abstract Instruction* ensures that the various different *Concrete Instructions* have a common interface.

- *Application*
  An *Application* consists (that is, contains via composition) a set of *Concrete Instructions* that it passes to the *Virtual Machine* to execute.

- *Application Control Block*
  There is one *Application Control Block* per executing application. The *Application Control Block* is basically an *Iterator* (see the Container-Iterator Pattern) for the *Sequencer*. It provides the information for the *Virtual Machine* to execute each *Application.*

- *Concrete Instruction*
  A *Concrete Instruction* is an instantiable class that represents the design language primitives. The instructions may be hand-generated by the programmer or automatically translated from another design language into a corresponding set of *Concrete Instructions.* Often this is done via a compiler so that a human readable form (either text, such as Java, or graphics, such as the UML) is translated into a more compact, portable compiled form.

- *Instruction Engine*
  The *Instruction Engine* translates the *Application,* one *Concrete Instruction* at a time, into instructions native to the target platform. This is most often done by calling subroutines (or functions or methods) that represent each *Concrete Instruction* and passing the relevant parameters. These subroutines then execute native target instructions to implement the *Concrete Instruction* in the design language.

- *Parameter*
  A *Parameter* is a class that consists primarily of a type-value pair, although it may have additional information, such as valid range and encoding format. Each *Concrete Instruction* has zero or more parameters that represent the values necessary for the *Concrete Instruction* to execute. In most languages, *Concrete Instructions* will have a fixed number of *Parameters*, but in other languages, the number of *Parameters* may be allowed to vary at run-time.

- *Real Machine*
  The *Real Machine* is not a software object but in fact represents the hardware CPU on which the *Virtual Machine* executes. Thus, it is shown as a node rather than an object (although it is also acceptable to show the *Real Machine* as an actor that associates with the *Instruction Engine*). The *Real Machine* executes not only the *Virtual Machine* but also the translated *Concrete Instructions*.

- *Sequencer*
  The *Sequencer* (aka the *Scheduler*) has a number of related responsibilities. It often loads (and in some cases, such as Java, compiles) the *Application* and initializes the *Virtual Machine* for execution. It also determines when to get the next *Concrete Instruction*, gets the next *Concrete Instruction*, and then passes it off to the *Instruction Engine* for execution. If the design language supports concurrency, then the *Sequencer* also manages that concurrency.

- *Virtual Machine*
  The *Virtual Machine* is a large-scale component that contains, via composition, both the *Sequencer* and the *Instruction Engine* as well as one *Application Control Block* for each *Application* executing. It manages the loading, unloading, and execution of the *Applications*.

4.7.5 Consequences

The advantages of this pattern are twofold. First, porting a particular application or a suite of applications to a novel hardware platform is greatly simplified, since it is sufficient to rewrite (or recompile) only the virtual machine. In addition, it greatly eases porting a suite of applications to a set of different hardware platforms. Furthermore, once the virtual machine for a particular platform exists, each application written for the virtual machine will now immediately execute on all platforms. This accounts for much of the success of the Java language. A Java application can be written once, and it will execute immediately on any Java virtual machine.

Another advantage of the Virtual Machine Pattern is that applications, which are stored in a tokenized format, are often very tiny compared to the sizes of natively compiled applications. This is because compiled applications normally each have their own set of libraries for I/O, user interface, mathematical calculations, and so on. In the Virtual Machine Pattern, these libraries are often contained within the virtual machine itself and so do not need to be replicated. Further, a single tokenized instruction may result in the execution of many hundreds of CPU instructions, and so the tokenized *Concrete Instruction* tends to be much more compact than the corresponding native assembly language.

These benefits come at a price, and performance is the most obvious and crucial one. A virtual machine is also typically fairly large. The Java virtual machine, for example, has about a 1.5-MB footprint. For smaller applications on memory-constrained devices, the resources may not exist for the virtual machine. When this is the case, the Microkernel Architecture Pattern may be preferable. Additionally, the creation of a virtual machine can be a great deal of work and may outweigh the benefits of the pattern if only a few applications or platforms need to be supported. Or the virtual machine approach can be implemented using a Microkernel Architecture Pattern so that it is scalable to run with selectable capability on different platforms. Notice, however, that in situations where the platform will run multiple applications at the same time, the Virtual Machine Pattern can *reduce* memory usage because the virtual machine itself provides much of the infrastructure of the applications and when using this pattern, this infrastructure is stored in memory in only once.

4.7.6 Implementation Strategies

Implementing virtual machines is a sizable task. In some sense, the virtual machine is an interpreter, executing one language by dynamically translating it to another during execution. However, a virtual machine is more than this because it provides a coherent (if nonexistent) target platform for a set of applications. Interpretation of the application is one aspect, certainly, but the virtual machine must also provide an abstraction of the underlying resource abstractions.

4.7.6.1 Reusability of the Virtual Machine

The whole point of the virtual machine is the ability of an application to run on the virtual machine regardless of the underlying platform. To achieve this goal, the virtual machine itself must be easily portable to a variety of underlying platforms. To be successful, the applications must be able to represent everything they can do in an abstract way that can be appropriately translated on all target platforms. If the application must constantly "go around" the virtual machine to implement some behavior directly on the target platform, then the goal of the virtual machine is at best compromised and, at worst, totally unrealized.

These are the keys to the successful *reusable* implementation of a virtual machine.

- *Using a portable language to write the virtual machine*
  Virtual machines are virtually always[3] themselves recompiled for the native environment on which they execute. This means that good compilers must exist for all of the target platforms (or they must be themselves written). For this reason, common languages, such as C or C++, are used to implement the virtual machine.

- *Encapsulation of the target platform idiosyncrasies*
  To easily port the virtual machine to a novel platform, most of the virtual machine should use platform-independent abstractions (much as the applications do). This means that the target platform idiosyncrasies are localized within small components or layers, and the rest of the virtual machine goes through those components when it must manipulate the underlying platform.

- *Use a Layered or Microkernel Architecture Pattern to organize the virtual machine*
  The encapsulation of the target platform leads naturally to a layered architecture of the virtual machine. Thus, to move to a novel environment, only the lowest platform-specific layer must be rewritten.

- *Extensible architecture*
  Layering is often not enough. Thought must be put into what aspects of the target platform are free to vary. These may be any of the following.
  - CPU instruction set
  - Support facilities (e.g., timers, special purpose hardware)
  - Operating system
  - Scheduling policies
  - Resource management policies (e.g., dynamic vs. fixed-sized heaps)

---

3. Pun intended.

- Communication media and protocols
- Middleware (e.g., Object Request Brokers)

4.7.6.2 Interacting with the Underlying Platform

For the most part, the applications should interact with the platform via the abstractions provided in the virtual machine. That means that the applications must be expressed in a language sufficiently rich to express these abstractions and their variants. The job of the virtual machine is, after all, to translate these abstract instructions in terms of concrete instructions on the CPU that utilize the features of the platform.

There will be circumstances (typically to achieve performance or other quality of service goals) in which the virtual machine mechanisms must be eschewed in favor of direct target platform invocation. Escape hatches are common in languages, such as the ability to insert assembly language statements directly in a C or C++ program. This makes the applications less portable, of course, but all of life is a compromise. The virtual machine must provide such an out, such as Java's so-called "native methods."

The virtual machine must provide a means for managing the resources of the target platform. These resources may be threads, memory, communications channels, or any other object that has a finite capacity to be shared.

4.7.6.3 Representing the Application

Most of the time, the application is precompiled to some intermediate form before being executed by the virtual machine. This has a number of advantages for the execution of the application. First, the application is represented in a format that is optimized for execution rather than optimized for human readability. Second, these compiled or, as they are sometimes called, *tokenized* applications require much less memory space for storage. Applications are often compiled from multiple sources, and this means that the virtual machine must only manipulate a single monolithic entity during execution. Since almost all virtual machines ultimately execute on a compiled form, precompilation removes the compilation time from the time necessary to load and execute the application. And finally, if the compilation is done elsewhere, the virtual machine itself can be smaller and simpler.

Another approach is called Just-In-Time (JIT) compilation. In this case, the JIT is actually a part of (or is invoked by) the virtual machine. This approach is used when the target environments are not memory or time constrained because the JIT compiler is invoked whenever the application is loaded. An advantage of the JIT compiler is that the application can be debugged on the executing platform by humans because it has retained its human-readable form. Clearly, such an approach is most useful when the target platforms interact directly with people and is least useful for deeply embedded, performance or memory size-critical environments.

4.7.6.4 Scheduling Applications

Some virtual machines abstract the scheduling policies of the underlying operating system. Some virtual machines do their own scheduling and run as a single task on the target system's OS. Still others expose the native OS's scheduling policies and require the application to be customized for the target.

Most virtual machines offer a particular set of scheduling policies (such as static priority preemption), but it is also common to have the ability to add user-defined scheduling policies as a plug-in to the virtual machine. Most commonly, though, a virtual machine provides a single scheduling policy and applications must be written to use it.

The simplest way to do that is to provide the scheduling abstractions commonly provided by the underlying OSes in the target domain. If the target domain is real-time and embedded systems, then the static priority-based preemption is the most common scheduling approach. However, most OSes also provide facilities to specify interrupt handlers (usually by providing parameterless function callbacks).

In terms of implementation of these facilities, the virtual machine commonly has an internal lightweight OS abstraction layer that knows how to create and destroy threads, get semaphores, manipulate event queues, get and release dynamic memory, and so on.

4.7.6.5 Debugging the Testing Facilities

Because the virtual machine provides an abstract execution environment, it is possible (and generally a *really* good idea) to build in symbolic debugging information into the application and debugging/

testing facilities. The compiler, whether it is offline or JIT, constructs the necessary symbol dereferencing information so that memory addresses can be mapped back to user symbols in the source language. "Source language" is the language in which the user entered the application, whether it is a text-based language, such as Java, or a graphical language, such as the UML class diagrams or Statecharts.

Typical facilities include execution control (run, stop, single step, set/remove breakpoint, and so on) and variable/attribute manipulation (monitor and set value). To implement this, the compiled application must have execution points at which debugging instructions can be inserted by the virtual machine.

4.7.7 Related Patterns

The virtual machine itself is often implemented using the layered or microkernel pattern.

4.8 COMPONENT-BASED ARCHITECTURE

A *component*, in the UML, is a run-time artifact that forms the basic replaceable unit of software. Although not explicitly represented as such in the UML metamodel, it is convenient to think of a component as a large-scale object that contains, via composition, objects that implement the component's interface. Components always have strong encapsulation (as you might expect, since they are meant to be replaceable) and well-defined, source-level language independent interfaces to which the components must conform. Examples of such components include static libraries, dynamic linkable libraries (DLLs), and OCX and ActiveX components.[4]

---

4. The difference between components and subsystems in the UML is subtle and ambiguous. Subsystems can be components and vice versa. Subsystems usually are the largest-scale pieces inside the system, typically containing multiple components. Components are the second-tier architectural pieces and may contain multiple subcomponents as well as use the services of other components. Components may also contain multiple threads by containing «active» objects. Each primitive object in a component typically executes in

A component-based system uses these large-scale objects as basic architectural units with the intent that the system can be managed by replacing the components piecemeal, as new revisions of the components become available or components optimized to different design criteria or using different algorithms become available.

Component-based systems have proven themselves to be very stable in the sense that (1) the architectural structure tends to remain the same over time as the system is maintained and modified, and (2) defects tend to be isolated to individual components, and so fixing the defects tends to have only local effects. The Component-Based Architecture Pattern is one way to organize a component-based system.

4.8.1 Abstract

Component-based systems offer some compelling advantages: ease of maintenance, isolation of defects, source-level language independence, ease of development, and ease of reusability. These advantages arise because of the nature of components: They are strongly encapsulated objects that provide language-independent, opaque interfaces. They do not differ greatly from the UML concept of a subsystem. Components are normally large-scale objects whose behavior is implemented in terms of smaller objects that the component owns via composition. The organizational principle of deciding which objects go into which components is also the same as subsystems: common run-time behavioral purpose. For example, components to add a specific GUI will contain typically many objects, but their run-time purpose—in this case, provide a consistent GUI—is the same.

Components differ from other objects in both the nature of the interface that they present—one that is source-language independent—and the nature of the applications into which they fit. Components provide strongly opaque interfaces and often provide both functional and configuration services. Because the whole idea of a component is *replaceability*, the component interface must be especially well documented. This includes not only the signature of the calling interface but also the pre- and postconditional invariants of the component, such as the performance properties of the component.

---

exactly one thread or is shared between threads within a component. A more rigorous (and hopefully useful) definition of components and subsystems is slated for UML 2.0, which is under development as of this writing.

The structure of component-based applications is different from other types of applications. Much of the flexibility and maintainability of component-based systems comes from the fact that such systems are composed of high-level replaceable pieces. This is similar to the construction of modern computer systems in which the knowledge of the layout or internal transistor and bus layout of chips is totally hidden from the client chips that communicate with the chip via its well-defined interface. Indeed, component-based systems are often said to have pluggable architectures into which components can be freely replaced, sometimes even while the system is running.

This means that each application can be structured from a relatively common set of components, much like a computer system is constructed from a set of well-understood chips and chip sets.

4.8.2 Problem

The Component-Based Architecture Pattern addresses the need for an architecture that is robust in the presence of maintenance and is highly reusable in a variety of circumstances.

4.8.3 Pattern Structure

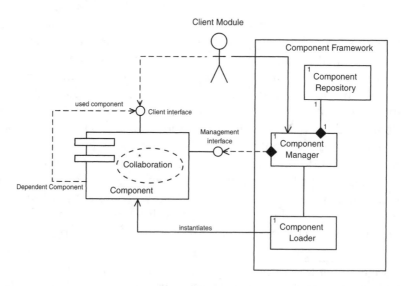

Figure 4-20: *Component-Based Architecture Pattern Structure*

4.8.4 Collaboration Roles

- *Client Interface*
  The *Client Interface* of the component provides the services offered by the component. These may include just the signature of the operation, but in general the interface should specify a contract between the client of the *Component* and the *Component* itself. This contract includes, in addition to the signature of the operations, preconditions and postconditions of each service and any exceptions thrown. These can be modeled as a statechart for the interface. The interface should be opaque—that is, it should not reveal anything about the internal implementation. This is crucial for *substitutability* of other *Components* that realize the same interface.

- *Collaboration*
  A *Collaboration* in this case refers to the collaboration of a set of semantic objects (objects defined in domains but instantiated in the component) that realize the use cases of the *Component*.

- *Component*
  A *Component* is a composite object that contains one or more *Collaborations*. That is, the *Component* is a container that provides an interface for the set of semantics objects within each collaboration contained within.

- *Component Framework*
  The *Component Framework* is a composition of the *Component Loader, Component Manager,* and *Component Repository*. It is responsible for the loading and management of the *Components*.

- *Component Loader*
  The *Component Loader* loads the *Components* in response to requests from the *Component Manager* and may be omitted if static linking is used.

- *Component Manager*
  The *Component Manager* manages the set of *Components* at runtime. A *Component Manager* is only required when dynamic linking of components is required. If *Components* are statically linked, then this object may be omitted. A *Component Manager* allows the swapping, loading, and unloading of *Components* as necessary, including chained *Components* (*Components* that depend on other *Components*).

- *Component Repository*
  All active *Components* register with the *Component Repository.* This allows the *Component Loader* to load the *Components* wherever it sees fit. When a *Component* or *Client Module* later wants to invoke a service on a loaded *Component*, it first checks the *Component Repository* to find out where it is. The *Component Repository* then returns a reference, handle, or pointer (implementation specific) to the desired *Component.* The type of reference returned is a defining property of the *Component* pattern instantiation. The *Component Repository* may also maintain a reference count for each *Component*, counting the number of clients registered to a given *Component.* When a new client registers for the *Component*, this count is augmented; when a client deregisters, the reference count is decremented. When the reference count is decremented to zero, the *Component* may be unloaded.

- *Management Interface*
  The *Management Interface* is an interface used by the *Component Framework.* The actual services provided by this interface will vary depending on the exact realization of the Component-Based Architecture Pattern. Typically, this will include the name and revision of the *Component* and a list of *Components* on which this *Component* depends (so they can be loaded as well).

4.8.5 Consequences

There are several consequences of using the Component-Based Architecture Pattern. The main advantage is that systems (and subsystems) may be constructed via *assembly* of a mixture of previously defined and newly developed components. This is similar to how hardware engineers typically construct digital electronics systems. The use of opaque, source-level language-independent interfaces greatly enhances reusability. There are many vendors providing reusable components today in a variety of domains: user interface, communications, distributed object middleware, and math libraries being the most common.

The primary disadvantage is potential inefficiency due to the use of opaque interfaces. The fact that an interface is opaque means that the client of a component is simply not allowed to rely on internal implementation detail of the component, disallowing some potential optimizations. Additionally, because functionality is packaged into relatively large-scale components, additional resources (such as CPU cycles or memory) may be required when only a few services from a component are actually used in the target system. The entire component (along with any other components required by the first) must be included in the system, even if only a few of the services of the component are invoked in the running system.

4.8.6 Implementation Strategies

Component-based design (CBD) is a very popular approach to constructing large complex systems quickly. In fact, I am one of three rotating authors writing a column on CBD for *Software Development* magazine (along with Bertrand Meyer and Clement Serpinski).[5] CBD is often implemented inside a framework in which components have a well-defined role. For example, Microsoft's Component Object Model (COM) and its variants COM+ and DCOM (Distributed COM) provide a common way of building and sharing components in monolithic and distributed systems on Microsoft operating system environments. CORBA (Common Object Request Broker Architecture—a standard owned by the Object Management Group) also provides a component model that is widely used on Microsoft, Unix, and other platforms. JINI is a plug-and-play standard for connecting Java-based devices into a network. Enterprise Java Beans (EJB) is another component standard for Java-based systems.

There are a great many variants of the Component-Based Architecture Pattern. We have represented one here that allows dynamic loading and unloading of components. Components may be static (statically linked, so that they are present in the load image of the application) or dynamic (loaded when necessary, such as load-on demand). Components themselves may be mostly data (such as configuration tables and databases), mostly behavioral (such as math libraries), or a combination of the two (such as GUI components, such as windows widgets). Some of the advantages of components are further realized through the use of COTS (commercial off-the-shelf) components versus custom-developed components. Such COTS components are typically constructed for a specific component architectural model (such as COM+ or EJB). If your system uses an already standardized component architecture, then there will be a

---

5. The column is called *Beyond Objects*. See *www.sdmagazine.com*.

wealth of potentially usable components available. New components must then be written with the commercial component architectural model in mind. There still may be advantages in creating your own component architecture, but if you can model or imitate one of the existing architectures, you'll be ahead of the game.

If you write components in any of these CBD environments, you must adhere to their standards for providing interfaces and services. If you're writing your own CBD environment, then you're free to construct your own. In any case, you must provide for these basic things.

- A standard way to invoke services provided by a component
- A standard way to query to identify the presence of a component and load-on demand, if necessary
- A source-language-independent means for specifying the interface to a component
- A way to identify the revision number for a component
- A way to identify the components on which a given component depends
- An infrastructure for loading and unloading components as necessary

Since components should have a program-language-independent means for specifying and using interfaces, some of the component architectures provide an Interface Description Language (IDL) for specifying interfaces. Different IDL compilers map the IDL description of the interface into the target programming language used by the components authors (on the server side) or users (on the client side).

In larger-scale CBD systems, it is common to classify the components based on the kinds of services they offer. The manner in which this is done leads us to the application of other patterns with the components. For example, it is very common to mix component patterns with a layered architecture pattern and realize different tiers of an n-tier layered architecture with components.

4.8.7 Related Patterns

Since the current revision of UML does not draw a strong distinction between subsystems and components (or, for that matter, between either of these and objects), components may be used in conjunction with any of the other structural architectural patterns. And the benefits of components are sufficiently compelling that one can in fact find examples of components used in conjunction with all of the other patterns in this chapter. For example, it is very common to mix the Component-Based Architecture Pattern and the Layered Pattern.

4.8.8 Sample Model

Figure 4-21 shows a simple example of a componentized application called *Control System.exe.* The system consists of three subsystems—*Display, Data Acquisition,* and *Data Management*—plus an infrastructure component framework. Each subsystem contains one or more

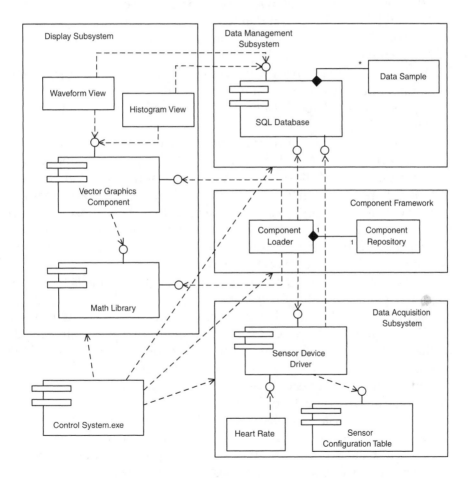

Figure 4-21: *Control System Sample Model*

components. The *Display Subsystem* contains two display objects relevant to the discussion here: the *Waveform View* and the *Histogram View* objects. These use the facilities of the *Vector Graphics* component to draw the data. This component could be a dynamically loaded component. The *Vector Graphics* component depends on the *Math Library* component for some functional capability, such as coordinate transformations. Both these components provide client interfaces; for the *Math Library,* the only direct client is the *Vector Graphics* component, whereas the semantic application objects are clients of the *Vector Graphics* component.

The *Data Acquisition* subsystem has a device driver component for the sensor hardware that in turn depends on the Sensor Configuration Table (which might be stored in ROM in our embedded application).

The *Data Management* component provides standard database management for the acquired sensor data. One would imagine that the *Data Acquisition* subsystem would link to the data management component to store incoming data. Similarly, the graphical view objects would link to the *Data Management* component to retrieve the data for display.

The *Component Framework* contains the *Component Loader* and *Component Repository.* When the *Control System.exe* application begins, it autoloads the Control Framework and then commands the Subsystems to initialize. The *Waveform::Display Subsystem* identifies its need for the *SQL Database Component.* It asks the *Component Framework* where it is. Since that component is not listed in the *Component Repository,* the *Component Loader* loads the component and notifies the *Waveform* object where it is.

The *Waveform* object also needs to use the *Vector Graphics* component. Again, it asks the *Component Framework.* The *Component Framework* cannot find it, so it loads the requested component. During its initialization, the *Vector Graphics* component discovers that it needs the *Math Library* component. So it then requests the location of the *Math Library.* Again, since it's not found, the *Component Loader* loads and installs the requested component, and the *Vector Graphics* component can complete its initialization.

When the *Histogram* object is initialized, it needs the same components as well. Since the components are already loaded, the *Component Framework* need not reload them—it merely notifies the requesting object of the component locations. This initialization sequence is shown in Figure 4-22.

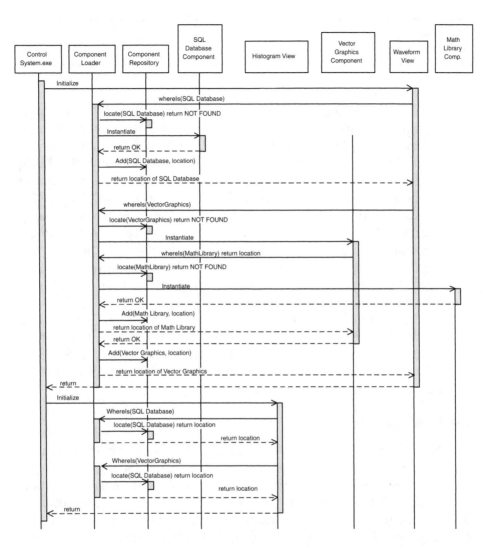

Figure 4-22: *Initialization of Display Objects Sequence Diagram*

4.9 ROOM PATTERN

ROOM (Real-Time Object-Oriented Methodology) [4] is an older methodology that predates the UML by several years. As pointed out by Jim Rumbaugh and Bran Selic, the UML is sufficiently general to model just about ANY other methodology, including ROOM [5]. These authors have, in fact, authored a paper defining a proprietary methodology, somewhat misleadingly called UML-RT.[6] UML-RT is basically nothing more than ROOM recast with window dressing. This is not to say that ROOM is bad or inapplicable in certain circumstances. It is really nothing more nor less than one of many architectural design patterns. As with all design patterns, it has both strengths and weaknesses, areas of good application and areas in which it is a poor pattern to use.

The ROOM Pattern identifies special object roles for bidirectional interfaces called *ports*[7] and rules governing the behavior of this interface, reified into classes called *protocol* classes. This provides strong encapsulation of interfaces and mediation and control of bidirectional associations among classes.

4.9.1 Abstract

The ROOM Pattern itself is a relatively heavyweight pattern, providing a well-structured interface and strong interface protection. All behavior in the ROOM Pattern is provided via statecharts[8] execution.

The ROOM Pattern is appropriate when the interaction of some large-scale objects is complex and requires special means to mediate and control. These objects may be within the same address space or distributed across address spaces.

---

6. I say *misleadingly* because although the methodology is called UML-RT, *time* actually appears nowhere in its specification!

7. UML 2.0 will likely have *Ports* as a first-order concept to facilitate the use of the ROOM pattern, although it appears (as of this writing) that the other roles will not be provided as first-order UML concepts. Generic classes may be used to create objects for these pattern roles as necessary.

8. ROOM itself uses only a subset of the UML Statechart model called ROOMCharts (which, for example, don't use and-states or multiple branch points from conditional pseudostates), but there is no reason inherent in the pattern why statechart semantics can't be used.

The interfaces are reified into *Port* classes, and the complex interaction among the objects is reified into *Protocol* classes that mediate how the ports interact. One special feature of the *Port* and *Protocol* classes is that unlike normal UML interfaces, these represent bidirectional interfaces.

The large-scale objects are called *Capsules*, which implement behavior specified by statecharts.[9] *Capsules* may contain subcapsules. Where appropriate, messages can be passed on from an outer *Capsule* port to an inner *Capsule* via a *Relay Port*. This has the advantage of consistency at different levels of abstraction (note the similarity with the Recursive Containment Pattern discussed earlier in this chapter) and the disadvantage of adding complexity over a simple UML association.

4.9.2 Problem

The ROOM Pattern addresses the needs of systems composed of a number of large-scale objects with opaque interfaces in which the large-scale objects have complex interactions. These large-scale objects may be distributed or not.

4.9.3 Pattern Structure

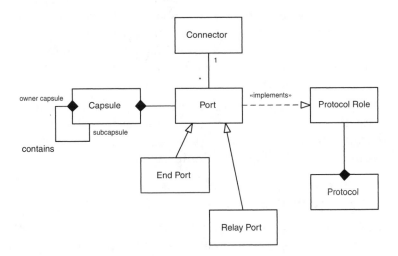

Figure 4-23: *ROOM Pattern Structure*

---

9. See previous footnote.

4.9.4 Collaboration Roles

- *Capsule*
  A large-scale class that provides a well-encapsulated behavior, accessible via *Port* classes.

- *Connector*
  A *Connector* connects two ports actively involved in message exchange. This is a reification of a UML *link* (an instance of an association).

- *End Port*
  An *End Port* indicates that a message stops at the specified capsule and invokes a signal on that capsule's statechart. In fact, all signals in this pattern either originate or terminate on *End Ports*.

- *Port*
  A *Port* represents an interface for a *Capsule* in a somewhat more relaxed manner than a UML interface. UML interfaces are named collections of operations that cannot have attributes. *Ports can* have attributes and structure. *Ports* relate tightly with *Protocols*. *Ports* are subclassed into *End Ports* and *Relay Ports*.

- *Protocol*
  A *Protocol* is a specification of desired or allowable sequences of message flow between two *Ports* sharing a *Connection*. Most *Protocols* are *binary*, meaning that they connect exactly two ports. In this case, the *Protocol* connected to one *Port* must be the inverse of the *Protocol* connected to the other. This is called the *Protocol Conjugate*.

- *Relay Port*
  A *Relay Port* is a port that passes messages on to an internal subcapsule. In a sense, they break the encapsulation boundary because they make the interface of an internal capsule visible from the outside of its containing capsule.

4.9.5 Consequences

ROOM, or as it is also known, UML-RT, is a proprietary methodology and as such is supported natively only by a single vendor. However, there is no reason at all why the ROOM pattern cannot be used with a standard UML tool. It is a relatively heavyweight pattern, but it does provide benefits as well. One benefit is that it models *both* sides of an interface, both the client and the server. UML itself only provides native modeling for the server side of the interface—that is, the object providing the services via the interface.

The use of port, connector, and protocol classes allows very good definition of complex interfaces. Protocol (and their protocol conjugate) classes are typically modeled using statecharts, which is a good way to model pre- and postconditions of the services (provided via the operations of the port and port conjugate classes). UML interfaces are essentially stateless-named collections of operations defined on a class. By abstracting these into separate port and protocol classes (rather than interfaces per se), they can have attributes and states, which makes them more powerful. Port classes are an elaboration of the Adapter or Interface Pattern, whereas protocol classes are a form of the Strategy or Policy Pattern.

The downside of this pattern is that all associations between the semantic classes (the capsules in this pattern) are mediated through an entire set of other classes. This greatly complicates otherwise simple relationships among classes with a heavyweight structure. Therefore, it is recommended that even when applied, the pattern is applied selectively to only large-scale semantic classes and used only when the interface between semantic classes is particularly complex or rich, especially in terms of pre- and postconditions.

In summary, users may find this pattern overly restrictive if over-applied or strictly applied (such as only allowing state-based behavior), but when applied in moderation to specific aspects of a system, it can be helpful in controlling certain interfaces when a heavyweight approach is called for.

4.9.6 Implementation Strategies

A port class is nothing more than an interface Adapter with a Protocol (same as the Policy or Strategy Pattern) class added to control the invocation of operations. The Capsule itself provides the implementation method for the operations of the ports. Relay port classes allow the Capsule to delegate the called operation to internal subcapsules, while End Port classes insert events into the Capsule's statechart to cause behavior. However, it is likely to be useful to implement End Port operations as calls to primitive operations when the invoked behavior is not stateful, as in either primitive or continuous behaviors [1] or when such behavior is delegated to the collaboration of objects owned by the Capsule via composition (as per the Recursive Containment or Hierarchical Control Patterns).

4.9.7 Related Patterns

The Adapter (aka Interface) Pattern separates out an interface from an implementation. Port classes are adapters that implement that adaptation in a particular fashion.

The Policy (aka Strategy) Pattern separates a cohesive set of logic rules from the behavior that uses those rules. Protocol classes provide interface rules for Ports and so are clearly Policy classes.

The ROOM pattern is similar to the Recursive Containment Pattern discussed earlier in this chapter. Both patterns use self-similar decomposition and strong interfaces to provide multiple layers of abstraction. The Recursive Containment Pattern is somewhat more general than the ROOM pattern.

4.9.8 Sample Model

Figure 4-24 shows a simple example of two objects communicating via ports and protocols. The *Master* is the sender in this case, while the *Slave* is the receiver. Each of these capsules[10] strongly aggregates a port (*iSender* and *iReceiver*, respectively), and each of these ports implements a protocol role. The *HiRel Protocol* class defines a "reliable communications protocol" between the sender and the receiver. The roles played by the sender and the receiver are, naturally enough, different. The *Socket* class serves the pattern role of connecting the two ports so that communications can take place.

Figure 4-25 shows just the port and connector classes, with their state behavior identified. Before a message can be sent, a connection must be formed. This connection is managed by the *Socket* class. Once a connection is requested of the *Socket* class, it notifies the other end of the communications link to connect. Once connected, both sides send events every 1000 ms to indicate the "liveness" of the con-

---

10. Note that the pattern roles are used as stereotype names on the class diagram. This is a fairly common idiom when instantiating patterns.

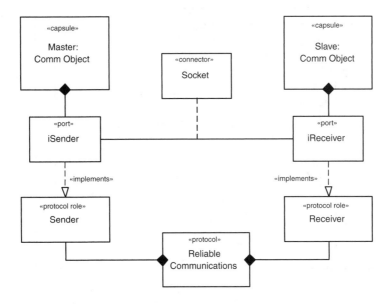

Figure 4-24: *ROOM Pattern Example Class Model*

nection. If the liveness at either end goes away for 1500 ms, then connection is considered broken, and both objects are notified of a disconnection.

Once the connection is established, the *iSender* class sends the message (in the *Transmitting* state). Once complete, it enters a state where it waits for an explicit acknowledgement from the receiver. If it gets an acknowledgement in less than 10 seconds, the *iSender* class goes back to its Ready state, the connection still active. If it doesn't receive an acknowledgement within 10 seconds of transmission, then the *iSender* class resends the message. To limit the number of retransmissions of the same message, an attribute of the *iSender* class, *tCount,* tracks the number of times the same message has been retransmitted. If it exceeds a preset limit, then an error is noted, and the *iSender* class goes back to its *Ready* state.

Note that if the roles can be reversed (that is, the Slave can initiate transmission and the Master can receive unsolicited communications), then both capsules will aggregate both protocol roles (they will both aggregate an *iSender* and an *iReceiver* class). Such a protocol is said to be *symmetric.*

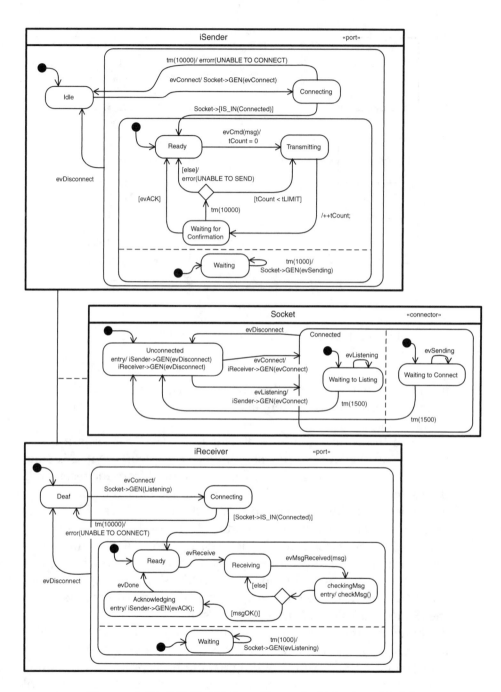

Figure 4-25: *ROOM Pattern Example Statechart Model*

4.10 References

[1] Douglass, Bruce Powel. *Doing Hard Time: Developing Real-Time Systems with UML, Objects, Frameworks and Patterns,* Reading, MA: Addison-Wesley, 1999.

[2] Gamma, E., R. Helm, R. Johnson, and J. Vlissides. *Design Patterns: Elements of Reusable Object-Oriented Software,* Reading, MA: Addison-Wesley, 1995.

[3] Buschmann, F., R. Meunier, H. Rohnert, P. Sommerlad, and M. Stal. *A System of Patterns: Pattern-Oriented Software Architecture,* New York: Wiley & Sons, 1996.

[4] Selic, B., G. Gullekson, and P. Ward. *Real-Time Object-Oriented Software,* New York: Wiley & Sons, 1994.

[5] Selic, B., and J. Rumbaugh. *Using UML to Model Complex Real-Time Systems* Rational Corporation white paper, *www.rational.com* March, 1998.

[6] Sickle, Ted. *Reusable Software Components,* Upper Saddle River, NJ: Prentice Hall, 1997.

[7] Herzum, P., and O. Sims. *Business Component Factory,* New York: Wiley & Sons, 2000.

[8] Brown, Alan. *Large-Scale Component-Based Development,* Upper Saddle River, NJ: Prentice Hall, 2000.

[9] Szyperski, Clemens. *Component Software: Beyond Object-Oriented Programming,* Reading, MA: Addison-Wesley, 1998.

Chapter 5

Concurrency Patterns

The following patterns are presented in this chapter.

- Message Queuing Pattern: Robust asynchronous task rendezvous
- Interrupt Pattern: Fast short event handling
- Guarded Call Pattern: Robust synchronous task rendezvous
- Rendezvous Pattern: Generalized task rendezvous
- Cyclic Executive Pattern: Simple task scheduling
- Round Robin Pattern: Fairness in task scheduling
- Static Priority Pattern: Preemptive multitasking for schedulable systems
- Dynamic Priority Pattern: Preemptive multitasking for complex systems

5.1 Introduction

This chapter focuses on the next aspect of architecture: concurrency. The concurrency architecture includes the control and scheduling of the architectural elements. This includes the management of resources that must be protected from simultaneous access.

5.2 CONCURRENCY PATTERN

In the UML, the basic unit of concurrency is the *thread*. Threads are associated with a stereotype of objects, called «active» objects; that is, an «active» object is special in the sense that it is the root of a thread of control.

The recommended way of adding concurrency into an object model is to identify the desired threads through the application of task identification strategies (see [7] for a list of several such strategies). Once a set of threads is identified, the developer creates an «active» object for each. The "passive" objects are then added to the «active» objects via the *composition* (strong aggregation) relation. The role of the «active» object is to run when appropriate and call or delegate actions to the passive objects that it owns. The passive objects execute in the thread of their «active» owner.

For example, in Figure 5-1a, we see a collaboration of objects. In architectural design, we add «active» objects to place these in different threads. The active objects accept messages (see the Message Queue Pattern following) and delegate them to the internally contained application objects for processing. All of the objects contained within the active object share the same thread and are invoked asynchronously by other application objects sending them messages or synchronously by directly calling their operations. If the callers are within the same thread, then they will use the active object's call stack and thread of control. If the caller is outside the active object, then the object will execute in its caller's thread of control. This can be a source of difficulty, as discussed in the Guarded Call Pattern later in this chapter. Figure 5-1b shows the resulting structure once

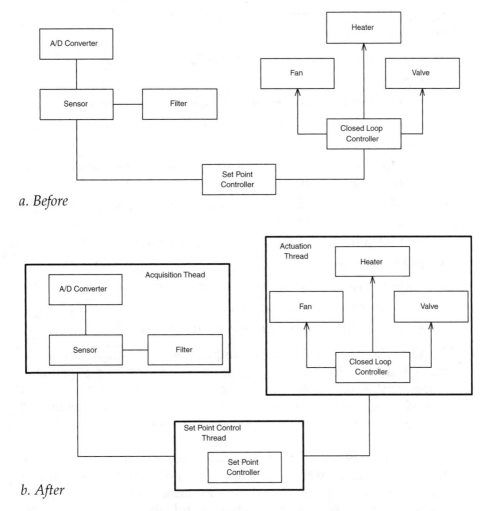

Figure 5-1: *Using «active» Objects*

the active objects are added. Note that notationally, active objects are shown using a standard class box with a heavy border line (although it is also common to use the guillemet notation "«active»"). There are many strategies to identify a good, perhaps even optimal thread set. Some of these strategies are discussed in [7].

The issues around concurrency management are quite varied. In the simplest case, the executing threads are completely independent.

In such cases, it is sufficient to identify the properties of the threads such as the following.

- Arrival pattern: periodic or aperiodic task execution?
- If periodic:
  - Period—the time between invocations of the thread
  - Jitter—the variation in the period
- If aperiodic
  - Minimum interarrival time—the minimum time between successive runs of the thread, or
  - Maximum burst length—the largest number of a string of arbitrarily close thread invocations, or
  - Probability distribution of thread invocations
- Execution time
  - Worst-case execution time (per thread invocation)
  - Average case execution time
  - Probability distribution of execution times

Of course, life is seldom that simple. The hard part of the concurrency model is that the threads are usually *not* really independent. They must coordinate, synchronize, and share information, and shared resources must be managed carefully to avoid corruption and erroneous computation. The concurrency patterns provided here provide some solutions to these commonly occurring problems.

It should be noted that the UML does not really distinguish between threads, tasks, and processes. These are all variations of the very same thing, but they differ in some aspects of their detailed properties (such as the task switch time and whether low-cost pointers can be used across the concurrency boundary). As the design progresses, the choices among the different thread weights will be made, but it is usually not crucial to do so early. The choices will be made to optimize thread safety and thread efficiency and should be deferred until the optimal set of threads is identified and modeled.

5.3 MESSAGE QUEUING PATTERN

The Message Queuing Pattern provides a simple means for threads to communicate information among one another. Although the communication is a fairly heavyweight approach to sharing information, it is the most common one because it is readily supported by operating systems and because it is the easiest to prove correct. This is because it does not share data resources that must be protected from mutual exclusion problems.

The mutual exclusion problem is illustrated in Figure 5-2. The upper part of the figure shows the structural object model, and the lower half shows a timing diagram. The «active» objects are shown with the heavy border (the standard UML icon for «active» objects). Both *Thread 1* and *Thread 2* share a common object, *Resource*. Let us assume that *Thread 1* runs periodically and requires three time cycles to write to it (as shown in the timing diagram). Thread 2 runs at some point and requires three time cycles to read it.

The timing diagram shown in Figure 5-2[1] shows the state of the objects along the y-axis and time along the x-axis. *Thread 1* runs for a little while and then enters the state of *Writing* as it modifies *Resource*. While *Resource* is being written to, it is in the state of *Partially Updated* until the writing is complete; then it is back into the state of *Correct*. Here are the events of interest on the timing diagram.

A. *Resource* is *Correct*; *Thread 1* starts to write to *Resource*, so it enters its state of *Partially Updated*.

B. *Thread 1* completes writing and returns to its *Working* state; *Resource* reenters its *Correct* state.

C. *Thread 1* starts writing to *Resource* again. *Resource* reenters its *Partially Updated* state.

D. *Thread 2* now runs and preempts *Thread 1*. *Resource* is in a *Partially Updated* state—that is, it is invalid. *Thread 2* reads the invalid value and processes it, possibly with catastrophic consequences.

---

1. It is anticipated that timing diagrams, such as the one in this figure, may be added in UML 2.0. I have written some preliminary specifications for timing diagrams for this purpose.

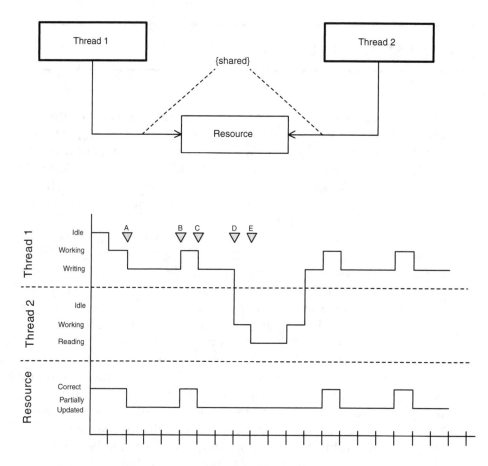

Figure 5-2: *The Mutual Exclusion Problem*

With mutual exclusion protection in place, at point D, *Thread 2* would not be allowed to read the value in *Resource*. It would be blocked from execution until *Thread 1* had completed its use of *Resource* (that is, it was back in its *Correct* state). If, however, *Thread 1* copies *Resource* and gives the copy to *Thread 2*, then there is no possibility of reading it when *Resource* is in an invalid condition.

5.3.1 Abstract

The Message Queuing Pattern uses asynchronous communications, implemented via queued messages, to synchronize and share information among tasks. This approach has the advantage of simplicity and does not display mutual exclusion problems because no resource is shared by reference. Any information shared among threads is *passed by value* to the separate thread. While this limits the complexity of the collaboration among the threads, this approach in its pure form is immune to the standard resource corruption problems that plague concurrent systems that share information *passed by reference*. In *passed by value* sharing, a copy of the information is made and sent to the receiving thread for processing. The receiving thread fully owns the data it receives and so may modify it freely without concern for corrupting data due to multiple writers or due to sharing it among a writer and multiple readers.

5.3.2 Problem

In most multithreaded systems, threads must synchronize and share information with others. Two primary things must be accomplished. First, the tasks must synchronize to permit sharing of the information. Second, the information must be shared in such a way that there is no chance of corruption or race conditions.[2]

5.3.3 Pattern Structure

The structure for the pattern is shown in Figure 5-3. The «active» object has the pattern role name *Thread*. Each *Thread* owns a message *Queue* that stores messages sent asynchronously to the *Thread*. When the *Thread* is active, it reads messages from the *Queue* and processes them, usually by dispatching them to internal object composing the *Thread* (not shown). Each *Queue* is protected by a mutual exclusion semaphore *(Mutex)*. Since the *Queue* itself is a shared resource (shared between the owning *Thread* and the *Thread* objects that want to send it messages), it must be protected from simultaneous access. This is the job of the *Mutex*.

The *Mutuex* has a lock() and a release() operation. When lock() is called, and the *Mutex* is currently not locked, it locks the *Mutex* and

---

2. A *race condition* is a condition in which a result depends on the order of execution, but the order of execution cannot be predicted.

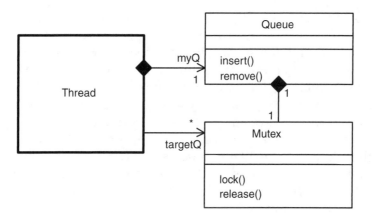

Figure 5-3: *Message Queuing Pattern*

allows the caller thread to continue.[3] If the *Mutex* is currently locked, the caller thread is suspended until the *Mutex* is unlocked in the future. This allows the original *Thread* to finish its use of the *Queue* unimpeded and makes sure the data in the *Queue* is not corrupted. Once the *Mutex* is released() by the original caller, the previously blocked *Thread* is now free to continue.

5.3.4 Collaboration Roles

- *Thread*
  The *Thread* object is «active»—that is, it is the root of an operating system thread, task, or process. It can both create messages to send to other *Threads* and receive and process messages when it runs. The scheduling policy for deciding when to execute the threads is not a part of this pattern—any reasonable scheduling policy will work.

- *Queue*
  The *Queue* is a container that can hold a number of messages. The *Queue* stores the messages waiting for its owner *Thread* until that

---

3. Note that the lock() operation has a non-interruptible portion so that between the checking for the locked state and locking the *Mutex* (going into the locked state), it cannot be interrupted by a preempting thread.

Thread is ready to run. The *Queue* itself runs in the thread of its caller—in other words, if it is called by its owner, it runs in that thread, but if called by a different thread—for example, to insert a message—then it executes that caller's thread. This makes the *Queue* a shared resource that requires protection. This is provided by the *Mutex*. The *Queue* provides insert() and remove() operations at minimum.

- *Mutex*
  The *Mutex* is a mutual exclusion semaphore. It provides a noninterruptible lock() operation and a release() operation. The *Mutex* provides protection from multiple access to the *Queue* contents. A single *Mutex* protects all *Queue* operations because they might return erroneous results otherwise. If a caller attempts to lock() the *Queue* (such as by calling *Queue::insert()* or *Queue::remove()*), and the *Queue* is unlocked, then the *Mutex* becomes locked until a subsequent call is made to *Mutex::release()*. If such an attempt is made when the *Queue* is already locked, then the caller thread immediately suspends, allowing the original thread to continue. An eventual call to *Mutex::release()* unlocks the *Mutex* and also unblocks the suspended thread, allowing it to run.

5.3.5 Consequences

This pattern has a number of advantages. It is such a common pattern that it is supported by virtually all real-time operating systems (see [8] for an example) and multitasking languages [4]. It is conceptually very simple and reasonably bulletproof. The primary disadvantages are that it is a relatively heavyweight approach to information passing among threads, it does not necessarily allow for highly efficient information sharing (since it is asynchronous, the receiving thread doesn't process the incoming message until it becomes ready to run), and information must be shared by value instead of by reference. This limits the complexity of the information sharing possible and doesn't allow for efficient use of large data structures.

5.3.6 Implementation Strategies

If the application uses an underlying operating system, the implementation of this pattern is very simple. Most real-time operating systems support this concurrency pattern easily and well.

5.3.7 Related Patterns

It is common to use this as the primary thread synchronization mechanism, but in special cases (involving high responsiveness) other patterns, such as the Interrupt Pattern or Guarded Call Pattern, are added for certain of the rendezvous.

Much of the time, the information to be shared cannot conveniently be passed by value. This may be due to the sheer size or amount of data, or it may be due to the use of the data as a single shared resource. When this is true, the Rendezvous Pattern works well to share data among several clients. This pattern can also be mixed with the Message Queuing Pattern.

5.3.8 Sample Model

Figure 5-4a shows a simple example of two active objects: *Sender* and *Receiver*. Constraints associated with the active object indicate their relative priority (to be used in the scenario in Figure 5-4b). Each strongly aggregates its own message queue. The *Sender* class issues messages to the *Receiver* class by posting a message to the *Receiver's* queue *(rQueue)*. This is most likely to be done via native OS message calls. Each message queue is a protected resource (again, most likely protected by the underlying OS) with an associated semaphore. When the *Sender* class sends a message to the *rQueue* class, the semaphore protects the resource from readers or writers until the message is successfully enqueued.

The scenario in Figure 5-4b illustrates how these classes collaborate. In this scenario, the *Sender* thread runs in response to an evRun event. The *Sender* class called the *rQueue::insert()* operation, which, in turn, locks the semaphore. While in the middle of the *rQueue::store()* operation, the thread is interrupted by the higher-priority *Receiver* thread.

Upon awakening, the *Receiver* attempts to check for incoming messages in its queue. It calls *rQueue::read()*, which, in turn, attempts to lock the semaphore. This fails, and the *Receiver* is automatically suspended or blocked, since the semaphore is already locked to the *Sender* thread. This allows the *Sender* thread to continue and complete the *store()* operation. Once complete, the *rQueue* releases its semaphore. This unblocks the *Receiver* thread, which now successfully locks the semaphore, reads the message now waiting in its

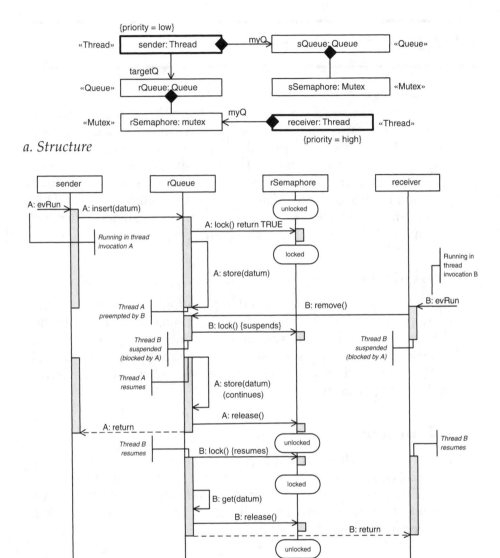

Figure 5-4: *Message Queuing Pattern Example*

queue, unlocks the semaphore, and processes the incoming message. The states of the semaphore itself are shown using the standard UML state-on-instance line notation in Figure 5-4b.

5.4 INTERRUPT PATTERN

Interrupts have much to recommend them. They occur when the event of interest occurs, they execute very quickly and with little overhead, and they can provide a means for timely response to urgent needs. This accounts for their widespread use in real-time and embedded systems. Nevertheless, they are not a panacea for timely response to aperiodic phenomena. There are circumstances in which they are highly effective, but there are other circumstances when their use can lead to system failure. This pattern explores those issues.

5.4.1 Abstract

In many real-time and embedded applications, certain events must be responded to quickly and efficiently, almost regardless of when they occur or what the system is currently doing. When those responses are relatively short and can be made atomic (noninterruptible), then the Interrupt Pattern can be an excellent design selection for handling those events.

5.4.2 Problem

In a system in which certain events are highly urgent, such as those that can occur at high frequencies or those in which the response must be as fast as possible, a means is needed to quickly identify and respond to those events. This can occur in many different kinds of systems from simple to complex.

5.4.3 Pattern Structure

Figure 5-5 shows the basic Interrupt Pattern structure. The machine itself (or operating system) provides an *Interrupt Vector Table*, which is nothing more than a linear array of address vectors (the size of which depends highly on the CPU). It is useful to model this as a class with Set and Get operations. The *Abstract Interrupt Handler* is a class that contains machinery to link into this *Interrupt Vector Table* as well as an operation to handle the interrupt when it occurs.

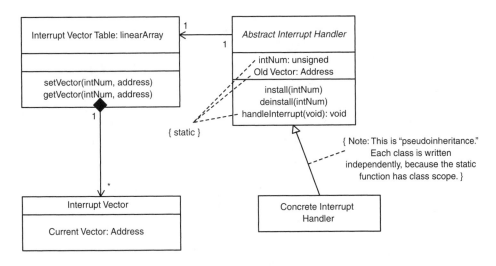

Figure 5-5: *Interrupt Pattern*

The behavior of the operations in the *Abstract Interrupt Handler* is very straightforward, as shown in the activity diagrams in Figure 5-6. Setting the interrupt handler to point to the *handleInterrupts(void)* method is nothing more than writing the function pointer to the right *Interrupt Vector* in the *Interrupt Vector Table.*

Sometimes the installation of a new interrupt handler does not remove the need to invoke the old handler as well. This is commonly called "chaining" of interrupt handlers. This done by calling the old handler, which is stored in the *Old Vector* attribute of *Interrupt Handler.*

Care must be taken that the interrupt routines are short so that other interrupts that may occur are not missed. If the processing of the interrupt handling must be long, the most common approach is to separate the interrupt handling into two phases: the handling of the event *per se* and the computational response. The event handling is done very quickly, and the event and any relevant information is enqueued to be handled by another thread at some time in the future. This allows the interrupt handler to reenable interrupts as quickly as possible while still permitting complex computation to take place as a result of the interrupt.

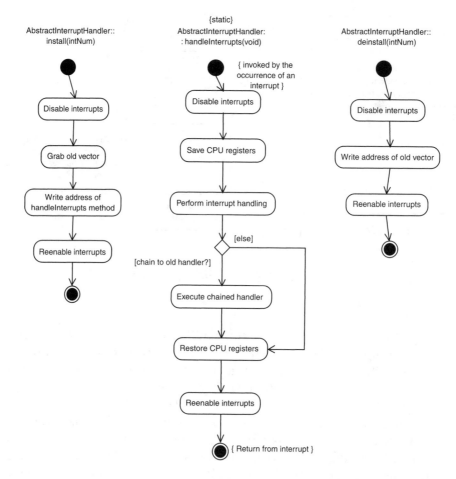

Figure 5-6: *Interrupt Handling Methods*

5.4.4 Collaboration Roles

- *Abstract Interrupt Handler*
  The *Abstract Interrupt Handler* defines the operations necessary to link up with the interrupt vector table as well as to sever that link. It provides a virtual operation *handleInterrupt(void)* that does that actual processing of the interrupt when it occurs. The actual method to implement this operation is provided by the *Concrete Interrupt Handler* subclass.

- *Concrete Interrupt Handler*
  The *Concrete Interrupt Handler* is a subclass of *Abstract Interrupt Handler*. It inherits all the machinery necessary to link and delink with the interrupt vector table. It additionally provides the method to do the actual work for handling the interrupt when it occurs. If necessary, it will chain (call) the previous interrupt handler. Care must be taken that interrupts are disabled during the interrupt handling itself and reenabled upon completion. Because the system may be doing anything when interrupted, all registers must be saved and restored as well so as not to corrupt other concurrent behaviors.

- *Interrupt Vector*
  The *Interrupt Vector* class is a simple abstract data type, representing a single function pointer. During boot, the *Vector Table* class initializes all interrupt handlers (typically to null interrupt handler that simply returns).

- *Interrupt Vector Table*
  The *Interrupt Vector Table* is little more than a simple array of *Interrupt Vectors*. It also includes, however, operations to initialize the vectors and set/get the vectors. (Although in practice it is more common for the set/get operations to be provided by the interrupt handler itself, some operating systems provide methods to do this. These methods are logically part of the *Interrupt Vector Table*.)

5.4.5 Consequences

These methods are most often used to queue responses for later (asynchronous processing). They are rarely used as the only concurrency strategy, but they can be used as such when the system is mostly idle and its functionality consists of a set of simple, short responses to events. Most often, these methods are used as an adjunct to another (primary) concurrency policy, providing highly efficient responses to extremely urgent events. However, care must be taken to ensure that the responses to the interrupts are short, since they typically must be atomic (noninterruptible).

When the responses to the interrupts can be made short, this pattern provides very fast, timely responses. When a longer response is required, but it can be partitioned into a fast response part and a longer, but allowably slower part, then it is common to use the interrupt handler to just receive and then queue the event for later, asynchronous processing by another task either running in the background or scheduled using another policy, such as priority-based preemption.

The downside of this pattern is that it is often used where inappropriate: when the responses are too long or when the system is so active that interrupting events are missed because the system has not completed its response to previous events.

Another difficulty is that it is relatively difficult to share information with other interrupt handlers. This is because such information must be protected from simultaneous access, but if the resource is currently being used, the interrupt handler *cannot* block (since it must be short or interrupts may be lost).

5.4.6 Implementation Strategies

Implementation of this pattern is only a little tricky. Most RTOSs provide an operation for the installation of an interrupt handler. It is important that the interrupt handler operation is parameterless and does not return a value. In most languages, parameters and return values are passed on the call stack. Since the return address is also on the call stack, listing parameters or a return value will mess up the call stack and not return the application to what it was doing before the interrupt handler was invoked.

It is also important to save all the CPU registers before your routine does *anything* else and restore them just prior to completing. Also, the routine must typically exit with a special Return From Interrupt (RTI) instruction rather than a normal Return (RET) instruction. This is often done by inserting assembly language instructions directly, prior to any executable statements in the interrupt handler and just after all executable statements in the routine. Some compilers offer the ability to mark class methods (using a nonstandard keyword such as *interrupt*) as interrupt handlers and automatically save and restore registers, terminate with an RTI instruction, and even pass CPU registers in pseudoparameters to make their contents available to the internals of the register. This is useful because one way to pass information to an interrupt routine is to load some specific CPU register(s) with the value(s) and then invoke the interrupt.

The *ConcreteInterruptHandler* class must be able to install, chain, and deinstall the interrupt handler method. By install, it is meant that the interrupt vector is replaced with a function pointer (the address of the method that will be receiving the interrupt). This is a little subtle in C++ because all methods (aka member functions) in C++ have an invisible (to the programmer) parameter passed call the *this pointer*. It is a pointer that points to the specific instance of the class in memory (which is, after all, only represented once for every class, but each instance has separate data). So even if you have a parameterless method in C++, there really is *still* a parameter passed on the stack.

The solution to this in C++ is to declare the method *static*, which means that it is the same for all instances of the class and can access only static data. Therefore, it doesn't need (or receive) the *this pointer* parameter.

In Figure 5-6 the *ConcreteInterruptHandler* class is shown inheriting from the *AbstractInterruptHandler* class. This clearly cannot work that way because static methods have classwide scope *including subclasses*. That is why it is annotated with a constraint indicating that we want to think about them as subclasses (since their structure is the same) but cannot implement them exactly that way due to C++ language characteristics. The simplest way to manage this is to simply write a set of *ConcreteInterruptHandlers* that all implement the same interface.

5.4.7 Related Patterns

It is possible to extend this pattern to coexist with other concurrency patterns, such as the Message Queuing Pattern in this chapter. Care must be taken to ensure a *balking rendezvous* is used when shared resources are activated. A balking rendezvous implements nonblocking semantics around resource sharing. Specifically, if the required resource is locked, the interrupt handler cannot block. It can do several things if it cannot pass on the information. For example, it can simply discard it. Another approach is for the client (but not the interrupt handler) to simply turn off interrupts when it is about to use the shared resource. Then the interrupt handler cannot be invoked, and the client is guaranteed to use the resource safely. When the client is done with the resource, it reenables interrupts. Of course, it is possible that interrupts may be lost. In most hardware, the system will retain a single interrupt if it occurs when interrupt handling is disabled. This means that if two interrupts occur during this time, one of them will be missed. Another strategy is for the interrupt handler to store the data locally and send it later when the interrupt handler is invoked again. Finally, the interrupt handler and client can agree on alternating two resources (commonly called "ping-pong" buffers), where the two resources are shared with the guarantee that the client will, at most, lock only one at a time.

5.4.8 Sample Model

Figure 5-7 illustrates the Interrupt Pattern with a simple example. Every 500ms, the temperature of the reactor core must be checked. If the temperature is less than or equal to some predetermined value, then life is good; the routine can terminate. If, however, the temperature is above that value, then the EmergencyAlert() operation of the SafetyExecutive object must be called. This operation is written in such a way that it is reentrant (in other words, always safe to call even if that or another operation of the SafetyExecutive object is called).

The object structure is shown in Figure 5-7a. The *Timer* and the *Thermometer* are shown as actors, since they represent actual hardware. The *Timer* is designed in hardware to invoke the *Timer Int Vector* when it fires. Figure 5-7b shows an example scenario. The *Timer* fires, invoking the *Timer Int Vector*, which invokes the *handleInterrupt()* operation of the *TempChecker* object. This interrupt handler then calls *Thermometer::getValue()* to get the current temperature. It then does a compare with its stored upper limit. The first time this occurs in the scenario, the test passes, so the interrupt handler simple does a return from interrupt. The second time, however, it fails. The operation then invokes *SafetyExecutive::EmergencyAlert()*, passing a parameter that indicates which failure occurred. This is a short (and, as mentioned previously, reentrant) routine that takes some corrective action, and eventually *the handleInterrupt()* operation returns.

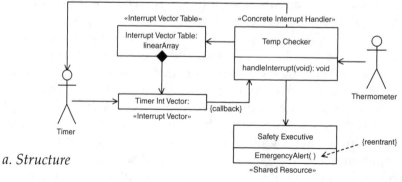

a. Structure

Figure 5-7: *Interrupt Pattern Example*

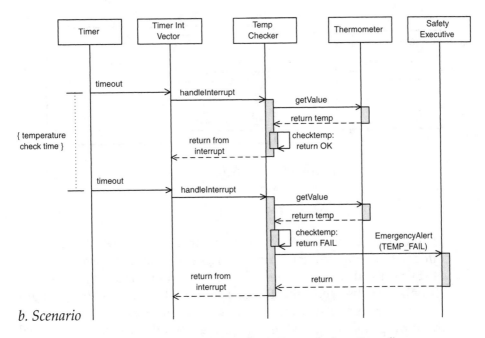

Figure 5-7: *Interrupt Pattern Example (continued)*

5.5 GUARDED CALL PATTERN

Sometimes asynchronous communication schemes, such as the Message Queuing Pattern, do not provide timely responses across a thread boundary. An alternative is to synchronously invoke a method of an object, nominally running in another thread. This is the Guarded Call Pattern (see Figure 5-8). It is a simple pattern, although care must be taken to ensure data integrity and to avoid synchronization and deadlock problems.

5.5.1 Abstract

The Message Queuing Pattern enforces an asynchronous rendezvous between two threads, modeled as «active» objects. In general, this approach works very well, but it means a rather slow exchange

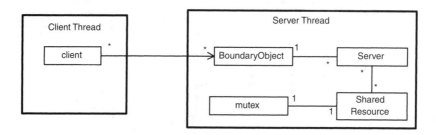

Figure 5-8: *Guarded Call Pattern*

of information because the receiving thread does not process the information immediately. The receiving thread will process it the next time the thread executes. This can be problematic when the synchronization between the threads is urgent (when there are tight time constraints). An obvious solution is to simply call the method of the appropriate object in the other thread, but this can lead to mutual exclusion problems if the called object is currently active doing something else. The Guarded Call Pattern handles this case through the use of a mutual exclusion semaphore.

5.5.2 Problem

The problem this pattern addresses is the need for a timely synchronization or data exchange between threads. In such cases, it may not be possible to wait for an asynchronous rendezvous. A synchronous rendezvous can be made more timely, but this must be done carefully to avoid data corruption and erroneous computation.

5.5.3 Pattern Structure

The Guarded Call Pattern solves this problem by guarding the access to the resource via the operation called across the thread boundary with a semaphore. If another thread attempts to access the resource while it is locked, the latter thread is blocked and must allow the previous thread to complete its execution of the operation. This simple solution is to guard *all* the relevant operations ("relevant" as defined to be accessing the resource) with a single mutual exclusion semaphore.

5.5.4 Collaboration Roles

- *Server Thread*
  This «active» object contains the *Server* objects that share the *Shared Resource* and protect them with the *Mutex*.

- *Client Thread*
  This «active» object contains (via the composition relation) the *Client* object that synchronously invokes the method, ultimately, on the *Server* objects. The *Client* runs in the thread of the *Client Thread*.

- *Boundary Object*
  The *Boundary Object* provides the protected interface to the *Server* objects; that is, it presents the operations the servers wish to provide across the thread boundary for a guarded call rendezvous. The boundary object combines *all* the operations together (because they may all affect the *Shared Resource*). If multiple different shared resources are to be protected, then the *Server Thread* can provide multiple *Boundary Objects*. The important concept is that the *Mutex* associated with the *Shared Resource* blocks any operation that attempts to use the *Shared Resource*.

- *Mutex*
  The *Mutex* is a mutual exclusion semaphore object that permits only a single caller through at a time. It can be explicitly locked and unlocked by the caller, but it is safer if the operations of the *Shared Resource* invoke it whenever a relevant service is called, locking it prior to starting the service and unlocking it once the service is complete. *Client Threads* that attempt to invoke a service when the services are already locked become blocked until the *Mutex* is in its unlocked state.

- *Server*
  Each *Server* object (and there may be many) has two relevant properties. First, it uses the *Shared Resource* object, and second, it may provide a service useable to a *Client* across the thread boundary that may use the *Shared Resource*.

- *Shared Resource*
  The *Shared Resource* object is any object that provides data or a service that is shared among multiple *Servers* in such a way that its integrity must be protected by the serialization of access. For objects that protect data in this way, it means that the *Servers* may

write to or in some way affect its value. For service objects, it often means that they provide an interface to some physical device or process that is changed by execution of the process, often in a nonreversible way.

5.5.5 Consequences

The Guarded Call Pattern provides a means by which a set of services may be safely provided across a thread boundary. This is done in such a way that even if several internal objects within the called thread share a common resource, that resource remains protected from corruption due to mutual exclusion problems. This is a synchronous rendezvous, providing a timely response, unless the services are currently locked. If the services are currently locked, then the resource is protected, but timely response cannot be guaranteed unless analysis is done to show that the service is schedulable (see [1] for a detailed description of such analytical techniques and [4], [5], and [6] for further description of those techniques).

The situation may be even simpler than required for this pattern. If the *Server* objects don't interact among each other with respect to the *Shared Resource*, then the Shared Resource itself may be contained directly within the *Server* object. In this case, the server objects themselves can be the boundary objects or the boundary objects can participate in a *Façade Pattern* (aka *Interface Pattern*). Then there is simply a *Mutex* object per *Server* object. This is a simpler case of this more general pattern.

5.5.6 Implementation Strategies

Both the *Client Thread and Server Thread* are «active» objects. It is typical to create an OS thread in which they run in their constructors and destroy that thread in their destructors. They both contain objects via the composition relationship. For the most part, this means that the «active» objects execute an event or message loop, looking for events or messages that have been queued for later asynchronous processing. Once an event or message is dequeued, it is dispatched to objects contained within it via composition, calling the appropriate operations on those objects to handle the event or message.

For the synchronous rendezvous, the «active» object allows other objects visibility to the Boundary objects (i.e., they are in its public interface) and their public operations.

5.5.7 Related Patterns

The rendezvous patterns presented in this chapter, Message Queuing, Interrupt, Guarded Call, and (the yet to come) Rendezvous Pattern may all be mixed, of course, albeit *carefully.* It is always easiest to have a single pattern for synchronization and data sharing among tasks, but there are valid reasons for mixing them as well. Care must be taken that race conditions are handled when accessing a *Server* object with more than one concurrency pattern. The religious use of a *Mutex* will solve most of these issues, provided that the system *can* block if the resource is currently locked. However, this is a really terrible idea if the blocking call is an interrupt handler.

If the Server is stateful (if its behavior is governed by a statechart), then the use of both asynchronous and synchronous event handling can lead to all sorts of "interesting" behavior. It is particularly important to remember that the semantics of event processing in statecharts is *run-to-completion.* That is, if a *Server* object is currently handling an incoming asynchronous event and executes state exit, transition, and state entry actions, this object cannot process other incoming events, whether they are synchronous or not, until that entire chain of actions completes. This is usually handled by protecting the event acceptor operation with a *Mutex* and executing the chain of actions under the auspices of that single operation. It can also be done by adding a *monitor* (similar to a Mutex) that locks the Server object until the event handler explicitly unlocks the Server once the action list is completely executed.

5.5.8 Sample Model

Figure 5-9a shows the model structure for the example. Three active objects encapsulate the semantic objects in this system. The *View Thread* object contains a view of the reactor temperature on the user interface. The *Alarming Thread* manages alarms in a different thread. And the *Processing Thread* manages the acquisition and filtering of the data itself. Stereotypes indicate the pattern roles.

Figure 5-9b walks through a scenario. Note that the messages use a thread prefix ("A:" or "B:") and the activation lines on the sequence diagram are coded with different fill patterns to indicate in which thread they belong. Points of interest are annotated with circled letters.

The scenario shows how the collision of two threads is managed in a thread-safe fashion. The first thread (A) starts up to get the value of the reactor temperature for display on the user interface. While processing that thread, the higher-priority thread (B) to acquire the

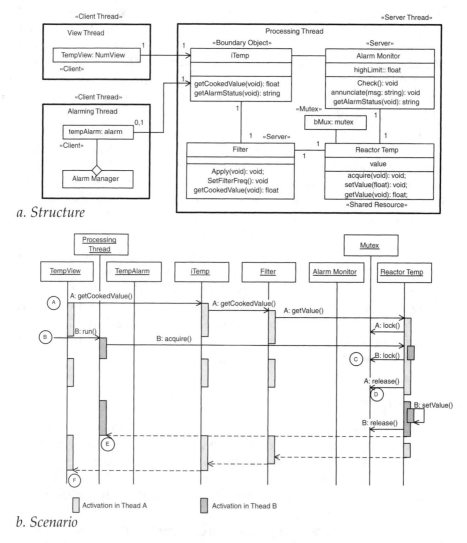

a. Structure

b. Scenario

Figure 5-9: *Guarded Call Pattern Example*

data begins. However, it finds the *Reactor Temp* object locked, and so it is suspended from execution until the *Mutex* is released. Once the *Mutex* is released, the higher-priority thread can now continue: The lock() operation succeeds, and the B thread continues until completion. Once thread B has completed, thread A can now continue, returning the (old) value to the *Temp View* object for display. Here are the points of interest for the scenario in Figure 5-9.

A. Thread A starts in *View Thread* to get the reactor temperature for display.

B. Thread B starts in *Processing Thread* to acquire and set a new value for the reactor temperature.

C. Since *Mutex* is already locked, thread B suspends and thread A continues.

D. Now that the *Mutex* is released, the higher-priority thread B can continue.

E. Thread B has completed, and now thread A can complete and return the (old) value for display.

F. Thread A is now complete.

5.6 RENDEZVOUS PATTERN

The Rendezvous Pattern (see Figure 5-10) is a simplified form of the Guarded Call pattern used to either synchronize a set of threads or permit data sharing among a set of threads. It reifies the synchronization of multiple threads as an object itself. There are many subtle variants of this pattern. The Rendezvous object may contain data to be shared as the threads synchronize, or it may simply provide a means for synchronizing an arbitrary number of threads at a synchronization point with some synchronization policy or precondition before allowing them all to continue independently. The simplest of these preconditions is that a certain number of threads have registered at their synchronization points. This special case is called the *Thread Barrier Pattern*.

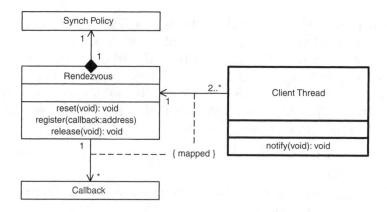

Figure 5-10: *Rendezvous Pattern*

5.6.1 Abstract

A *precondition* is something that is specified to be true prior to an action or activity. Preconditions are a type of constraint that is usually generative—that is, it can be used to generate code either to force the precondition to be true or to check that a precondition is true. In fact, the most common way to ensure preconditions in UML or virtually any design language is through the use of state machines. A state is a precondition for the transitions exiting it.

The Rendezvous Pattern is concerned with modeling the preconditions for synchronization or rendezvous of threads. It is a general pattern and easy to apply to ensure that arbitrarily complex sets of preconditions can be met at run-time. The basic behavioral model is that as each thread becomes ready to rendezvous, it registers with the *Rendezvous* class and then blocks until the *Rendezvous* class releases it to run. Once the set of preconditions is met, then the registered tasks are released to run using whatever scheduling policy is currently in force.

5.6.2 Problem

The problem addressed by this pattern is to codify a collaboration structure that allows any arbitrary set of preconditional invariants to be met for thread synchronization, independent of task phasings, scheduling policies, and priorities.

5.6.3 Pattern Structure

The basic behavioral model is that as each thread becomes ready to rendezvous, it registers with the *Rendezvous* class and then blocks until the *Rendezvous* class releases it to run. Once the set of preconditions is met, then the registered tasks are released to run, using whatever scheduling policy is currently in force. The rendezvous itself is abstracted into a class, as is the set of preconditions. This approach provides a great deal of flexibility in modeling arbitrarily complex preconditional invariants.

5.6.4 Collaboration Roles

- *Callback*
  The *Callback* object holds the address of the *Client Thread*. This is so the *Rendezvous* object can notify all the threads that have registered when the preconditions are met. This callback may be an object address, a URL, or any other means that enables the *Rendezvous* object to unambiguously signal the *Client Thread* when the preconditions are met. Some RTOSs provide named events on which target threads may *pend()*; when that named event is posted(), all threads waiting on it are released.

- *Client Thread*
  There are at least two *Client Threads*. When they reach their synchronization point, they register with the *Rendezvous* object and pass their callback. The *notify()* operation is called by dereferencing the callback; this signals the *Client Thread* that the preconditions have been met and it is now free to continue.

- *Rendezvous*
  The *Rendezvous* object manages the Thread Synchronization. It has a register(callback:address) operation that the *Client Threads* invoke to indicate that they have reached their synchronization point.

- *Synch Policy*
  The *Synch Policy* reifies the set of preconditions into a single concept. The simplest *Synch Policy* is nothing more than the registration count reaching some predetermined, expected value; that is, it counts the threads that have registered, and when the registration count reaches a set value, the precondition is met. This is called the Thread Boundary Pattern. For more complex synchronization

policies, the *Synch Policy* object may employ a statechart to capture the richness of the required policy.

5.6.5 Consequences

This is a simple pattern that can be widely applied for various policies for thread synchronization. It scales up well to arbitrary numbers of threads and to arbitrarily complex synchronization policies.

5.6.6 Implementation Strategies

The *Synch Policy* and *Rendezvous* classes are stateful and most likely to be implemented as statecharts. In the case of the Thread Barrier Pattern specialization, it is enough to simply implement a counting machine. Figure 5-11 shows a simple counting machine statechart that counts. It begins to synch (process *evSynch* events) in its *Counting* state. After each event, it increments its *Count* attribute. If it equals or exceeds the expected number of threads waiting to rendezvous, then the *else* clause is taken, and the *Synch Policy* object sends an *evReleaseAll* event to the *Rendezvous* object.

The *Rendezvous* class accepts *register* messages from the associating *Client Thread* objects; when it receives a register message, it sends an *evSynch* event to the Synch Policy object. When the Rendezvous

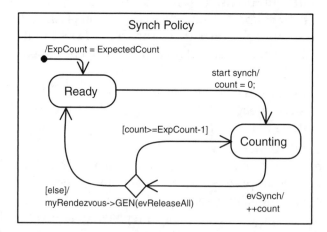

Figure 5-11: *Thread Barrier Synch Policy Statechart*

object receives an *evReleaseAll* event, it iterates over the list of *Call-back* objects, sending each a *notify* message, informing it that the synchronization is complete and the thread is free to continue.

The *Callback* class is little more than the storage of an address of some kind. In some cases, it will literally be the address of the notify operation, to be called directly, or in a thread-safe way, using the Guarded Call Pattern. In other cases, the *notify* message will be sent to that thread's event queue to be processed when the thread is scheduled to run by the operating system. In still other cases, such as when using a component infrastructure, such as COM or CORBA, the callback will contain the object ID, which the component infrastructure will dereference to locate the proper object.

5.6.7 Related Patterns

This pattern can be mixed with the other thread management patterns, such as the Message Queue and Guarded Call patterns, as well as the other nonconcurrency model architectural patterns, such as the Component and Layered Patterns.

5.6.8 Sample Model

Figure 5-12a shows an example with three threads, each of which controls a different aspect of a robot arm: two joints and a manipulator. When each of the three threads is ready, they are all allowed to proceed. Figure 5-12b shows the flow of a scenario. Note how each thread (other than the last) is blocked until the *Rendezvous* object releases them all. Then they will be scheduled by the OS according to its scheduling policy.

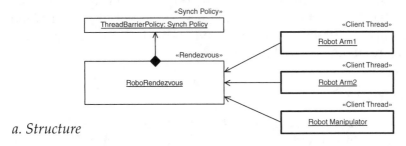

a. Structure

Figure 5-12: *Rendezvous Pattern Example (continued)*

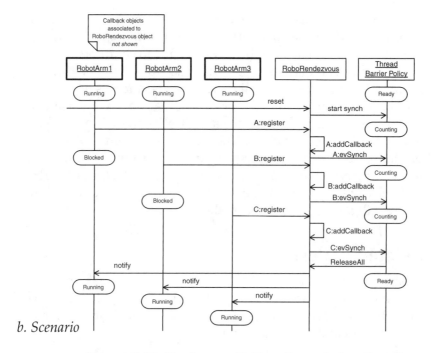

b. Scenario

Figure 5-12: *Rendezvous Pattern Example (continued)*

5.7 CYCLIC EXECUTIVE PATTERN

For very small systems, or for systems in which execution pre-dictability is crucial, the Cyclic Executive Pattern is a commonly used approach. It is used a lot in both small systems and in avionic flight systems for both aircraft and spacecraft applications environments. Although not without difficulties, its ease-of-implementation makes this an attractive choice when the dynamic properties of the system are stable and well understood.

5.7.1 Abstract

A Cyclic Executive Pattern has the advantage of almost mindless simplicity coupled with extremely predictable behavior. This results in a number of desirable properties for such systems. First, implementation of this pattern is so easy it is hard to get it wrong, at least in any gross way. Also, it can be written to run in highly memory-constrained systems where a full RTOS may not be an option.

5.7.2 Problem

In many very small applications, not only is a full RTOS not required, it may not even be feasible due to memory constraints. Often, the only RTOS support that is really required is the ability to run a set of more or less independent tasks. The simplest way to accomplish this is to run what is called an "event loop" or Cyclic Executive that simply executes the tasks in turn, from the first to the last, and then starts over again. Each task runs if it has something to do, and it relinquishes control immediately if not.

Another issue occurs when the execution time for a set of tasks is constant and it is desirable to have a highly predictable system. "Highly predictable" means you can predict the assembly language instruction that will be executing at any point in the future, based solely on the time.

5.7.3 Pattern Structure

You can see from Figure 5-13 just how simple this pattern is. The set of threads is maintained as an ordered list (indicated by the constraint on the association end attached to the *Abstract Thread* class). The Cyclic Executive merely executes the threads in turn and then restarts at the beginning when done. When the Scheduler starts, it must instantiate *all* the tasks before cycling through them.

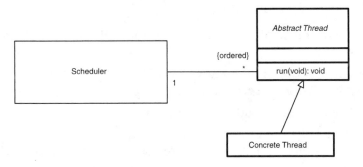

Figure 5-13: *Cyclic Executive Pattern*

5.7.4 Collaboration Roles

Because of the simplicity of this pattern, it is often used in the absence of a real operating system. Thus, it is common to directly implement all the classes in the pattern even though they would be provided by an operating system if one were used.

- *Abstract Thread*
  The *Abstract Thread* class is an abstract (noninstantiable) super-class for *Concrete Thread*. *Abstract Thread* associates with the *Scheduler*. Since *Concrete Thread* is a subclass, it has the same interface to the *Scheduler* as the *Abstract Thread*. This enforces interface compliance.

- *Concrete Thread*
  The *Concrete Thread* is an «active» object most typically constructed to contain passive "semantic" objects that do the real work of the system. The *Concrete Thread* object provides a straightforward means of attaching these semantic objects into the concurrency architecture. *Concrete Thread* is an instantiable subclass of *Abstract Thread*.

- *Scheduler*
  This object initializes the system by loading the entire set of tasks and then running each of them in turn in perpetuity. It is generally up to the tasks themselves to relinquish control of the CPU to the *Scheduler* when they are finished.

5.7.5 Consequences

The best applications of the Cyclic Executive Patterns have a number of properties in common.

- The number of tasks is constant throughout the run-time of the system.
- The amount of time a given task tasks each cycle is either unimportant or consistent from cycle to cycle.
- The tasks are mostly independent.
- Usage of resources shared among the tasks can be guaranteed to be complete when each task relinquishes control to the *Scheduler*.
- There exists a sequential ordering of tasks that is known to be adequate for all situations.

When any of these properties is seriously violated, it is likely that another solution may be preferable to the Cyclic Executive Pattern.

The primary advantage of this pattern is its simplicity. Its primary disadvantages are its lack of flexibility, instability to violations of its assumptions, and nonoptimality. Tasks cannot be added or removed during run-time, so its applicability is limited to systems with a small number of tasks that run iteratively for the lifetime of the system. Computation of schedulability is a straightforward matter: the time of the cycle is equal to the time for each task completion (worst case or average case may be used, depending on the nature of the task deadlines). If the deadline for each task is less than the total cycle time, then the system will be schedulable.

However, response to incoming events is far from optimal. When an event comes in regardless of which task is currently executing, it must wait until the appropriate task is running before it is handled. Therefore, all events must have a deadline greater than or equal to the cycle time. The Cyclic Executive Pattern is likewise unstable: It cannot usually be predicted which tasks will fail in an overload situation because it depends on which task is executing when the event occurs. There is no notion of criticality or urgency in the Cyclic Executive—all tasks are equally important. There have been case studies, such as the BSY-1 Trainer [14], that were not schedulable using a Cyclic Executive Pattern but became easily schedulable when a Static or Dynamic Priority Pattern was used.

When the system is sensitive to time, then the cycle must frequently be tuned each time a task is added or modified. This *tuning* is a manual process involving reordering of tasks, decomposition of tasks into smaller tasks, grouping of tasks together (composition), adding or removing NOP (no-op) CPU instructions, and so on—normally proceeding by trial-and-error. Another issue with the application of this pattern is that a single misbehaving task can halt the entire system by not returning control to the *Scheduler.*

5.7.6 Implementation Strategies

The implementation of this pattern is very straightforward and should present no difficulties to the implementer. Because the Concrete Threads are run-to-completion, there is no need for more than a single stack. Shared resources may be implemented as global variables. The common assumption is that each task releases all its used resources before relinquishing control. If this is not true, and resources are to be shared across tasks, then some mechanism must be put in place, such as semaphores, to ensure the integrity of the resource.

5.7.7 Related Patterns

There are a couple of variants of the Cyclic Executive Pattern (see Figure 5-14) that are employed with great success. One of these is to

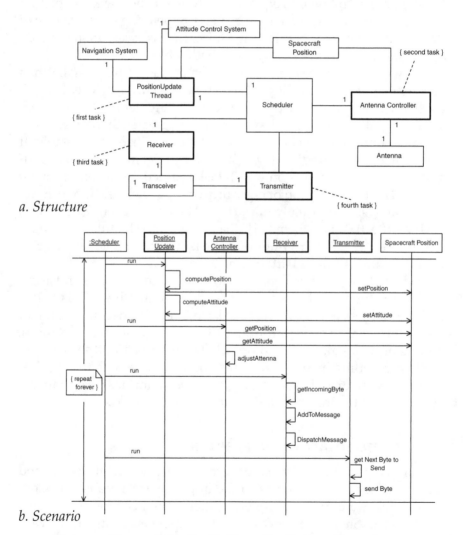

a. Structure

b. Scenario

Figure 5-14: *Cyclic Executive Pattern Example*

use a time-trigger for the start of the cycle for the Cyclic Executive. This "Triggered Cyclic Executive Pattern" is useful when the start of the execution of the task set must occur at a specific time, such as when highly regular and tightly controlled polling must occur. This variant is similar to the primary Cyclic Executive Pattern, except that a system timeout occurs to start each cycle. When the Cyclic Executive Pattern is inappropriate, then one of the other scheduling patterns may be used instead.

5.8 ROUND ROBIN PATTERN

The Round Robin Pattern employs a "fairness" scheduling doctrine that may be appropriate for systems in which it is more important for all tasks to progress than it is for specific deadlines to be met. The Round Robin Pattern is similar to the Cyclic Executive Pattern except that the former does employ preemption based on time.

5.8.1 Abstract

Most of the literature of real-time systems has focused on hard real-time systems (primarily because of its computation tractability). Hard real-time systems have tasks that are either time-driven (periodic) or event-driven (aperiodic with well-defined deadlines, after which the tasks are late). Such systems are inherently "unfair" because in an overload situation, low-priority tasks are selectively starved. There are other systems where individual deadlines are not as crucial as overall progress of the system. For such systems, a priority-based preemption approach may not be preferred.

5.8.2 Problem

The Round Robin Pattern addresses the issue of moving an entire set of tasks forward at more or less equal rates, particularly tasks that do not complete within a single scheduling cycle.

5.8.3 Pattern Structure

The Round Robin Pattern is a simple variation of the Cyclic Executive Pattern. The difference is that the *Scheduler* has the ability to preempt running tasks and does so when it receives a tick message from its associated *Timer*. Two forms of the Round Robin Pattern are shown in Figure 5-15. The complete form (Figure 5-15a) shows the infrastructure classes *Task Control Block* and *Stack*. The simplified form (Figure 5-15b) omits these classes.

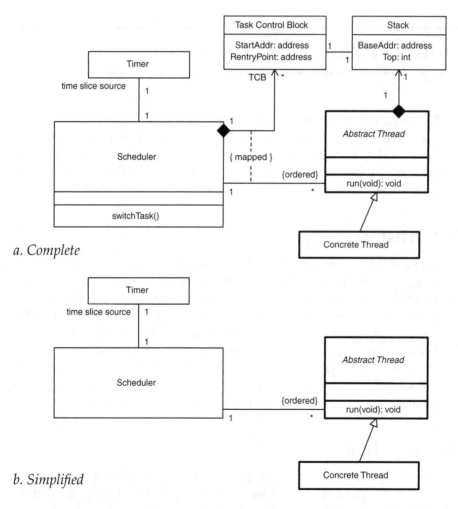

Figure 5-15: *Round Robin Pattern*

5.8.4 Collaboration Roles

- *Abstract Thread*
  The *Abstract Thread* class is an abstract (noninstantiable) superclass for *Concrete Thread*. *Abstract Thread* associates with the *Scheduler*. Since *Concrete Thread* is a subclass, it has the same interface to the *Scheduler* as the *Abstract Thread*. This enforces interface compliance.

- *Concrete Thread*
  The *Concrete Thread* is an «active» object most typically constructed to contain passive "semantic" objects that do the real work of the system. The *Concrete Thread* object provides a straightforward means of attaching these semantic objects into the concurrency architecture. *Concrete Thread* is an instantiable subclass of *Abstract Thread*.

- *Scheduler*
  This object initializes the system by loading the entire set of tasks and then running each of them in turn in perpetuity. The tasks may voluntarily relinquish control to the *Scheduler,* or they may be preempted when the *Scheduler* receives a Tick message from the *Timer.*

- *Stack*
  The *Stack* is a control-and-data stack as used in standard programming languages to store "automatic" variables, function return values, and return addresses. The Round Robin Pattern needs a stack per Thread because each Thread may be interrupted in the middle of arbitrary operation execution and will need to resume where it leaves off when the task is restarted.

- *Task Control Block*
  The *Task Control Block* object stores information about each task for the *Scheduler*. This includes the initial starting address (stored in the attribute *StartAddr*) and the entry point after preemption (stored in the *RentryPoint* attribute). There is a matching *Task Control Block* for every *Concrete Thread* object in the system, indicated by the {mapped} constraint.

- *Timer*
  This object sends periodic ticks to the *Scheduler* to tell it when to switch the task with the active focus. In most cases, this is implemented as a front-end to a hardware-based timer. The *Scheduler* typically configures the *Timer* prior to system execution by defining the time slice period. The *Timer* event is caught by an interrupt, which causes the *Scheduler* to execute the *switchTask*() operation.

5.8.5 Consequences

The Round Robin Pattern is, like the Cyclic Executive Pattern, *fair*, in that all the tasks get a chance to run. Unless the tasks use critical sections (and turn off interrupts and task switching), the Round Robin Pattern has an advantage over the Cyclic Executive Pattern in that a misbehaving task won't stop the entire system from running because the *Timer* will interrupt each task when it is time to perform a task switch. Also, like the Cyclic Executive Pattern, the Round Robin Pattern is suboptimal in terms of response to incoming events and unstable in the sense that you can't predict which task will fail in an overload situation. This pattern does scale up better than the Cyclic Executive pattern to larger numbers of tasks but not as well as priority-based preemption patterns. As the number of threads grows, the relative time each task gets for a time slice shrinks. This results in thrashing when the number of tasks grows too large, and the system will spend an increasing percentage of its time switching tasks. Note that even if a task has nothing to do, it still gets a time slice, and this can result in even more thrashing. Since data-sharing mechanisms are rudimentary, complex models may be difficult to implement with this pattern.

5.8.6 Implementation Strategies

This pattern is easily implemented as a Cyclic Executive Pattern with a hardware timer-driven interrupt and a few more simple parts. The *Concrete Thread* can prevent preemption during a critical section by temporarily disabling interrupts. Care must be taken, however, that interrupts don't get permanently disabled and stop task switching from ever occurring. This pattern does not assume run-to-completion semantics, so in general, each task will need a separate *Stack* for automatic variables, return values, and return addresses as well as a *Task Control Block* to store the reentry address for the preempted task.

5.8.7 Related Patterns

The Round Robin Pattern is a bit more complex than the Cyclic Executive Pattern, but it is not as complex as the priority-based preemption patterns, such as Static Priority Pattern and Dynamic Priority Pattern, discussed next in this chapter.

5.8.8 Sample Model

Figure 5-16 shows a simple two-task model implemented with the Round Robin Pattern. In this simple case, when the *Scheduler* is run, it configures the *Timer* with the proper period and then executes each task in turn for the time slice. Initially, it uses the default run() operation on the tasks; subsequently, it will merely jump directly to

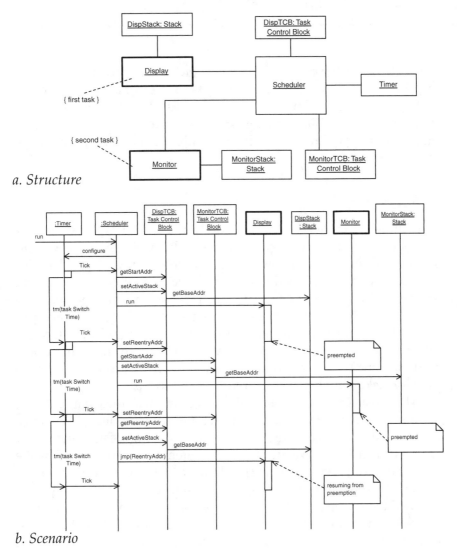

Figure 5-16: *Round Robin Pattern Example*

where that task left off. Prior to executing the task, the relevant task's stack is set active, and the stack pointer is set with the current top of stack.

5.9 STATIC PRIORITY PATTERN

The static priority pattern is the most common approach to scheduling in a real-time system. It has the advantages of being simple and scaling fairly well to large numbers of tasks. It is also simple to analyze for schedulability, using standard rate monotonic analysis methods (see [1], [6], and [7] for details on the analytic methods themselves).

5.9.1 Abstract

Two important concepts in the design of real-time systems are urgency and criticality. *Urgency* refers to the nearness of a deadline, while *criticality* refers to how important the meeting of that deadline is in terms of system functionality or correctness. It is clear that these are distinctly different concepts, yet what operating systems typically provide to deal with both of these issues is a single concept: priority. The operating system uses the priority of a task to determine which tasks should run preferentially when more than one task is ready to run. That is, the operating system always runs the highest-priority task of all the tasks currently ready to run.

The most common approach to assigning priorities in a real-time system is to define the priority of each task during design. This priority is called *static* because it is assigned during design and never changed during the execution of the system. This approach has the advantages of (1) simplicity, (2) stability, and, (3) if good policies are used in the selection of the tasks and their priorities, optimality.

By *stability*, we mean that in an overloaded situation, we can predict which tasks will fail to meet their deadlines (that is, the lower-priority ones). By *optimality*, we mean that if the task set can be scheduled using other approaches, then it can also be scheduled using static priority assignment. We will discuss a common optimal approach to priority assignment later in this section.

5.9.2 Problem

When we say "real-time" we mean that predictably timely execution of behavior is essential to correctness. This constraint can arise from any number of real-world problems, such as the length of time a safety-critical system can tolerate a fault before an "incident" occurs or the stability characteristics of a PID control loop.[4] By far, the most common way to model time for such systems is to assign a time interval, beginning with an incoming event or the start of the thread execution and ending with the completion of the task invocation. This is called a *deadline*. It is a common simplification that is used because systems can be easily analyzed for schedulability, given the periodicity,[5] the worst-case execution time, and deadline for all tasks in the system, as long as the priority of the tasks is also known.

5.9.3 Pattern Structure

Figure 5-17 shows the basic structure of the pattern. Each «active» object (called *Concrete Thread* in the figure) registers with the *Scheduler* object in the operating system by calling *createThread* operation and passing to it, the address of a method defined. Each *Concrete Thread* executes until it completes (which it signals to the OS by calling *Scheduler::return()*), it is preempted by a higher-priority task being inserted into the *Ready Queue,* or it is blocked in an attempt to access a *Shared Resource* that has a locked *Mutex* semaphore.

The upper part of the figure shows the complete pattern. In most cases, the details of the scheduler and its associations are not of interest to the modeler (because they are being provided by a COTS[6]

---

4. Proportional integral-differential. This is a very common means for controlling systems that do not display reactive (i.e., stateful) behavior but instead must be dynamically controlled through a continuous range of values. PID controllers tend to be very sensitive to the timely execution of corrective measures to deviations from set values; if the execution is delayed, this can put the system in what is called an "unstable" condition, leading to complete systems failure.

5. Or the minimum interarrival time for nonperiodic tasks.

6. Commercial Off-The-Shelf.

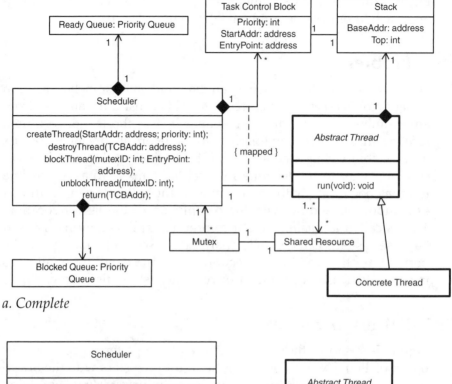

a. Complete

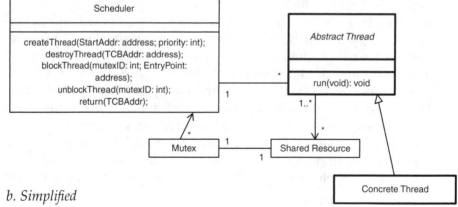

b. Simplified

Figure 5-17: *Static Priority Pattern*

operating system). When the infrastructure is not of interest, then this leads to the simplified form of the pattern shown in the lower half of the figure.

5.9.4 Collaboration Roles

Note that this discussion includes objects typically provided by the operating system: *Scheduler, Mutex, Ready Queue,* and *Blocked Queue.* If you are using a particular OS, then the interface may differ from what is shown here. Nevertheless, the gist of the operation remains the same for the vast majority of operation systems. For embedded systems in which you are writing the scheduler, this pattern can be used as is.

- *Abstract Thread*
  The *Abstract Thread* class is an abstract (noninstantiable) superclass for *Concrete Thread. Abstract Thread* associates with the *Scheduler.* Since *Concrete Thread* is a subclass, it has the same interface to the *Scheduler* as the *Abstract Thread.* This enforces interface compliance.

- *Blocked Queue*
  The *Blocked Queue* is a priority queue of Task Control Block (TCB) references. When a task is blocked (that is, prohibited from execution until a required resource is available), a reference to it is put into this queue. When the task is unblocked (the required resource becomes available), it is removed from the *Blocked Queue* and put into the *Ready Queue.*

- *Concrete Thread*
  The *Concrete Thread* is an «active» object most typically constructed to contain passive "semantic" objects that do the real work of the system. The *Concrete Thread* object provides a straightforward means of attaching these semantic objects into the concurrency architecture. *Concrete Thread* is an instantiable subclass of *Abstract Thread.*

- *Mutex*
  The *Mutex* is a mutual exclusion semaphore object that permits only a single caller through at a time. The operations of the *Shared Resource* invoke it whenever a relevant service is called, locking it prior to starting the service and unlocking it once the service is complete. *Threads* that attempt to invoke a service when the services are already locked become blocked until the *Mutex* is in its unlocked state. This is done by the *Mutex* semaphore signaling the *Scheduler* that a call attempt was made by the currently active thread, the *Mutex* ID (necessary to unlock it later when the *Mutex*

is released), and the entry point—the place at which to continue execution of the *Thread*.

- *Ready Queue*
  The *Ready Queue* holds references to TCBs for tasks that are currently ready to run. Whenever the highest-priority task in the *Ready Queue* is a higher priority than the currently running task (or when the currently running task terminates), then that task's TCB reference is removed from the *Ready Queue* and the referenced task executes. If a *Thread* is executing and a higher priority *Thread* is placed in the *Ready Queue*, then the currently executing *Thread* is preempted—that is, it stops executing and is put back into the *Ready Queue*, and the higher-priority *Thread* executes preferentially.

- *Scheduler*
  This object orchestrates the execution of multiple threads based on their priority according to a simple rule: Always run the ready thread with the highest priority. Some schedulers may be more complex than this, but this is the basic rule. When the «active» *Thread* object is created, it (or its creator) calls the *createThread* operation to create a thread for the «active» object. Whenever this thread is executed by the *Scheduler*, it calls the *StartAddr:address* (except when the thread has been blocked or preempted, in which case it calls the *EntryPoint* address).

- *Shared Resource*
  A resource is an object shared by one or more *Threads*. For the system to operate properly in all cases, all shared resources must either be reentrant (meaning that corruption from simultaneous access cannot occur) or they must be protected. Protection via mutual exclusion semaphores is discussed in the Guarded Call Pattern. In the case of a protected resource, when a *Thread* attempts to use the resource, the associated *Mutex* semaphore is checked, and if locked, the calling task is placed into the *Blocked Queue*. The task is terminated with its reentry point noted in the TCB.

- *Stack*
  Each *Abstract Thread* has a *Stack* for return addresses and passed parameters. This is normally explicit at the assembly language level within the application thread, but it is an important part of the scheduling infrastructure.

- *Task Control Block (TCB)*

  The TCB contains the scheduling information for its corresponding *Thread* object. This includes the priority of the thread, the default start address, and the current entry address, if it was preempted or blocked prior to completion. The *Scheduler* maintains a TCB object for each existing *Thread*. Note that TCB typically also has a reference off to a call and parameter stack for its *Thread*, but that level of detail is not shown in Figure 5-17.

5.9.5 Consequences

This pattern represents a common approach for task threads to interface with a scheduler. UML uses the notion of «active» objects to model threads. This pattern may be adjusted to use various different scheduling approaches, such as priority-based preemption or round robin policies.

In this pattern, priorities are allocated at design time. This means that the running system cannot dynamically reallocate priorities in response to changing conditions. For most systems, this is adequate because care is taken to ensure that the system is scheduled under worst-case conditions. However, this does limit the scalability of the approach. Static priorities may be applied to all sizes of systems where the environment and desired system response is highly predictable.

The most common policy for the selection of priorities is *rate monotonic scheduling* or RMS. The fundamental assumptions of RMS are that tasks are periodic and infinitely preemptable and that task deadlines occur at the end of the period.

When these are true, RMS assigns the priorities of the tasks based on their period—the shorter the period, the higher the priority. This scheduling approach is demonstrably optimal and stable. It is optimal in the sense that if the task set can be scheduled using another policy, then it can also be scheduled using RMS. It is stable in the sense that in the presence of an overload situation, which tasks will fail is predictable: The lower-priority tasks will fail.

When the first assumption is violated—that is, some of the tasks are not periodic but are instead event-driven—then the most common approach is to determine the *minimum interarrival time* for the event-driven threads and use that as if that were the period. While this is useful, it most often results in overdesigned systems that could be designed using less expensive parts if other approaches were used. For a description of the various approaches, see [1], [6], and [7].

When the second assumption is violated (deadlines are not necessarily at the end of the period), then a simple adaptation of RMS is used, called *Deadline Monotonic Scheduling,* or DMS. In this case, priorities are set based on the length of the deadline rather than the period of the task.

5.9.6 Implementation Strategies

This is the typical application of this pattern.

- Identify the objects in one or more collaborations.
- Apply some thread identification policies.
- Add the "passive" objects from the realizing collaborations into the «active» objects via composition relations.
- Adjust the associations across «active» object boundaries as necessary to ensure thread safety such as by applying the Rendezvous Patterns discussed previously in this chapter.

Most of the infrastructure of this pattern is provided by a real-time operating system: *Blocked Queue, Ready Queue, Scheduler, Mutex,* and *Task Control Block.* As an implementer of the pattern on top of an existing operating system, you only need be concerned with *Abstract Thread, Concrete Thread,* and *Shared Resource.* Of course, if you're writing your own *Scheduler,* then you will have to construct the OS objects as well.

5.9.7 Related Patterns

Although this pattern is used frequently, additional patterns are typically added to address other issues in the management of multiple concurrent threads. Specifically, additional patterns should be applied to manage synchronization and the sharing of information (Message Queuing Pattern, Guarded Call Pattern, Rendezvous Pattern) and concurrent resource management (Static Allocation Pattern, Fixed Sized Buffer Pattern, Priority Inheritance Pattern). Also the Dynamic Priority Pattern (next) is an alternative to this pattern in terms of a scheduling policy.

In the general (and common) case, resources must be shared among the threads. In order to ensure the integrity of the shared resource, it is very common to implement a blocking policy; that is when a higher-priority task needs a resource currently owned by a lower-priority task, the higher-priority task is blocked until the resource is released. Doing this in a naïve way can result in unschedulable systems due to a well-known problem called unbounded priority inversion. The resource-sharing patterns Priority Inheritance, Highest Locker, and Priority Ceiling Protocol specifically address this issue.

5.9.8 Sample Model

Figure 5-18 uses the simplified pattern form from Figure 5-17b. In this case, three threads are spawned (in other words, the active objects are created, and in each the constructor creates a thread from the OS in which to execute). The active objects (shown with the standard UML notation, a heavy border) share passive objects. Passive objects are objects that execute in the thread of their caller. In this case, both the *DataAcqThread* and the *FilteringThread* share the *RawData* resource, while the *FilteringThread* and the *DisplayThread* share the *CookedData* resource. Both resources use a mutex semaphore to serialize their access to avoid information corruption.

The threads run at different (static) priorities: the *DataAcqThread* runs at the highest priority, the *DisplayThread* at the next highest, and the *FilteringThread* runs at the lowest priority. The *Scheduler* tells each task when to run. Figure 5-18b shows a typical execution of this model.

A. The *Scheduler* runs the *DisplayThread*. The *DisplayThread* gets data from the *CookedData* resource.

B. *DisplayThread* completes.

C. The *Scheduler* runs the *FilteringThread*. It plans to get some raw data, filter it, and then store the results as cooked data. However, it gets preempted by the higher-priority task *DataAcqThread* during its use of the *RawData* resource.

D. The *Scheduler* runs the *DataAcqThread*. Since this is a higher priority than the *FilteringThread*, the latter is preempted. The former tries to write data to the *RawData* resource.

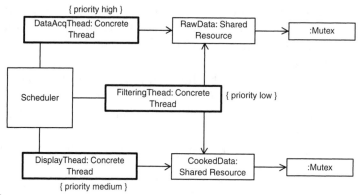

a. Structure

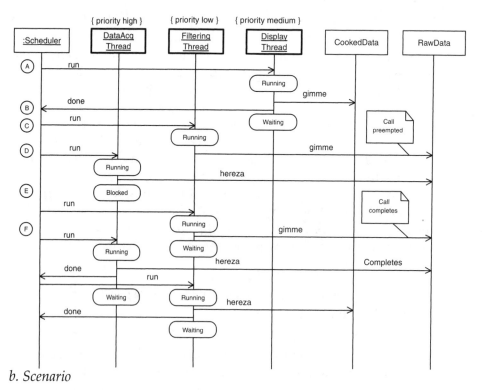

b. Scenario

Figure 5-18: *Static Priority Pattern Example*

E. The *Mutex* on *RawData* (not shown) blocks the *DataAcqThread* as it attempts to write the data to the *RawData* resource. This is necessary to preserve the integrity of the resource.

F. The *FilteringThread* is allowed to run (because the higher-priority task is blocked) until it releases the resource. Once the RawData resource is released, the *DataAcqThread* is unblocked and immediately preempts the *FilteringThread*. Once the *DataAcqThread* completes, the *FilteringThread* is allowed to continue. It updates the CookedData Resource and then terminates.

5.10 DYNAMIC PRIORITY PATTERN

The Dynamic Priority Pattern is similar to the Static Priority Pattern except that the former automatically updates the priority of tasks as they run to reflect changing conditions. There are a large number of possibly strategies to change the task priority dynamically. The most common is called *Earliest Deadline First,* in which the highest-priority task is the one with the nearest deadline. The Dynamic Priority Pattern explicitly emphasizes *urgency* over *criticality.*

5.10.1 Abstract

As mentioned in the previous section, the two most important concepts around schedulability are urgency and criticality, but what operating systems typically provide to manage *both* is a single value: priority. In the Static Priority Pattern, priorities are set at design time, usually reflecting a combination of the urgency and criticality of the two. In the Dynamic Priority Pattern, the priority of a task is set at run-time based solely on the urgency of the task.

The Dynamic Priority Pattern sets the priority of each task as a function of the time remaining until its deadline—the closer the deadline, the higher the priority. Another common name for such a scheduling policy is *Earliest Deadline First,* or EDF. Such a strategy is demonstrably *optimal.* This means that if the task set can be scheduled by any approach, then it can also be scheduled by this one.

However, the Dynamic Priority Pattern isn't *stable;* this means that it is impossible to predict at design time which tasks will fail in an overload situation.

The Dynamic Priority Pattern is best suited for task sets that are at least of approximately equal criticality so that urgency is the overriding concern. It is also well suited for highly complex situations in which it may be impossible to predict the set of tasks that will be running simultaneously. In such complex situations, it is difficult or impossible to construct optimal static priorities for the tasks.

5.10.2 Problem

For small real-time systems, the permutations of tasks that will be running are known, and the tasks themselves are stable: Their deadlines are consistent from task invocation to task invocation, and their execution time is roughly the same as well. This simplifies the analysis well enough to permit each computation of the schedulability of the system in absolute terms. In a complex system, such as fully symmetric multitasking systems, in which the assignment of a task to a processor isn't known until execution time, such analysis is difficult or impossible. Furthermore, even if the analysis can be done, it is complicated work that must be completely redone to add even a single task to the analysis.

5.10.3 Pattern Structure

The pattern structure is shown in Figure 5-19. It structurally the same as the Static Priority Pattern, but the *Abstract Thread* class also contains an attribute called *Deadline.* This is normally the duration of time from the invocation of the task until the point in time at which the task becomes late. It is specified as a duration, but the *Scheduler* will compute an absolute deadline from this (in the task's Task Control Block) and then order the task execution based on a policy of nearest deadline first. When a new task becomes ready to run, it is inserted in the ready queue based on its next deadline.

5.10.4 Collaboration Roles

As in the previous pattern, note that this discussion includes objects typically provided by the operating system: *Scheduler, Mutex, Ready*

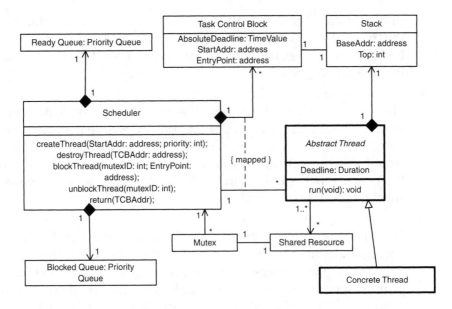

Figure 5-19: *Dynamic Priority Pattern*

Queue, and *Blocked Queue.* If you are using a particular OS, then the interface may differ from what is shown here. Nevertheless, the gist of the operation remains the same for the vast majority of operation systems. For embedded systems in which you are writing the scheduler, this pattern can be used as is.

- *Abstract Thread*
  The *Abstract Thread* class is an abstract (noninstantiable) superclass for *Concrete Thread*. *Abstract Thread* associates with the *Scheduler*. Since *Concrete Thread* is a subclass, it has the same interface to the *Scheduler* as the *Abstract Thread*. This enforces interface compliance. The *Abstract Thread* class has a *Deadline* attribute that is of type *Duration*. This is the length of time after the invocation of the task that the execution of the task must be complete. The *Scheduler* will use this value to compute the task's next deadline (stored in the *Task Control Block's AbsoluteDeadline* attribute) to determine the task's current priority.

- *Blocked Queue*
  The *Blocked Queue* is a priority queue of Task Control Block (TCB) references. When a task is blocked (prohibited from execution

until a required resource is available) a reference to it is put into this queue. When the task is unblocked (the required resource becomes available), it is removed from the *Blocked Queue* and put into the *Ready Queue*.

- *Concrete Thread*
  The *Concrete Thread* is an «active» object most typically constructed to contain passive "semantic" objects that do the real work of the system. The *Concrete Thread* object provides a straightforward means of attaching these semantic objects into the concurrency architecture. *Concrete Thread* is an instantiable subclass of *Abstract Thread*.

- *Mutex*
  The *Mutex* is a mutual exclusion semaphore object that permits only a single caller through at a time. The operations of the *Shared Resource* invoke it whenever a relevant service is called, locking it prior to starting the service, and unlocking it once the service is complete. *Threads* that attempt to invoke a service when the services are already locked become blocked until the *Mutex* is in its unlocked state. This is done by the *Mutex* semaphore signaling the *Scheduler* that a call attempt was made by the currently active thread, the *Mutex* ID (necessary to unlock it later when the *Mutex* is released), and the entry point—the place at which to continue execution of the *Thread*.

- *Ready Queue*
  The *Ready Queue* holds references to TCBs for tasks that are currently ready to run. Whenever the highest-priority task in the *Ready Queue* is a higher priority than the currently running task (or when the currently running task terminates), then that task's TCB reference is removed from the *Ready Queue*, and the referenced task executes. If a *Thread* is executing and a high-priority *Thread* is placed in the *Ready Queue*, then the currently executing *Thread* is preempted—that is, it stops executing and is put back into the *Ready Queue*, and the higher-priority *Thread* executes preferentially.

- *Scheduler*
  This *Scheduler* is very similar to the *Scheduler* in the Static Priority Pattern. It still orchestrates the execution of multiple threads based on their priority. The difference is that this *Scheduler* computes priority dynamically as function of the nearness of task

deadlines. This is a straightforward computation of the *Abstract Thread's* deadline attribute. When the task becomes ready to run, the next deadline is calculated (and stored in the TCB) and the tasks are scheduled based on the nearness of the next deadline for the task.

- *Shared Resource*
  A resource is an object shared by one or more *Threads*. For the system to operate properly in all cases, all shared resources must either be reentrant (meaning that corruption from simultaneous access cannot occur) or they must be protected. Protection via mutual exclusion semaphores is discussed in the Guarded Call Pattern. In the case of a protected resource, when a *Thread* attempts to use the resource, the associated *Mutex* semaphore is checked, and if locked, the calling task is placed into the *Blocked Queue*. The task is terminated with its reentry point noted in the TCB.

- *Stack*
  Each *Abstract Thread* has a *Stack* for return addresses and passed parameters. This is normally explicit at the assembly language level within the application thread but is an important part of the scheduling infrastructure.

- *Task Control Block (TCB)*
  The TCB contains the scheduling information for its corresponding *Thread* object. This includes the priority of the thread, the default start address and the current entry address, if it was preempted or blocked prior to completion. The *Scheduler* maintains a TCB object for each existing *Thread*. Note that TCB typically also has a reference off to a call and parameter stack for its *Thread*, but that level of detail is not shown in Figure 5-19. The TCB has the attribute *AbsoluteDeadline* that holds the next deadline for that task.

5.10.5 Consequences

Dynamic priority scheduling is optimal but not stable. By "optimal" it is meant that if the tasks can be scheduled by any algorithm, they can also be scheduled by this algorithm. By "unstable" it is meant that it cannot be predicted a priori which tasks will fail in an overload situation.

The Dynamic Priority Pattern scales well to large numbers of threads under conditions that defy static analysis. The Static Priority

Patterns work well for less dynamic situations in which the worst case can be known and planned for. In highly complex system, particularly with fully symmetric multitasking architectures, this may not be the case.

5.10.6 Implementation Strategies

The implementation of this pattern is only slightly more complex to implement than the Static Priority Pattern. In the Static Priority Pattern, the *Concrete Thread* must contain the priority as a constant value. The Scheduler then uses this static priority to arrange the priority queue of TCBs. With the dynamic priority pattern, the *Concrete Thread* must contain instead the deadline of the task relative to the start of the task (this is shown as the *Deadline* attribute). When the *Concrete Thread* becomes ready to run, the Scheduler must compute the next *AbsoluteDeadline* from that and store this value in the TCB. This attribute is used as the sorting criterion for the Scheduler's priority queue.

5.10.7 Related Patterns

This pattern is less common than the related Static Priority Pattern. And like the Static Priority Pattern, this pattern is typically mixed with any number of other patterns as well, such as resource management patterns. As with the Static Scheduling Pattern, the hard part of scheduling occurs when resources must be shared. The resource sharing patterns Priority Inheritance, Highest Locker, and Priority Ceiling Protocol specifically address the problems that can occur with unbounded priority inversion.

5.10.8 Sample Model

Figure 5-20 is the *same* model as used for the Static Priority Pattern in the previous section. The *Deadline* attributes are shown with their specific deadline values that result in equivalent but not necessarily identical scheduling for the tasks. For example, if the *DataAcqThread* becomes ready to run, under the Static Priority Pattern, it will preempt either of the two threads regardless of how near their deadlines are. With the Dynamic Priority Pattern, however, the *DataAcqThread* will only preempt currently running threads if its next deadline is, in fact, closer to their deadlines. Both approaches are schedulable in

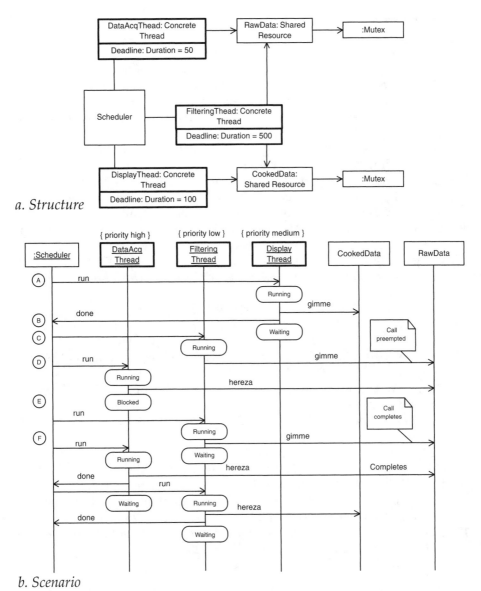

a. Structure

b. Scenario

Figure 5-20: *Dynamic Priority Pattern Example*

this case. In the Static Priority Pattern, in an overload situation, it is predictable which thread will be late: the lowest-priority thread *(FilteringThread)*. Which thread will be late in an overload situation cannot, however, be predicted if the Dynamic Priority Pattern is used.

5.11 References

[1] Klein, M., T. Ralya, B. Pollak, R. Obenza, and M. Harbour. *A Practitioner's Handbook for Real-Time Analysis: Guide to Rate Monotonic Analysis for Real-Time Systems*, Norwell, MA: Kluwer Academic Press, 1993.

[2] Pinedo, Michael. *Scheduling: Theory, Algorithms, and Systems*, Englewood Cliffs, NJ: Prentice Hall, 1995.

[3] Gomma, Hassan. *Software Design Methods for Concurrent and Real-Time Systems*, Reading, MA: Addison-Wesley, 1993.

[4] Oaks, S. and H. Wong. *Java Threads*, Sebastopol, CA: O'Reilly Press, 1997.

[5] Stankovic, J., M. Spuri, K. Ramamritham, and G. Buttazzo. *Deadline Scheduling for Real-Time Systems*, Norwell, MA: Kluwer Academic Press, 1998.

[6] Briand, L., and D. Roy. *Meeting Deadlines in Hard Real-Time Systems*, Los Alamitos, CA: IEEE Computer Society, 1999.

[7] Douglass, Bruce Powel. *Doing Hard Time: Developing Real-Time Systems with UML, Objects, Frameworks, and Patterns*, Reading, MA: Addison-Wesley, 1999.

[8] Gallmeister, B. *POSIX.4*, Sebastopol, CA: O'Reilly Press, 1995.

[9] Pope, Alan. *The CORBA Reference Guide: Understanding the Common Object Request Broker Architecture*, Reading, MA: Addison-Wesley, 1998.

[10] Aklecha, Vishwajit. *Object-Oriented Frameworks Using C++ and CORBA Gold Book*, Scottsdale, AZ: Coriolis Press, 1999.

[11] Rubin, W., and M. Brain. *Understanding DCOM*, Upper Saddle River, NJ: Prentice Hall, 1999.

[12] Mowbry, T., and R. Malveau. *CORBA Design Patterns*, New York: Wiley & Sons, 1997.

[13] Gamma, E., R. Helm, R. Johnson, and J. Vlissides. *Design Patterns: Elements of Reusable Object-Oriented Software*, Reading, MA: Addison-Wesley, 1995.

[14] Ralya, T. E. "IBM BSY-1 Trainer" in *An Analytical Approach to Real-Time Systems Design in Ada, Tutorial for Trai-Ada'89,* Conference held at David L. Lawrence Convention Center, Pittsburgh, PA, Oct. 23–26, 1989.

[15] Noble, J., and C. Weir. *Small Memory Software: Patterns for Systems with Limited Memory*, Boston, MA: Addison-Wesley, 2001.

Chapter 6

Memory Patterns

The following patterns are presented in this chapter.

- Static Allocation Pattern: Allocates memory up front
- Pool Allocation Pattern: Preallocates pools of needed objects
- Fixed Sized Buffer Pattern: Allocates memory in same-sized blocks
- Smart Pointer Pattern: Makes pointers reliable
- Garbage Collection Pattern: Automatically reclaims lost memory
- Garbage Compactor Pattern: Automatically defragments and reclaims memory

6.1 Memory Management Patterns

Much of the difficulty in building complex real-time and embedded system centers around managing shared resources in ways that are simultaneously efficient and robust. The patterns in this chapter focus on efficient management of memory as a resource and the robust sharing of general software resources (modeled as objects) to ensure schedulability of the overall system.

6.2 STATIC ALLOCATION PATTERN

The Static Allocation Pattern applies only to simple systems with highly predictable and consistent loads. However, where it *does* apply, the application of this pattern results in systems that are easy to design and maintain.

6.2.1 Abstract

Dynamic memory allocation has two primary problems that are particularly poignant for real-time and embedded systems: nondeterministic timing of memory allocation and deallocation and memory fragmentation. This pattern takes a very simple approach to solving both these problems: *disallow dynamic memory allocation*. The application of this pattern means that all objects are allocated during system initialization. Provided that the memory loading can be known at design time and the worst-case loading can be allocated entirely in memory, the system will take a bit longer to initialize, but it will operate well during execution.

6.2.2 Problem

Dynamic memory allocation is very common in both structured and object design implementations. C++, for example, uses *new* and *delete*, whereas C uses *malloc* and *free* to allocate and deallocate memory, respectively. In both these languages, the programmer must explicitly perform these operations, but it is difficult to imagine any sizable program in either of these languages that doesn't use pointers to allocated memory. The Java language is even worse: *All* objects are allocated in dynamic memory, so all object creation implicitly uses dynamic memory allocation. Further, Java invisibly deallocates memory once it is no longer used, but when and where that occurs is not under programmer control.[1]

As common as it is, dynamic memory allocation is somewhat of an anathema to real-time systems because it has two primary difficulties. First, allocation and deallocation are nondeterministic with respect to time because generally they require searching data structures to find free memory to allocate. Second, deallocation is not without problems either. There are two strategies for deallocation: explicit and implicit. Explicit deallocation can be deterministic in terms of time (since the system has a pointer to its exact location), and the programmer must keep track of all conditions under which the memory must be released and explicitly release it. Failure to do so correctly is called a *memory leak,* since not all memory allocated is ultimately reclaimed, so the amount of allocable storage decreases over time until system failure. Implicit deallocation is done by means of a *Garbage Collector*—an object that either continuously or periodically scans memory looking for lost memory and reclaiming it. Garbage collectors *can* be used, but they are more nondeterministic than allocation strategies, require a fair amount of processing in and of themselves, and may require *more* memory in some cases (for example, if memory is to be compacted). Garbage collectors *do*, on the other hand, solve the most common severe defects in software systems.

The third issue around dynamic memory is fragmentation. As memory is allocated in blocks of various sizes, the deallocation order is usually unrelated to the allocation order. This means that what was once a contiguous block of free memory ends up as a hodgepodge of free and used blocks of memory. The fragmentation increases the longer the system runs until eventually a request for a block of memory cannot be fulfilled because there is no single block large enough to fulfill the request, even though there may be more

---

1. This is not true in the two competing real-time Java specifications but is true for generic Java.

than enough total memory free. This is a serious problem for all real-time and embedded systems that use dynamic memory allocation—not just for those that must run for longer periods of time between reboots.

6.2.3 Pattern Structure

Figure 6-1 shows the basic structure for this pattern. It is structurally very simple but can handle systems of arbitrary size via nesting levels of abstraction. The *System Object* starts the initialization process and creates the highest-level *Composite Objects*. They have composition relations to other *Composite Objects* or to *Primitive Objects*. The latter are defined to be objects that do not create other objects dynamically. Composition relations are used because they clearly identify the creation/deletion responsibilities.

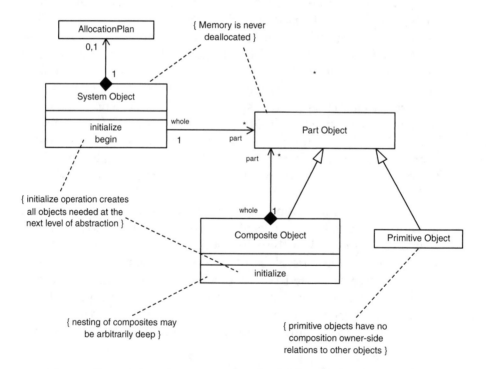

Figure 6-1: *Static Allocation Pattern*

6.2.4 Collaboration Roles

- *Allocation Plan*
  The *Allocation Plan*, if present, identifies the *order* in which the largest system composite objects should be allocated. If not present, then the system can allocate objects in any order desired.

- *Composite Object*
  A *Composite Object*, by definition within this pattern, is an object that has composition relations to other objects. These other objects may either be composites or primitive objects. A *Composite Object* is responsible for the creation of all objects that it owns via composition. There is a constraint on this object (and the *System Object* as well) that memory cannot be deallocated. Composites may be composed of other composites, but, as stated in the UML specification, each object owned via a composition relation may only belong to one such relation. This means that the creation responsibility for every object in the system is clearly identified in the pattern.

- *Part Object*
  This is a superclass of *Composite Object* and *Primitive Object*. This allows both *System Object* and *Composite Object* to contain, via composition, both *Composite Objects* and *Primitive Objects*.

- *Primitive Object*
  A *Primitive Object* is one that does not allocate any other objects. All *Primitive Objects* are created by composites.

- *System Object*
  The *System Object* is structurally the same as a *Composite Object*, except that it may own an *Allocation Plan* and is the highest abstraction possible in the system. Its responsibility is to "kick-start" the system by creating and initializing the primary pieces of the system (the highest level *Composite Objects*), which in turn create *their* pieces, and so on. Once the objects all are created, the *System Object* then begins system execution by running the *begin* operation.

6.2.5 Consequences

The Static Allocation Pattern is useful when the memory map can be allocated for worst case at run-time. This means that (1) the worst case is known and well understood, and (2) there is enough system memory to handle the worst case. Systems that work well with this pattern typically don't have much difference between worst and average case; that is, they have a consistent memory load for all execution profiles. System behavior is likewise relatively simple and straightforward. This means that the systems using this pattern will usually be small. The need to allocate the memory for all possible objects means that it can easily happen that more memory will be required than if dynamic allocation was used. Therefore, the system must be relatively immune to the cost of memory. When the cost of memory is very small with respect to overall cost, this pattern may be applicable.

There are a number of consequences of the Static Allocation Pattern. First of all, because creation of all objects takes place at startup, the execution of the system after initialization is generally faster than when dynamic allocation is used, sometimes *much* faster. Run-time execution is usually more predictable as well because of the removal of one of the primary sources for system nondeterminism. Further, since no deallocation is done, there is no memory fragmentation whatsoever.

Since all allocation is done at start time, there may be a noticeable delay from the initiation of startup until the system becomes available for use. In some systems that must have a very short startup time, this may not be acceptable. An ideal system run-time profile is that the system can handle a long start time but must provide minimum response time once operation has begun.

6.2.6 Implementation Strategies

This pattern is very easy to implement. In many cases, a separate initialize method may not be required—and the constructor of each of the composites may be used.

6.2.7 Related Patterns

Other patterns in this chapter address these same issues but provide somewhat different benefits and consequences. See, for example, Pool Allocation, Fixed Sized Buffer, Garbage Collector, and Garbage Compactor Patterns.

6.2.8 Sample Model

Figure 6-2 shows a simple example using instances of a fully constructed system. Figure 6-2a shows the instance structure with an object diagram, and Figure 6-2b shows how the Static Allocation Pattern works on startup. You can see how the creation process is delegated to the composite objects of decreasing abstraction until the primitive objects are constructed.

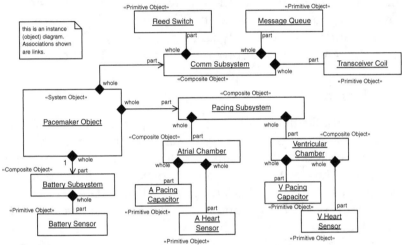

a. Structure

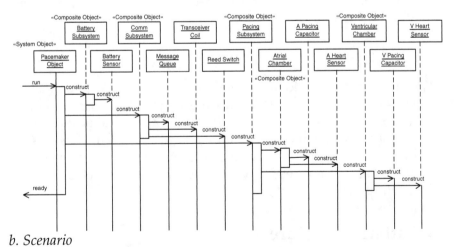

b. Scenario

Figure 6-2: *Static Allocation Pattern Example*

6.3 POOL ALLOCATION PATTERN

The Static Allocation Pattern only works well for systems that are, well, *static* in nature. Sometimes you need sets of objects for different purposes at different times during execution. When this is the case, the Pool Allocation Pattern works well by creating pools of objects, created at startup, available to clients upon request. This pattern doesn't address needs for dynamic memory but still provides for the creation of more complex programs than the Static Allocation Pattern.

6.3.1 Abstract

In many applications, objects may be required by a large number of clients. For example, many clients may need to create data objects or message objects as the system operates in a complex, changing environment. The need for these objects may come and go, and it may not be possible to predict an optimal dispersement of the objects even if it *is* possible to bound the total number of objects needed. In this case, it makes sense to have pools of these objects—created but not necessarily initialized and available upon request. Clients can request them as necessary and release them back to the pool when they're done with them.

6.3.2 Problem

The prototypical candidate system for the Pooled Allocation Pattern is a system that cannot deal with the issues of dynamic memory allocation, but it is too complex to permit a static allocation of all objects. Typically, a number of similar, typically small, objects, such as events, messages, or data objects, may need to be created and destroyed but are not needed a priori by any particular clients for the entire run-time of the system.

6.3.3 Pattern Structure

Figure 6-3 shows the Pooled Allocation Pattern. The parameterized class *Generic Pool Manager* is instantiated to create the specific *Pooled-*

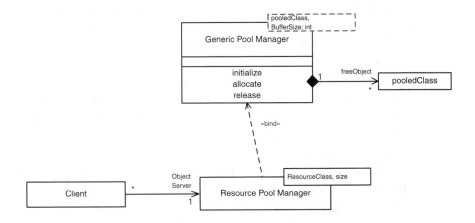

Figure 6-3: *Pooled Allocation Pattern*

Class required. The instantiated class is shown as *Resource Pool Manager*. Typically, there will be a number of such instantiated pools in the system, although only one for any specific *PooledClass* type. Each pool creates and then manages its set of objects, allocating them (and returning a pointer, reference, or handle to the allocated object to the client) and releasing them (putting the released object back into the freeObject list) upon request. Usually, the entire set of pools is created at system startup and never deleted. This removes the problems associated with dynamic memory allocation but preserves many of the benefits.

6.3.4 Collaboration Roles

- *Client*
  The *Client* is any object in the system that has a need to use one or more objects of class *resourceClass*. To request an object, they call *ResourcePool::allocate()* and give the object back to the pool by calling *ResourcePool::release()*. As we will see later in the Implementation Strategies section, in C++, the *new()* and *delete()* operators may be overridden to call the *allocate()* and *release()* operations to hide the infrastructure from the client.

- *Generic Pool Manager*
  Generic Pool Manager is a parameterized (template) class that uses the formal parameters *pooledClass* and *BufferSize* to specify the

class of the objects pooled and the number of them to create, respectively. The operations of *Generic Pool Manager* are written to work in terms of these formal parameters.

- *PooledClass*
  PooledClass is a formal parameter to the *Generic Pool Manager* parameterized class. Practically, it may be realized with just about any object desired, but most often, they are simple, small classes used by a variety of *clients*.

- *Resource Pool Manager*
  The *Resource Pool Manager* class is the instantiated *Generic Pool Manager,* in which a specific class *(ResourceClass)* and a specific number of objects *(size)* are passed as actual parameters. There may be any number of such instantiations in the system but only one per *Resource Class.*

6.3.5 Consequences

The Pooled Allocation Pattern has a number of advantages over the Static Allocation Pattern. Since memory is allocated at startup and never deleted, there is no problem with the nondeterministic timing of dynamic memory allocation during run-time or memory fragmentation. The system, however, can handle nondeterministic allocation of certain classes of objects. Thus, the pattern scales to more complex systems than does the Static Allocation Pattern. It is especially applicable to systems where a number of common objects may be needed by many different clients, but it cannot be determined at design time how to distribute these objects. This pattern allows the objects to be distributed on an as-needed basis during the execution of the system. Because all pooled objects are created at system startup, the decision about the optimal number of different kinds of objects must be made at design time. For example, it might be decided that as a worst case, 1000 message objects, 5000 data sample objects, and so forth, may be required. If this turns out to be an erroneous decision, the system may fail at startup or later during execution. Further, the system cannot grow to meet new system demands, so the pattern is best applied to systems that are well understood and relatively predictable in their demands on system resources.

A note for Java programmers: This pattern is particularly helpful for Java applications because memory is never released. This pattern avoids fragmentation and the run-time overhead for object allocation, but the garbage collector will still take up some time even though it won't find objects to delete.

6.3.6 Implementation Strategies

This common pattern is fairly easy to implement. To make the pattern easier to use in C++, it is common to rewrite *new* and *delete operators* to use the pool manager for the various *pooledClass* types. That way, the issue of dynamic versus pooled allocation can be hidden from the application programmer.

Code Segment 6-1: C++ Pooled Allocation Implementation Strategy

```
#include <list>
using namespace std;

class PoolEmpty {
}; // exception type to be thrown

// note: list is a container from the C++ STL
template <class Resource, int nElements>
class GenericPool {
        list<Resource* > freeList;
public:
        GenericPool(void) {
        for (int j=0; j<nElements; j++) {
                freeList.push_back(new Resource);
                };
        };

    Resource* allocate(void) {
                Resource* R;
                if (freeList.size() > 0) {
                        R = freeList.begin();
                        // get the first one.
                        freeList.pop_front();
                        // remove it from the free list
            return R
                        // and pass it back to the client
                } else {
                throw new PoolEmpty;
                };
        };

        void release(Resource* R) {
                freeList.push_back(R);
```

```
        };
};
class BusMessage {
        string s;
};
int main(void)
{
        GenericPool<BusMessage, 1000> busMessagePool;
        return 0;
}
```

Additionally, this pattern can be mixed with the Factory Pattern of [1] to create the correct subtypes, if desired.

Java has no parameterized types, but it does have collections (arrays) plus some methods for manipulating arrays (in java.util) that are modeled after the Standard Template Library of C++. There are many implementation solutions available. A very simple one was used in Code Segment 6-2. In this example, the LinkedList class from java.util was used to hold the created *BusMessage* objects. When a client allocates it, the object is removed from the list and passed back to the client. When the client wishes to return the object to the pool, it merely calls *BusMessagePool.release()*, and the object is reinserted into the pool.

Code Segment 6-2: Java Implementation Strategy for Pools

```
import java.util.*;

class BusMessage {
  private String s;
  };

class PoolEmpty extends Exception {
};

public class BusMessagePool{
  private LinkedList freeList = new LinkedList();

  public BusMessagePool() {

    for (int j=0; j<1000; j++)

      freeList.addLast(new BusMessage());

  };

  //
```

```
// allocate() gives the client a reference to a
// BusMessage object and removes it from the free list
public BusMessage allocate() throws PoolEmpty {
  BusMessage B;
  if (freeList.size() > 0) {
    B = (BusMessage) freeList.getFirst();
                              // get the first one.
    freeList.removeFirst(); // remove it from the
                            // free list and pass
    return B;               // it back to the
                            // client
    } else {
    throw new PoolEmpty();
    };
  };
  // release() returns the passed BusMessage object back
into the pool
  public void release(BusMessage Carcass) {
    freeList.addFirst(Carcass);
    };
}
```

Whatever the underlying basis for the pools, there must be a separate *Resource Pool Manager* for each kind of *pooledClass*. In C++, this is simply a matter of binding a different class to the formal parameter list of the *ResourcePool* template. In Java, this can be done by creating different lists using the LinkedList containers.

6.3.7 Related Patterns

The Pooled Allocation Pattern is but one of many approaches to managing memory allocation. The Static Allocation Pattern can be used for systems that are simpler, and the Dynamic Allocation Pattern and its variants can be used for more complex needs. The Abstract Factory Pattern [1] can be used with this pattern to provide a means for Pooled Allocation for different environments.

6.3.8 Sample Model

Figure 6-4a shows the object model for a system running a class model derived from the pattern shown in Figure 6-3. Figure 6-4b shows a scenario of the objects as they run. The first message shows the creation of the TempDataPool object, which in turn creates the

1000 TempData objects that it will manage. The other part of the object model shows three clients of the TempDataPool.

- *TempSensor* This is a thermometer that records the temperature every ½ second and in doing so, allocates a TempData object to store the information. This object reports the temperature (by passing a reference to the allocated TempData object), first to the

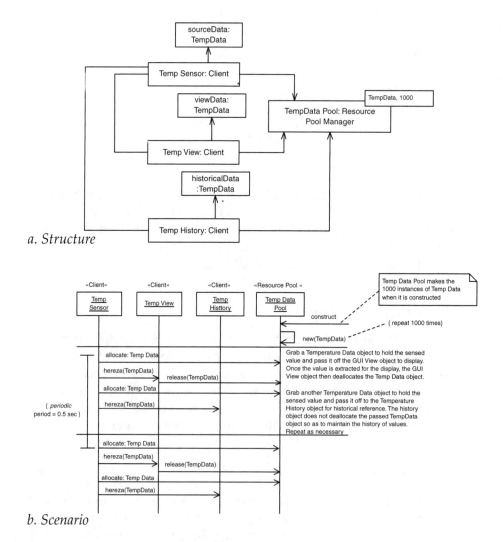

Figure 6-4: *Pooled Allocation Pattern Example*

TempView, a GUI view object, and then to TempHistory, which manages the history of Temperature over the last several seconds.

- *TempView*   This is a GUI object that displays the temperature to a user on a display. Once it has displayed the value, it releases the TempData object that was passed back to the pool

- *TempHistory*   This maintains a history of the last ten seconds of temperature data. Thus, for the first 20 samples, it does not delete the TempData objects passed to it, but subsequently, it releases the oldest TempData object it owns when it receives a new one.

6.4 FIXED SIZED BUFFER PATTERN

Many real-time and embedded systems are complex enough to be unpredictable in the order in which memory must be allocated and too complex to allocate enough memory for all possible worst cases. Such systems would be relatively simple to design using dynamic memory allocation. However, many such systems in the real-time and embedded world must function reliably for long periods of time—often years or even decades—between reboots. That means that while they are complex enough to require dynamic random allocation of memory, they cannot tolerate one of the major problems associated with dynamic allocation: fragmentation. For such systems, the Fixed Sized Buffer Pattern offers a viable solution: fragmentation-free dynamic memory allocation at the cost of some loss of memory usage optimality.

6.4.1 Abstract

The Fixed Sized Buffer Pattern provides an approach for true dynamic memory allocation that does not suffer from one of the major problems that affect most such systems: memory fragmentation. It is a pattern supported by most real-time operating systems directly. Although it requires static memory analysis to minimize nonoptimal memory usage, it is a simple and easy to implement approach.

6.4.2 Problem

One of the key problems with dynamic memory allocation is memory fragmentation. Memory fragmentation is the random intermixing of free and allocated memory in the heap. For memory fragmentation to occur, the following conditions must be met.

- The order of memory allocation is unrelated to the order in which it is released.
- Memory is allocated in various sizes from the heap.

When these preconditions are met, then memory fragmentation will inevitably occur if the system runs long enough. Note that this is not a problem solely related to object-oriented systems, functionally decomposed systems written in C are just as affected as those written in C++.[2] The problem is severe enough that it will usually lead to system failure if the system runs long enough. The failure occurs even when analysis has demonstrated that there is adequate memory because if the memory is highly fragmented, there may be more than enough memory to satisfy a request, but it may not be in a contiguous block of adequate size. When this occurs, the memory allocation request fails even though there is enough total memory to satisfy the request.

6.4.3 Pattern Structure

There are two ways to fix dynamic allocation so that it does not lead to fragmentation: (1) correlate the order of allocation and deallocation, or (2) do not allow memory to be allocated in any but a few specific block sizes. The basic concept of the Fixed Sized Buffer Pattern is to *not* allow memory to be allocated in any random block size but to limit the allocation to a set of specific block sizes.

Imagine a system in which you can determine the worst case of the total number of objects needed (similar to computing the worst-case memory allocation) as well as the largest object size needed. If the entire heap was divided into blocks equal to the largest block

---

2. Although it should be noted that the problem is potentially even worse with Java because *all* objects in Java are allocated on the heap, whereas "automatic variable" objects are allocated on the stack in C++.

ever needed, then you could guarantee that if there is *any* memory available, then the memory request could be fulfilled.

The cost of such an approach is the inefficient use of available memory. Even if only a single byte of memory were needed, a worst-case block would be allocated, wasting most of the space within the block. If the object sizes were randomly distributed between 1 byte and the worst case, then overall, ½ of the heap memory would be wasted when the heap was fully allocated. Clearly, this is wasteful, but the advantage of this approach is compelling: There will *never* be failure due to the fragmentation of memory.

To minimize this waste, the Fixed Sized Buffer Pattern provides a finite set of fixed-sized heaps, each of which offers blocks of a single size. Static analysis of the system can usually reveal a reasonable allocation of memory to the various-sized heaps. Memory is then allocated from the smallest block-sized heap that can fulfill the request. This compromise requires more analysis at design time but allows the designer to "tune" the available heap memory to minimize waste. Figure 6-5 shows the basic Fixed Sized Buffer Pattern.

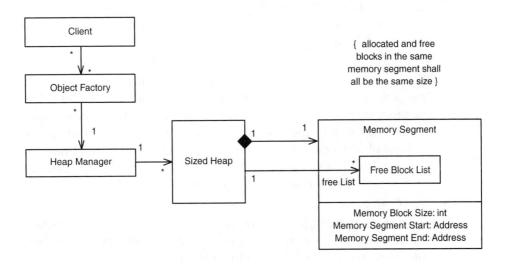

Figure 6-5: *Fixed Sized Buffer Pattern*

6.4.4 Collaboration Roles

- *Client*
  The *Client* is the user of the objects allocated from the fixed sized heaps. It does this by creating new objects as needed. In C++ this can be done by overwriting the global new and delete operators. In other languages, it may be necessary to explicitly call Object-Factory.new() and ObjectFactory.delete().

- *Free Block List*
  This is a list of the unallocated blocks of memory within a single *Memory Segment.*

- *Heap Manager*
  This manages the sized heaps. When a request is made for a block of memory for an object, it determines the appropriate *Sized Heap* from which to request it. When memory is released, the *Heap Manager* can check the address for the memory block to determine which memory segment (and hence which free list) it should be added back into.

- *Memory Segment*
  A *Memory Segment* is a block of memory divided into equal-sized blocks, which may be allocated or unallocated. Only the free blocks must be listed, though. When memory is released, it is added back into the free list. The *Memory Segment* has attributes that provide the size of the blocks it holds and the starting and ending addresses for the *Memory Segment.*

- *Object Factory*
  The *Object Factory* takes over the job of allocation of memory on the heap. It does this by allocating an appropriately sized block of memory from one of the *Sized Heaps* and mapping the newly created object's data members into it and then calling the newly created object's constructor. Deleting an object reverses this procedure: The destructor of the object is called, and then the memory used is returned to the appropriate *Free Block List.*

- *Sized Heap*
  A *Sized Heap* manages the free and allocated blocks from a single *Memory Segment.* It returns a reference to the memory block when allocated, moves the block to the allocated list, and accepts a reference to an allocated block to free it. Then it moves *that* block to the free list so that subsequent requests can use it.

6.4.5 Consequences

The use of this pattern eliminates memory fragmentation. However, the pattern is suboptimal in terms of total allocated memory because more memory is allocated than is actually used. Assuming a random probability of memory size needs, on the average, half of the allocated memory is wasted. The use of *Sized Heaps* with appropriately sized blocks can alleviate some of this waste but cannot eliminate it. Many RTOSs support fixed sized block allocation out-of-the-box, simplifying the implementation.

6.4.6 Implementation Strategies

If you use an RTOS, then most of the pattern is provided for you by the underlying RTOS. In that case, you need to perform an analysis to determine the best allocation of your free memory into various-sized block heaps. If you rewrite global new and delete operators so that they use the *Object Factory* object rather than the default operators, then the use of sized heaps can be totally hidden from the clients.

6.4.7 Related Patterns

This pattern allows true dynamic allocation but without the problems of memory fragmentation. The issues of nondeterministic time are minimized but still present. However, there is no protection against memory leaks (clients neglecting to release inaccessible memory), inappropriate access to released memory, and the potentially critical issue of wasted memory. In simpler cases, the pooled allocation, or even static allocations patterns, may be adequate. If time predictability is not a major issue, then the Garbage Collector pattern may be a better choice, since it does protect against memory leaks.

6.4.8 Sample Model

Figure 6-6a shows a structural example of an instance of this pattern. In this case, there are three block-sized heaps: 128-byte blocks, 256-byte blocks, and 1024-byte blocks. Figure 6-6b presents a scenario in which a small object is allocated, followed by a larger object. After this, the smaller object is deleted.

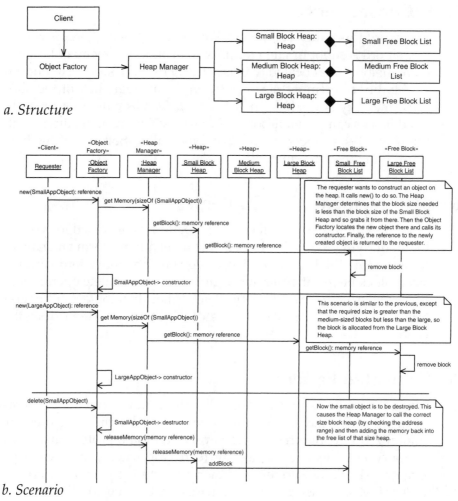

a. Structure

b. Scenario

Figure 6-6: *Fixed Sized Buffer Pattern Example*

6.5 SMART POINTER PATTERN

In my experience over the last couple of decades leading and managing development projects implemented in C and C++, pointer problems are by far the most common defects and the hardest to identify.

They are common because the pointer metaphor is very low level and requires precise management, but it is easy to forget about when dealing with all possible execution paths. Inevitably, somewhere a pointer is destroyed (or goes out of scope), but the memory is not properly freed (a memory leak), memory is released but nevertheless accessed (dangling pointer), or memory is accessed but not properly allocated (uninitialized pointer). These problems are notoriously difficult to identify using standard means of testing and peer reviews. Tools such as Purify and LINT can identify "questionable practices," but sometimes they flag so many things it is virtually impossible to use the results. The Smart Pointer Pattern is an approach that is mechanistic (medium scope) rather than architectural (large scope) but has produced excellent results.

6.5.1 Abstract

Pointers are by far the most common way to realize an association between objects. The most common implementation of a navigable association is to use a pointer. This pointer attribute is dereferenced to send messages to the target object. The problem with pointers per se is that they are not objects; they are just data. Because they are not objects, the primitive operations you can perform on them are not checked for validity. Thus, we are free to access a pointer that has never been initialized or after the memory to which it points has been freed. We are also free to destroy the pointer without releasing the memory, resulting in the loss of the now no-longer-referenceable memory to the system.

The Smart Pointer Pattern solves these problems by making the pointer itself an object. Because a Smart Pointer is an object, it can have constructors and destructors and operations that can ensure that its preconditional invariants ("rules of proper usage") are maintained.

6.5.2 Problem

In many ways, pointers are the bane of the programmer's existence. If they weren't so incredibly useful, we would have discarded them a long time ago. Because they allow us to dynamically allocate, de-allocate, and reference memory dynamically, they form an important part of the programmer's toolkit. However, their use commonly results in a number of different kinds of defects.

- Memory leaks—destroying a pointer before the memory they reference is released. This means that the memory block is never put back in the heap free store, so its loss is permanent, at least until the system is rebooted. Over time, the available memory in the heap free store (that is, memory that can now be allocated by request) shrinks, and eventually the system fails because it cannot satisfy memory requests.

- Uninitialized pointer—using a pointer as if it was pointing to a valid object (or memory block) but neglecting to properly allocate the memory. This can also occur if the memory request is made but refused.

- Dangling pointer—using a pointer as if it was pointing to a valid object (or memory block) but *after* the memory to which it points has been freed.

- Pointer arithmetic defects—using a pointer as an iterator over an array of values but inappropriately. This can be because the pointer goes beyond the bounds of the array (in either direction), possibly stepping on memory allocated to other objects, or becoming misaligned, pointing into the middle of a value rather than at its beginning.

These problems arise because pointers are inherently *stupid*. They are only data values (addresses), and the operations defined on them are primitive and without checks on their correct use. If only they were *objects*, their operations could be extended to include validity checks and they could identify or prevent inappropriate use.

6.5.3 Pattern Structure

The basic solution of the Smart Pointer Pattern is to reify the pointer into an object. Once a pointer comes smart, or potentially smart, its operations can ensure that the preconditions of the pointer (it points to valid memory) are met. Figure 6-7a shows the simple structure of this pattern, and Figure 6-7b shows a common variant.

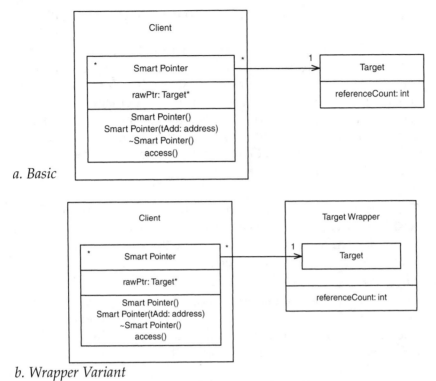

a. Basic

b. Wrapper Variant

Figure 6-7: *Smart Pointer Pattern*

6.5.4 Collaboration Roles

- *Client*
  The *Client* is the object that at the analysis level simply has an association to the *Target* object. If this is a bidirectional association, then *both* these objects have smart pointers to the other.

- *Smart Pointer*
  The *Smart Pointer* is an object that contains the actual pointer *(rawPtr)* as an attribute, as well as constructor, destructor, and access operations. The access operations will usually be realized by overriding pointer dereference operators ([] and →) in C++, to hide the fact that a smart pointer is being used. The *Target:: referenceCount* attribute keeps track of the number of smart pointers that are referring to the specific target object. It's important to know

this so you can determine when to destroy the dynamically created *Target*.

The *Smart Pointer* has two constructors. The default constructor creates a corresponding *Target* and sets *referenceCount* to the value 1. The second constructor initializes the *rawPtr* attribute to the value of the address passed in and increments the *Target:: referenceCount*. The destructor decrements the *Target::reference-Count*; if it decrements to 0; then the *Target* is destroyed. In principle, the *Target::referenceCount* must be referred to by all *Smart Pointers* that point to the *same* object.

- *Target*
  The *Target* is the object providing the services that the *Client* wishes to access. In the basic form of the pattern (Figure 6-7a), *Target* also has a *reference count* attribute that tracks the number of *Smart Pointers* currently referencing it.

- *Target Wrapper*
  In the Smart Pointer Pattern variant in Figure 6-7b, the *Target* object is not at all aware of Smart Pointers or reference counts. The *Target Wrapper* object contains via composition, the *Target* object, and it owns the *referenceCount* attribute.

6.5.5 Consequences

This is a mechanistic-level design pattern; that means it optimizes individual collaborations. The main advantage of applying this pattern is that it is a simple means to ensure that objects are destroyed when they are no longer accessible—that is, when all references to them have been (or are being) destroyed. This requires some discipline on the part of the programmers. If the *Target* object is being referenced by *both* smart and raw pointers, then this pattern will break with potential catastrophic consequences. On the other hand, using the pattern can be codified into an easily checked rule: Use no raw pointers; that is, validate during code reviews.

To ensure robustness in the presence of multithreaded access to an object (*Smart Pointers* exist in multiple threads that reference the same *Target*), then care must be taken in the creation of constructors and destructors. The simplest way to handle them is to make them atomic (prevent task switching during the construction or destruction of a *Smart Pointer*). You can do this easily by making the first operation in the constructor a call to the OS to prevent task switching (just don't forget to turn it back on when you're done!). The destructor must be similarly protected. Otherwise, there is a possibility that the object may be destroyed *after* you checked that it was valid and a *Smart Pointer* is now pointing to a *Target* that no longer exists.

Finally, there is one situation in which *Smart Pointers* may be correctly implemented but still may result in memory leakage. The *Smart Pointer* logic ensures that whenever there is no *Smart Pointer* pointing to a *Target*, the *Target* will be deleted. However, it is possible to define small cycles of objects that contain *Smart Pointers*, but the *entire cycle* cannot be accessed by the rest of the application. In other words, it is *still* possible to get a memory leak if the collaboration of objects has cycles in it. Figure 6-8 shows how this can happen.

Object *Obj3* and *Obj5* form a cycle. If *Obj2* and *Obj4* are destroyed, the reference counts associated with *Obj3* and *Obj5* decrement down to 1 rather than 0, and these two objects are unable to be referenced by the remainder of the application. Since their reference counts are greater than 1, they cannot be destroyed, but neither can the application invoke services of these objects because there are no references to these objects outside the cycle itself.

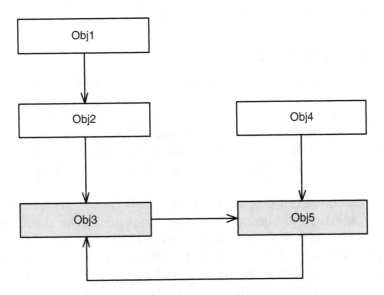

Figure 6-8: *Smart Pointer Cycles*

The easiest way to handle the problem is to ensure that no *Target* itself references another object that could ever reference the original. This can usually be deduced from drawing class diagrams of the collaborations and some object diagrams resulting from the execution of the class diagram. If cycles cannot be avoid, then it might be better to avoid using the Smart Pointer Pattern for those cycles specifically.

6.5.6 Implementation Strategies

This pattern is simple and straightforward to implement and should create no problems. If you desire a Smart Pointer Pattern that can handle cyclic object structures, then this can be solved at the cost of increased complexity and processing resource usage. A good discussion of these methods is provided in [2].

6.5.7 Related Patterns

There are more elaborate forms of the Smart Pointer in [2], although they are expressed as algorithms defined on the Smart Pointer rather than patterns per se, as it is here. When cycles are present but the benefits of the Smart Pointer Pattern (protection against pointer defects) are strongly desired, the Garbage Collector or Compacting Garbage Collector Patterns may be indicated.

6.5.8 Sample Model

Figure 6-9 shows a simple application of this pattern. Two clients of the HR Sensor object exist: one object that displays the values and another that tracks values to do trending analysis. When the HR Display object runs, it creates an HR Sensor object via a Wrapped Sensor object. The HR Display object also notifies the HR Trend object to begin tracking the heart rate information (via the Wrapped Sensor object).

Later, the HR Display is destroyed. It calls the delete operation on the Wrapped Sensor class. The Wrapped Sensor decrements its reference count but does not delete the HR Sensor because the reference count is greater than zero (the HR Trend DB still has a valid reference to it). Later on, when the HR Trend DB removes the last pointer to the HR Sensor object, the HR Sensor object is finally deleted.

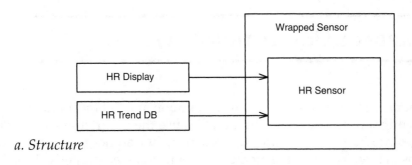

a. Structure

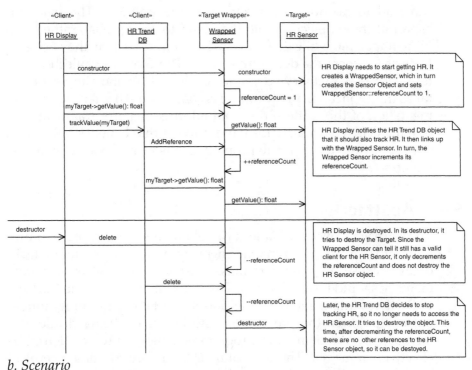

b. Scenario

Figure 6-9: *Smart Pointer Pattern Example*

6.6 GARBAGE COLLECTION PATTERN

Memory defects are among the most common and yet most difficult to identify errors. They are common because the programming languages provide very low access to memory but do not provide the means to identify when the memory is being accessed properly. This can lead to memory leaks and dangling pointers. The insidious aspect of these defects is that they tend to have global, rather than local, impact, so while they can crash the entire system, they leave no trace as to where the defect may occur. The Garbage Collection Pattern addresses memory access defects in a clean and simple way as far as the application programmer is concerned. The standard implementation of this pattern does not address memory fragmentation (see the Garbage Compactor Pattern to get that benefit), but it does allow the system to operate properly in the face of poorly managed memory.

6.6.1 Abstract

The Garbage Collection Pattern can eliminate memory leaks in programs that must use dynamic memory allocation. Memory leaks occur because programmers make mistakes about when and how memory should be deallocated. The solution offered by the Garbage Collection Pattern removes the defects by taking the programmer out of the loop—the programmer no longer explicitly deallocates memory. By removing the programmer, that source of defects is effectively removed. The costs of this pattern are run-time overhead to identify and remove inaccessible memory and a loss of execution predictability because it cannot be determined at design time when it may be necessary to reclaim freed memory.

6.6.2 Problem

The Garbage Collection Pattern addresses the problem of how we can make sure we won't have any memory leaks. Many high-availability or high-reliabilty systems must function for long periods of time without being periodically shut down. Since memory leaks lead to unstable behavior, it may be necessary to completely avoid them in such systems. Furthermore, reference counting Smart Pointers (see Smart Pointer Pattern, earlier in this chapter) have the disadvantages that they require programmer discipline to use correctly and cannot be used when there are cyclic object references.

6.6.3 Pattern Structure

Figure 6-10 shows the pattern for what is called *Mark and Sweep* garbage collection. In Mark and Sweep, garbage collection takes place in two phases: a marking phase, followed by a reclamation phase. When objects are created, they are marked as *live objects*. The marking phase is begun in response to a low memory or an explicit request to perform garbage collection. In the marking phase, each of the *root* objects is searched to find all live objects. Objects that cannot be reached in this way are marked as dead. In the subsequent sweep phase, all the objects marked as dead are reclaimed. The garbage collector must stop normal processing before performing its duties, reducing the predictability of real-time systems.

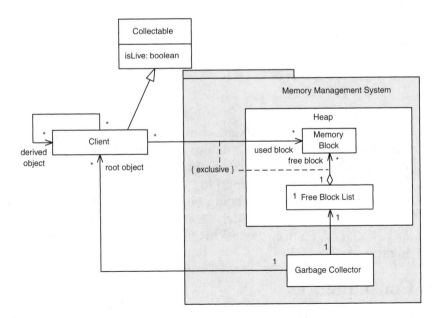

Figure 6-10: *Garbage Collection Pattern (Mark and Sweep)*

6.6.4 Collaboration Roles

- *Client*
  The *Client* is the user-defined object that allocates memory (generally, although not necessarily, in the form of objects). It is a subclass of *Collectable* and contains pointers to *derived objects*, allowing the *garbage collector* to search from the so-called *root objects* to all derived objects. When created, the object is marked as live with is *isLive* attribute, inherited from *Collectable.* On the second pass, all objects not marked as live are removed—that is, added back to the heap free memory.

- *Collectable*
  This is the base class for *Client,* and it provides the *isLive* Boolean attribute used during the garbage collection process.

- *Free Block List*
  A list of free blocks from which requests for dynamic memory are fulfilled.

- *Garbage Collector*
  The *Garbage Collector* manages the reclamation of memory by searching the object space starting with the root objects, looking at all blocks to ensure their liveness, and removing all those that are no longer live—in other words, those that cannot be reached in some fashion from a root or derived object.

- *Heap*
  The *Heap* is the owner of all the *Memory Blocks* and the *Free Block List.*

- *Memory Block*
  The *Memory Block* is just like it sounds: a block (normally of arbitrary size, in which case it contains a *size* parameter) of memory, usually, although not necessarily, associated with an object. *Memory Blocks* may be pointed to by the *Free Block List,* in which case they are not currently being pointed to by a *Client* or may be pointed to by a *Client,* in which case they are not pointed to by the *Free Block List.* Hence, the {exclusive} constraint on the relations to those classes.

6.6.5 Consequences

This architectural pattern removes the vast majority of memory-related problems by effectively eliminating memory leaks and dangling pointers. It is *still* possible to do bad pointer arithmetic, but they account for a relatively small number of defects compared to the first two memory-management defects. Further, there is much less need to do pointer arithmetic when memory is collected and managed for you. The use of this pattern removes these user defects by eliminating reliance on the user to correctly deallocate memory. The garbage collector runs episodically when a "low-memory" condition is detected and deallocates all inaccessible memory. Following garbage collection, all non-NULL pointers and references are valid, and all unreferenced memory is freed. The pattern correctly identifies and handles circular references, unlike the *Smart Pointer Pattern*.

Since this pattern uses a two-pass mark-and-sweep algorithm, it takes a nontrivial amount of time to do a complete memory cleanup. This has two negative consequences. First, considerable processing time and effort may be required to perform the memory reclamation, and it cannot, in general, be predicted how much time and effort will be required. Second, because it is done in response to a low-memory condition (such as a request for memory that cannot be fulfilled), *when* it occurs is likewise unpredictable. This means that while the approach scales up to large-scale system well in terms of managing complexity, it may not work well in systems with hard real-time constraints.

Another difficulty with this approach is that it does not affect *fragmentation*, a key problem in systems that must run for long periods of time. Memory will be reclaimed properly, but it will result in fragmented free space. This means that although enough memory may be free to fulfill a request for memory, there may not be a single contiguous block available to fulfill the request. In fact, with this pattern (and most other memory management patterns) fragmentation increases monotonically the longer the system runs. The *Garbage Compactor Pattern*, described in the next section, addresses this need.

6.6.6 Implementation Strategies

As with all such patterns, the simplest way to use this pattern is to *buy* it. Some languages, such as Java, provide memory management systems that use garbage collection out of the box. Where such languages are not available, the implementation of such a memory management schema can be done easily in the naïve case and with more difficulty in the more optimized case.

A common optimization is to allow the application objects to explicitly request a garbage collection pass when it is convenient for the application, such as when the application is quiescent. For example, if the concurrency model is managed by a cyclic executive (see the *Cyclic Executive Pattern*), then at the end of the cycle, if there is sufficient time, a memory cleanup may be performed. If it cannot be guaranteed that the garbage collection will complete before the next cycle occurs, the garbage collector may be preemptable, so that it is stopped prior to completion, allowing the application to run and meet its deadlines. When using such a strategy, be careful that you do not assume that the object marked as live on the previous pass has remained live.

6.6.7 Related Patterns

When the inherent unpredictability of the system cannot be tolerated, another approach, such as the *Smart Pointer Pattern* or *Fixed Size Allocation Pattern*, should be used. To eliminate memory fragmentation, the *Garbage Compactor Pattern* works well. The Static Allocation Pattern does not have fragmentation, and the Fixed Sized Allocation Pattern does its best to minimize fragmentation. The Smart Pointer Pattern cannot handle circular references, but the Garbage Collection and Garbage Compactor Patterns do.

6.6.8 Sample Model

Figures 6-11a, b, and c show instance snapshots of allocated memory. In the figures, Ob1 and Ob2 are root objects, known to the Garbage Collector. These might be, for example, initial instances created in the main() of the application. Objects Ob1a, Ob1b, and Ob1c are *derived* objects that can be found by traversing the links from Ob1 and Ob2 in Figure 6-11a. In Figure 6-11b, the link from Ob1 to Ob1a is broken. This means that Ob1a and Ob1b are no longer accessible to the system, since they cannot be found through a traversal of links from root objects. Note that Ob1c remains accessible via the link through the root object Ob2. In Figure 6-11c, we see that the memory used by Ob1a and Ob1b is reclaimed, and only accessible objects remain.

Figure 6-12 shows how the garbage collector proceeds. First, every object in the heap is marked as dead. Subsequently, each root

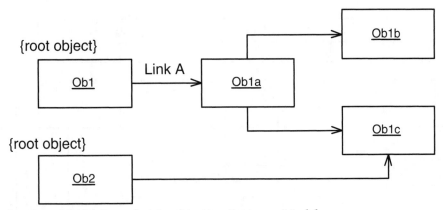

a. Instance Model Snapshot 1—Starting Instance Model

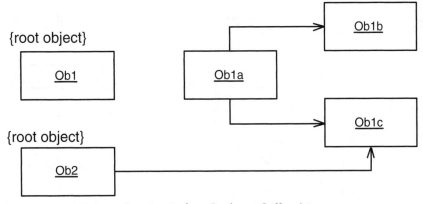

b. Instance Model Snapshot 2—Before Garbage Collection

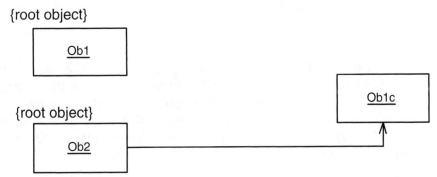

c. Instance Model Snapshot 3—After Garbage Collection

Figure 6-11: *Garbage Collection Pattern*

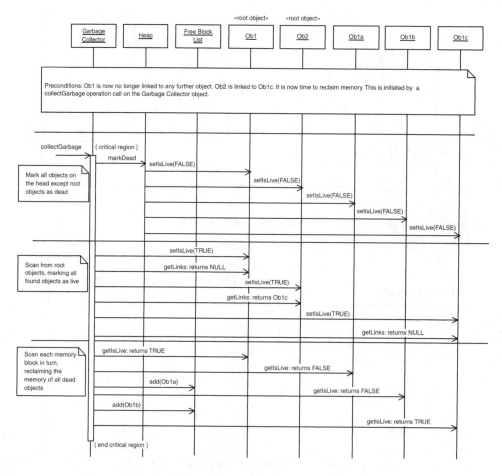

Figure 6-12: *Garbage Collection Pattern Example Scenario*

object is searched. As objects are found, they are marked as live by setting the *isLive* attribute to TRUE. In the second pass, the garbage collector does a linear search through all the allocated memory blocks, removing those that are still marked dead. This is done by first calling the object's destructor (if one exists) and then adding the object to be deleted to the *Free Block List*.

6.7 GARBAGE COMPACTOR PATTERN

6.7.1 Abstract

The Garbage Compactor Pattern is a variant of the Garbage Collection Pattern that also removes memory fragmentation. It accomplishes this goal by maintaining two memory segments in the heap. During garbage collection, live objects are moved from one segment to the next, so in the target segment, the objects are juxtapositioned adjacent to each other. The free memory in the segment then starts out as a contiguous block.

6.7.2 Problem

The Garbage Collection Pattern solves the problem of programmers forgetting to release memory by every so often finding inaccessible objects and removing them. The pattern has a couple of problems, including maintaining the timeliness of the application and fragmentation. Fragmentation means that the free memory is broken up into noncontiguous blocks. If the application is allowed to allocate blocks in whatever size they may be needed, most applications that dynamically allocate and release blocks will eventually get into the situation where although there is enough total memory to meet the allocation request, there isn't a single contiguous block large enough. At this point, the application fails. Garbage collection per se does not solve this problem just because it finds and removes dead objects. To compact memory, the allocated blocks must be moved around periodically to leave the free memory as a single, large contiguous block.

6.7.3 Pattern Structure

Figure 6-13 shows the structural pattern for *copying garbage collection*. A copying garbage collector works in a single phase. It is initiated in the same way as a mark and sweep garbage collector. As it searches the object space from the root objects, it copies all the live objects it finds to another memory space. It is more efficient than mark and sweep because a single phase is all that is necessary, and it also

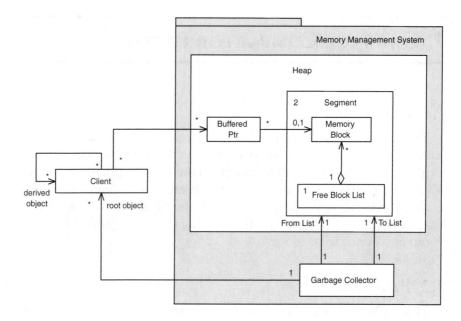

Figure 6-13: *Garbage Compactor Pattern*

eliminates memory fragmentation because it compacts memory as it moves the referenced objects. The copying garbage collector must update object references as it moves objects. This pattern requires twice as much memory as the mark and sweep pattern because it must always maintain both a *from space* and a *to space* (although they will reverse roles on subsequent invocations of the garbage collector). In addition, a copying garbage collector requires that user objects reference heap objects via double buffering—that is, their pointers must point to pointers owned by the heap. This allows the garbage collector to update its internal pointer references to the actual location of the heap object as it moves around. Either that, or the garbage collector must have references to the user objects and modify their pointers *in vivo* when the referenced heap object is relocated.

6.7.4 Collaboration Roles

- *Buffered Ptr*
  The *Buffered Ptr* is an intermediary between one object's reference to the object being referenced. This is required because the

Garbage Compactor must update the references to the objects as it moves them. This is far simpler if the actual references to the memory location are under its control rather than the object's clients.

- *Client*
  The *Client* is the user-defined object that allocates memory (generally, although not necessarily, in the form of objects). During the collection process, root objects are searched, and objects found during the search are moved as they are found.

- *Free Block List*
  A list of free blocks from which requests for dynamic memory are fulfilled.

- *Garbage Compactor*
  The *Garbage Compactor* manages the reclamation of memory by searching the object space starting with the root objects and copying the found objects from the current memory segment to the target memory segment. Dead objects are not copied and are thus automatically reclaimed.

- *Heap*
  The *Heap* is the owner of all the *Segments* and *Buffered Ptrs*. The heap fills all memory requests from the currently *active segment* and ignores the *inactive segment*. The roles the two segments play swap each time the *Garbage Compactor* performs the garbage compaction process.

- *Memory Block*
  The *Memory Block* is just like it sounds: a block (normally of arbitrary size, in which case it contains a *size* parameter) of memory usually, although not necessarily, associated with an object. *Memory Blocks* may be pointed to by the *Free Block List*—in which case they are not currently being pointed to by a *Client*—or may be pointed to by a *Client* (via a *Buffered Ptr*)—in which case they are not pointed to by the *Free Block List*.

- *Segment*
  The heap maintains two segments that are alternatively swapped in terms of use. The one in use is called the *active segment*, and the other is called the *inactive segment*. From the *Garbage Compactor's* point of view, which is taken during the compaction process, one

is the *from segment* and the other is the *target segment.* The *Active Segment* is used to fill all requests for dynamic memory allocation. During compaction, all live objects are copied from the *from segment* to the *target segment,* and then the *target segment* is set to be the *Heap's active segment.*

6.7.5 Consequences

The most noticeable consequence of using the Garbage Compactor Pattern is that the programmers don't need to deallocate their objects (the Garbage Compactor does it for them) and that fragmentation does not monotonically increase the longer the system runs. Fragmentation increases for a while but is reduced to zero when the Garbage Compactor runs. Since the Garbage Compactor runs when a request for memory cannot be satisfied, this means that if there is enough total memory to meet a request, the request will always be satisfied.

Another highly noticeable consequence of this pattern, at least in terms of memory requirements, is that the pattern requires twice as much memory as the *Garbage Collection Pattern.* Assuming that each *Segment* is large enough to hold the worst-case memory needs at any moment in time, the pattern requires two such segments. This makes this approach inappropriate when there are tight memory size requirements.

Doing pointer arithmetic with the Garbage Compactor Pattern is a chancy thing for a number of reasons. However, since the main reason for doing pointer arithmetic is to manage memory, this should not cause many difficulties.

Of course, the length of time necessary to run the compactor is an issue for any application in which timeliness is a concern. There is a small amount of overhead for the double buffering of the pointers, but the major timeliness impact comes from the time and cycles necessary to identify the live objects and copy them to the target memory segment. This pattern requires more CPU cycles to run than the Garbage Collection Pattern because of the overhead of copying objects, but with care, it may be possible to run the garbage collector piecemeal to implement an incremental garbage compactor at the cost of recomputing which objects in the From segment are still live.

Because the reclaimed objects are not destroyed per se, their destructors are not called. If there are finalizing behaviors required of the objects (other than the normal release of memory), then the programmer must still manually ensure these behaviors are invoked before removing their references to the objects.

6.7.6 Implementation Strategies

There are a number of small details to be managed by the memory management system in this pattern. The use of *Buffered Ptrs* allows the *Garbage Compactor* to move the objects and then update the location in a single place. If the source language is interpreted, such as Java, then the virtual machine can easily manage the double pointer referencing required of the client objects (in other words, their pointers are to *Buffered Ptrs*, which ultimately point to the actual memory used). If the source language produces native code, then the *new* operator must be rewritten to not only allocate the *Memory Block* per se but also create a *Buffered Pts* as well.

6.7.7 Related Patterns

As with the Garbage Collection Pattern, this pattern can seriously impact the predictability of timeliness of systems using it. When timeliness is a primary concern, the Static Allocation, Fixed Sized Buffer, or Smart Pointer Patterns may be better. The Garbage Collection Pattern has the benefit of removing memory leaks, and it requires less memory than the Garbage Compactor Pattern, but it doesn't address memory fragmentation. The Static Allocation and Fixed Sized Allocation Patterns remove or reduce fragmentation but are not immune to memory leaks.

6.7.8 Sample Model

The example shown in Figure 6-14 is the same as for the previous pattern. Figure 6-15 shows a scenario of the system as it collects the garbage. We see that when the Garbage Collector is started, it first requests Segment 2 (the target segment) to initialize itself so that it is ready to begin copying memory into itself. Because it always starts empty, there is no fragmentation within the segment

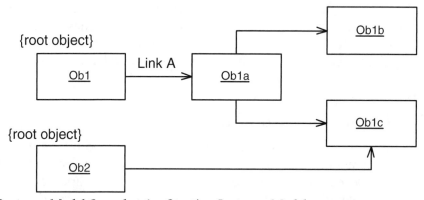

a. Instance Model Snapshot 1—Starting Instance Model

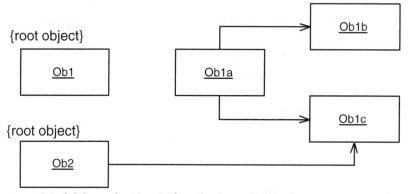

b. Instance Model Snapshot 2—Before Garbage Collection

c. Instance Model Snapshot 3—After Garbage Collection

Figure 6-14: *Garbage Compactor Pattern*

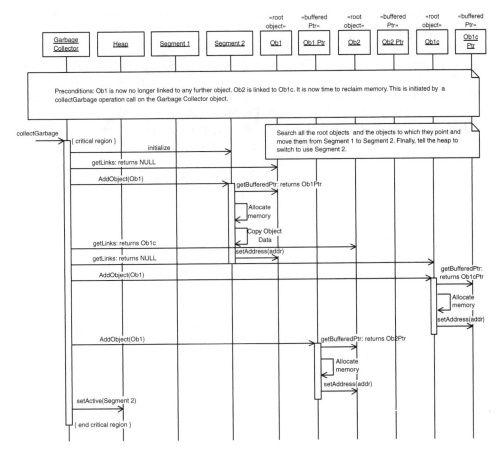

Figure 6-15: *Garbage Compactor Pattern Example Scenario*

as memory blocks are allocated one after another in a contiguous fashion.

Then the garbage collector searches the root objects. As it finds a root object, it asks if it has any valid links. First, in the case of Ob1, it finds two valid links, so the Garbage Collector can pass the object Ob1 off to the AddObject operation of the target segment (Segment 2). The segment, in turn, gets the location of the buffer pointer for the memory, allocates a new memory block to store Ob1's data, and then copies the object from the original segment. Finally it updates Obj1's buffered pointer to point to its data's new location.

6.8 References

[1] Gamma, E., R. Helm, R. Johnson, and J. Vlissides. *Design Patterns: Elements of Reusable Object-Oriented Software*, Reading, MA: Addison-Wesley, 1995.

[2] Jones, R., and R. Lins. *Garbage Collection: Algorithms for Automatic Dynamic Memory Management*, West Sussex, England: John Wiley & Sons, 1996.

[3] Noble, J., C. Weir. *Small Memory Software: Patterns for Systems with Limited Memory*, Reading, MA: Addison-Wesley, 2001.

Chapter 7

Resource Patterns

The following patterns are presented in this chapter.

- Critical Section Pattern: Uses resources run-to-completion
- Priority Inheritance Pattern: Limits priority inversion
- Highest Locker Pattern: Limits priority inversion
- Priority Ceiling Pattern: Limits priority inversion and prevents deadlock
- Simultaneous Locking Pattern: Prevents deadlock
- Ordered Locking Pattern: Prevents deadlock

7.1 Introduction

One of the distinguishing characteristics of real-time and embedded systems is the concern over management of finite resources. This chapter provides a number of patterns to help organize, manage, use, and share such resources. There is some overlap of concerns with the patterns in this and other chapters. For example, the Smart Pointer Pattern provides a robust access to resources of a certain type: those that are dynamically allocated. However, that pattern has already been discussed in Chapter 6. Similarly, the synchronization of concurrent threads may be thought of as resource management, but it is dealt with using the Rendezvous Pattern from Chapter 5. This chapter focuses on patterns that deal with the sharing and management of resources themselves and not the memory they use. To this end, we'll examine a number of ways to manage resources among different, possibly concurrent, clients.

A *resource*, as used here, is a thing (an object) that provides services to clients that have finite properties or characteristics. This definition is consistent with the so-called Real-Time UML Profile [1], where a resource is defined as follows.

> An element that has resource services whose effectiveness is represented by one or more Quality of Service (QoS) characteristics.

The QoS properties are the quantitative properties of the resource, such as its capacity, execution speed, reliability, and so on. In real-time and embedded systems, it is this quantifiable finiteness that must be managed. For instance, it is common for a resource to provide services in an atomic fashion; this means that the client somehow "locks" the resource while it needs it, preventing other clients from accessing that resource until the original client is done. This accomplishes the more general purpose of *serialization* of resource usage, crucial to the correct operation in systems with concurrent threads. This is often accomplished with a mutex semaphore (see the Guarded Call Pattern in Chapter 5) or may be done by serializing the requests themselves (see the Message Queuing Pattern, also in Chapter 5).

The management of resources with potentially many clients is one of the more thorny aspects of system design, and a number of patterns have evolved or been designed over time to deal specifically with just that.

The first few patterns (Priority Inheritance, Highest Locker, Priority Ceiling) address the schedulability of resources in a priority-based pre-emptive multitasking environment, which can be a major concern for real-time systems design. In static priority scheduling approaches (see, for example, the Static Priority Pattern in Chapter 5), the priorities of the tasks are known at design time. The priority of the task determines which tasks will run preferentially when multiple tasks are ready to run—the highest-priority task that is ready. This makes the timing analysis of such systems very easy to compute, as long as certain assumptions are not violated too badly. These assumptions are the following.

- Tasks are periodic with the deadlines coming at the end of the periods.
- Infinite preemptibility—a lower-priority task can be preempted immediately when a higher-priority task becomes ready to run.
- Independence—tasks are independent from each other.

When these conditions are true, then the following standard rate monotonic analysis formula may be applied.

$$\sum_{n} \frac{C_j}{T_j} \leq n \left(2^{\frac{1}{n}} - 1 \right)$$

Note that it is "2 raised to the power of (1/n)", where C_j is the worst-case amount of time required for task j to execute, T_j is its period, and n is the number of tasks. [2], [3] If the inequality is true, then the system is *schedulable*—that is, the system will *always* meet its deadlines. Aperiodic tasks are generally handled by assuming they are periodic and using the minimum arrival time between task invocations as the period, often resulting in an overly strong but sufficient condition. The assumption of infinite pre-emptibility is usually not a problem if the task has very short critical sections during which it cannot be preempted—short with respect to the execution and period times. The problem of independence is, however, much stickier.

If resources are sharable (in the sense that they can permit simultaneous access by multiple clients), then no problem exists. However many, if not most, resources cannot be shared. The common solution to this problem was addressed in the Guarded Call Pattern of Chapter 5 using a mutual-exclusion semaphore to serialize access to the resource. This means that if a low-priority task locks a resource and then a higher-priority task that needs the resource becomes ready to run, it must *block* and allow the low-priority task to run until it can release the resource so that the higher-priority task can run. A simple example of this is shown in the timing diagram in Figure 7-1.

In the figure, Task 1 is the higher-priority task. Since Task 2 runs first and locks the resource, when Task 1 is ready to run, it cannot because the needed resource is unavailable. It therefore must block and allow Task 2 to complete its use of the resource. During the period of time between marks C and D, Task 1 is said to be *blocked*. A task is blocked when it is prevented from running by a lower-priority task. This can only occur when resources are shared via mutual exclusion.

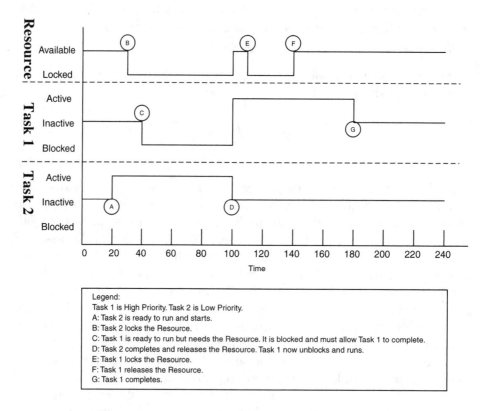

Legend:
Task 1 is High Priority. Task 2 is Low Priority.
A: Task 2 is ready to run and starts.
B: Task 2 locks the Resource.
C: Task 1 is ready to run but needs the Resource. It is blocked and must allow Task 1 to complete.
D: Task 2 completes and releases the Resource. Task 1 now unblocks and runs.
E: Task 1 locks the Resource.
F: Task 1 releases the Resource.
G: Task 1 completes.

Figure 7-1: *Task Blocking[1]*

---

1. A note about notation. These are *timing diagrams*. They show linear time along the X-axis and "state" or "condition," a discrete value, along the Y-axis. For more information, see [4].

The problem with blocking is that the analysis of the timeliness becomes more difficult. When Task 1 is blocked, the system is said to be in a state of *priority inversion* because a lower-priority task has the thread focus even though a higher-priority task is ready to run. One can imagine third and fourth tasks of intermediate priority that don't share the resource (and are therefore able to preempt Task 2) running and preempting Task 2, thereby lengthening the amount of time before Task 2 releases the resource and allowing Task 1 to run. Because an arbitrary number of tasks can be fit in the priority scheme between Task 1 and Task 2, this problem is called *unbounded priority inversion* and is a serious problem for the schedulability of tasks. Figure 7-2 illustrates this problem by adding intermediate-priority Tasks X and Y to the system. Note that for some period of time, Task 1, the highest-priority task in the system, is blocked by *all three* remaining tasks.

To compute the schedulability for task sets with blocking, the modified RMA inequality is used.

$$\sum_j \frac{C_j}{T_j} + \max\left(\frac{B_1}{T_1}, \cdots, \frac{B_{n-1}}{T_{n-1}}\right) \leq n\left(2^{\frac{1}{n}} - 1\right)$$

where B_j is the blocking time for task j—that is, the worst-case time that the task can be prevented from execution by a lower-priority task owning a needed resource. The problem is clear from the inequality—unbounded blocking means unbounded blocking time, and nothing useful can be said about the ability of such a system to meet its deadlines.

Unbounded priority inversion is a problem that is addressed by the first three patterns in this chapter. Note that priority inversion is a necessary consequence of resource sharing with mutual exclusion locking, but it can be bounded using these patterns.

These first three patterns solve, or at least address, the problem of resource sharing for schedulability purposes, but for the most part they don't deal with the issue of deadlock. A deadlock is a condition in which clients of resources are waiting for conditions to arise that cannot in principle ever occur. An example of deadlock is shown in Figure 7-3.

In Figure 7-3, there are two tasks, Task 1 and Task 2, that share two resources, R1 and R2. Task 1 plans to lock R2 and then lock R1 and release them in the opposite order. Task 2 plans to lock R1 and then R2 and release them in the reverse order. The problem arises when Task 1 preempts Task 2 when it has a single resource (R1) locked. Task 1 is a higher

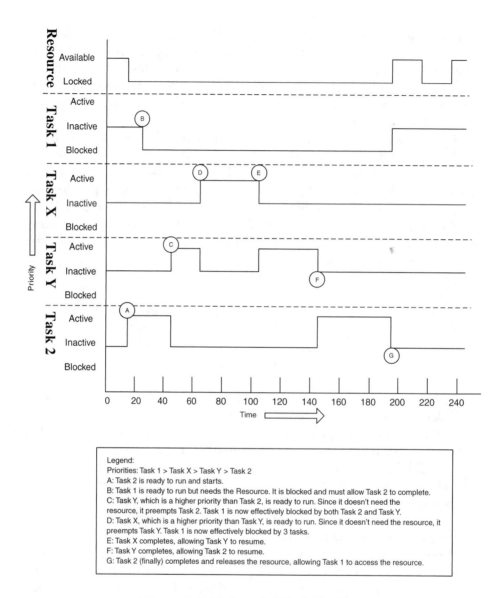

Figure 7-2: *Unbounded Task Blocking*

Legend:
Priorities: Task 1 > Task X > Task Y > Task 2
A: Task 2 is ready to run and starts.
B: Task 1 is ready to run but needs the Resource. It is blocked and must allow Task 2 to complete.
C: Task Y, which is a higher priority than Task 2, is ready to run. Since it doesn't need the resource, it preempts Task 2. Task 1 is now effectively blocked by both Task 2 and Task Y.
D: Task X, which is a higher priority than Task Y, is ready to run. Since it doesn't need the resource, it preempts Task Y. Task 1 is now effectively blocked by 3 tasks.
E: Task X completes, allowing Task Y to resume.
F: Task Y completes, allowing Task 2 to resume.
G: Task 2 (finally) completes and releases the resource, allowing Task 1 to access the resource.

priority, so it can preempt Task 1, and it doesn't need a currently locked resource, so things are fine. It goes ahead and locks R2. Now it decides that it needs the other resource, R1, which, unfortunately is locked by the

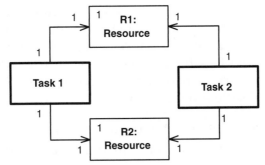

a. Deadlocked Class Structure

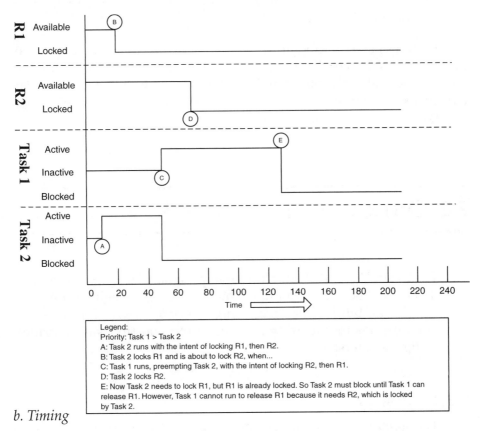

Legend:
Priority: Task 1 > Task 2
A: Task 2 runs with the intent of locking R1, then R2.
B: Task 2 locks R1 and is about to lock R2, when...
C: Task 1 runs, preempting Task 2, with the intent of locking R2, then R1.
D: Task 2 locks R2.
E: Now Task 2 needs to lock R1, but R1 is already locked. So Task 2 must block until Task 1 can release R1. However, Task 1 cannot run to release R1 because it needs R2, which is locked by Task 2.

b. Timing

Figure 7-3: *Deadlock*

blocked task, Task 2. So Task 1 cannot move forward and must block in order to allow Task 2 to run until it can release the now needed resource (R1). So Task 2 runs but finds that it now needs the other resource (R2) owned by the blocked Task 1. At this point, each task is waiting for a condition that can never be satisfied, and the system stops.

In principle, a deadlock needs the following four conditions to occur.

1. Mutual exclusion (locking) of resources
2. Resources are held (locked) while others are waited for
3. Preemption while holding resources is permitted
4. A circular wait condition exists (for example, P1 waits on P2, which waits on P3, which waits on P1)

The patterns for addressing deadlock try to ensure that at least one of the four necessary conditions for deadlock cannot occur. The Simultaneous Locking Pattern breaks condition 2, while the Ordered Locking Pattern breaks condition 4. The Priority Ceiling Pattern is a pattern that solves both the scheduling problem and the deadlock problem.

7.2 CRITICAL SECTION PATTERN

The Critical Section Pattern is the simplest pattern to share resources that cannot be shared simultaneously. It is lightweight and easy to implement, but it may prevent high priority tasks, even ones that don't use *any* resources, from meeting their deadlines if the critical section lasts too long.

7.2.1 Abstract

This pattern has been long used in the design of real-time and embedded systems whenever a resource must have at most a single owner at any given time. The basic idea is to lock the Scheduler whenever a resource is accessed to prevent another task from simultaneously accessing it. The primary advantage of this pattern is its simplicity, both in terms of understandability and in terms of implementation. It becomes less applicable when the resource access may take a long time because it means that higher-priority tasks may be blocked from execution for a long period of time.

7.2.2 Problem

The main problem addressed by the Critical Section Pattern is how to robustly share resources that may have, at most, a single owner at any given time.

7.2.3 Pattern Structure

Figure 7-4 shows the basic structural elements in the Critical Section Pattern.

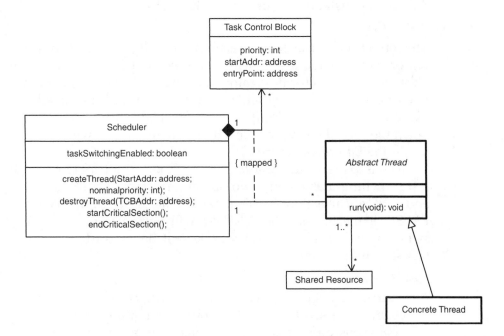

Figure 7-4: *Critical Section Pattern*

7.2.4 Collaboration Roles

- *Abstract Thread*
  The *Abstract Thread* class is an abstract (noninstantiable) super-class for *Concrete Thread*. *Abstract Thread* associates with the *Scheduler*. Since *Concrete Thread* is a subclass, it has the same interface to the *Scheduler* as the *Abstract Thread*. This enforces interface compliance. The *Abstract Thread* is an «active» object, meaning that when it is created, it creates an OS thread in which to run. It contains (that is, it has composition relations with) more primitive application objects that execute in the thread of the composite «active» object.

- *Concrete Thread*
  The *Concrete Thread* is an «active» object most typically constructed to contain passive "semantic" objects (via the composition relation) that do the real work of the system. The *Concrete Thread* object provides a straightforward means of attaching these semantic objects into the concurrency architecture. *Concrete Thread* is an instantiable subclass of *Abstract Thread*.

- *Scheduler*
  This object orchestrates the execution of multiple threads based on some scheme requiring preemption. When the «active» *Thread* object is created, it (or its creator) calls the *createThread* operation to create a thread for the «active» object. Whenever this thread is executed by the *Scheduler*, it calls the StartAddr address (except when the thread has been blocked or preempted—in which case it calls the *EntryPoint* address).

  In this pattern, the *Scheduler* has a Boolean attribute called taskSwitchingEnabled and two operations, startCriticalSection() and endCriticalSection(), which manipulate this attribute. When FALSE, it means that the *Scheduler* will not perform any task switching; when TRUE, tasks will be switched according to the task scheduling policies in force.

- *Shared Resource*
  A resource is an object shared by one or more *Threads* but cannot be reliably accessed by more than one client at any given time. All operations defined on this resource that access any part of the resource that is not simultaneously sharable (its nonreentrant parts) should call *Scheduler.startCriticalSection()* before

they manipulate the internal values of the resource and should call *Scheduler.endCriticalSection()* when they are done.

- *Task Control Block*
The TCB contains the scheduling information for its corresponding *Thread* object. This includes the priority of the thread, the default start address, and the current entry address if it was preempted or blocked prior to completion. The *Scheduler* maintains a TCB object for each existing *Thread.* Note that TCB typically also has a reference off to a call and parameter stack for its *Thread,* but that level of detail is not shown in Figure 7-4.

7.2.5 Consequences

The designers and programmers must show good discipline in ensuring that every resource access locks the resource before performing any manipulation of the source. This pattern works by effectively making the current task the highest-priority task in the system. While quite successful at preventing resource corruption due to simultaneous access, it locks out all higher-priority tasks from executing during the critical section, even if they don't require the use of the resource. Many systems find this blocking delay unacceptable and must use more elaborate means for resource sharing. Further, if the initial task that locks the resource neglects to deescalate its priority, then all other tasks are permanently prevented from running. Calculation of the worst-case blocking for each task is trivial with this pattern: It is simply the longest critical section of any single task of lesser priority.

It is perhaps obvious, but should nevertheless be stated, that when using this pattern a task should never suspend itself while owning a resource because task switching is disabled so that in a situation like that no tasks are permitted to run at all. This pattern has the advantage in that it avoids deadlock by breaking the second condition (holding resources while waiting for others) as long as the task releases the resource (and reenables task switching) before it suspends itself.

7.2.6 Implementation Strategies

All commercial RTOSs have a means for beginning and ending a critical section. Invoking this Scheduler operation prevents all task switching from occurring during the critical section. If you write your own RTOS, the most common way to do this is to set the Disable Interrupts bit on your processor's flags register. The precise details of this vary, naturally, depending on the specific processor.

7.2.7 Related Patterns

As mentioned, this is the simplest pattern that addresses the issue of sharing nonreentrant resources. Other resource sharing approaches, such as Priority Inheritance, Highest Locker, and Priority Ceiling Patterns, solve this problem as well with less impact on the schedulability of the overall system but at the cost of increased complexity. This pattern can be mixed with all of the concurrency patterns from Chapter 5, except the Cyclic Executive Pattern, for which resource sharing is a nonissue.

7.2.8 Sample Model

An example of the use of this pattern is shown in Figure 7-5. This example contains three tasks: Device Test (highest priority), Motor Control (medium priority), and Data Processing (lowest priority). Device Test and Data Processing share a resource called Sensor, whereas Motor Control has its own resource called Motor.

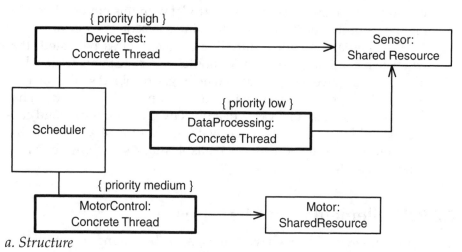

a. Structure

Figure 7-5: *Critical Section Pattern Example*

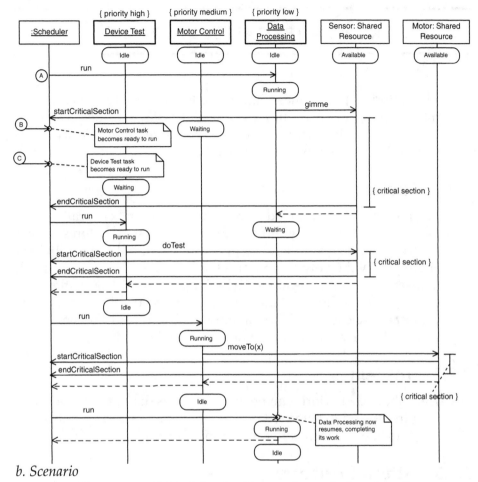

b. Scenario

Figure 7-5: *Critical Section Pattern Example (continued)*

The scenario starts off with the lowest-priority task, Data Processing, accessing the resource that starts up a critical section. During this critical section both the Motor Control task and the Device Test task become ready to run but cannot because task switching is disabled. When the call to the resource is almost done, the *Sensor.gimme()* operation makes a call to the scheduler to end the critical section. The scenario shows three critical sections, one for each of the running tasks. Finally, at the end, the lowest-priority task is allowed to complete its work and then returns to its Idle state.

7.3 PRIORITY INHERITANCE PATTERN

The Priority Inheritance Pattern reduces priority inversion by manipulating the executing priorities of tasks that lock resources. While not an ideal solution, it significantly reduces priority inversion at a relatively low run-time overhead cost.

7.3.1 Abstract

The problem of unbounded priority inversion is a very real one and has accounted for many difficult-to-identify system failures. In systems running many tasks, such problems may not be at all obvious, and typically the only symptom is that occasionally the system fails to meet one or more deadlines. The Priority Inheritance Pattern is a simple, low-overhead solution for limiting the priority inversion to at most a single level—that is, at most, a task will only be blocked by a single, lower-priority task owning a needed resource.

7.3.2 Problem

The unbounded priority inversion problem is discussed in the chapter introduction in some detail. The problem addressed by this pattern is to bound the maximum amount of priority inversion.

7.3.3 Pattern Structure

Figure 7-6 shows the structure of the pattern. The basic elements of this pattern are familiar: Scheduler, Abstract Task, Task Control Block, and so on. This can be thought of as an elaborated subset of the Static Priority Pattern, presented in Chapter 5. Note the use of the «frozen» constraint applied to the Task Control Block's *nominalPriority* attribute. This means the attribute is unchangeable once the object is created.

7.3.4 Collaboration Roles

*   *Abstract Thread*
    The *Abstract Thread* class is an abstract (noninstantiable) superclass for *Concrete Thread*. *Abstract Thread* associates with the *Scheduler*.

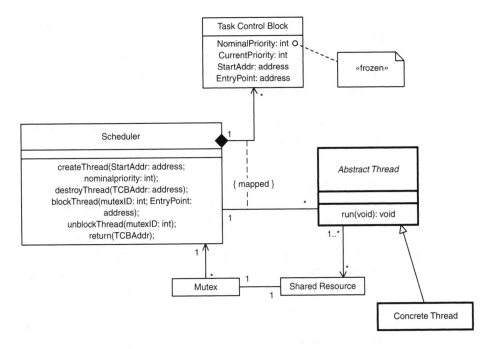

Figure 7-6: *Priority Inheritance Pattern*

Since *Concrete Thread* is a subclass, it has the same interface to the *Scheduler* as the *Abstract Thread*. This enforces interface compliance. The *Abstract Thread* is an «active» object, meaning that when it is created, it creates an OS thread in which to run. It contains (that is, it has composition relations with) more primitive application objects that execute in the thread of the composite «active» object.

- *Concrete Thread*
  The *Concrete Thread* is an «active» object most typically constructed to contain passive "semantic" objects (via the composition relation) that do the real work of the system. The *Concrete Thread* object provides a straightforward means of attaching these semantic objects into the concurrency architecture. *Concrete Thread* is an instantiable subclass of *Abstract Thread*.

- *Mutex*
  The *Mutex* is a mutual exclusion semaphore object that permits only a single caller through at a time. The operations of the *Shared Resource* invoke it whenever a relevant service is called, locking it

prior to starting the service and unlocking it once the service is complete. *Threads* that attempt to invoke a service when the services are already locked become blocked until the *Mutex* is in its unlocked state. This is done by the *Mutex* semaphore signaling the *Scheduler* that a call attempt was made by the currently active thread, the *Mutex* ID (necessary to unlock it later when the *Mutex* is released), and the entry point—the place at which to continue execution of the *Thread*.

- *Scheduler*
  This object orchestrates the execution of multiple threads based on their priority according to a simple rule: Always run the ready thread with the highest priority. When the «active» *Thread* object is created, it (or its creator) calls the *createThread* operation to create a thread for the «active» object. Whenever this thread is executed by the *Scheduler*, it calls the StartAddr address (except when the thread has been blocked or preempted, in which case it calls the *EntryPoint* address).

  In this pattern, the *Scheduler* has some special duties when the *Mutex* signals an attempt to access a locked resource: Specifically, it must block the requesting task (done by stopping that task and placing a reference to it in the *Blocked Queue* (not shown—for details of the *Blocked Queue*, see Static Priority Pattern in Chapter 5), and it must elevate the priority of the task owning the resource to that of the highest priority *Thread* being blocked. This is easy to determine since the *Blocked Queue* is a priority FIFO—the highest-priority blocked task is the first one in that queue. Similarly, when the *Thread* releases the resource, the *Scheduler* must lower its priority back to its nominal priority.

- *Shared Resource*
  A *Shared Resource* is an object shared by one or more *Threads*. For the system to operate properly in all cases, all shared resources must either be reentrant (meaning that corruption from simultaneous access cannot occur) or they must be protected. In the case of a protected resource, when a *Thread* attempts to use the resource, the associated *Mutex* semaphore is checked, and if locked, the calling task is placed into the *Blocked Queue*. The task is terminated with its reentry point noted in the TCB.

- *Task Control Block*
The TCB contains the scheduling information for its corresponding *Thread* object. This includes the priority of the thread, the default start address and the current entry address, if it was preempted or blocked prior to completion. The *Scheduler* maintains a TCB object for each existing *Thread*. Note that TCB typically also has a reference off to a call and parameter stack for its *Thread,* but that level of detail is not shown in Figure 7-6. The TCB tracks both the current priority of the thread (which may have been elevated due to resource access and blocking) and its nominal priority.

7.3.5 Consequences

The Priority Inheritance Pattern handles well the problem of priority inversion when at most a single resource is locked at any given time and prevents unbounded priority inversion in this case. This is illustrated in Figure 7-7. With naïve priority management, Task 1, the highest-priority task in the system, is delayed from execution until Task 2 has completed. Using the Priority Inheritance Pattern, Task 1 completes as early as possible.

When there are multiple resources that may be locked at any time, this pattern exhibits behavior called *chain blocking*. That is, one task may block another, which blocks another, and so on. This is illustrated in the only slightly more complex example in Figure 7-8. The timing diagram in Figure 7-8b shows that Task 1 is blocked by Task 2 *and* Task 3 at Point G.

In general, the Priority Inheritance Pattern greatly reduces unbounded blocking. In fact, though, the number of blocked tasks at any given time is bounded only by the lesser of the number of tasks and the number of currently locked resources. There is a small amount of overhead to pay when tasks are blocked or unblocked to manage the elevation or depression of the priority of the tasks involved. Computation of a single task's worst-case blocking time involves computation of the worst-case chain blocking of all tasks of lesser priority.

This pattern does not address deadlock issues at all, so it is still possible to construct task models using this pattern that have deadlock.

Another consequence of the use of the priority inheritance patterns (Priority Inheritance Pattern, Highest Locker Pattern, and Priority Ceiling Pattern) is the overhead. The use of semaphores and

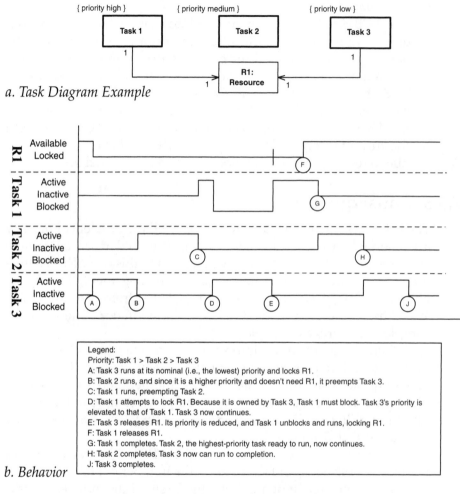

a. Task Diagram Example

b. Behavior

Legend:
Priority: Task 1 > Task 2 > Task 3
A: Task 3 runs at its nominal (i.e., the lowest) priority and locks R1.
B: Task 2 runs, and since it is a higher priority and doesn't need R1, it preempts Task 3.
C: Task 1 runs, preempting Task 2.
D: Task 1 attempts to lock R1. Because it is owned by Task 3, Task 1 must block. Task 3's priority is elevated to that of Task 1. Task 3 now continues.
E: Task 3 releases R1. Its priority is reduced, and Task 1 unblocks and runs, locking R1.
F: Task 1 releases R1.
G: Task 1 completes. Task 2, the highest-priority task ready to run, now continues.
H: Task 2 completes. Task 3 now can run to completion.
J: Task 3 completes.

Figure 7-7: *Priority Inheritance Pattern*

blocking involves task switching whenever a locked mutex is requested and another task switch whenever a waited-for mutex is released. In addition, the acts of blocking and unblocking tasks during those task context switches involves the manipulation of priority queues. Further, the use of priority inheritance means that there is some overhead in the escalation and deescalation of priorities. If blocking occurs infrequently, then this overhead will be slight, but if there is a great deal of contention for resources, then the overhead can be severe.

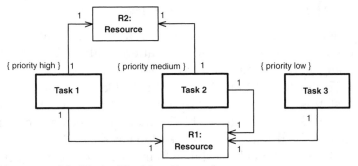

a. Task Diagram with Chain-Blocking Example

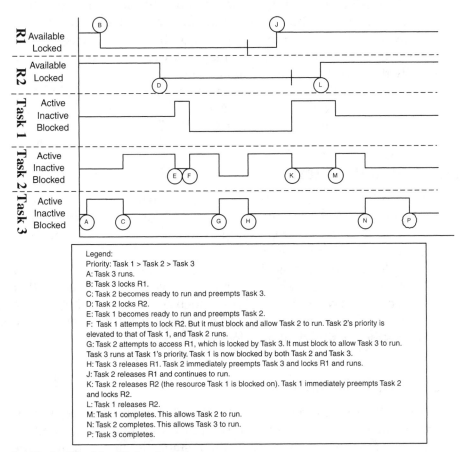

Legend:
Priority: Task 1 > Task 2 > Task 3
A: Task 3 runs.
B: Task 3 locks R1.
C: Task 2 becomes ready to run and preempts Task 3.
D: Task 2 locks R2.
E: Task 1 becomes ready to run and preempts Task 2.
F: Task 1 attempts to lock R2. But it must block and allow Task 2 to run. Task 2's priority is elevated to that of Task 1, and Task 2 runs.
G: Task 2 attempts to access R1, which is locked by Task 3. It must block to allow Task 3 to run. Task 3 runs at Task 1's priority. Task 1 is now blocked by both Task 2 and Task 3.
H: Task 3 releases R1. Task 2 immediately preempts Task 3 and locks R1 and runs.
J: Task 2 releases R1 and continues to run.
K: Task 2 releases R2 (the resource Task 1 is blocked on). Task 1 immediately preempts Task 2 and locks R2.
L: Task 1 releases R2.
M: Task 1 completes. This allows Task 2 to run.
N: Task 2 completes. This allows Task 3 to run.
P: Task 3 completes.

b. Chain-Blocking Behavior

Figure 7-8: *Priority Inheritance Pattern*

7.3.6 Implementation Strategies

Some RTOS directly support the notion of priority inheritance, and so it is very little work to use this pattern with such an RTOS. If you are using an RTOS that does not support it, or if you are writing your own RTOS, then you must extend the RTOS (many RTOSs have API for just this purpose) to call your own function when the mutex blocks a task on a resource. The *Scheduler* must be able to identify the priority of the thread being blocked (a simple matter because it is in the Task Control Block for the task) in order to elevate the priority of the task currently owning the resource.

It is possible to build in the nominal priority as a constant attribute of the Concrete Thread. When the Concrete Thread always runs at a given priority, then the constructor of the «active» object should do exactly that. Otherwise, the creator of that active object should specify the priority at which that task should run.

In virtually all other ways, the implementation is very similar to the implementation of standard concurrency patterns, such as the Static Priority Pattern presented in Chapter 5.

7.3.7 Related Patterns

The Priority Inheritance Pattern exists to help solve a particular problem peculiar to priority-based preemption multitasking, so all of the concurrency patterns having to do with that style of multitasking can be mixed with this pattern.

While this pattern is lightweight, it greatly reduces priority inversion in multitasking systems. However, there are other approaches that can reduce it further, such as Priority Ceiling Pattern and Highest Locker Pattern. In addition, Priority Ceiling Pattern also removes the possibility of deadlock.

7.3.8 Sample Model

Figure 7-9 provides an example to illustrate how the Priority Inheritance Pattern works. States of the objects are shown using standard UML—that is, as state marks on the instance lifelines. Some of the returns are shown, again using standard UML dashed lines. Showing that a call cannot complete is indicated with a large X on the call—*not* standard UML, but clear as to its interpretation.

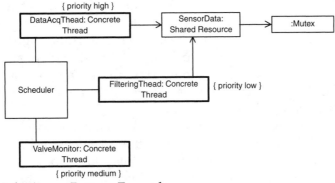

a. Priority Inheritance Pattern Example

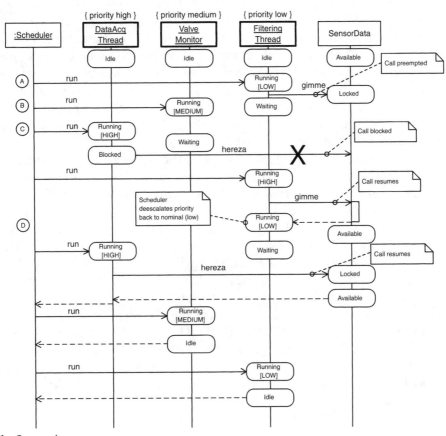

b. Scenario

Figure 7-9: *Priority Inheritance Pattern*

The flow of the scenario in Figure 7-9b is straightforward. All tasks begin the scenario in the Idle state. Then, at point A, the *FilteringThread* task becomes ready to run. It runs at its nominal priority, which is LOW (the priority of the thread is shown inside square brackets in the Running state mark—again, not quite standard UML, but parsimonious). It then calls the resource *SensorData* that then enters the Locked state.

At point B, the *ValveMonitor* task becomes ready to run. It preempts the *FilteringThread* because the former is of higher priority. The *ValveMonitor* task runs for a while, but at point C, task *DataAcqThread* becomes ready to run. Since it is the highest priority, it preempts the *ValveMonitor* thread. *DataAcqThread* object then tries to access the *SensorData* object and finds that it cannot because the latter is locked with a *Mutex* semaphore (not shown in the scenario). The *Scheduler* then blocks the *DataAcqThread* thread and runs the *FilteringThread* at the same priority as *DataAcqThread* because the *FilteringThread* inherits the priority from the highest blocking task—in this case the *DataAcqThread* task. Note at this point, the medium-priority task, *ValveMonitor,* is in the state Waiting. Without priority inheritance, if *DataAcqThread* is blocked, the *ValveMonitor* would run because it has the next highest priority.

At point D, *FilteringThread's* use of the resource is complete, and it releases the resource (done at the end of the *SensorData.gimme* operation). As it returns, the *Mutex* signals the *Scheduler* that it is now available, so the Scheduler deescalates *FilteringThread's* priority to its nominal value (LOW) and unblocks the highest-priority task, *DataAcqThread.* This task now runs to completion and returns. The *Scheduler* then runs the next highest-priority waiting task, *ValveMonitor,* which runs until it is done and returns. Finally, the lowest-priority task, *FilteringThread,* gets to complete.

The worst-case blocking time for the *DataAcqThread* task is then the amount of time that *FilteringThread* locks the *SensorData* resource. Without the Priority Inheritance Pattern, the worst-case blocking for *DataAcqThread* task would be the amount of time *FilteringThread* locks the *SensorData* resource plus the amount of time that *ValveMonitor* executes.

7.4 HIGHEST LOCKER PATTERN

The Highest Locker Pattern defines a *priority ceiling* with each resource. The basic idea is that the task owning the resource runs at the highest-priority ceiling of all the resources that it currently owns, provided that it is blocking one or more higher-priority tasks. This limits priority inversion to at most one level.

7.4.1 Abstract

The Highest Locker Pattern is another solution to the unbounded blocking/unbounded priority inversion problem. It is perhaps a minor elaboration from the Priority Inheritance Pattern, but it is different enough to have some different properties with respects to schedulability. The Highest Locker Pattern limits priority inversion to a single level as long as a task does not suspend itself while owning a resource. In this case, you may get chained blocking similar to the Priority Inheritance Pattern. Unlike the Priority Inheritance Pattern, however, you cannot get chained blocking if a task is preempted while owning a resource.

7.4.2 Problem

The unbounded priority inversion problem is discussed in the chapter introduction in some detail. The problem addressed by this pattern is to limit the maximum amount of priority inversion to a single level—that is, there is *at most* a single lower-priority task blocking a higher-priority task from executing.

7.4.3 Pattern Structure

The Highest Locker Pattern is shown in Figure 7-10. The structural elements of the pattern are the same as for the Priority Inheritance Pattern, with the addition of an attribute *priorityCeiling* for the *SharedResource*.

The pattern works by defining each lockable resource with a priority ceiling. The priority ceiling is just greater than the priority of the

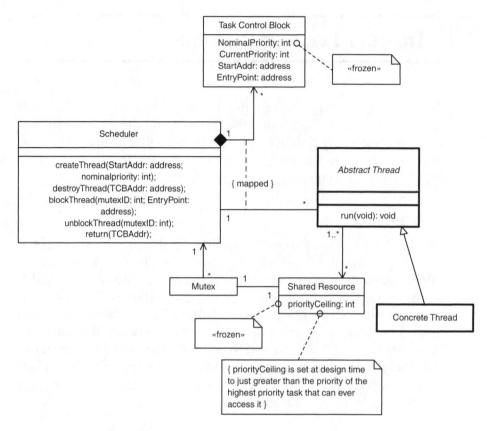

Figure 7-10: *Highest Locker Pattern*

highest-priority client of the resource—this is known at design time in a static priority scheme. When the resource is locked, the priority of the locking task is augmented to the priority ceiling of the resource.

7.4.4 Collaboration Roles

- *Abstract Thread*
  The *Abstract Thread* class is an abstract (noninstantiable) super-class for *Concrete Thread*. *Abstract Thread* associates with the

Scheduler. Since *Concrete Thread* is a subclass, it has the same interface to the *Scheduler* as the *Abstract Thread*. This enforces interface compliance. The *Abstract Thread* is an «active» object, meaning that when it is created, it creates an OS thread in which to run. It contains (that is, it has composition relations with) more primitive application objects that execute in the thread of the composite «active» object.

- *Concrete Thread*
  The *Concrete Thread* is an «active» object most typically constructed to contain passive "semantic" objects (via the composition relation) that do the real work of the system. The *Concrete Thread* object provides a straightforward means of attaching these semantic objects into the concurrency architecture. *Concrete Thread* is an instantiable subclass of *Abstract Thread*.

- *Mutex*
  The *Mutex* is a mutual exclusion semaphore object that permits only a single caller through at a time. The operations of the *Shared Resource* invoke it whenever a relevant service is called, locking it prior to starting the service and unlocking it once the service is complete. *Threads* that attempt to invoke a service when the services are already locked become blocked until the *Mutex* is in its unlocked state. This is done by the *Mutex* semaphore signaling the *Scheduler* that a call attempt was made by the currently active thread, the *Mutex* ID (necessary to unlock it later when the mutex is released), and the entry point—the place at which to continue execution of the *Thread*.

- *Scheduler*
  This object orchestrates the execution of multiple threads based on their priority according to a simple rule: Always run the ready thread with the highest priority. When the «active» *Thread* object is created, it (or its creator) calls the *createThread* operation to create a thread for the «active» object. Whenever this thread is executed by the *Scheduler*, it calls the StartAddr address (except when the thread has been blocked or preempted—in which case it calls the *EntryPoint* address).

  In this pattern, the *Scheduler* has some special duties when the *Mutex* signals an attempt to access a locked resource. Specifically, it must block the requesting task (done by stopping that task and placing a reference to it in the *Blocked Queue* (not shown—for details of the *Blocked Queue*, see the Static Priority Pattern in Chapter 5), and it must elevate the priority of the task owning the resource to the *Shared Resource's priorityCeiling*.

- *Shared Resource*
A resource is an object shared by one or more *Threads*. For the system to operate properly in all cases, all *Shared Resources* must either be reentrant (meaning that corruption from simultaneous access cannot occur), or they must be protected. In the case of a protected resource, when a *Thread* attempts to use the resource, the associated *Mutex* semaphore is checked, and if locked, the calling task is placed into the *Blocked Queue*. The task is terminated with its reentry point noted in the TCB.

  The *SharedResource* has a constant attribute (note the «frozen» constraint in Figure 7-10), called priorityCeiling. This is set during design to just greater than the priority of the highest-priority task that can ever access it. In some RTOSs, this means that the priority will be one more (when a larger number indicates a higher priority), and in some it will be one less (when a lower number indicates a higher priority). This ensures that when the resource is locked, no other task using that resource can preempt it.

- *Task Control Block*
The TCB contains the scheduling information for its corresponding *Thread* object. This includes the priority of the thread, the default start address, and the current entry address if it was preempted or blocked prior to completion. The *Scheduler* maintains a TCB object for each existing *Thread*. Note that TCB typically also has a reference off to a call and parameter stack for its *Thread*, but that level of detail is not shown in Figure 7-10. The TCB tracks both the current priority of the thread (which may have been elevated due to resource access and blocking) and its nominal priority.

7.4.5 Consequences

The Highest Locker Pattern has even better priority inversion-bounding properties than the Priority Inheritance Pattern. It allows higher-priority tasks to run, but only if they have a priority higher than the priority ceiling of the resource. The priority ceiling can be determined at design time for each resource by examining the clients of a given resource and identifying to which active object they belong and selecting the highest from among those. The priority ceiling is this value augmented by one. Computation of worst-case blocking is the length of the longest critical section (that is, resource locking time) of any task of lesser priority as long as a task never suspends itself while owning a resource.

The pattern has the disadvantage that while it bounds priority inversion to a single level, that level happens more frequently than with some other approaches. For example, if the lowest-priority task locks a resource with the highest-priority ceiling, and during that time an intermediate priority task becomes ready to run, then it is blocked even though in this case one would prefer that the normal priority rules apply. One way to handle that is to elevate the priority of the task owning the resource only when another task attempts to lock it; until then, the locking tasks runs at its nominal priority.

In this pattern, care must be taken to ensure that a task never suspends itself while owning a resource. It is fine if it is preempted, but voluntary preemption while owning a resource can lead to chain blocking, a problem previously identified with the Priority Inheritance Pattern in the previous section. If the system allows tasks to suspend themselves while owning a resource, then the computation of worst-case blocking is computed in the same way as with the Priority Inheritance Pattern—the longest case of chain blocked must be traversed.

This pattern avoids deadlock as long as no task suspends itself while owning a resource because no other task is permitted to wait on the resource (condition 4). This is because the locking task runs at a priority higher than any of the other clients of the resource. As previously noted, there is also a consequence of computational overhead associated with the Highest Locker Pattern.

7.4.6 Implementation Strategies

Fewer RTOSs support the Highest Locker Pattern more than the basic Priority Inheritance Pattern. Implementation of this pattern in your own RTOS is fairly straightforward, with the addition of priority ceiling attributes in the *Shared Resource*. When the mutex is locked, it must notify the *Scheduler* to elevate the priority of the locking task to that resource's priority ceiling.

7.4.7 Related Patterns

The Highest Locker Pattern exists to help solve a particular problem peculiar to priority-based preemption multitasking, so all of the concurrency patterns having to do with that style of multitasking can be mixed with this pattern.

7.4.8 Sample Model

In the example shown in Figure 7-11, there are four tasks with their priorities shown using constraints, two of which, *Waveform Draw* and *Message Display*, share a common resource, *Display*. The tasks, represented as active objects in order of their priority, are *Message Display* (priority Low), *Switch Monitor* (priority Medium Low), *Waveform Draw* (priority Medium High), and *Safety Monitor* (priority Very High), leaving priority High unused at the outset. *Message Display* and *Waveform Draw* share *Display*, so the priority ceiling of *Display* is just above *Waveform Draw* (that is, High).

The scenario runs as follows: First, the lowest-priority task, *Message Display*, runs, calling the operation *Display.displayMsg()*. Because the *Display* has a mutex semaphore, this locks the resource, and the *Scheduler* (not shown in Figure 7-11) escalates the priority of the locking task, *Message Display*, to the priority ceiling of the resource—that is, the value High.

While this operation executes, first the *Switch Monitor* and then the *Waveform Draw* tasks both become ready to run but cannot because the *Message Display* task is running at a higher priority than either of them. The *Safety Monitor* task becomes ready to run. Because it runs at a priority Very High, it can, and does, preempt the *Message Display* task.

After the *Safety Monitor* task returns control to the *Scheduler*, the *Scheduler* continues the execution of the *Message Display* task. Once it releases the resource, the mutex signals the *Scheduler*, and the latter deescalates the priority of the *Message Display* task to its nominal priority level of Low. At this point, there are two tasks of a higher priority waiting to run, so the higher-priority waiting task (*Waveform Draw*) runs, and when it completes, the remaining higher-priority task (*Switch Monitor*) runs. When this last task completes, the *Message Display* task can finally resume its work and complete.

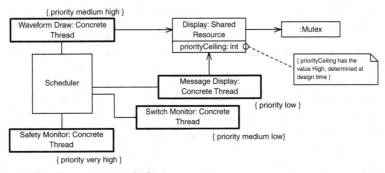

a. Highest Locker Pattern Example

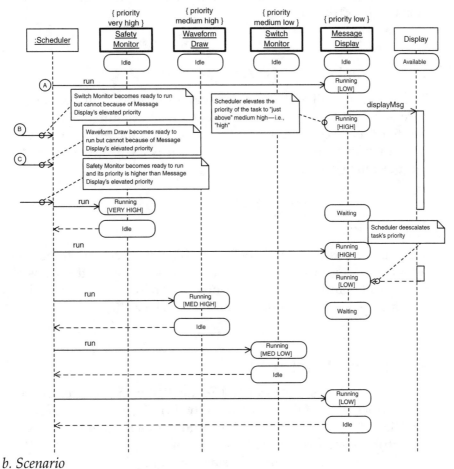

b. Scenario

Figure 7-11: *Highest Locker Pattern*

7.5 PRIORITY CEILING PATTERN

The Priority Ceiling Pattern, or Priority Ceiling Protocol (PCP) as it is sometimes called, addresses both issues of bounding priority inversion (and hence bounding blocking time) and removal of deadlock. It is a relatively sophisticated approach, more complex than the previous methods. It is not as widely supported by commercial RTOSs, however, and so its implementation often requires writing extensions to the RTOS.

7.5.1 Abstract

The Priority Ceiling Pattern is used to ensure bounded priority inversion and task blocking times and also to ensure that deadlocks due to resource contention cannot occur. It has somewhat more overhead than the Highest Locker Pattern. It is used in highly reliable multitasking systems.

7.5.2 Problem

The unbounded priority inversion problem is discussed in the chapter introduction in some detail. The Priority Ceiling Pattern exists to limit the maximum amount of priority inversion to a single level and to completely prevent resource-based deadlock.

7.5.3 Pattern Structure

Figure 7-12 shows the Priority Ceiling Pattern structure. The primary structural difference between the Priority Ceiling Pattern and the Highest Locker Pattern is the addition of a System Priority Ceiling attribute for the Scheduler. Behaviorally, there are some differences as well. The algorithm for starting and ending a critical section is shown in Figure 7-13.

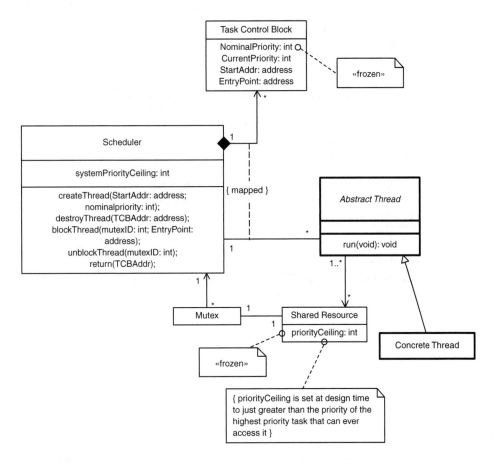

Figure 7-12: *Priority Ceiling Pattern*

7.5.4 Collaboration Roles

- *Abstract Thread*
  The *Abstract Thread* class is an abstract (noninstantiable) super-class for *Concrete Thread*. *Abstract Thread* associates with the *Scheduler*. Since *Concrete Thread* is a subclass, it has the same interface to the *Scheduler* as the *Abstract Thread*. This enforces interface compliance. The *Abstract Thread* is an «active» object, meaning that when it is created, it creates an OS thread in which to run. It

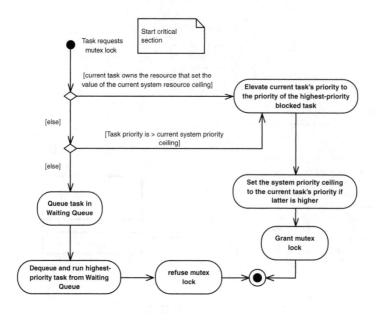

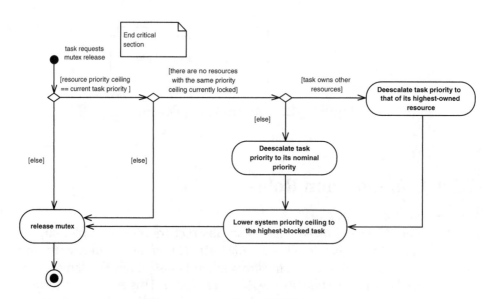

Figure 7-13: *Priority Ceiling Pattern Resource Algorithm*

contains (that is, it has composition relations with) more primitive application objects that execute in the thread of the composite «active» object.

- *Concrete Thread*
  The *Concrete Thread* is an «active» object most typically constructed to contain passive "semantic" objects (via the composition relation) that do the real work of the system. The *Concrete Thread* object provides a straightforward means of attaching these semantic objects into the concurrency architecture. *Concrete Thread* is an instantiable subclass of *Abstract Thread*.

- *Mutex*
  The *Mutex* is a mutual exclusion semaphore object that permits only a single caller through at a time. The operations of the *Shared Resource* invoke it whenever a relevant service is called, locking it prior to starting the service and unlocking it once the service is complete. *Threads* that attempt to invoke a service when the services are already locked become blocked until the *Mutex* is in its unlocked state. This is done by the *Mutex* semaphore signaling the *Scheduler* that a call attempt was made by the currently active thread, the *Mutex* ID (necessary to unblock the correct *Thread* later when the *Mutex* is released), and the entry point—the place at which to continue execution of the *Thread*. See Figure 7-13 for the algorithms that control locking, blocking, and releasing the *Mutex*.

- *Scheduler*
  This object orchestrates the execution of multiple threads based on their priority according to a simple rule: Always run the ready thread with the highest priority. When the «active» *Thread* object is created, it (or its creator) calls the *createThread* operation to create a thread for the «active» object. Whenever this thread is executed by the *Scheduler*, it calls the StartAddr address (except when the thread has been blocked or preempted—in which case it calls the *EntryPoint* address).

  In this pattern, the *Scheduler* has some special duties when the *Mutex* signals an attempt to access a locked resource. Specifically, under some conditions, it must block the requesting task (done by stopping that task and placing a reference to it in the *Blocked Queue* (not shown—for details of the *Blocked Queue*, see the Static Priority Pattern in Chapter 5), and it must elevate the priority of the highest-priority blocked *Thread* being blocked. This is easy to determine, since the *Blocked Queue* is a priority FIFO—the highest-priority blocked task is the first one in that queue. Similarly, when the *Thread* releases the resource, the *Scheduler* must lower its priority back to its nominal priority. The *Scheduler* maintains the value of the highest-priority ceiling of all currently locked resources in its attribute *systemPriorityCeiling*.

- *Shared Resource*
  A resource is an object shared by one or more *Threads*. For the system to operate properly in all cases, all *Shared Resources* must either be reentrant (meaning that corruption from simultaneous access cannot occur), or they must be protected. In the case of a protected resource, when a *Thread* attempts to use the resource, the associated mutex semaphore is checked, and if locked, the calling task is placed into the *Blocked Queue*. The task is terminated with its reentry point noted in the TCB.

  The *SharedResource* has a constant attribute (note the «frozen» constraint in Figure 7-12), called priorityCeiling. This is set during design to just greater than the priority of the highest priority task that can ever access it. In some RTOSs, this means that the priority will be one more (when a larger number indicates a higher priority), and in some it will be one less (when a lower number indicates a higher priority). This ensures that when the resource is locked, no other task using that resource can preempt it.

- *Task Control Block*
  The TCB contains the scheduling information for its corresponding *Thread* object. This includes the priority of the thread, the default start address and the current entry address if it was preempted or blocked prior to completion. The *Scheduler* maintains a TCB object for each existing *Thread*. Note that TCB typically also has a reference off to a call and parameter stack for its *Thread*, but that level of detail is not shown here. The TCB tracks both the current priority of the *Thread* (which may have been elevated due to resource access and blocking) and its nominal priority.

7.5.5 Consequences

This pattern effectively enforces the desirable property that a high-priority task can at most be blocked from execution by a single critical section of a lower-priority task owning a required resource.

It can happen in the Priority Ceiling Pattern that a running task may not be able to access a resource even though it is not currently locked. This will occur if that resource's priority ceiling is less than the current system resource ceiling.

Deadlock is prevented by this pattern because condition 4 (circular wait) is prevented. Any condition that could potentially lead to circular waiting is prohibited. This does mean that a task may be prevented from accessing a resource even though it is currently unlocked.

There is also a consequence of computational overhead associated with the Priority Ceiling Pattern. This pattern is the most sophisticated of the resource management patterns presented in this chapter and has the highest computational overhead.

7.5.6 Implementation Strategies

Rather few RTOSs support the Priority Ceiling Pattern, but it can be added if the RTOS permits extension, particularly when a mutex is locked or released. If not, you can create your own Mutex and System Resource Ceiling classes that intervene with the priority management prior to handing off control to the internal RTOS scheduler. If you are writing your own scheduler, then the implementation should be a relatively straightforward extension of the Highest Locker Pattern.

7.5.7 Related Patterns

Because this pattern is the most sophisticated, it also has the most computational overhead. Therefore, under some circumstances, it may be desirable to use a less computational, if less capable, approach, such as the Highest Locker Pattern, the Priority Inheritance Pattern, or even the Critical Section Pattern.

7.5.8 Sample Model

A robotic control system is given as an example in Figure 7-14a. There are three tasks. The lowest-priority task, *Command Processor*, inserts commands into a shared resource, the *Command Queue*. The middle-priority task, *Safety Monitor*, performs periodic safety monitoring, accessing the shared resource *Robot Arm*. The highest-priority task, *Robotic Planner*, accepts commands (and hence must access the *Command Queue*) and also moves the arm (and therefore must access

Robot Arm). Note that the resource ceiling of both resources must be the priority of the highest-priority task in this case because it accesses both of these resources.

Figure 7-14b shows a scenario for the example. At point A, the *Command Processor* runs, putting set of commands into the *Command Queue*. The call to the *Command Processor* locks the resource successfully because at this point, there are no locked resources. While this is happening, the *Safety Monitor* starts to run at point B. This preempts the *Command Processor* because it is a higher priority, so *Command Processor* goes into a waiting state because it's ready to run but cannot because a higher-priority task is running. Now the *Safety Monitor* attempts to access the second resource, *Robot Arm*. Because a resource is currently already locked with same priority ceiling (found by the Scheduler examining its *systemPriorityCeiling* attribute), that call is blocked. Note that the *Safety Monitor* is prevented from running even though it is trying to access a resource that is not currently locked but *could* start a circular waiting condition, potentially leading to deadlock. Thus, the access is prevented.

When the resource access to *Safety Monitor* is prevented, the priority of the *Command Processor* is elevated to Medium, the same level as the highest-blocked task. At point C, *Robot Planner* runs, preempting the *Command Processor* task. The *Robot Planner* invokes *Command Queue.Get()* to retrieve any waiting commands but finds that this resource is locked. Therefore, its access is blocked, and it is put on the blocked queue, and the *Command Processor* task resumes but at priority High.

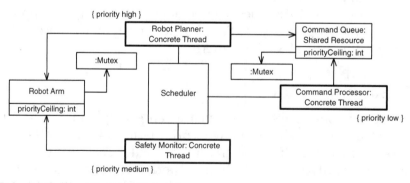

a. Priority Ceiling Pattern Example

Figure 7-14: *Priority Ceiling Pattern*

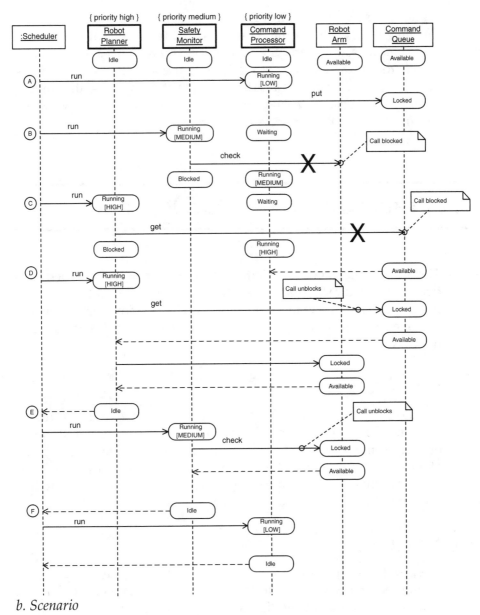

b. Scenario

Figure 7-14: *Priority Ceiling Pattern*

When the call to *Command Queue.put()* finally completes, the priority of the *Command Processor* task is deescalated back to its nominal priority—Low (point D). At this point in time, there are two tasks of higher priority waiting to run. The higher priority of them, *Robot Planning* runs at its normal High priority. It accesses first the *Command Queue* resource and then the *Robot Arm* resource. When it completes, the next highest task ready to run is *Safety Monitor*. It runs, accessing the *Robot Arm* resource. When it completes, the lowest-priority task, *Command Processor* is allowed to complete its work and return control to the OS.

7.6 SIMULTANEOUS LOCKING PATTERN

The Simultaneous Locking Pattern is a pattern solely concerned with deadlock avoidance. It achieves this by breaking condition 2 (holding resources while waiting for others). The pattern works in an all-or-none fashion. Either all resources needed are locked at once or none are.

7.6.1 Abstract

Deadlock can be solved by breaking any of the four conditions required for its existence. This pattern prevents the condition of holding some resources by requesting others by allocating them all at once. This is similar to the Critical Section Pattern. However, it has the additional benefit of allowing higher-priority tasks to run if they don't need any of the locked resources.

7.6.2 Problem

The problem of deadlock is such a serious one in highly reliable computing that many systems design in specific mechanisms to detect it or avoid it. As previously discussed, deadlock occurs when a task is waiting on a condition that can never, in principle, be satisfied. There are four conditions that must be true for deadlock to occur, and it is sufficient to deny the existence of any one of these. The Simultaneous Locking Pattern breaks condition 2, not allowing any task to lock resources while waiting for other resources to be free.

7.6.3 Pattern Structure

Figure 7-15 shows the structure of the Simultaneous Locking Pattern. The special structural aspect of this pattern is the collaboration role *MultiResource*. Each *MultiResource* has a single mutex semaphore that locks only when the entire set of aggregated *Shared Resources* is available to be locked. Similarly, when the semaphore is released, all the aggregated *Shared Resources* are released.

7.6.4 Collaboration Roles

- *MultiResource*
  This object aggregates an entire set of resources needed (or possibly needed) by a *Resource Client*. *MultiResource* explicitly locks and unlocks the set of resources. This locking and unlocking action should be a noninterruptible critical section. If any of the aggregated *Shared Resources* is not available during the locking process,

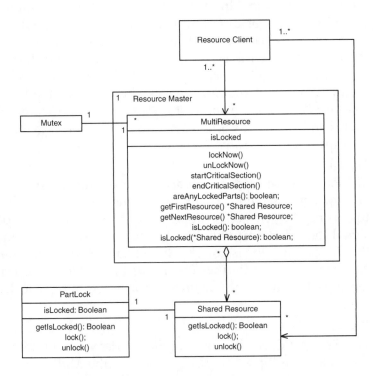

Figure 7-15: *Simultaneous Locking Pattern*

then the *MultiResource* must release all of the Shared Resources it successfully locked. *MultiResource* must define operations *startCriticalSection()* and *endCriticalSection* to prevent task switching from occurring during the locking or unlocking process. Also, *areAnyLockedParts()* returns TRUE if any of the *Shared Resources* aggregated by the *MultiResource* are still locked. For walking through the *Shared Resources,* the *MultiResource* also has the operations *getFirstResource()* and *getNextResource(),* both of which return a pointer to a *Shared Resource* (or NULL if at the end of the list) and *isLocked(*Shared Resource),* which returns TRUE only if the referenced *Shared Resource* is currently locked by the *MultiResource.* If either unlocked or not aggregated by the *MultiResource,* then it returns FALSE. Two more operations, *lockNow()* and *unlockNow(),* simply set the *isLocked* attribute of the *MultiResource* without checking the status of the aggregated parts.

- *Mutex*
The *Mutex* is a mutual exclusion semaphore object that associates with *MultiResource.* In this pattern the shared resources are locked for a longer duration than with the priority inheritance-based patterns. This is because *Resource Client* needs to own all the resources for the entire critical section so that the *Resource Client* never owns a resource while trying to lock another. The policy is that the *Mutex* is only locked if *all* of the required *Share-Resource PartLocks* are successfully locked. *Mutex* is an OS-level mutex and signals the *Scheduler* to take care of blocking tasks that attempt to lock the *SharedResource.*

- *PartLock*
The *PartLock* is a special mutual exclusion semaphore that associates to *Shared Resource.* This *Mutex* is queryable as to its lock status, using the *getIsLocked()* operation. This semaphore does not signal the *Scheduler* unlike the *Mutex,* because there is no need; the OS-level locking is done by the *Mutex* and not by the *PartLock.* Nevertheless, the *MultiResource* needs to be able to ascertain the locking status of all the resources before attempting to lock any of them.

- *Resource Client*
The *Resource Client* is a user of *Shared Resource* objects. It locks potentially multiple *Shared Resources* via the *MultiResource.* The policy enforced in this pattern is that all resources used in a criti-

cal section must be locked at the same time, or the entire lock will fail. The *Resource Client* is specifically prohibited from locking one resource and later, while still owning that lock, attempting to lock another. Put another way, an attempt to lock a set of resources is only permitted if the *Resource Client* currently owns no locks at all, and if any of the requested resources are unavailable, the entire lock will fail and the *Resource Client* must wait and block on the set of resources (that is, it blocks on the mutex owned by its associated *MultiResource*).

*   *ResourceMaster*
    The *ResourceMaster* orchestrates the locking and unlocking of *Mutexes* associated with *MultiResources*. Whenever a *MultiResource* locks a *Mutex*, the *ResourceMaster* searches its list of all *MultiResources* and locks any that share one of the *SharedResources*. That way, if a *Thread* tries to lock its *MultiResource* and another one owns a needed *SharedResource*, the *Thread* can block on the *Mutex* of its associated *MultiResource*. Conversely, when a *MultiResource* releases all of its *Shared Resources*, that *MultiResource* notifies the *ResourceMaster* and it tracks down all of the other *MultiResources* and sees if it can unlock them as well (it may not be able to if another *MultiResource* has locked a *SharedResource* unused by the first).

*   *Shared Resource*
    A resource is a part object owned by the *MultiResource* object. In this pattern, a *Shared Resource* does not connect to a *Mutex* because it is not locked individually. As implied by its name, the same *Shared Resource* object may be an aggregated part of different *MultiResource* objects. The pattern policy is that no resource that is aggregated by one *MultiResource* is allowed to be directly locked by a *Thread*, although it may be accessed by a *Thread* to perform services. The *Shared Resource* contains operations to explicitly lock, unlock, and to query its locked status, and these simply invoke services in the associated *PartLock*.

7.6.5 Consequences

The Simultaneous Locking Pattern prevents deadlock by breaking condition 2, required for deadlock to occur—namely locking some resources while waiting for others to become available. It does this by locking all resources needed at once and releasing them all at once. This resource management pattern can easily be used in most scheduling patterns, such as the Static Priority Pattern.

There are two primary negatives to the use of this pattern. First, priority inversion is not bounded. A higher-priority task is free to preempt and run as long as it doesn't use any currently locked resource. This pattern could be mixed in with the priority inheritance pattern to address that problem.

The second issue is that this pattern invokes some computational overhead, which may become severe in situations in which there are many shared resources. Each time a request to lock a resource is made, each of the *Shared Resources* must be locked *and* all of the other *MultiResources* must be checked to see if they aggregate any of these locked *Shared Resources*. Any *MultiResource* that shares one of the just-locked *Shared Resources* must itself be locked. On release of a lock on a particular *MultiResource,* all of its *Shared Resources* must be unlocked, and then each of the other *MultiResources* must be examined using the *areAnyLockedParts()* operation. If it returns TRUE, then that *MultiResource* must remain locked; otherwise is must be unlocked.

Another issue is that programmer/designer discipline is required not to access the *Shared Resources* without first obtaining a lock by going through the *MultiResource* mechanism. Because *Shared Resources* don't use standard OS mutexes for locking (since we don't want *Threads* blocking on them rather then the *MultiResources*), it is possible to directly access the *Shared Resource,* bypassing the locking mechanisms. This is a Bad Idea. One possible solution to enforce the locking is to propagate all of the operations from the resources to the *MultiResource,* make the operations public in the *MultiResource* and private in the *Shared Resource,* and making the *MultiResource* a friend of the *Shared Resource.* This adds some additional computational overhead, but in some languages the propagated operations could be made inline to minimize this. Alternatively, each *Shared Resource* could be told, during the locking process, who its owner is. Then on each service call, the owner would have to pass an owner ID to prove it had rights to request the service.

7.6.6 Implementation Strategies

Care must be taken that the locking of all the resources in *MultiResource.lock()* and *MultiResource.unlock()* must be done in a critical section to prevent deadlock condition 2 from occurring. Other than that, the implementation of this pattern is straightforward.

7.6.7 Related Patterns

This pattern removes deadlock by breaking condition 2 required for deadlock. There are other approaches to avoiding deadlock. One of this is presented in the Ceiling Priority Pattern and another in the Ordered Locking Pattern, both presented in this chapter. This pattern is normally mixed with a concurrency management policy, such as the Static Priority Pattern, but other patterns can be used as well. If it is desirable to limit priority inversion, then this pattern can be mixed with the Priority Inheritance Pattern.

7.6.8 Sample Model

Figure 7-16a shows a simple example of the application of this pattern. Two *Concrete Threads*, *Machine 1* and *Machine 2*, share three resources: *MsgQueue 1* (Machine 1 only), *Command Queue* (both), and *MsgQueue 2* (Machine 2 only). To avoid the possibility of a deadlock occurring, the Simultaneous Locking Pattern is used. Two *MultiResources* (*Multi 1* and *Multi 2*) are created as composite parts of an instance of *Resource-Master*. Figure 7-16b shows the behavior when *Machine 1* locks its

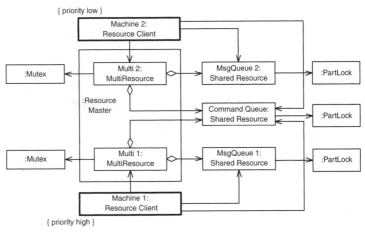

a. Simultaneous Locking Pattern Example

Figure 7-16: *Simultaneous Locking Pattern (continued)*

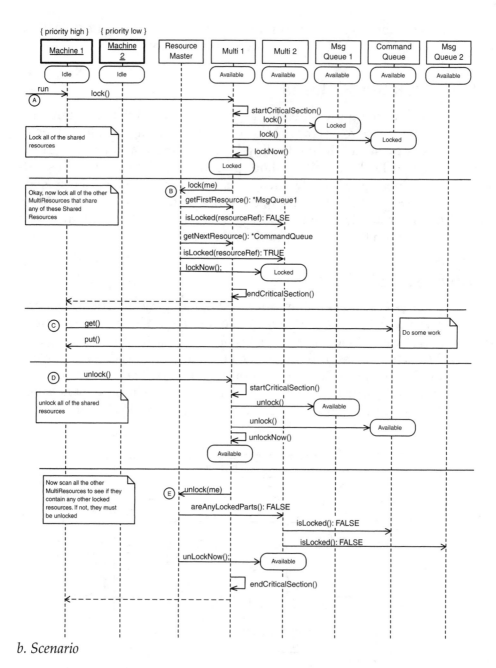

b. Scenario

Figure 7-16: *Simultaneous Locking Pattern (continued)*

resources, does some work (moving messages from the *Command Queue* to *MsgQueue 1*), and then unlocks the resources.

What is not shown is what happens if *Machine 2* runs during the execution of the get() and put() operations, but it is clear that as soon as *Machine 2* attempts to lock its *MultiResource*, it will be blocked.

7.7 ORDERED LOCKING PATTERN

The Ordered Locking Pattern is another way to ensure that deadlock cannot occur—this time by preventing condition 4 (circular waiting) from occurring. It does this by ordering the resources and requiring that they always be accessed by any client in that specified order. If this is religiously enforced, then no circular waiting condition can ever occur.

7.7.1 Abstract

The Ordered Locking Pattern eliminates deadlock by ordering resources and enforcing a policy in which resources must be allocated only in a specific order. Unlike "normal" resource access, but similar to the Simultaneous Locking Pattern, the client must explicitly lock and release the resources, rather than doing it implicitly by merely invoking a service on a resource. This means that the potential for neglecting to unlock the resource exists.

7.7.2 Problem

The Ordered Locking Pattern solely addresses the problem of deadlock elimination, as does the previous Simultaneous Locking Pattern.

7.7.3 Pattern Structure

Figure 7-17a shows the structural part of the Ordered Locking Pattern. Each *Resource Client* aggregates a *Resource List,* which contains an ordered list of Resource IDs currently locked by the *Thread.*

Figure 7-17b uses UML activity charts to show the algorithms for locking and unlocking the resource. The basic policy of resource locking is that each resource in the entire system has a unique integer-valued identifier, and a *Thread* may *only* lock a resource whose ID is greater than that of the highest resource it currently owns. An attempt to lock a resource with a lower-valued ID than the highest-

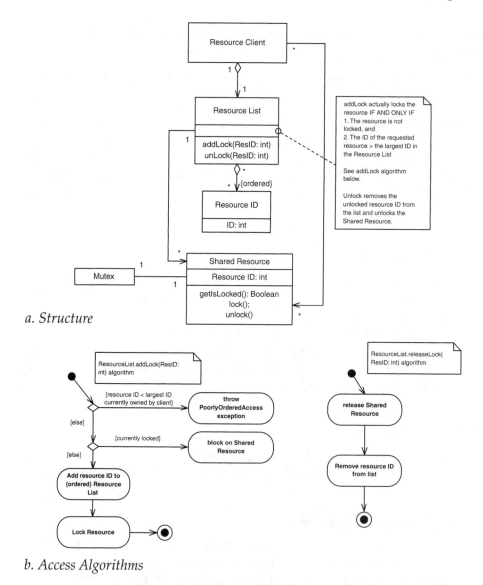

a. Structure

b. Access Algorithms

Figure 7-17: *Ordered Locking Pattern*

valued resource you currently own causes the *Resource List* to throw a *PoorlyOrderedAccess* exception, indicating a violation of this policy. Sometimes a *Resource Client* may block on a resource that it needs because it is locked, and that is perfectly fine. But it can never happen that a circular waiting condition can occur (required for deadlock) because it would require that at least one *Resource Client* would have to block waiting for the release of a resource whose ID is lower than its highest-owned resource.[2]

7.7.4 Collaboration Roles

- *Mutex*
  The *Mutex* is a mutual exclusion semaphore object that associates with *Shared Resource*. If a Shared Resource is currently locked when requested by a *Resource Client* (via its *Resource List*), then the *Resource Client* blocks on that resource.

- *Resource Client*
  A *Resource Client* is an object (which may be «active») that owns and locks resources. It aggregates a *Resource List* to manage the locking and unlocking of those resources.

- *Resource ID*
  The *Resource ID* is a simple part objected aggregated by *Resource List*. It merely contains the ID of a corresponding *Shared Resource* currently locked by the *Thread*. When the *Shared Resource* is unlocked by the *Resource List*, its ID is removed from the list.

- *Resource List*
  The *Resource List* manages the locking and unlocking of *Shared Resources* according to the algorithm shown in Figure 7-17b. When a *Resource Client* wants to lock a resource, it makes the request of the *Resource List*. If the ID of the required resource is greater than any currently owned resource, and then if it is unlocked, the *Resource List* locks it and adds it to the list. If it is locked, then the *Thread* blocks on the resource.

- *Shared Resource*
  A resource is an object shared by one or more *Resource Client*. In this pattern, each *Shared Resource* has a unique integer-valued

---

2. The proof is left as an exercise for the reader.

identifier. This identifier is used to control the order in which *Shared Resources* may be locked. If a *Shared Resource* itself uses other *Shared Resources,* then it may *only* do so if the called *Shared Resource* identifiers are of higher value than its own.

7.7.5 Consequences

This pattern effectively removes the possibility of resource-based deadlocks by removing the possibility of condition 4—circular waiting. For the algorithm to work any ordering of *Shared Resources* will do provided that this ordering is global. However, some orderings are better than others and will result is less blocking overall. This may take some analysis at design time to identify the best ordering of the *Shared Resources.* As mentioned above, if *Shared Resources* are themselves *Resource Clients* (a reasonable possibility), then they should *only* invoke services of *Shared Resources* that have higher-valued IDs than they do. If they invoke a lower-valued *Shared Resource,* then they are in effect violating the ordered locking protocol by the transitive property of locking (if A locks B and then B locks C, then A is in effect locking C).

While draconian, one solution to the potential problem of transitive violation of the ordering policy is to enforce the rule that a *Shared Resource* may never invoke services or lock other *Shared Resources.* If your system design does allow such transitive locking, then each transitive path must be examined to ensure that the ordering policy is not violated. The Ordered Locking Pattern does not address the issue of bounding priority inversion as do some other patterns here.

7.7.6 Implementation Strategies

One memory-efficient implementation for *Resource List* is to use an array of integers to hold the *Resource IDs.* The array only needs to be as large as the maximum number of resources held at any one time. For an even more memory-efficient implementation (but at the cost of some computational complexity), a bit set can be used. The bit set must have the same number of bits as maximum *Resource ID* value. Setting and unsetting the bit is computationally lightweight, but checking to see if there is a greater bit set is a little more computationally intensive.

7.7.7 Related Patterns

There are two other patterns here that prevent deadlock. The Simultaneous Locking Pattern locks all the needed resources in a single critical section; other *Resource Clients* that need to run can do so as long as they don't request any of the same *Shared Resources*. If a small subset of the resources need to be locked at any given time or if the sets needed for different *Resource Clients* overlap only slightly, then the Simultaneous Locking Pattern works well.

The Priority Ceiling Pattern solves the deadlock problem as well, although the algorithm is significantly more complex. For that added sophistication, the Priority Ceiling Pattern also bounds priority inversion to a single level.

7.7.8 Sample Model

The example shown in Figure 7-18a provides a simple illustration of how the pattern works. *Client 1* uses three *Shared Resources: SR1* (ID=0), *SR3* (ID=2), and *SR4* (ID=3). *Client 2* uses three *Shared Resources: SR2* (ID=1), *SR3* (ID=2), and *SR4* (ID=3). They both, therefore, share SR2, SR3, and SR4.

Note that in the absence of some scheme to prevent deadlock (such as the use of the Ordered Locking Pattern), deadlock is easily possible in this configuration. Suppose *Client 1* ran and locked SR2, and when it was just about to lock SR3, *Client 2* (running in a higher-priority thread) preempts *Client 1*. *Client 2* now locks SR3 and tries to lock SR2. It cannot, of course, because it is already locked (by *Client 1*), and so it must block and allow *Client 1* to run until it releases the resource. However, now *Client 1* cannot successfully run because it needs SR3, and it is locked by *Client 2*. A classic deadlock situation. This particular scenario is not allowed with the Ordered Locking Pattern. Figure 7-18b shows what happens when this scenario is attempted.

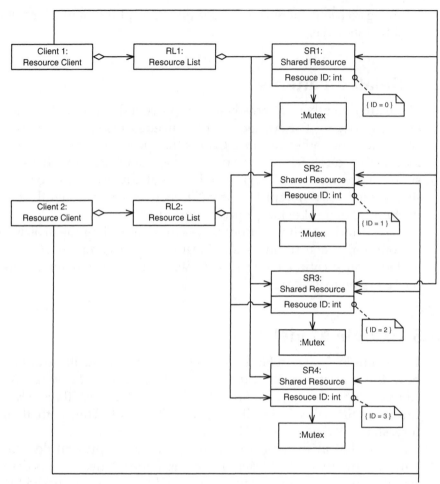

a. Ordered Locking Pattern Example

Figure 7-18: *Ordered Locking Pattern*

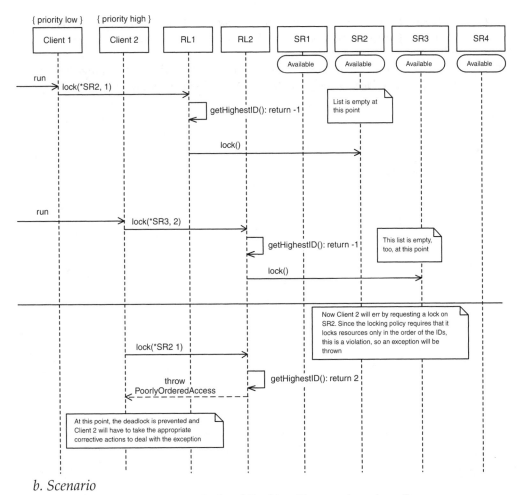

b. Scenario

Figure 7-18: *Ordered Locking Pattern (continued)*

7.8 References

[1] *Response to the OMG RFP for Schedulability, Performance, and Time, Revised Submission,* Boston, MA: Object Management Group OMG Document Number: ad/2001-06-14, 2001.

[2] Klein, M., T. Ralya, B. Pollak, R. Obenza, and M. Harbour. *A Practitioner's Handbook for Real-Time Analysis: Guide to Rate Monotonic Analysis for Real-Time Systems,* Norwell, MA: Kluwer Academic Press, 1993.

[3] Douglass, Bruce Powel. *Doing Hard Time: Developing Real-Time Systems with UML, Objects, Frameworks and Patterns*, Reading, MA: Addison-Wesley, 1999.

[4] Douglass, Bruce Powel. *Real-Time UML 2nd Edition: Developing Efficient Objects for Embedded Systems*, Boston, MA: Addison-Wesley, 2000.

Chapter 8

Distribution Patterns

The following patterns are presented in this chapter.

- Shared Memory Pattern: Using multiported memory to share global data and send messages
- Remote Method Call Pattern: Synchronous message passing across processor boundaries
- Observer Pattern: Efficient invocation of services with multiple clients
- Data Bus Pattern: Providing a common virtual medium for sharing data
- Proxy Pattern: Using the Observer Pattern between processors
- Broker Pattern: Sharing services when object location is unknown at design time

8.1 Introduction

Distribution is an important aspect of architecture. It defines the policies, procedures, and structure for systems that may, at least potentially, exist on multiple address spaces simultaneously. Distribution comes in two primary forms: asymmetric and symmetric. Asymmetric distribution architectures are those in which the binding of the objects to the address spaces is known at design time. Most real-time and embedded systems are of this kind because it is simpler and requires less overhead. Symmetric distribution architectures are dynamic in the sense that which address space in which an object will execute isn't known until run-time. While this is more complex, it is also a great deal more flexible and allows dynamic load balancing.

For both asymmetric and symmetric architectures, distribution architecture also exists at multiple levels of abstraction. The application level of abstraction simply maps the objects to the address space and worries about the *application protocol*—the rules by which these application-level objects share information and control. These application protocols are abstract and are implemented on top of a wide variety of deployment bus and network architectures. This latter aspect includes the communication protocol, and it deals with the more concrete means by which the application protocols are implemented.

The ISO communications model is one that identifies seven different layers in what is called the *protocol stack,* each having a virtual protocol with a corresponding layer in the other address space. This is a common view but by no means the only one. It is common for many of these layers to be skipped and the application objects that need to communicate to take care of these things, such as reliable delivery and ensuring the data format is correct. There are a great many ways that communications protocols have been successfully deployed in real-time and embedded systems.

In this chapter, we deal with distribution architectures at the application level, which we refer to as *collaboration architecture.* At the application level, the collaboration architecture focuses on how the objects find and communicate with each other without specific regard to the details of how the communication actually takes place. Distribution can also be discussed at the level of the underlying communication transport protocol. At the communications protocol level, the protocol architecture deals with the primary strategies for managing the timely, reliable exchange of information.

The underlying transportation protocol moves the data from processor to processor, sometimes under the direct control of the application objects, sometimes in a manner that is transparent to the application objects. Different communications protocols have different performance, schedulability, and predictability characteristics. The communications protocol should be chosen with the desired properties to support the required qualities of service of the overall system.

For example, CDMA (collision detect multiple access) protocols allow for multimastering of the communications bus. When different network nodes attempt to send a message at the same time, a collision arises; in this case, both nodes stop attempting to transmit and try again at random times. The consequence of this design decision is that above about 30 percent bus utilization, virtually all the time is spent managing collisions and very little time is spent actually transmitting information.

TDMA (time division multiple access) protocols give nodes a slice of the overall communication cycle into which they may transmit. This gives predictable response times but may not scale up to large numbers of nodes.

Other protocols are based on priorities; CAN bus protocol and SCSI are two examples of priority-based systems. In such protocols, some of the bandwidth is spent arbitrating who has control over the bus. Both of these priority schemes are based in what is called a *bit domance protocol*. A sender not only puts out bits onto the bus but also listens to see if what was written is what actually appears. If it sends a nondominant bit but hears a dominant bit, then it assumes it has lost the arbitration and drops off. The CAN bus uses bits in the message that are used to specify the transmission priority, and so different nodes may send messages of various priorities. In the SCSI protocol, the priority is tied to the node address. In high-utilization environments, such protocols can be highly efficient.

Besides deciding which messages may be transmitted, protocols are also concerned with reliability of transfer. The communication media used by the protocols is inherently unreliable, so protocols may layer additional logic on top of the basic transmission-reception scheme to add reliability. UDP, part of the TCP/IP protocol suite, is an *unreliable* means for communication in that if a message is lost or becomes corrupted, there is no mechanism for retransmission. TCP, on the other hand, is referred to as a reliable communications protocol because the sender will retry for a fixed number of times if it does not receive a message acknowledging the reception of the transmission. Many protocols also include redundancy on the message contents, often in the form of checksums or cyclic redundancy checks (CRCs) to identify if a message gets corrupted in transit.

Another issue with the communication infrastructure has to do with the interpretation and representation of information. A distributed system is often composed of a heterogeneous assortment of processors with different representations of data types. For example, the primitive *int* data type might be 8-bits, 16-bits, 32-bits, or 64 bits, as well as stored in "big endian" or "little endian" forms. In order to construct truly interoperative systems, the knowledge of the data representations should be hidden from the client and server processors. This is usually done by the Presentation Layer in an OSI-compliant communications protocol or by calling explicit data filters to convert from local storage format to a special transmission format called *network format*.

When sending a message, the sender takes a message and *marshals* it— that is, constructs a datagram or message in a form that can be sent across the communications protocol, which includes such things as the sender and receiver addresses, message size, error-checking codes, and, of course, the information itself. Part of this process is taking the information stored in the *local format* of the sending machine and recasting it into a universal format called *network format*. Once received, the message is demarshalled, the error codes are checked, the bits and fields used for the transmission are discarded, and the information is reformatted into the local format of the receiver. In this case, the sender and the receiver do not need to have knowledge of how each other stores information locally.

8.2 SHARED MEMORY PATTERN

The Shared Memory Pattern uses a common memory area addressable by multiple processors as a means to send messages and share data. This is normally accomplished with the addition of special hardware—specifically, multiported RAM chips.

8.2.1 Abstract

The Shared Memory Pattern is a simple solution when data must be shared among more than one processor, but timely responses to messages and events between the processors are not required. The pattern almost always involves a combined hardware/software solution. Hardware support for single CPU-cycle semaphore and memory access can avoid memory conflicts and data corruption, but usually some software support to assist the low-level hardware features is required for robust access. If the data to be shared is read-only, as for code that is to be executed on multiple processors, then such concurrency protection mechanisms may not be required.

8.2.2 Problem

Many systems have to share data between multiple processors—this is the essence of distribution, after all. In some cases, the access to the data may persist for a long period of time, and the amount of data shared may be large. In such cases, sending messages may be an inefficient method for sharing such information. Multiple computers may need to update this "global" data, such as in a shared database, or they may need to only read it, as is the case with executable code that may run on many processors or configuration tables. A means by which such data may be effectively shared is needed.

8.2.3 Pattern Structure

The Shared Data Pattern addresses these concerns by using a shared memory device to store the information to be shared. The pattern shown in Figure 8-1 actually shows two patterns of usage: singular global data and shared message queues. A particular instance may be either or both of these subpatterns. The physical devices are shown using their standard UML notation—three-dimensional boxes—whereas the software classes are shown using their standard rectangular forms.

8.2.4 Collaboration Roles

- *Data Client*
  The *Data Client* instance exists on a single processor and accesses the *Global Data* object. There are generally *Data Client* objects accessing the same *Global Data* object on at least two different processors. In addition, a *Data Client* may be the recipient of *Message* objects from a *Receiver*.

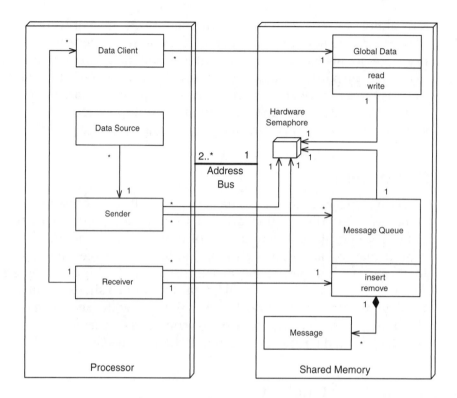

Figure 8-1: *Shared Memory Pattern*

- *Data Source*
  The *Data Source* instance exists on a single processor and inserts *Messages* to a *Message Queue* object in *Shared Memory*.

- *Global Data*
  The *Global Data* object is shared among at least two, but possibly many more, *Data Clients* running on different processors. It associates with a *Hardware Semaphore* to ensure data integrity.

- *Hardware Semaphore*
  This is a hardware-supported semaphore that can be locked or unlocked within a single memory cycle. The semaphore does not usually physically prevent the memory from being accessed but provides a readable flag as to its logical accessibility. The *Hardware Semaphore* is physically a part of the *Shared Memory* device. The *Shared Memory* device typically provides multiple *Hardware*

Semaphores that may be used to logically protect different objects existing in the RAM.

- *Message*
  A *Message* object encapsulates a UML logical message that is to be sent to a *Receiver*. This may be a request for a service to be performed or a request for information.

- *Message Queue*
  A *Message Queue* manages a set of *Message* objects from possibly many *Senders* to a single *Receiver*. It is common to have as many *Message Queue* objects are there are *Processors*; each *Message Queue* normally queues *Messages* only for a single *Receiver*. Access to the queue is protected via a *Hardware Semaphore*.

- *Processor*
  This is a physical CPU executing the code. There are at least two *Processors* in this pattern. Objects shown within the *Processor* node are executing in the local memory of that *Processor*.

- *Receiver*
  Most commonly, each *Processor* has only a single *Receiver*. The *Receiver's* task is to check whether there are *Messages* waiting for it in its corresponding *Message Queue* and, if there are, to remove them and dispatch them to the appropriate *Data Client* objects.

- *Sender*
  Each *Processor* usually has a single *Sender* object. The *Sender* must identify which *Message Queue* in which to insert messages it is given to send. In the most common case, each *Message Queue* stores *Messages* for a single recipient *Processor*.

- *Shared Memory*
  This is a physical RAM device that is shared among the processors.

8.2.5 Consequences

This solution requires the use of specialized memory, so it is mostly used for applications in systems in which hardware and software are being codesigned. It is generally not a COTS (Commercial Off The Shelf) solution. The hardware solution may limit the number of separately lockable blocks (because of the fixed limit on the hardware semaphores). The RAM chips used for this purpose usually allow only a single Processor to have access at a given time, but the hardware semaphores must be explicitly set and unset by the software to indicate availability. Because of potential race conditions, after a semaphore is locked, it must subsequently be read to ensure that the write succeeded.

The patterns works well when there is a relatively large store of data that must be persistently available to multiple processors. Since the data is stored in a globally accessible space, it can be read and written as often as necessary with low overhead. Because the clients poll the shared memory to see when there is new data for them, this pattern may not result in a timely delivery of messages.

8.2.6 Implementation Strategies

The most common implementation of this pattern has exactly two processor nodes sharing a single shared memory device, but other deployment (physical) architectures with more processors are possible. This memory device provides multiple hardware semaphores that the designer is free to use as desired. The hardware selection must take into account the power, memory, and heating requirements. A typical choice is the Cypress CY7C037/38, a 64K x 19bit dual-port static RAM chip [1].

For the semaphores, the software must use a firm policy of ensuring accessibility before reading or writing the memory. This is done by checking the semaphore. The CY7C037/38 chip works when the Processor, wanting to lock the shared memory object, writes a "0" to the appropriate semaphore and then reads its status. If it reads back a "0," then it succeeded; if it reads a "1," then it failed (because the semaphore was already locked). If there are more distinct memory objects to lock than there are hardware semaphores, then additional software semaphores may be created, and one of the hardware semaphores may be used to protect access to the block of software semaphores. The software semaphores must only be examined after successfully locking the semaphore block.

8.2.7 Related Patterns

When a timely response is required, a Remote Method Call Pattern may be used to push through a message. When there are potentially many clients for a datum, an Observer pattern may be more appropriate.

8.2.8 Sample Model

The structural model of the example is shown in Figure 8-2a. There are two processors: a User Controller processor that takes inputs from a switch and a Knob and sends to them to the Motor object on the Actuation Processor. This is done, of course, via the Shared Memory device that contains a Message Queue for storing such messages until the Receiver is ready to read them.

Figure 8-2b shows a simple scenario of usage. In this case, there is no contention to be mediated. The Switch sends an OnMsg by invoking the send() operation on the Sender. This in turn results in it being stored in the queue. Note that the Sender explicitly manipulates the hardware semaphore to ensure that it can write to the queue safely. It does this by attempting to lock the semaphore and then explicitly checking to see if it succeeded (and in this scenario, it did). Then the Knob sends a TurnRightMsg in the same fashion.

Eventually, the Receiver checks the Message Queue for messages. First, it locks the semaphore in the same fashion as the Sender. Once that succeeds, it then discovers two messages are waiting. Each is dequeued and passed on to the ultimate receiver.

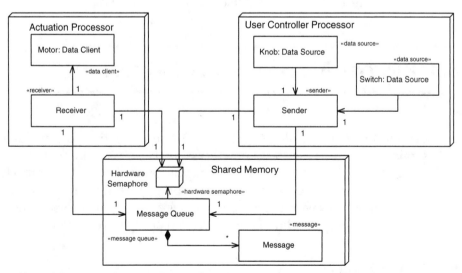

a. Shared Memory Pattern Example

Figure 8-2: *Shared Memory Pattern (continued)*

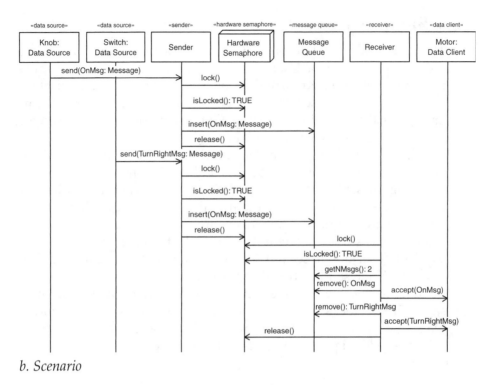

b. Scenario

Figure 8-2: *Shared Memory Pattern (continued)*

8.3 REMOTE METHOD CALL PATTERN

Remote Procedure Calls (RPCs) are a common method for invoking services synchronously between processors. The object-oriented equivalent, Remove Method Calls, work in the same way. This approach requires underlying OS support, but it works much the same way that local method calls work: The client invokes a service on the server and waits in a blocked condition until the called operation completes.

8.3.1 Abstract

RPCs are provided by Unix-based [2] and other operating systems such as VxWorks [3] as a more abstract and usable form of Interprocess Communications (IPC). RPCs allow the invocation of services across a network in a way very similar to how a local service would be invoked. In the object-oriented world, we refer to RMCs (Remote Method Calls), but the concept is the same: provide a means to invoke services across a network in a manner as similar as possible to how they are invoked locally.

8.3.2 Problem

The programming model used to invoke services locally is very well understood: dereference an association (most commonly implemented as a pointer or reference) and invoke the service. This is done in a synchronous fashion—the caller blocking until the server completes the request and returns whatever values were requested. What is needed is a means to do the same thing even when the client and server are not colocated.

8.3.3 Pattern Structure

Figure 8-3 shows the basic structure for the Remote Method Call Pattern. Ultimately, the *Client* wants to invoke a service on the *Server*. It does so by invoking a *Client Stub* that knows how to marshal the service request in terms of the underlying transport protocol and the network data representation format. The *Server Stub* listens for service requests (usually by registering with the server-side OS with a specific port number), demarshals the request, and invokes the specified method on the server. When it completes, the *Server Stub* then issues a return() to the *Client Stub,* returning any requested values via the underlying transport protocol, which are ultimately returned to the waiting client. From the client's point of view, it is very much like calling a local method except that a few special operations must be invoked first to set up the logical connection between the *Client Stub* and *Server Stub.*

Note that if the underlying operating system already supports RPCs, then the application developer really only needs to be concerned with the *Client* and *Server* classes and how to invoke the remote procedure call mechanism from the OS. If the underlying OS does not support RPCs natively, then the application developer must explicitly construct all the classes in the pattern.

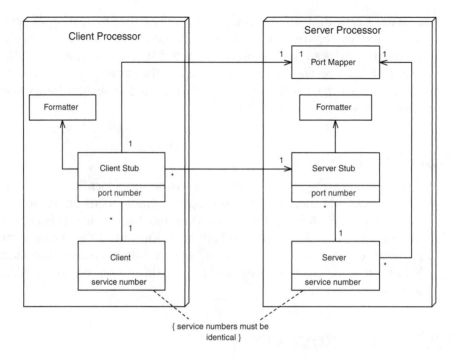

Figure 8-3: *Remote Method Call Pattern*

8.3.4 Collaboration Roles

- *Client*

  The *Client* is the object wanting to invoke the method. The *Client* invokes the service synchronously—that is, it *blocks,* remaining suspended, until the service on the remote processors has completed and the *Client* had been notified of that completion.

  The *Client* associates with as many *Client Stubs* as remote methods that it wants to invoke, one *Client Stub* per remote method. How the service is invoked is OS specific, but commonly special OS calls are provided for this purpose. The *Client* and *Server* must agree on the service number of the method, since this is how the requested service will be identified. The format of the service number is specific to the RPC implementation, but commonly it includes three distinct values: a server program number, a server program version number, and a procedure number.

- *Client Stub*

  The *Client Stub* contains knowledge of how to invoke the remote service, mapping from the simple request from the *Client* into a series of messages sent over the network. For this to function, the *Client Stub* must know the *port number* of the service. During setup, the *Client Stub* will query the *Port Mapper* for the port number of the service, also represented as a value called the *service number*. The service number may include the program number, the program version number, and the procedure number.

  A *Client Stub* is most often created through a protocol compiler, compiling a specification of the requested service into a stub that performs the marshalling of the request and the demarshalling of the response. It may also be written by hand. The *Client Stub* waits for the response from the *Server Stub* via OS calls or by running as a daemon.

- *Formatter*

  The *Formatter* takes the local representation of the data in the parameter list and changes the format into network format (for messages to be transmitted) or from network format into local format (for received messages). If RPCs are directly supported in your OS, then a set of formatters will be provided for the standard primitive types. For more complex data and object types, you must provide your own.

- *Port Mapper*

  The *Port Mapper* binds ports to addresses and returns a port number (address) for a specified service request. A port is a logical communications channel, and it is usually identified with a number. A server specifies a service number and registers it with the *Port Mapper*, who allocates a port for it and returns it to the *Server*. If the OS supports RPCs, then it will provide a built-in *Port Mapper* for the *Servers* to use.

- *Server*

  The *Server* provides the method to be invoked by the remote *Client*. In order to publish this service, the *Server* must register the service with the *Port Mapper*, who allocates a port number for it. The *Server Stub* monitors this port number (via OS services) waiting for requests.

- *Server Stub*
  The *Server Stub* monitors its specified port number for requests. This is generally done via OS calls (or by running as a daemon), waiting for a network message with a matching port number. When a request is received, the message is demarshalled with the help of the *Formatter,* and the request is passed on to the *Server* for processing. When the invoked method completes, the *Server Stub* issues a response message back to the *Client Stub,* which then notifies the waiting *Client.* Return values coming from the *Server* are put into network format (with the aid of the *Formatter*) and back into client-side local format (with the aid of the client-side *Formatter*) for consumption of the *Client.*

8.3.5 Consequences

RMCs simplify the process of client-server communication over a network. The writing of the Clients and Servers is greatly simplified and, although the stubs are protocol specific, they tend to be simplified as well over IPC programming, especially when protocol compilers are used. Of course, timing is delayed over local calls because of the necessity to translate into network data format and back and because of network delays. Further, more elaborate error handling may be required because networking infrastructure is inherently less reliable than local calls. If timeliness or reliability of service completion is important, then the underlying transport protocol should be selected with those requirements in mind. ONC RPC, for example, is implemented with UDP, an "unreliable" protocol. TCP can be used instead, but the application developer must use lower-level calls to achieve this.

8.3.6 Implementation Strategies

As mentioned, many OSs support RPCs "out of the box" and provide programming library support for RPCs, including protocol compilers. The interested reader is referred to references [2] and [3] for programming on specific platforms.

The Client and Server must agree on the *service number* because this identifies the method to be invoked. As an example, with ONC RPC, the server registers with a call to

```
int registerrpc(u_long prognum, u_long versnum, u_long
procnum, char *(*procname)(), xdrproc_t inproc,
xdrproc_t outproc)
```

where

- *prognum* is the number of the server program providing the procedure to be invoked.
- *versnum* is the version number of the program.
- *procnum* is the number of the procedure to be published.
- *procname* is the procedure to be invoked when a request is made.
- *inproc* is the data formatting filter to be invoked to convert incoming parameters to local format.
- *outproc* is the data formatting filter to be invoked to convert outgoing responses to network format.

In this case, the service number is represented as three distinct u_long values, *prognum*, *versnum*, and *procnum*.

To wait for requests, a server in an ONC RPC system makes a call to svc_run() to go to sleep and wait for requests. On the client side, the *Client* must make a request that results in the transmission of a network message. In ONC RPC, it does this by invoking the callrpc().

```
int callrpc(char *host, u_long prognum, u_long versnum,
u_long procnum, char *(*procname)(), xdrproc_t inproc,
char *in, xdrproc_t outproc, char *out)
```

where

- *host* is the name of the server machine.
- *in* points to the parameter list for the requested service (in ONC RPC, this is a single parameter).
- *out* points to the return value.

The other parameters are equivalent to their counterparts in the registerrpc() call.

When the selected OS does not support RPCs, then the infrastructure may be added, including the *Port Manager, Client Stub,* and *Server Stub.*

8.3.7 Related Patterns

The RMC pattern provides similar capabilities as the Shared Memory Pattern, but it does so at a higher level of abstraction. Further, it doesn't require specialized hardware support (other than a network or bus), but it is most commonly provided in Unix and related operating systems. It requires the *Client* and *Server* to use identical numbering conventions for the program, version, and procedures (commonly achieved by using shared include files).

The RMC pattern makes no attempt to optimize network traffic and is a call-on-demand or *pull* approach; that is, the *Server* merely responds to a request from the *Client*. The Observer pattern provides a *push* approach in which the *Clients* registers with the *Server* for notification when data-of-interest has changed. The RMC pattern is preferred when it is not data that is being shared but rather invocation of a service that just happens to be remotely located.

8.3.8 Sample Model

The simple three-processor model shown in Figure 8-4 illustrates the pattern. If the example is deployed on Unix operating systems that support RPCs, then the application developer is really only concerned with three of the classes: *Alarm Manager, Sensor Control,* and *Motion Sensor.* The rest are created and managed invisibly for him or her by the operating systems. The operating system-created classes are shown with a dashed-line border. If you are realizing the pattern

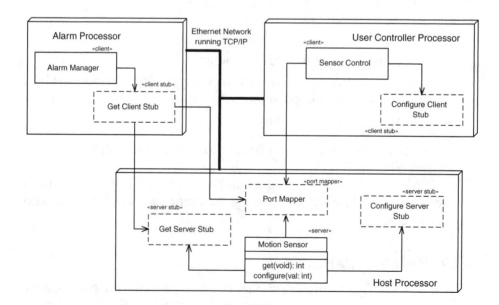

Figure 8-4: *Remote Method Call Example*

without operating system support, then you will implement these classes as well.

The scenario in Figure 8-5 shows a typical application of this pattern using the model structure shown in Figure 8-4. To differentiate between the messages visible to the application-level classes and those visible only to the infrastructure classes, the application-level messages are shown in bold, and the messages among the infrastructure are shown lightfaced. In addition, the thick line at the left of the

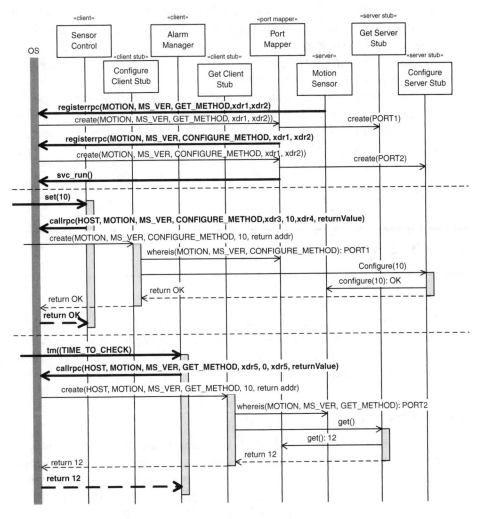

Figure 8-5: *Remote Method Call Scenario*

sequence diagram (called a "collaboration boundary") represents all objects other than those explicitly shown. In this case, it represents the underlying OS and networking structures that are not explicitly shown on the diagram.

We can see that the *Motion Sensor* object acts as a server. It registers with the OS via registerrpc() operation for both methods (get() and configure()) it wants to publish. Then it goes to sleep, waiting for the client requests via the svc_run() operation call.

The *Sensor Control* client calls the *Motion Sensor::configure()* operation via the RPC mechanism. The infrastructure takes care of the details, including the creation of the *Configure Client Stub,* which queries the Host *Port Mapper* to identify the logical port and then invokes the *Configure Client Stub.* This object in turn calls the desired operation and returns the value OK.

Later, the *Alarm Manager* receives a timeout event, and it goes to get the sensor value. It does this, naturally, via the RPC mechanism in a way very similar to the previous case. From the application viewpoint, very little must be done to invoke the methods on the remove server object.

8.4 OBSERVER PATTERN

The Observer Pattern is perhaps arguably more of a mechanistic design than architectural design pattern. However, it will serve as the basis for other distribution collaboration architecture patterns, and so it is included here.

8.4.1 Abstract

The Observer Pattern (aka "Publish-Subscribe") addresses the specific issue of how to notify a set of clients in a timely way that a value that they care about has changed, especially when the notification process is to be repeated for a relatively long period of time. The basic solution offered by the Observer Pattern is to have the clients "subscribe" to the server to be notified about the value in question according to some policy. This policy can be "when the value changes," "at least every so often," "at most every so often," etc. This minimizes computational effort for notification of clients and across a communications bus and minimizes the bus bandwidth required for notification of the appropriate clients.

8.4.2 Problem

The problem addressed by the Observer Pattern is how to notify some number of clients in a timely fashion of a data value according to some abstract policy, such as "when it changes," "every so often," "at most every so often," and "at least every so often." One approach is for every client to query the data value but this can be computationally wasteful, especially when a client wants to be notified only when the data value changes. Another solution is for the server of this information to be designed knowing its clients. However, we don't want to "break" the classic client-server model by giving the server knowledge about its clients. That makes the addition of new clients a design change, making it more difficult to do dynamically at run-time.

8.4.3 Pattern Structure

Figure 8-6 shows the structure of the Observer Pattern. The structure is very simple, expressing a very simple idea; that the solution is to dynamically couple the client to the server with a subscription policy. The server contains that data of interest, and clients register or deregister for it. When a client registers, it supplies a way to send that information to the client. Classically, this is a callback (method address), but it can also be an object ID or some other means to pass the value back to the client. When the policy indicates the data should be sent to the clients, the server looks up all the registered clients and sends it to the clients

This pattern is what is classically deemed a "mechanistic" design pattern because the scope of the application of the pattern is "collaborationwide" rather than "systemwide." However, it is used as a basis for more elaborate patterns that employ its principle across distributed architectures, and so it is included here.

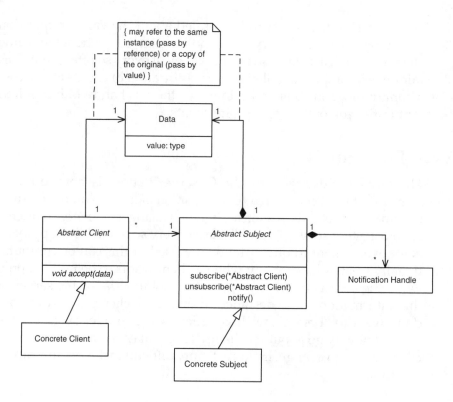

Figure 8-6: *Observer Pattern*

8.4.4 Collaboration Roles

- *Abstract Client*
  The *Abstract Client* associates with the *Abstract Subject* so that it can invoke *subscribe()* and *unsubscribe()* as necessary. It contains an *accept()* operation called to accept the information required via the subscription, the address (as a *Notification Handle*) of which is passed to the *Abstract Subject* instance to which it connects. There are many different ways to specify how to notify the client when new or updated information is available, but callbacks (pointers to an accept() operation of the client) are the most common.

- *Abstract Subject*
  The *Abstract Subject* acts as a server of information desired by the *Abstract Clients*. It accepts *subscribe* and *unsubscribe* requests from

its clients. When the policy dictates that the *Abstract Subject* must notify its clients, it walks the client list to notify each. As noted in the Implementation Strategies sections, a number of implementation means may be used to notify the subscribed clients.

- *Notification Handle*
  The *Notification Handle* stores information for each client so that the *Abstract Subject* can notify the *Abstract Client* of the value stored in the *Data* class. The most common implementation strategy for object communication is to use a pointer (or a reference) to the *Abstract Client::accept()* operation. However, there are other means to implement *Notification Handles,* such as local object identifiers, protocol-specific remote object IDs, network node port numbers, or even URLs.

- *Concrete Client*
  The *Concrete Client* is an application-specific subclass of the *Abstract Client.* The pattern is applied by subclassing the *Abstract Client* and adding application-specific semantics into the new subclass.

- *Concrete Subject*
  The *Concrete Subject* is an application-specific subclass of the *Abstract Subject* class. The pattern is applied by subclassing the *Abstract Subject* and adding application-specific semantics to the subclass.

- *Data*
  The *Data* class contains the information that the *Abstract Subject* knows and the *Abstract Client* wants to know. The *Data* object containing the appropriate value may be shared with the clients either "by reference" (such as passing a pointer to the single instance of the *Data* object) or "by value" (copying the *Data* object for each of the subscribing clients).

8.4.5 Consequences

The Observer Pattern simplifies the process of managing the sharing of values among a single server with possibly many clients. The simplification occurs in a number of ways. First, the Observer Pattern has run-time flexibility. It is easy at run-time to change the number of subscribers as well as the identity of the subscribers because the

Abstract Subject does not need to have any information about its clients prior to their subscription. Further, all this information that the *Abstract Subject* needs can be provided by the clients during the subscription process. Second, a single policy to the timely or efficient updating of the clients can be centralized in the server and not replicated in the potentially many clients. This means that the code that implements the notification policy needs to be running in only a single place (the server) rather than many places (the individual clients).

8.4.6 Implementation Strategies

The primary points of variation in implementation of the Observer Pattern are in the formulation of the notification Handle, the implementation of the notification policy, and the type of data sharing.

The most common means for implementing object associations is a pointer (in C or C++) or a reference (in C++ or Java). A callback is a virtualized association and may use the same implementation. In this case, the one-to-many composition relation between the *Abstract Subject* and the *Notification Handle* classes is implemented using an array or list of function pointers. When the server and the clients are not in the same address space, we use a Proxy Pattern, which is discussed later in the chapter.

The notification policy may be built in to the *Abstract Subject* and potentially overridden in the *Concrete Subject* subclasses, or the Strategy Pattern may be employed. To use the Strategy Pattern, the notification policy is reified as a separate class that instructs the *Abstract Subject* when it is appropriate to notify the registered clients. The following are the most common notification policies.

- When the relevant data (*Data.value*) changes
- Periodically
- Both at the time of change and periodically

The last primary implementation issue is how to pass the information around. The two primary approaches are by reference and by value. When passed by reference, the most common implementation is to pass a pointer or reference to the single *Data* object owned by the server. In this pattern it is important to ensure that the clients only read the information; it should only be modified by the *Abstract*

Subject. Further, if the data is to be shared among clients that may reside in different threads, then care must be taken to protect the data from corruption due to mutual exclusion problems. The resource management patterns from Chapter 5, such as the Guarded Call Pattern, can be used to ensure the resource's integrity is maintained. When the data is shared by value, then a copy of the *Data* object is made for each subscriber—who then has the explicit responsibility to destroy that object when it is no longer needed. This approach has the advantage that data protect issues go away but the disadvantage that more memory is needed and, the issues around dynamic allocation, such as lack of timeliness predictability and memory fragmentation, must be dealt with.

8.4.7 Related Patterns

The Observer Pattern is a simple approach that may be elaborated to address sharing of information between a single server and a set of clients. It serves as the founding concept for the Data Bus, Proxy, and Broker Patterns, for example.

8.4.8 Sample Model

Figure 8-7 shows a straightforward example of this simple pattern. Figure 8-7a shows the class structure of the model. Central to that structure is the *Wheel Sensor,* which acts as the «concrete subject», and the *Cruise Control, Speedometer,* and the *Antispin Controller* act as «concrete clients».

Figure 8-7b shows an example scenario of the execution of the structure shown in Figure 8-7a. In this scenario, each of the clients registers with the server by calling its subscribe operation. Later, when an *evGetData* event is sent to the server, it walks the *Callback List* to find all the registered clients and sends them the data. This is done by calling the *Callbacklist::getFirst* and *CallbackList::getNext()* operations; these return a pointer to a client, which may then be dereferenced and the target object's *accept()* function called. When the *CallbackList::getNext()* operation returns NULL, then the walk through the list is complete. At the end of the scenario, the *Antispin Controller* is sent an *evDisable* event, and so it unsubscribes from the server.

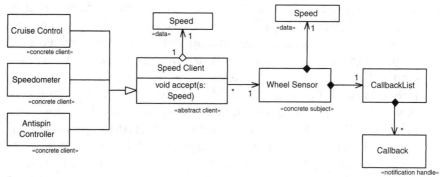

a. Structure

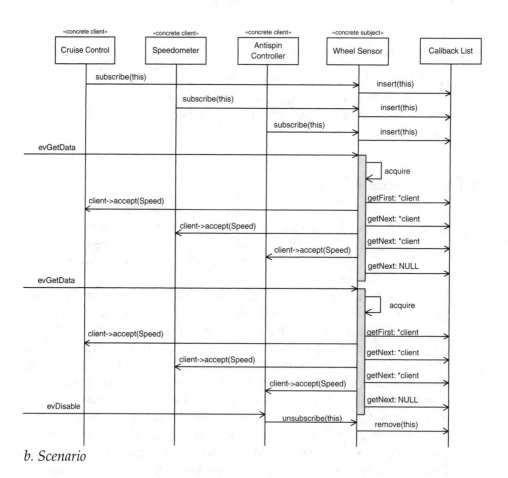

b. Scenario

Figure 8-7: *Observer Pattern Example*

8.5 Data Bus Pattern

The Data Bus Pattern further abstracts the Observer Pattern by providing a common (logical) bus to which multiple servers post their information and where multiple clients come to get various events and data posted to the bus. This pattern is useful when a large number of servers and clients must share data and events and is easily supported by some hardware bus structures that broadcast messages, such as the CAN (Control Area Network) bus architectures.

8.5.1 Abstract

The Data Bus Pattern provides a single locale (the "Data Bus") for the location of information to be shared across multiple processors. Clients desiring information have a common location for pulling information as desired or subscribing for pushed data. The Data Bus Pattern is basically a Proxy Pattern with a centralized store into which various data objects may be plugged.

8.5.2 Problem

Many systems need to share many different data among a mixture of servers and clients, some of whom might not be known when the client or data is designed. This pattern solves the problem by providing a central storage facility into which data that is to be shared may be plugged along with metadata that describes its contents.

8.5.3 Pattern Structure

The pattern comes in both "push" and "pull" varieties. In the pull version, the client objects check the *Data Bus* for new data of concern. To get new or updated information, the *Concrete Client* number queries the *Data Bus* for the information again. Figure 8-8 shows the structure of the pull version of the Data Bus Pattern. In the push version, shown in Figure 8-9, the *Listener* objects register with the *Data Bus,* just as the client objects subscribe with the server in the Observer Pattern. The *Listener* objects are subsequently notified

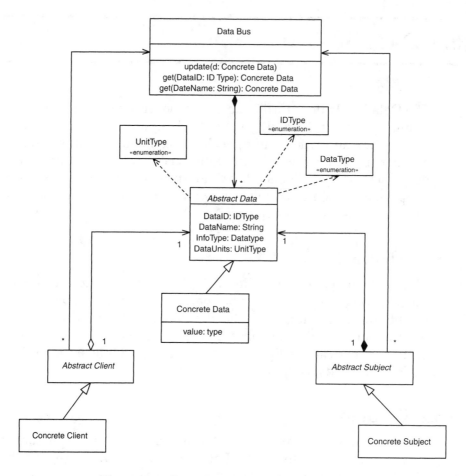

Figure 8-8: *Data Bus Pattern (Pull Version)*

according to some policy, just as when that datum is updated to the *Data Bus*.

The pattern also contains *metadata*—that is, information about the data. The metadata in this pattern are the data types, ID types, and units of the data objects stored. The metadata is useful because it allows data to be identified and properly used, even when it is published in a different type of unit from how its clients wish to manipulate it. The metadata serves to further decouple the client implementation from the server's.

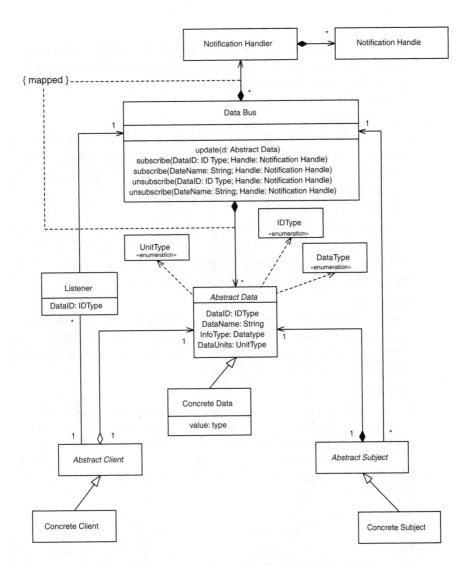

Figure 8-9: *Data Bus Pattern (Push Version)*

8.5.4 Collaboration Roles

- *Abstract Data*
  The Abstract Data class specifies the basic structure of all data objects that may be plugged into the Data Bus. The important attributes are the following.

Data ID: ID Type

The *Data ID* identifies which datum this is as an enumerated value. For example, the *Data ID Type* might be {Wheelspeed=0, EngineSpeed=2, EngineTemperature=3, OilTemperature=4, Oil-Pressure=5}.

Data Name: String

The *Data Name* provides an alternative means to identify the datum of concern. The advantage of using this approach is that this is an inherently extensible data type at the expense of computational effort to parse and search strings.

Info Type: Data Type

The *Info Type* is the primitive type of the information, as opposed to its name, which is provided by the first two attributes. This is an enumerated type of the primitive types available. For example, it might be {SHORT, INT, LONG, FLOAT, DOUBLE, STRING}.

Data Units

This attribute identifies the application units for the datum in question, also stored as an enumerated type. For example, if the data represents a weight, then units might be one of {GRAM, KILOGRAM, OUNCE, POUND, TON}.

- *Abstract Client*

  In the pull version, the *Abstract Client* requests specified *Data* from the *Data Bus* when it wants to check for new or updated data. In the push version, the *Listener* subscribes to the *Data Bus* and notifies its associated *Abstract Client* when it has new data. The *Listener* specifies the *Data ID* (or the *Data Name*) to which it wishes to subscribe.

- *Abstract Subject*

  The *Abstract Subject* provides the *Data* that plug into the *Data Bus*. There are typically many different *Abstract Subjects*, and each *Abstract Subject* may, in fact, provide multiple different *Data* objects. Each *Data* object is distinguished on the basis of its *Data ID* and/or its *Data Name* attribute. Most commonly, a *Data* object with a specific *Data ID* is only provided by a single *Abstract Subject* instance.

- *Concrete Data*

  This is the specific *Data* subclass that defines a systemwide unique datum. It will have a unique *Data ID* and *Data Name*. The subclass includes the typed attribute *value*.

- *Concrete Client*

  This is the specific subclass of the *Abstract Client* that uses the Data objects it gets from one or more *Abstract Subjects* via the *Data Bus*.

- *Concrete Subject*

  The *Concrete Subject* is an instantiable subclass of *Abstract Subject*.

- *Data Bus*

  The *Data Bus* provides the centralized locale for the *Data* objects to be shared. The *Data Bus* does not know the specific subclasses of the *Data* class that will be plugged into it or even how many different *Data* objects will be held.

  In the push version of the pattern, the *Data Bus* object strongly aggregates a set of *Notification Lists*—one for each different unique *Data ID* or *Data Name*. This is shown in Figure 8-9 with the {mapped} constraint, meaning that there is a Notification List for every different *Data* object aggregated by the *Data Bus*.

  The *Data Bus* object provides a number of important operations.

  get(DataID: ID Type): Concrete Data

  In the pull version, the *get* operation finds the specified data by the *Data ID* and returns it to the calling *Abstract Client*.

  get(DataName: String): Concrete Data

  In the pull version, the *get* operation finds the specified data by the *Data Name* attribute and returns it to the calling *Abstract Client*.

  Subscribe(DataID: ID Type; Handle: Notification Handle)

  In the push version, the *Listener* subscribes or unsubscribes to the requested data. This can be done by calling this operation and passing in the *Data ID*.

  Subscribe(DataName: String; Handle: Notification Handle)

  This operation works the same as the other *Subscribe* operation except that it uses the *Data Name* rather than the *Data ID*.

  Unsubscribe(DataID: ID Type; Handle: Notification Handle)

  This operation allows a *Listener* to unsubscribe to a specific *Datum*. The *Data ID* specifies which *Datum*, and the *Handle* specifies which client.

  Unsubscribe(DataName: String; Handle: Notification Handle)

  This operation serves the same purpose as the previous unsubscribe operation but uses the *Data Name* to identify the *Datum* of interest.

update(d: Concrete Data)

The operation update() replaces the existing *Data* object with the same *Data ID* (or *Data Name*) if one exists. If not, then the *Data* object is added to the list of available *Data* objects.

*   *Data Type*

This is an enumeration of primitive data types used to represent the values in the *Concrete Data* objects, such as *int, long, float, double, string,* and so on. This metadata allows subscribers to deal with the data in different formats.

*   *ID Type*

The *ID Type* identifies the logical name of the *Concrete Data* in the system. There may be many objects with type *int*, but the *Data Type* allows the specific information carried by the *Data* objects to be known. This is an enumeration type—for example, {Wheelspeed=0, EngineSpeed=2, EngineTemperature=3, OilTemperature=4, OilPressure=5}.

*   *Listener*

The *Listener* object monitors the *Data Bus* via periodic polling for new *Data* objects with a specific *Data ID* or *Data Name*. The *Listener* only appears in the push version of the pattern.

*   *Notification List*

In the push version of the pattern, the *Data Bus* must maintain a list of subscribers for each *Data* object with a unique *Data ID* or *Data Name*. Each *Notification List* manages a list of subscribers, and each subscriber has a unique *Notification Handle* to identify how the data may be pushed to it when appropriate.

*   *Notification Handle*

This object serves the same function as in the Observer Pattern: provides a means for the *Data Bus* to send the data to the *Abstract Client* when it must. In this case, the *Notification Handles* must be implemented in such a way as to cross address space boundaries, such as an *Object ID* with a processor address known to the underlying communications protocol.

*   *Unit Type*

The *Unit Type* is an enumerated type of units appropriate for the data, such as {OUNCES, POUNDS, GRAMS, KILOGRAMS, INCHES, FEET, YARDS, MILES, CENTIMETERS, METERS, KILOMETERS, DEGREES_F, DEGREES_C } or whatever may be appropriate for the application.

8.5.5 Consequences

The Data Bus pattern has an advantage in that there is always a *single* location for clients to go and acquire required data and for servers to publish their data. The Data Bus doesn't understand the semantics of the data that it serves to the clients, but it can manage an arbitrarily large set of different data objects and types. The Data Bus is very extensible, and new data object types may be added even at run-time without modification of the Data Bus and its closely related classes. All that is required is creating the appropriate *Concrete Subject* and *Concrete Client* and adding the enumerated *Data ID* to the *ID Type* and possibly adding additional unit values to the *Unit Type*.

The Data Bus location, or at least knowledge of how to send it messages, must be known at design time. The location of the Data Bus must be rich enough to store all the instances of the subclasses of the *Abstract Data* class. The traffic required to manage the serving of all the information contained by the Data Bus may limit that node's capacity to do other work. The push version of the pattern is a bit more complicated but minimizes traffic over the underlying communications media because data is only sent out to the subscribed clients and only when it is appropriate to do so. The pull version, while a bit simpler, may result in more overall bus traffic to do repeated queries for data that may not have changed.

This pattern is useful for symmetric architectures, especially when the servers are located on "unconvenient" processors, such as those with low capacity to manage the required communications traffic or those that may be relatively inaccessible to the clients.

8.5.6 Implementation Strategies

The Data Bus may be implemented on top of a regular data base server if desired, but many embedded systems lack the resources for that approach. Because the Data Bus is potentially remote, the Abstract Subject, Abstract Client, and Listener class must know how to marshal messages to communicate with the Data Bus. That infrastructure is protocol-specific and is not represented in the pattern.

8.5.7 Related Patterns

The Observer Pattern offers capabilities similar to the push version of the Data Bus Pattern but only locally—that is, within the same address space. The Proxy Pattern may be thought of as a distributed version of the Observer Pattern and offers capabilities similar to the Data Bus Pattern. In both of these alternatives, the servers and clients ultimately link directly with each other, requiring the clients to know *a priori* how to contact the servers. Thus, these latter patterns are more appropriate for asymmetric distribution architectures wherein the location of the objects is known at design time. The Data Bus Pattern provides these capabilities for a symmetric architecture, which permits dynamic load balancing to occur as the system runs.

8.5.8 Sample Model

Figure 8-10 shows the four-processor system as an example of the pull version of the pattern. The system controls a motor, monitors its output speed, and provides a user interface. The fourth processor manages the repository: the Data Bus and its aggregated Data objects.

The User Control Processor contains an instance of class *Motor Controller* that takes the input from a Knob and uses it to set the output speed of the Motor. *Motor Controller* acts as a concrete server for the SetMValue (set motor value) information. The *Motor Controller* updates this information to the Data Bus object on the Repository processor. The *Motor* object running on the Motor Control Processor is a client for this information and uses it as the commanded speed of the motor. It gets that information from the *Data Bus*.

The Monitoring Processor contains the instance of the *Motor Sensor* class. This class monitors the true output speed of the motor and acts as a server for ActualMValue (actual motor value). It writes this value out to the Data Bus where it is pulled by the *Motor View* object running on the User Control Processor.

The Motor View is a client for both the SetMValue and the ActualMValue data objects. This object displays the commanded (SetMValue) and the true (ActualMValue) speeds for the motor on the user display. It gets this information from the Data Bus in the normal (pull) way.

Note that the Data objects SetMValuex and ActualMValuex are all instances of the class *Motor Speed*. For clarity reasons, the object names differ on the different processors (because they are, after all, different objects even if they have identical values). For example, SetMValue0 is the instance owned by the Data Bus, while SetMValue1 is owned by the server (*Motor Controller*), SetMValue2 is

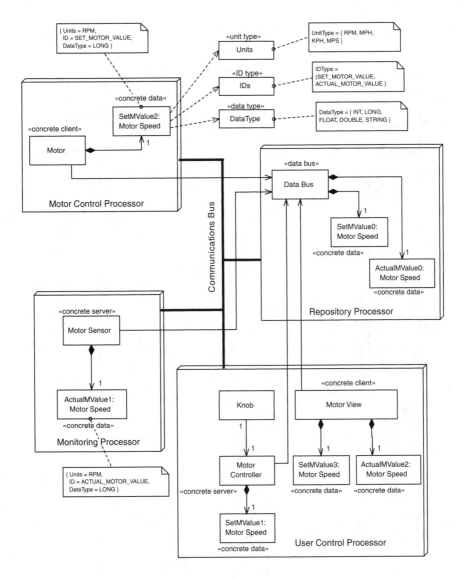

Figure 8-10: *Data Bus Pattern Example Structure*

owned by the *Motor* client, and SetMValue3 is owned by the *Motor View* client. The *Motor Speed* class depends on the Units, IDs, and Data Type classes, all enumerated types, as shown in the figure.

Figure 8-11 shows a scenario of the structural model shown in Figure 8-10. The scenario begins with the *Motor Controller* receiving a

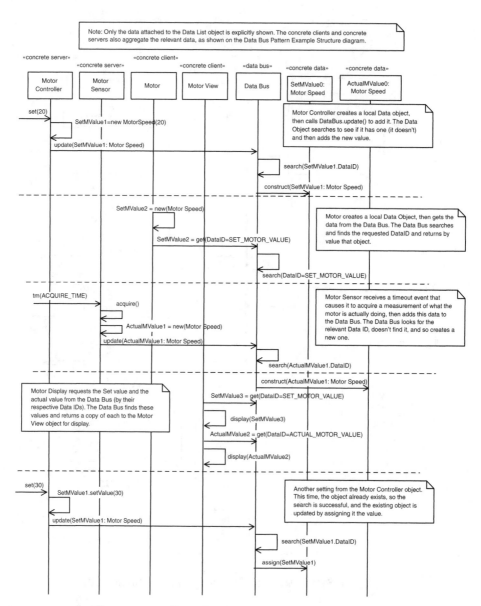

Figure 8-11: *Data Bus Pattern Example Scenario*

set value from the *Knob*. It creates a local instance of *Motor Speed* called *SetMValue1*. It then invokes *DataBus.update()*. The *Data Bus* object searches for the presence of the specified DataID (which it doesn't find), and then it creates a local copy of it called *SetMValue0*.

Later, when the *Motor* queries the *Data Bus* for the set value, the *Data Bus* finds the requested data object and returns it.

The *Motor Sensor* receives a timeout (shown as a tm(ACQUIRE_TIME) message in the scenario), and it then acquires the data, creates the *ActualMValue1* instance, and updates the *Data Bus* in a very similar fashion to the previous example.

Later, the *Motor View* object requests both the set value and the actual value for display. The *Data Bus* has both values and returns them, in turn, to the *Motor View*. Finally, the *Motor Controller* receives another set value, and the *Data Bus* object updates the existing value of the *SetMValue0* instance on the Repository Processor.

8.6 PROXY PATTERN

The Proxy Pattern abstracts the true server from the client by means of a "stand-in" or surrogate class providing a separation of a client and a server, allowing the hiding of specified properties of the server from the clients.

8.6.1 Abstract

The Proxy Pattern abstracts the true server from the client by means of a "stand-in" or surrogate class. There are a number of reasons why this may be useful, such as to hide some particular implementation properties from the clients and thus allow them to vary transparently to the client. For our purposes here, the primary reason to use the Proxy Pattern is to hide the fact that a server may be actually located in another address space from its client. This allows the server to be located in any accessible location, and the clients need not concern themselves with how to contact the true server to access required information or services.

8.6.2 Problem

The design of modern embedded systems must often be deployed across multiple address spaces, such as different processors. Often such details are subject to change during the design process or, even worse, during the implementation of the system. It is problematic to "hard-code" the knowledge that a server may be remote because this may change many times as the design progresses. Further, the clients and servers may be redeployed in other physical architectures and using different communications media. If the clients are intimately aware of these design details, then porting the clients to the new platforms is more difficult.

The two primary problems addressed by the Proxy Pattern are the transparency of the potential remoteness of the servers and the hiding and encapsulation of the means by which to contact such remote servers.

8.6.3 Pattern Structure

The Proxy Pattern, shown in Figure 8-12, clearly shows its lineage from the Observer Pattern. Indeed, the Proxy Pattern differs primarily in that it adds a proxy between the *Abstract Client* and the *Abstract Subject*.

The pattern has two sides. In the first side, the *Client-side Proxies* subscribe to the *Server-side Proxies*, which publish the data under the command of the *Concrete Servers*. When the *Concrete Servers* call the send() operation, all the remote *Client-side Proxies* are notified of the new data.

On the other side, the *Concrete Clients* subscribe in turn to the *Client-side Proxies*, just as in the Observer Pattern, where *Concrete Clients* subscribe to *Concrete Servers*. When these *Client-side Proxies* are notified of new data, they walk their notification lists to send the data to all their local subscribers.

Although the structure of the pattern emphasizes the exchange of *Data* objects, this is only one kind of service that can be performed via the Proxy Pattern. In fact, any service may be published by the server and accessed via the proxy classes, even if no data is actually exchanged.

8.6.4 Collaboration Roles

- *Abstract Client*
  The *Abstract Client* associates with the *Client-side Proxy* so that it can invoke the latter's *subscribe()* and *unsubscribe()* operations as

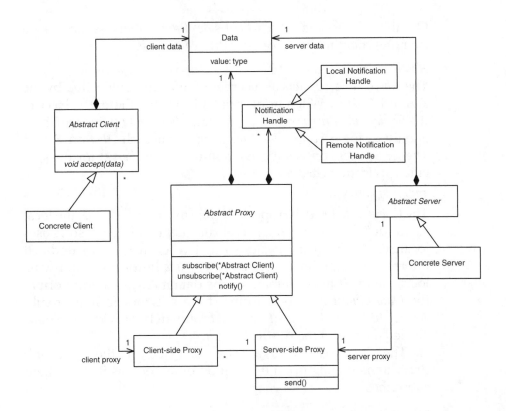

Figure 8-12: *Proxy Pattern*

necessary. It contains an *accept()* operation called to accept the information required via the subscription, the address (as a *Notification Handle*) of which is passed to the *Client-side Proxy* instance to which it connects.

- *Abstract Proxy*
  The *Abstract Proxy* provides the general mechanisms to handle client subscriptions and data delivery. It aggregates, via composition, zero-to-many *Notification Handle* objects (to notify the instances of its clients) and *Data* object. It has two subclasses: one to service the application clients and one to service the application server. On the client-side, the proxy acts in the same fashion as the *Abstract Subject* class in the Observer Pattern: Clients subscribe to receive the data that is subsequently "pushed" to them.

On the server-side, the *Client-side Proxy* subclass acts as a (remote) client to the *Server-side* Proxy subclass.

- *Abstract Server*
  The *Abstract Server* acts as a server of information desired by the *Abstract Clients*. When appropriate, it pushes the data object to the *Server-side Proxy* by calling the latter's *send()* operation. There is only a single *Server-side Proxy* object for each *Abstract Server*. The *Abstract Server* is subclassed into *Concrete Server* for the specific application classes.

- *Client-side Proxy*
  The *Client-side Proxy* is a specialized proxy that serves as the local "stand-in" for the remote server. Its clients are local, so it uses localized *Notification Handles* so that when it receives updated information from its associated *Server-side Proxy*, it can notify its local clients. It must unmarshal the data messages and reformat the *Data Object* into local format from network format. It subscribes to the *Server-side Proxy* that ultimately provides the marshalled data from the *Abstract Server*.

  The *Client-side Proxy* usually subscribes to the *Server-side Proxy* immediately upon its creation or as soon as its first client subscribes.

- *Concrete Client*
  The *Concrete Client* is an application-specific subclass of the *Abstract Client*. The pattern is applied by subclassing the *Abstract Client* and adding application-specific semantics into the new subclass.

- *Concrete Server*
  The *Concrete Subject* is an application-specific subclass of the *Abstract Server* class. The pattern is applied by subclassing the *Abstract Server* and adding application-specific semantics to the subclass.

- *Data*
  The *Data* class contains the information that the *Abstract Server* knows and the *Abstract Client* wants to know. The *Data* object containing the appropriate value may be shared with the clients by value, since it must be at least *potentially* delivered to different address spaces.

- *Local Notification Handle*
  This subclass of the *Notification Handle* class is used by the *Client-side Proxy* class. Most commonly, callbacks (pointers to the accept() method of the *Client-side Proxy* class) are used for the *Local Notification*.

- *Notification Handle*
  The *Notification Handle* stores information for each client so that the *Abstract Proxy* can notify its clients of the value stored in the *Data* class.

- *Remote Notification Handle*
  This subclass of the *Notification Handle* class is used by the *Server-side Proxy* class to store the required information to contact its remote clients, instances of the *Client-side Proxy* class.

- *Server-side Proxy*
  The *Server-side Proxy* provides encapsulation of the *Abstract Server* from the communications media and protocols. It manages remote subscriptions from *Client-side Proxy* objects and notifies them when data is "pushed" to it by the *Abstract Server*. It is responsible for marshalling the information into a network or bus message and converting the data values into network format. The *Server-side Proxy* usually subscribes to the *Abstract Subject* immediately upon its creation.

8.6.5 Consequences

The Proxy Pattern does a good job of isolating the subject from knowledge that the server may be remote. The advantage is that the clients are simplified, not having to deal differently with remote and local clients. The Proxy Pattern also encapsulates the knowledge of how to contact the servers into the proxy classes so that should the communications media change, fewer classes must be updated.

Because there are usually many fewer client-proxy instances (one per data type per address space) than client instances, the traffic on the communications media is minimized. One message is sent across the bus or network for each proxy, rather than one per client. This reduces bus traffic, a common bottleneck in embedded and real-time systems. Bus traffic is reduced even further because of the use of a subscription policy, resulting in transmission of the data only when necessary, as opposed to polling for the data.

8.6.6 Implementation Strategies

On the local (client-proxy) side, the same implementation strategies used for the Observer Pattern apply here. The *Abstract Client* objects subscribe to the *Client-side Proxies* in the same way as in the Observer Pattern. For the remote (server) side, the implementation is generally highly protocol-specific. The *Server-side Proxy* marshals the messages from the *Abstract Server* and invokes the communications system to transmit them to its clients, the remote *Client-side Proxy* objects. The *Server-side Proxy* can do this because the *Client-side Proxy* objects subscribe to the *Server-side Proxy.*

Note that in this case, the *Client-side Proxy* objects must know a priori how to contact the *Server-side Proxy* for the desired information. Thus, this pattern is especially useful on asymmetric distribution architectures—that is, architectures in which the locations of objects are known at design-time.

Note also that both the *Client-side Proxy* and the *Server-side Proxy* classes aggregate *Notification Handle* objects via composition. This latter class will typically be subclassed into "local" and "remote" flavors as an optimization. *Local Notification Handles* may be simple function pointers to the accept() method of the *Concrete Client* class. *Remote Notification Handles* must rely on the underlying transport protocol for message delivery.

8.6.7 Related Patterns

This pattern is an extension of the Observer Pattern to deal with situations in which the servers are in a different address space from their clients. In the special case in which the server and its clients are known to be in the same address space, the Observer Pattern would be a preferable choice because of its simplicity.

The Proxy Pattern here requires a priori knowledge as to the location of the server, although not on the part of the clients. This means that the client proxies know how to subscribe to the server proxy. This is the case in asymmetric distribution architectures in which the address spaces where objects will run is known at design-time. The objects then use this design-time knowledge to simplify their task.

For symmetric distribution architectures, in which the locations of the servers are not known at design time, the Data Bus Pattern centralizes the shared information. The Broker Pattern, described next, allows the clients to dynamically locate the desired servers after locating them through the object request broker.

8.6.8 Sample Model

The example for the Proxy Pattern is shown in Figures 8-13 and 8-14. Figure 8-13 shows the structure of the collaboration and the mapping of the objects onto the physical architecture. Figure 8-14 shows how such a system behaves.

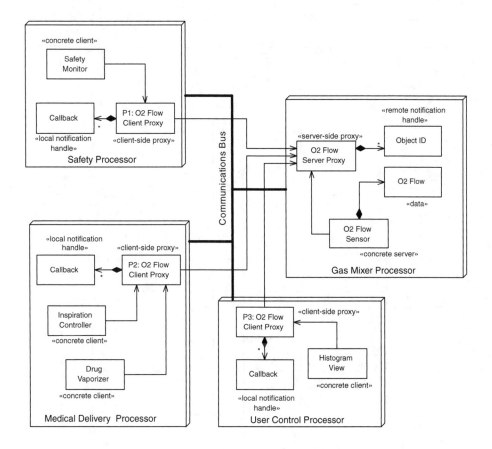

Figure 8-13: *Proxy Pattern Example Structure*

Figure 8-13 shows four nodes: the Gas Mixer, Safety, Medical Delivery, and User Control processors. The Gas Mixer contains the server, an object of class *O2 Flow Sensor.* This connects with a server-side proxy class *O2 Flow Server Proxy.* This proxy aggregates Object IDs to use as addresses on the bus connecting the nodes running a custom communications protocol. This bus (shown as the heavy lines connecting the nodes) provides the physical means to deliver the messages among the objects running on different processors.

The Gas Mixer Processor contains the *O2 Flow Sensor,* which acts as a server for the data. The *O2 Flow Sensor* invokes *O2 Server Proxy::send()* to send the data to all the registered clients. This is done by walking the

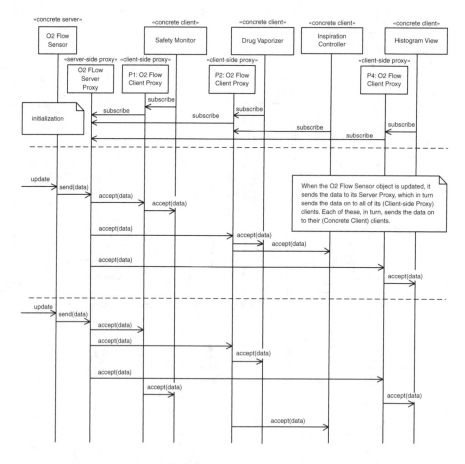

Figure 8-14: *Proxy Pattern Example Scenario*

notification handle list (which holds Object IDs that the lower-level communications protocol uses for message delivery) and sending a message to each registered client (the *O2 Flow Client Proxies*).

There are four clients of the *O2 Flow* data object: the *Safety Monitor* running on the Safety Processor, the *Inspiration Controller* and the *Vaporizer* running on the Medical Deliver Processor, and *Histogram View* running on the User Control Processor. Each processor that contains at least one client also has a single *O2 Flow Client Proxy* instance to obtain the value from the *O2 Flow Server Proxy*.

The scenario shown in Figure 8-14 shows the clients subscribing to their client proxies and the client proxies subscribing to the server proxy. Later, when the *O2 Flow Sensor* receives an update, it invokes the *O2 Flow Server Proxy::send()* operation, which walks the *Notification Handle* list (not shown to save space), and for each registered client proxy, it sends the data. In turn, the receiving client proxy walks *its* client list for the ultimate delivery of the data.

Note: Although the send() operation walks the list of subscribers (*Remote Notification Handles*) in a serial fashion, the delivery of the messages is generally asynchronous, and you cannot determine the arrival order of the messages from the sending order. This is because the objects in different addresses usually operate in different threads, so relative order cannot be determined. That is why in the second update a different deliver order is shown with respect to the delivery of the data to the concrete clients.

8.7 Broker Pattern

The Broker Pattern may be thought of as a symmetric version of the Proxy Pattern—that is, it provides a Proxy Pattern in situations where the location of the clients and servers are not known at design time.

8.7.1 Abstract

The Broker Pattern extends the Proxy Pattern through the inclusion of the *Broker*—an "object reference repository" globally visible to both the clients and the servers. This broker facilitates the location of the servers for the clients so that their respective locations need not be known at design time. This means that more complex systems that can use a symmetric deployment architecture, such as is required for dynamic load balancing, can be employed.

8.7.2 Problem

In addition to the problems addressed by the Proxy Pattern (such as communication infrastructure transparency), a limitation of most of the distribution patterns is that they require a priori knowledge of the location of the servers. This limits their use to asymmetric distribution architectures. Ideally, the solution should provide a means that can locate and then invoke services at the request of the client, including subscription to published data.

8.7.3 Pattern Structure

Figure 8-15a shows the basic structure for the Broker Pattern, containing only the key elements—the *Broker, Client, Client-side Proxy, Server,* and *Server-side Proxy.* Figure 8-15b shows the complete structure, including the *Notification Handles* and *Data* objects. Similar to the Remote Method Call Pattern, the easiest implementation from the application developer's point of view is to use a commercial middleware product, such as a CORBA Object Request Broker (ORB). However, sometimes it is desirable to implement a lightweight *Broker* pattern, and in this case, the infrastructure classes may themselves be implemented by the application developer.

The pattern comes in two flavors: the dynamic and static dispatch versions. In the dynamic dispatch version, the *Broker* mediates all service requests so that there is never a direct linkage between the *Client* (or the *Client-side Proxy*) and the *Server* (or the *Server-side Proxy*). In the static version, the *Broker* serves up a reference address for the *Server,* and then the *Client-side Proxy* uses this information to connect directly with the *Server-side Proxy* for the duration of the session. The *Broker* is only recontacted if the connect link between the proxies breaks.

Note also that just as with the Proxy Pattern, sharing *Data* objects is just one kind of service invocation. It is also possible to invoke services as a one-time request that causes some action to occur on the server-side without transmission of information.

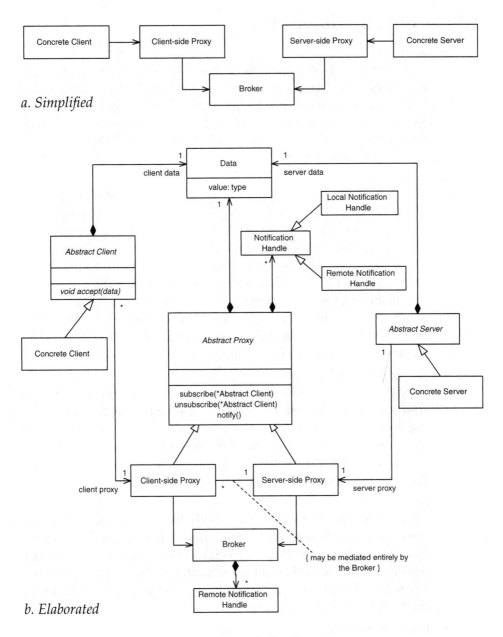

Figure 8-15: *Broker Pattern*

8.7.4 Collaboration Roles

- *Abstract Client*
  The *Abstract Client* associates with the *Client-side Proxy* so that it can invoke the latter's *subscribe()* and *unsubscribe()* operations as necessary. It contains an *accept()* operation called to accept the information required via the subscription, the address (as a *Notification Handle*) of which is passed to the *Client-side Proxy* instance to which it connects.

- *Abstract Proxy*
  The *Abstract Proxy* provides the general mechanisms to handle client subscriptions and data delivery. It aggregates, via composition, zero-to-many *Notification Handle* objects (to notify the instances of its clients) and the *Data* object. It has two subclasses: one to service the application clients and one to service the application server. On the client-side, the proxy acts in the same fashion as the *Abstract Subject* class in the Observer Pattern—clients subscribe to receive the data that is subsequently "pushed" to them. On the server-side, the *Client-side Proxy* subclass acts as a client to the *Server-side* Proxy subclass.

- *Abstract Server*
  The *Abstract Server* acts as a server of information desired by the *Abstract Clients*. When appropriate, it pushes the data object to the *Server-side Proxy* by calling the latter's *accept()* operation. There is only a single *Server-side Proxy* object for each *Abstract Server*. The *Abstract Server* is subclassed into *Concrete Server* for the specific application classes.

- *Broker*
  Concrete Servers (which register with the aid of the *Server-side Proxy*) use the *Broker* to advertise their services. *Concrete Clients* (via their *Client-side Proxy* objects) either request the services directly from the *Broker* (which dispatches them) or request the address and then contact the *Server-side Proxy* directly, depending on the type of *Broker* employed.

- *Client-side Proxy*
  The *Client-side Proxy* is a specialized proxy that serves as the local "stand-in" for the remote server. Its clients are local, so it uses localized *Notification Handles* so that when it receives updated information from its associated *Server-side Proxy*, it can notify its

local clients. It subscribes to the *Server-side Proxy* that ultimately provides the marshalled data from the *Abstract Server*. The *Client-side Proxy* must unmarshal the messages, extract the *Data* object, and format it into client local format.

In the Broker Pattern, the *Client-side Proxy* either queries the *Broker* for the address of the *Server-side Proxy* and then subscribes directly to the *Server-side Proxy* (static linkage model) or subscribes via the *Broker*, which sends the request on to the *Server-side Proxy* at the behest of the *Client-side Proxy*.

- *Concrete Client*
  The *Concrete Client* is an application-specific subclass of the *Abstract Client*. The pattern is applied by subclassing the *Abstract Client* and adding application-specific semantics into the new subclass.

- *Concrete Server*
  The *Concrete Subject* is an application-specific subclass of the *Abstract Server* class. The pattern is applied by subclassing the *Abstract Server* and adding application-specific semantics to the subclass.

- *Data*
  The *Data* class contains the information that the *Abstract Server* knows and the *Abstract Client* wants to know. The *Data* object containing the appropriate value may be shared with the clients by value since it must be at least *potentially* delivered to different address spaces.

- *Local Notification Handle*
  This subclass of the *Notification Handle* class is used by the *Client-side Proxy* class. Most commonly, callbacks (pointers to the accept() method of the *Client-side Proxy* class) are used for the *Local Notification*.

- *Notification Handle*
  The *Notification Handle* stores information for each client so that the *Abstract Proxy* can notify its clients of the value stored in the *Data* class.

- *Remote Notification Handle*
  This subclass of the *Notification Handle* class is used by the *Server-side Proxy* class to store the required information to contact its remote clients, instances of the *Client-side Proxy* class. The *Broker*

stores the *Remote Notification Handles* of the registered Servers so that these addresses can either be used by the *Client-side Proxies* or be used at their request.

- *Server-side Proxy*
  The *Server-side Proxy* provides encapsulation of the *Abstract Server* from the communications media and protocols. It manages remote subscriptions from *Client-side Proxy* objects and notifies them when data is "pushed" to it by the *Abstract Server.* The *Client-side Proxy* classes register with the *Broker* so that *Clients* can find them. The *Server-side Proxy* must take the *Data* object passed to it from the *Concrete Server,* reformat it into network format, and marshal a message to send to the *Client-side Proxy.*

8.7.5 Consequences

The Broker Pattern is a very effective means for hiding the remoteness of clients and servers. While not completely successful in hiding all the details, it nevertheless greatly simplifies the creation of systems with symmetric distribution architectures. There are a number of middleware products that supply ORBs (Object Request Brokers), which give good, and even real-time, performance. In addition, systems constructed with this distribution architecture are highly scalable and hide the underlying details of the processors, their locations, and the communications media. There is good software support for the creation of models using commercial middleware ORBs.

Commercial ORBs do require a minimum amount of resources that may exceed those available in smaller systems. For these cases, it may be possible to use smaller, less capable ORBs or write one from scratch that includes only the desired capabilities.

8.7.6 Implementation Strategies

As with the Remote Method Call (RMC) Pattern, protocol compilers greatly facilitate the creation of the proxies. In the Broker Pattern, protocols between clients and servers are written in *Interface Description Languages* (IDLs). Commercial ORBs, such as those based on CORBA, provide IDL compilers that generate the necessary source-level language statements to implement the model elements.

It is also possible to work at a level above IDL. Some commercial UML tools can use stereotypes on the model classes to identify the interface classes (proxies) and automatically generate the IDL and then run the appropriate IDL compilers as a part of generating the distributed application.

Figure 8-16 shows a very simple example captured in the Rhapsody UML tool.[1] In this simple model, a class called *Server_Interface* contains an attribute *a* (of type *int*) that we want to share with remote clients. We indicate this sharing by stereotyping the class as a «CORBAInterface». The tool then generates the CORBA IDL necessary to publish this data via a CORBA ORB. The class *Client_Interface* contains an operation *getA()* that wants to read the data. By stereotyping

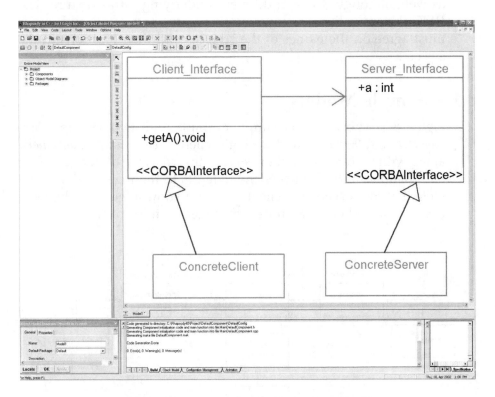

Figure 8-16: *Simple CORBA Example Model*

---

1. Rhapsody is a complete UML design automation tool targeted primarily at real-time and embedded application development, available from I-Logix. See *www.ilogix.com*.

that class as well, the tool can generate the necessary IDL and even automatically invoke the IDL compiler.

8.7.7 Related Patterns

The Broker Pattern may be thought of as an elaborate Proxy Pattern. The Proxy Pattern is an asymmetric pattern in that the clients require knowledge of the locations of the servers, whereas in the Broker Pattern, the clients may dynamically discover the relations. This makes the Broker Pattern more scalable than the Proxy Pattern but also somewhat more heavyweight.

The Remote Method Call Pattern is similar to the Proxy Pattern as well, although it uses a different underlying infrastructure. The RMC Pattern is likewise asymmetric because the clients and server must agree on the names of the services and their locations in the system.

8.7.8 Sample Model

Figure 8-17 shows a very simple example with two servers (*Thermometer* and *Furnace*) and a single client (*Temperature Controller*), along with their associated proxies. In this case, the dynamic broker *ORB* handles and dispatches the requests to the registered servers. Note that the servers and clients have no knowledge as to the locations of each other—it is entirely managed by the broker.

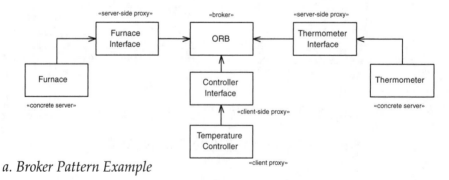

a. Broker Pattern Example

Figure 8-17: *Broker Pattern*

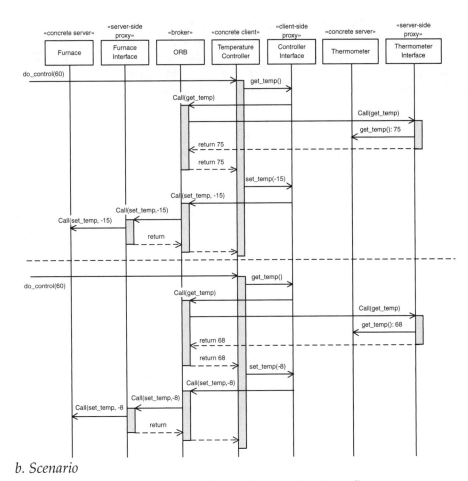

b. Scenario

Figure 8-17: *Broker Pattern (continued)*

8.8 References

[1] *www.cypress.com*
[2] Bloomer, John. *Power Programming with RPC,* Sebastopol, CA: O'Reilly and Associates, 1992.
[3] *VxWorks Programmer's Guide, Version 5.3.1,* Alameda, CA: Wind River Systems, 1997.

[4] Gamma, E., R. Helm, R. Johnson, and J. Vlissides. *Design Patterns: Elements of Reusable Object-Oriented Software,* Reading, MA: Addison-Wesley, 1995.

[5] Pope, Alan. *The CORBA Reference Guide: Understanding the Common Object Request Broker Architecture,* Reading, MA: Addison-Wesley, 1998.

[6] Mowbray, T., and R. Malveau. *CORBA Design Patterns,* New York: John Wiley & Sons, 1997.

Chapter 9

Safety and
Reliability Patterns

The following patterns are presented in this chapter.

- Protected Single Channel Pattern: Safety without heavyweight redundancy
- Homogeneous Redundancy: Protection against random faults
- Triple Modular Redundancy: Protection against random fault with continuation of functionality
- Heterogeneous Redundancy Pattern: Protection against random and systematic faults without a fail-safe state
- Monitor-Actuator Pattern: Protection against random and systematic faults with a fail-safe state
- Sanity Check Pattern: Lightweight protection against random and systematic faults with a fail-safe state
- Watchdog Pattern: Very lightweight protections and timebase fault and detection of deadlock with a fail-safe state
- Safety Executive Pattern: Safety for complex systems with complex mechanisms to achieve fail-safe states

9.1 Introduction

Safety may be defined as *freedom from accident or losses* [1], whereas reliability refers to the probability that a system will continue to function for a specified period of time. A safe system may fail frequently as long as it does not cause accidents, while the reliability of a system does not refer at all to the consequences of failure if it should occur. The differences between these two concepts escape many working in the development of real-time and embedded systems, but they can be illustrated with a simple example. A handgun is considered a very reliable device, but it is still dangerous and prone to accidents. On the other hand, my 1972 Plymouth station wagon is not very reliable (since it doesn't even run), but it *is* very safe as it sits in my garage.[1]

However, safety and reliability have one important aspect in common: their handling requires redundancy of some kind in the design of systems. This redundancy is necessary to both identify the dangerous condition or fault and to take corrective action. To this end, there are a number of common approaches—patterns—that are used to manage both safety and reliability. This redundancy may be used to enhance safety or reliability, or sometimes both, depending on the management policy. This chapter identifies and illustrates a number of these patterns in common use in the development of real-time and embedded systems.

Faults come in two flavors: systematic and random. Systematic faults (known as "errors" or "design faults"[2]) are mistakes made at either design or build time. Random faults (known as "failures") occur because something that at one time worked is now broken. Mechanical and electronic hardware exhibit both kinds of faults, while software only exhibits systematic faults. The patterns in this chapter use redundancies in different ways to address safety or reliability.

Many, but not all, safety-critical systems have a condition of existence known to be safe—a so-called fail-safe state. For example, the fail-safe state for an automobile cruise control system is OFF; the fail-safe state for a drill press is OFF. A fail-safe state is usually "off" or depowered, although it may provide reduced, nonsafety-related monitoring. Not all

---

1. I suppose it *could* cause an accident if you *fell* on it.
2. Although some software companies insist on calling them "features," we will not follow that trend.

systems have a fail-safe state. It may be inappropriate to turn off or depower a jet engine during flight, for example.

When a system has a fail-safe state, safety and reliability are at odds, since the safest thing for the system to do is enter the fail-safe state. If there is no fail-safe state, then enhancing reliability may (and typically will) improve safety as well. This results in a number of different patterns that may be used in different application systems for different reasons. The overlap between safety and reliability is illustrated in Figure 9-1.

Given that similar means are used to ensure both safety and reliability, what *are* the differences? First of all, safety measures are aimed at improving safety via the detection of unsafe conditions and taking appropriate actions. To this end, in safety-critical systems, the monitoring is usually of the physical environment and not so much of the system per se. Further, safety actions are aimed at improving safety. If the system has a fail-safe state and the system detects a potential hazard, then the correct thing to do is to invoke the fail-safe state. If the system does not have a fail-safe state, then standard reliability mechanisms are used.

Reliable systems generally focus on ensuring that they are executing properly: They have, by definition, *high availability.* To accomplish that, reliable systems rely on system self-tests, either on power up (called Power On Self Test, or POST) or during execution (called Built In Test, or

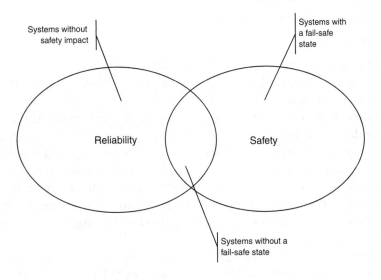

Figure 9-1: *Safety Versus Reliability*

BIT) or, most commonly, both. When a fault is detected, the system limps along as best it can. This may mean switching to a backup channel or reducing functionality. In many systems both safety and reliability are important, so compromises are reached, combining both approaches to improve reliability and safety.

Notice that I haven't used the term *software safety*. Safety is a *system* issue and can be addressed through software, hardware, or more usually, a combination of the two. Although safety and reliability always require some level of redundancy, care must be taken in how the redundancy is applied. Redundancy is of no use if the portion of the system at fault is shared in the redundant copies—this is called a *common mode fault*. It is important that a fault in one channel does not affect the functioning of the alternative channels if safety and reliability are to be improved.

9.1.1 Handling Faults

Faults are ultimately identified in these patterns using redundancy built into the pattern, and they are usually handled in one of these ways.

- Retrying an operation (feedback fault correction)
- Using information redundancy built into the data itself to correct the fault (feedforward error correction)
- Going to a fail-safe state
- Alerting monitoring personnel
- Restarting the system

Feedback error correction systems protect only against random, transient faults unless coupled with another mechanism. The fault can be identified in a number of ways. First, the data may itself contain information to detect the errors, such as by storing a cyclic redundancy check with the data that detects when the data is corrupted or by storing multiple copies of the information (often in one's-complement format) and comparing these copies prior to the use of the data. Most commonly, however, in safety-critical systems, the error is detected through independent monitoring of the actuation or resulting output of the system. Once the fault is detected, the data may be reacquired or recomputed, or the computation process can restart.

Feedforward error correction uses the properties or structure of the data to correct and possibly to identify the fault. This may be done with an odd number of channels and a voting policy (see the Triple Modular

Redundancy Pattern) or using codes with sufficient Hamming distance to identify single- or dual-bit errors. Armed with this information, the system may be able to compute not only that the data was corrupted but what the original uncorrupted value was. Then the system can correct the corrupted data and continue with the computation at hand.

Some systems have a fail-safe state—that is, a condition known to always be safe and given the detection of a safety-related fault or a safety hazard transition to that state. Often such a state is OFF or depowered, although it may be one with limited functionality (such as monitoring only). For example, a failure in an automotive cruise control results in the system being turned off, or a failure in a patient ventilator may result in notifying the attending physician and only providing monitoring, not therapy.

If there are monitoring personnel and the fault tolerance time for the specific identified fault is within the expected reaction time of the monitoring personnel, then alarming can be used to raise awareness of the fault or hazardous condition. For example, a breathing circuit failure for a patient ventilator has a fault tolerance time of about five minutes (more if the patient is breathing pure oxygen), so notifying the attending physician can be an effective way of dealing with that condition. However, an overpressure situation can only be tolerated for about 250 milliseconds, so alarming would be inappropriate for that fault.

Finally, a common strategy is to restart the entire system in the hope that the fault was a transient one. For this strategy to be appropriate, the system must be able to tolerate a reboot both in terms of the length of time it takes for the system to come back on line but also any potential hazards induced through the immediate loss of system functionality.

9.2 PROTECTED SINGLE CHANNEL PATTERN

Complete redundancy is costly. Sometimes it is costly in terms of recurring cost (cost per shipped system) because hardware is replicated. Sometimes it is costly also in development cost (due to diverse, or n-way, redundancy). Not all safety-critical and high-reliability systems need the heavy weight and expensive redundancy required by some safety and reliability patterns. The Protected Single Channel Pattern is a lightweight means to get some safety and reliability by adding additional checks and actions (and possibly some level of redundant hardware as well).

9.2.1 Abstract

The Protected Single Channel Pattern uses a single channel to handle sensing and actuation. Safety and reliability are enhanced through the addition of checks at key points in the channel, which may require some additional hardware. The Protected Single Channel Pattern will not be able to continue to function in the presence of persistent faults, but it detects and may be able to handle transient faults.

9.2.2 Problem

Since redundancy is expensive in recurring cost, and the safety and reliability requirements of some systems may not be as high as with others, a means is needed to improve safety and reliability in an inexpensive manner even if the improvements in safety and reliability are not as great as with some other approaches.

9.2.3 Pattern Structure

Figure 9-2a shows the open loop version of the pattern, and Figure 9-2b shows the closed-loop version of the pattern. The largest-scale structure is the «channel», which is of the same size and scope of a typical subsystem. It is internally composed of components that handle input and output processing, internal data transformation, and data integrity checks (and, in the case of the closed-loop control, actuation monitoring). Safety and reliability policies are distributed within the *Data Transformation* component(s).

9.2.4 Collaboration Roles

- *Actuator (Actor)*
  The *Actuator* is the actual hardware actuator that performs the actions of the channel. This might be a heater, motor, switch,

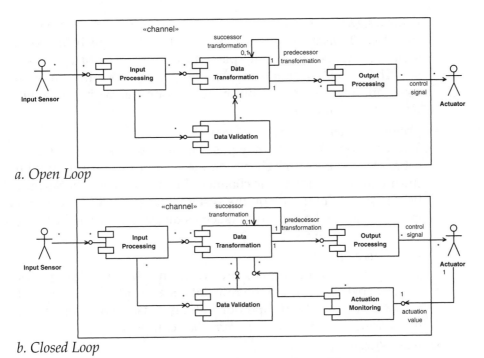

a. Open Loop

b. Closed Loop

Figure 9-2: *Protected Single Channel Pattern*

relay, fan, hydraulic press, anesthetic vaporizer, or any other device that carries out the will of the system to perform a safety or reliability-relevant function. There may be multiple actuators being controlled by a single channel.

- *Channel*
  The *channel* is an "end-to-end" subsystem that goes all the way from the acquisition of relevant data to the performance of the actuation based on that data. Normally it transforms data serially, possibly by combining it with other data. If one datum flows through the entire *channel* before the next is acquired, it is called a *serial channel*. If the *channel* typically contains many data, each of which may be in different stages of transformation at any given time, it is called a *parallel channel*.

- *Data Transformation*
  The *Data Transformation* component (which may also be a simple object) does a single transformation step on the data in the execution of a possible complex algorithm to compute the appropriate

control signals sent to the *Actuator*. The channel may contain multiple *Data Transformation* components; if so, they are arranged in series and work on the data passed from predecessor to successor. The last *Data Transformation* component does not have an association to a successor but instead associates with the *Output Processing* component.

- *Data Validation*
  This component (which may in some cases be a simple object or set of objects) performs checks on the system and its information during the execution of the channel's behavior. These checks may be performed internally on the system hardware (RAM tests, for example) or on the data itself (such as range checks, CRC checks, data inversion checks).

- *Input Processing*
  The *Input Processing* component (which may be a single object or a set of objects) is where the raw data is acquired from the *Input Sensor* and possibly grouped or initially massaged before being transformed by the *Data Transformation* component(s).

- *Input Sensor (Actor)*
  This actor is the source of information used to (ultimately) control the actuator. It might be a thermometer, pressure sensor, photodetector, switch, or any other kind of sensor that is used to monitor either the actual environment or the proper functioning of the system. This is typically *not* monitoring the actuator per se, although it may be monitoring the effect of the actuator. To avoid a common mode fault condition, the input sensor should not be within the actuator or be used by the actuator. There may be multiple *Input Sensors*.

- *Output Processing*
  The *Output Processing* component (which may be a simple object or set of objects) does the last stage of the data transformation, taking the computed outputs and translating them into service requests on the actuator itself. The *Output Processing* component may be thought of as a device driver for the *Actuator*.

9.2.5 Consequences

The Protected Single Channel Pattern (PSCP) is a lightweight means of providing some level of safety and reliability in the presence of either systematic or random faults. Typically, the PSCP can only continue to provide services in the presence of *transient* faults—that is, faults that are due to singular events (such as electromagnetic corruption of data inside the system or corrupted data) that do not permanently affect the system. The approach is inexpensive in both recurring cost (because only portions of the channel are redundant) and in development cost.

This pattern is appropriate for systems with a fail-safe or that do not need to continue to function in the presence of a persistent fault or when the system is cost-sensitive. Because the Protected Single Channel Pattern has many points at which a single fault can cause the loss of the entire system, it is not applicable to all safety-relevant systems.

9.2.6 Implementation Strategies

The implementation issues center around identifying the faults that can lead to system dysfunction or to a hazard and mitigating them with redundancy-in-the-small. This can be done in several ways. The data itself may be stored redundantly, for example. When the data is written, a CRC may be computed. When the data is read, the CRC is checked before the data is used. Or the data itself may be stored multiple times. One common approach is to store a copy of the data in inverted format (one's complement) because stuck-at RAM faults can be detected in this way, whereas an identical second copy might not detect it. Semantic knowledge of the data can be used to detect faulty data as well, such as with range checking. A drug delivery system that computes dosage based on patient weight should look askance at a patient weight of 500 Kg. Data inversion is yet another approach to detect invalid data. This approach applies a second algorithm to the end of a computational stream to recompute the original value; if they don't match, then the data or computation must be corrupt. Other approaches use monitoring of the output results to detect faults.

9.2.7 Related Patterns

If the system must be able to operate in the presence of permanent faults (whether random or systematic), then one of the heavier-weight patterns, such as Homogeneous Redundancy or Heterogeneous Redundancy Patterns, should be used. If it is only necessary to protect against random faults, then the Homogeneous Redundancy Pattern may be used. If protection is needed from both random and systematic faults, then the Heterogeneous Redundancy Pattern gives better coverage.

9.2.8 Sample Model

Figure 9-3 shows an example of the Protected Single Channel Pattern, putting in place "redundancy-in-the-small" at a couple of

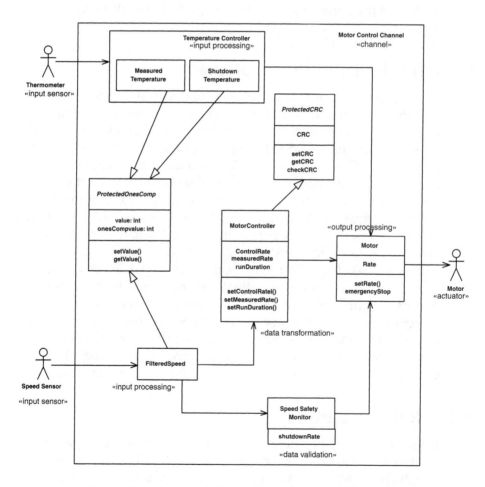

Figure 9-3: *Protected Single Channel Pattern Example*

points in the channel. Two safety-related superclasses appear: *ProtectedOnesComp* and *ProtectedCRC*. The former protects its safety-relevant attributes by storing the value twice—once in normal form and once in one's-complement form—during a set operation. A get operation reads the one's-complement form, bit-inverts it, and then compares it to the original value. If the comparison works, then the value is presumed to be okay. The *ProtectedCRC* class uses a cyclic redundancy check over its attribute values to identify in vivo corruption. This is useful when the attribute is large or when several attributes are protected at once. The concrete classes subclass these abstract superclasses, and the get and set operations should work without change. Note that the *TemperatureController* is a composite class containing two parts, each of which is a subclass of *ProtectedOnesComp*. That way, it can detect corruption of both the shutdown and measured temperatures.

The *Safety Speed Monitor* class examines the input from the Speed Sensor actor, and when it exceeds a threshold, it calls the *emergencyStop* operation on the *Motor* class. You can see that adding these small classes provides the ability to detect certain kinds of errors—those that result in detectable data corruption. Other errors are not detected, however, illustrating the weakness of this pattern. For example, a problem in the ROM or the CPU will disable both the actuation and the safety monitoring. This is called a *common mode fault,* as discussed earlier.

9.3 HOMOGENEOUS REDUNDANCY PATTERN

The Homogeneous Redundancy Pattern is primarily a pattern to improve reliability by offering multiple channels. These channels can operate in sequence, as in the Switch To Backup Pattern (another name for this pattern), or in parallel, as in the Triple Modular Redundancy Pattern, described later. The pattern improves reliability by addressing random faults (failures). Since the redundancy is homogeneous, by definition any systematic fault in one copy of the system is replicated in its clones, so it provides no protection against systematic faults (errors).

9.3.1 Abstract

An obvious approach to solving the problem of things breaking is to provide multiple copies of that thing. In safety and reliability architectures, the fundamental unit is called a *channel*. A channel is a kind of subsystem, or run-time organizational unit, which is end-to-end in its scope, from the monitoring of real-world signals to the control of actuators that do the work of the system. The Homogeneous Redundancy Pattern replicates channels with a switch-to-backup policy in the case of an error.

9.3.2 Problem

The problem addressed by the Homogenous Redundancy Pattern is to provide protection against random faults—that is, failures—in the system execution and to be able to continue to provide functionality in the presence of a failure. The primary channel should continue to run as long as there are no problems. In the case of failure within the channel, the system must be able to detect the fault and switch to the backup channel.

9.3.3 Pattern Structure

The pattern structure is shown in Figure 9-4. We see that the two channels are identical in structure (hence the pattern name). The checking components implement a switch-to-backup policy by invoking the other channel when an error is detected in the currently operating channel.

9.3.4 Collaboration Roles

- *Actuation Validation*
  The purpose of this component is to compare the output to the commanded output and determine when some application-specific fault condition has occurred: If it has, switch to the other channel. The *Actuation Validation* component may be a simple data comparison, but in general, actuation lags commanded validation, and the gain on the actuation is not infinite, so the *Actuation Validation* component must consider time lag, inertia, and accuracy limits when deciding whether the actuation is in error.

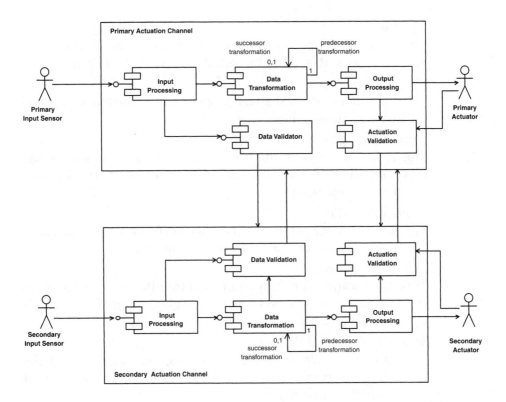

Figure 9-4: *Homogeneous Redundancy Pattern*

- *Primary Actuator*
  The *Actuator* actor is the actual device performing the actuation.

- *Data Transformation*
  This component is the same as in the Protected Single Channel Pattern: It performs a single transformation step on the input data.

- *Data Validation*
  This component is the same as in the Protected Single Channel Pattern: It validates that the data is correct or reasonable, except that it stops the processing on the current channel and begins it on the second channel when a fault is detected.

- *Input Processing*
  This component is the same as in the Protected Single Channel Pattern. It acquires and possibly performs initial processing on the raw data.

- *Input Sensor*
  This is the source of information used to (ultimately) control the actuator, just as it is in the Protected Single Channel Pattern.

- *Output Processing*
  This component does the last stage of data transformation and controls the *Actuator* itself.

- *Primary Actuation Channel*
  This is one of two replicated channels, the one used as a default. It is normally self-tested on startup, at reset, or every 24 hours, whichever comes first.

- *Primary Actuator*
  The *Actuator* actor is the actual device performing the actuation. The *Primary Actuator* is the one used by default.

- *Primary Input Sensor*
  This is the source of information used to (ultimately) control the actuator, just as it is in the Protected Single Channel Pattern. This is the primary, or default, *Input Sensor.*

- *Secondary Actuation Channel*
  This is one of two replicated channels, the one used as the backup. It is normally self-tested on startup, at reset, or every 24 hours, whichever comes first.

- *Secondary Actuator*
  The *Actuator* actor is the actual device performing the actuation. This is the backup of the first *Actuator.*

- *Secondary Input Sensor*
  This is the source of information used to (ultimately) control the actuator, just as it is in the Protected Single Channel Pattern. This is the backup *Input Sensor.*

9.3.5 Consequences

The Homogenous Redundancy Pattern has a number of advantages. It is conceptually simple and easy to design. It provides good coverage for random (that is, hardware and transient) faults, although only if the hardware is itself replicated. It is usually a simple matter to get good isolation of faults and to eliminate common mode faults. The pattern applies when random faults occur at a significantly higher rate than systematic faults, such as in rough or arduous physical environments. It also is useful for safety-critical or high-reliability systems that must continue to operate in the presence of faults.

The disadvantages of the pattern are primarily the higher recurring cost and a lack of coverage for systematic faults. Because the electronic and mechanical hardware must be duplicated for maximal coverage, each shipping system must bear the cost of additional hardware components. Furthermore, since the channels are clones, any systematic fault in one channel must, by definition, appear in the other. The pattern runs a single channel and switches over to a backup channel only when a fault is detected. This means that the computation step is lost when a fault is detected and either the data is lost or recovery time to redo the computation must be taken into account in time-critical situations.

9.3.6 Implementation Strategies

The implementation of this pattern is only a bit more work than the implementation of a nonredundant system. To remove common fault modes, the computing hardware (CPU, memory, etc.) as well as mechanical systems should be replicated. The only special work is the logic to identify the faults and switch to the alternative channel when a fault is detected.

9.3.7 Related Patterns

To eliminate much of the recurring cost of this pattern, you can use the Protected Single Channel Pattern. To add coverage of systematic faults as well, one of the heterogeneous redundancy patterns can be used. The Triple Modular Redundancy Pattern (TMR) also provides reliability in the presence of random faults, just like the Homogeneous Redundancy Pattern, but TMR does not have to restart a computation when a failure is detected. However, TMR is a more expensive design pattern to apply.

9.3.8 Sample Model

The model shown in Figure 9-5 is a simple system that provides closed-loop control of gas flow, such as for a respirator, based on sensed O_2 concentration and gas flow rate. The sensor drivers get the information from the sensors themselves. The next component in

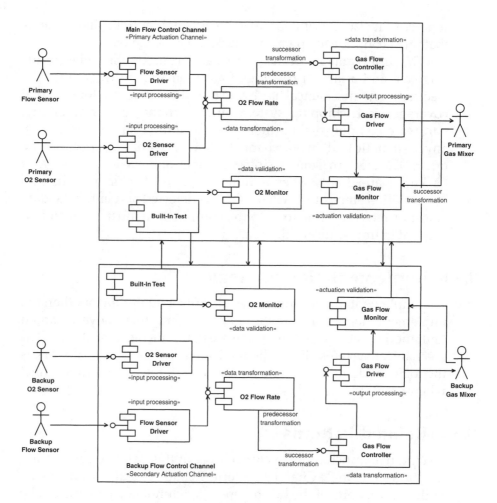

Figure 9-5: *Homogeneous Redundancy Pattern Example*

line, the *O2 Flow Rate* component, computes the O_2 flow rate from this information. This information is fed into the *Gas Flow Controller,* which oversees the delivery of sufficient gas to respirate the patient and then commands the Gas Flow Driver to set the gas flow on the Gas Mixer.

Faults and hazards are detected by two components: the O2 Monitor and the Gas Flow Monitor. If either the O_2 concentration or delivered gas flow is too low, then the backup channel is activated.

The two channels—*Main Flow Controller Channel* and *Backup Flow Controller Channel*—are identical. If one detects a fault or hazardous condition, the alternative channel is activated. Remember that the channel itself has logic to initiate, do power on self test and built-in tests, and shut down.

Note that the flow rate received from the Gas Mixer actor comes from a different source than the Flow Sensor. This independence means that if one is broken (and if we assume a single point fault), then it will be detected.

9.4 TRIPLE MODULAR REDUNDANCY PATTERN

The Triple Modular Redundancy Pattern (TMR, for short) is a pattern used to enhance reliability and safety in situations where there is no fail-safe state. The TMR pattern offers an odd number of channels (three) operating in parallel, each in effect checking the results of all the others. The computational results or resulting actuation signals are compared, and if there is a disagreement, then a two-out-of-three majority wins policy is invoked.

9.4.1 Abstract

The TMR pattern is a variation of the Homogeneous Redundancy Pattern that operates three channels in parallel rather than operating a single channel and switching over to an alternative when a fault is detected. By operating the channels in parallel, the TMR pattern detects random faults as outliers (assuming a single point failure and common mode fault independence of the channels) that are discarded as erroneous automatically. The TMR pattern runs the channels in parallel and at the end compares the results of the computational channels together. As long as two channels agree on the output, then any deviating computation of the third channel is discarded. This allows the system to operate in the presence of a fault and continue to provide functionality.

9.4.2 Problem

The problem addressed by the Triple Modular Redundancy Pattern is the same as the Homogeneous Redundancy Pattern—that is, to provide protection against random faults (failures) with the additional constraint that when a fault is detected, the input data should not be lost, nor should additional time be required to provide a correct output response.

9.4.3 Pattern Structure

Figure 9-6 shows the replicated structure of the Triple Modular Redundancy Pattern. Similar to the Homogeneous Redundancy Pattern, the channel contains a set of objects that process incoming data in a series of transformational steps. What's different about the TMR pattern is that the channels typically do not cross-check each other at strategic points. Rather, the set of three channels operate completely in parallel, and only the final resulting outputs are compared. If the system contains a single point failure and the channels have success-

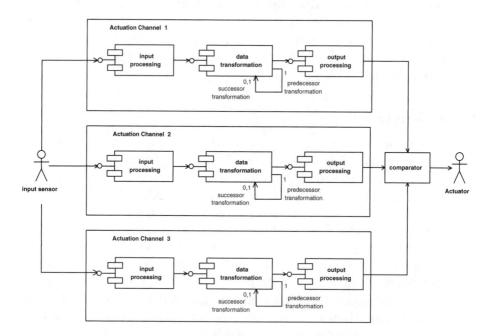

Figure 9-6: *Triple Modular Redundancy Pattern*

fully achieved independence of common mode faults, then a failure will result in *at most* a single channel producing an incorrect result. The other two channels, unaffected by the fault, will continue to produce the correct result. The comparator implements a winner-take-all policy so that the two channels producing the correct results will win.

9.4.4 Collaboration Roles

- *Actuation Channel 1, 2, 3*
  The three channels are all replicated homogeneous structures. They all process the same input data and perform identical operations, all the channels executing in parallel. Because the pattern provides only single point failure protection, each channel is normally self-tested on startup, at reset, or every 24 hours, whichever comes first.

- *Actuator*
  The *Actuator* actor is the actual device performing the actuation.

- *Comparator*
  The *Comparator* takes the three outputs (one per channel) and implements a majority-wins policy, discarding data from one channel if it deviates significantly from the other two. The *Comparator* just takes into account computational and time-lag jitter when it compares the values and decides which differences are significant and which are not.

- *Data Transformation*
  This component is the same as in the Protected Single Channel Pattern: It performs a single transformation step on the input data.

- *Input Processing*
  This component is the same as in the Protected Single Channel Pattern. It acquires and possibly performs initial processing on the raw data.

- *Input Sensor*
  This is the source of information used to (ultimately) control the actuator, just as it is in the Protected Single Channel Pattern.

- *Output Processing*
  This component does the last stage of data transformation and controls the *Actuator* itself.

9.4.5 Consequences

Similar to the Homogeneous Redundancy Pattern, the Triple Modular Redundancy Pattern can only detect random faults. Since the channels are homogeneous, then *by definition* any systematic fault in one channel must be present in both of the others. This can be addressed by having heterogeneous channels, if desired. The sensors and actuators can also be replicated, if desired, to provide even stronger fault tolerance. The comparator may be triple-replicated as well, but it is perhaps more common to use a single, highly reliable comparator.

Because the channels execute in parallel, the source data is also replicated in each channel. In the case of an error, only the erroneous channel's output is discarded; the other channels' output is used, so the failure does not result in the loss of data, nor does it necessitate the recomputation of the output. This makes the TMR pattern time efficient in the presence of faults.

TMR has a rather high recurring cost because the hardware and software in the channels must be replicated. The development cost is not very high because the channels are homogeneous. The TMR pattern is a common one in applications where reliability needs are very high and worth the additional cost to replicate the channels. In many applications, the systems are safety-critical without a fail-safe state, so enhancing reliability also enhances safety.

9.4.6 Implementation Strategies

The development of the TMR pattern is not much more difficult than a nonredundant channel. It is common to replicate the hardware and software in toto to avoid common mode faults so that each channel uses its own memory, CPU, crystal, and so on.

9.4.7 Related Patterns

Because there are three replicated channels, this pattern has one of the highest recurrent costs. The Protected Single Channel Pattern is much less expensive, but it does not provide functionality in the presence of a fault. A Homogeneous Redundancy Pattern can be used if the data can be lost when a failure occurs or when it is okay to reexecute the failed computational step. If protection against systematic faults is desired, then this pattern can use heterogeneous redundancy (independent designs for each channel, each meeting the same functional and quality-of-service requirements), but, of course, this triples the development effort. One of the other heterogeneous redundancy patterns can be used as well if it gives adequate fault and safety protection.

9.4.8 Sample Model

Figure 9-7 shows a typical example of a TMR system: the Speed Computation Subsystem (SCS) for a locomotive train. Clearly, this is has a high safety level, since trains pack an incredible amount of kinetic energy. The Engine Control system uses the speed information to compute engine speed to calculate whether it is in the right place at the right time. In this application, there is a fail-safe state

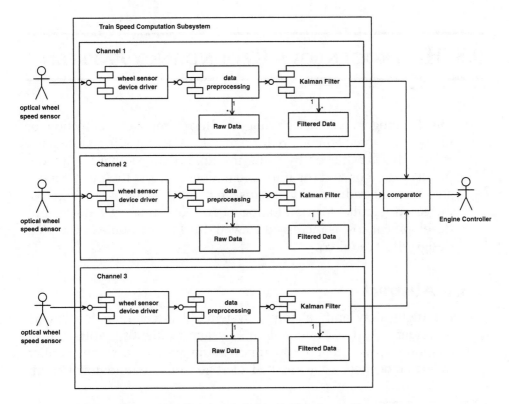

Figure 9-7: *Triple Modular Redundancy Example*

(stopped) that the Engine Controller can switch to if the entire SCS fails, although it is very expensive to do so if unnecessary. In this example, the SCS has three replicated channels, each of which processes an optical wheel speed sensor, stores a queue of raw data values, and then uses this history with a Kahlman filter to calculate the position of the train when the Engine Controller receives the computed speed (this is important in high-speed train systems, since they can rapidly change speed). In this case, the TMR pattern uses homogeneous redundancy so that the SCS can easily detect failures in one channel. If protection against systematic faults is also desired, one can easily imagine one channel processing optical wheel sensor data while another uses a Doppler radar (using surface reflection from the track to compute velocity), and yet another uses Balise sensors embedded in the track, with each channel having independently written filters to compute predicted speed.

9.5 HETEROGENEOUS REDUNDANCY PATTERN

The Heterogeneous Redundancy Pattern[3] improves detection of faults over homogeneous redundancy by also detecting systematic faults. This is achieved by using multiple channels that have independent designs and/or implementations. This is the most expensive kind of redundancy because not only is the recurring cost increased (similar to the Homogeneous Redundancy Pattern) but development cost is increased as well due to the doubled or tripled design effort required.

9.5.1 Abstract

For high-safety and reliability systems, it is common to provide redundant channels to enable the system to identify faults and to continue safe and reliable operation in the presence of faults. Similar to its homogeneous cousin, the Heterogeneous Redundancy Pattern

---

3. Also known as *Diverse Redundancy* and *N-way Programming*.

provides redundant channels as an architectural means to improve safety and reliability. What sets the Heterogeneous Redundancy Pattern apart is that the channels are not mere replicas but are constructed from independent designs. This means that identical design errors are unlikely to appear in multiple channels. The primary downside of this pattern is its high design development cost that comes on top of the high recurring cost typical of heavyweight redundant channels.

There are a number of useful variants of the Heterogeneous Redundancy Pattern that provide the detection of both kinds of faults but are lower cost and may not provide continued operation in the presence of faults. See, for example, the Monitor-Actuator and Sanity Check Patterns.

9.5.2 Problem

The Heterogeneous Redundancy Pattern provides protection against both kinds of faults—systematic errors as well as random failures. Assuming that the design includes independence of faults, the pattern provides single fault safety in the same way as the Homogeneous Redundancy Pattern—that is, when the primary channel detects a fault, the secondary channel takes over.

9.5.3 Pattern Structure

The reader will no doubt notice the close resemblance between Figure 9-8 and Figure 9-4. Indeed, the pattern is almost identical, with the primary difference being that the components of the two channels are the result of independent design efforts. The independent design effort may use the same algorithm with different teams or—even better—different algorithms with different teams.

9.5.4 Collaboration Roles

- *(Primary or Secondary) Actuation Validation*
  The purpose of this component is to compare the output to the commanded output and determine when some application-specific fault condition has occurred. If it has, switch to the other channel. The *Actuation Validation* component may be a simple

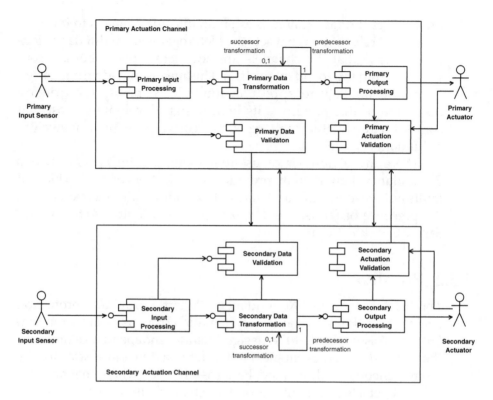

Figure 9-8: *Heterogeneous Redundancy Pattern*

data comparison, but in general, actuation lags commanded validation, and the gain on the actuation is not infinite, so the *Actuation Validation* component must consider time lag, inertia, and accuracy limits when deciding whether the actuation is in error.

Since each entity in the pattern appears in both channels (although independently designed and implemented), the corresponding entities are discussed in the same bullet. However, the primary entity is the one that works if the primary channel is active, and the secondary entity is the one working if the secondary channel is active.

- *(Primary or Secondary) Actuator*
 The *Actuator* actor is the actual device performing the actuation.

- *(Primary or Secondary) Data Transformation*
  This component is the same as in the Protected Single Channel Pattern: It performs a single transformation step on the input data.

- *(Primary or Secondary) Data Validation*
  This component is the same as in the Protected Single Channel Pattern: It validates that the data is correct or reasonable, except that it stops the processing on the current channel and begins it on the second channel when a fault is detected.

- *(Primary or Secondary) Input Processing*
  This component is the same as in the Protected Single Channel Pattern. It acquires and possibly performs initial processing on the raw data.

- *(Primary or Secondary) Input Sensor*
  This is the source of information used to (ultimately) control the actuator, just as it is in the Protected Single Channel Pattern.

- *(Primary or Secondary) Output Processing*
  This component does the last stage of data transformation and controls the *Actuator* itself.

- *(Primary or Secondary) Actuation Channel*
  This is one of two replicated channels, the one used as a default. It is normally self-tested on startup, at reset, or every 24 hours, whichever comes first.

9.5.5 Consequences

This pattern has two "heavyweight" channels. This means both are relatively expensive to design and construct, and either can perform the actuation processing with similar levels of fidelity. Similar to the Homogeneous Redundancy Pattern, this pattern has a high recurring cost due to the inclusion of additional hardware support for the redundancy. However, in addition to this, the Heterogeneous Redundancy Pattern also has a high development cost because multiple independent designs must be performed, usually with different teams to provide independence of systematic faults. This is generally considered the safest architectural pattern and the most expensive as well. With only two channels, however, it may have lower availability than with the Triple Modular Redundancy Pattern. To enhance availability, a Triple Modular Redundancy Pattern may be used with heterogeneous channels to get the best (and the worst) of both worlds.

9.5.6 Implementation Strategies

The implementation of this pattern requires fault independence. That means that the hardware components must be replicated in both channels (CPU, memory, and so on). It is common to replicate the computing hardware rather than use different CPUs, but different computing hardware does give a slightly increased level of safety. The sensors and actuators are, however, usually different hardware implementations, often using different technologies. It is best if the software is not only designed by different teams but also uses different algorithms. Nancy Leveson [1] has noted that simply using independent teams doesn't provide total independence of systematic faults, since the teams will tend to make mistakes in the same portions of the application (such as the hard parts).

9.5.7 Related Patterns

As mentioned earlier, this is a very expensive pattern to implement. Reduced cost can be had at the expense of reducing safety coverage as well. A Homogeneous Redundancy Pattern can be used with the effect of lowering the ability to detect systematic faults and lowering development cost. A Triple Modular Redundancy Pattern implemented with heterogeneous channels improves availability over the Heterogeneous Redundancy Pattern but at the cost of increasing both the development and recurring cost by one third. When protection should be provided but the system does not need to continue operation in the presence of a fault, then a lower-weight solution, such as the Monitor-Actuator or Sanity Check Pattern may be used.

9.5.8 Sample Model

Figure 9-9 shows the Speed Computation Subsystem, just as in the last section, but this time it is done using a Heterogeneous Redundancy Pattern rather than a TMR pattern. In this case, the subsystem operates in a switch-to-backup mode rather than running the channels simultaneously, and there are only two channels instead of

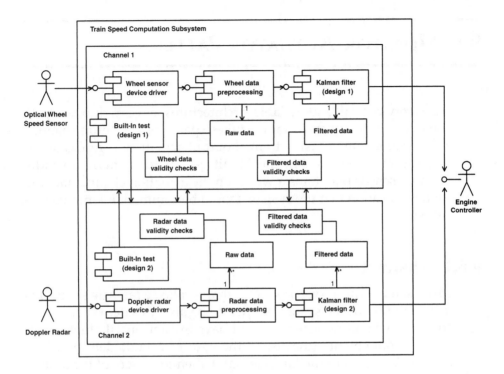

Figure 9-9: *Heterogeneous Redundancy Pattern Example*

three. Note that different sensor technology is used—in one case, an optical wheel sensor is used, while in the other, a Doppler radar is used. These sensing technologies have different failure modes (the optical sensor is sensitive to the reduction in wheel size over time due to friction, while the Doppler radar has dropouts due to different reflection surfaces).

Note that the Engine Controller is not replicated. A train system has a fail-safe mode (OFF), so it is assumed that the design of the Engine Controller would include logic that would shut down the engines and engage the brakes should speed data stop being delivered. Thus, it is enough *for the subsystem* design to ensure that only correct data or no data is delivered to the Engine Controller.

9.6 MONITOR-ACTUATOR PATTERN

All safety-critical and reliable architectures have redundancy in some form or another. In some of these patterns, the entire channel, from original data sensing to final output actuation, is replicated in some form or another. In the Monitor-Actuator Pattern, an independent sensor maintains a watch on the actuation channel looking for an indication that the system should be commanded into its fail-safe state.

9.6.1 Abstract

Many safety-critical systems have what is called a fail-safe state. This is a condition of the system known to be always safe. When this is true, and when the system doesn't have extraordinarily high availability requirements (that is, in the case of a fault detection it is appropriate to enter the fail-safe state), then the safety of the system can be maintained at a lower cost than some of the other patterns discussed in this chapter. The Monitor-Actuator Pattern is a specialized form of the Heterogeneous Redundancy Pattern because the redundancy provided is different from the primary actuation channel: It provides monitoring, typically of the commanded actuation itself (although it may also monitor the internal operation of the actuation channel as well).

Assuming fault independence and a single point fault protection requirement, the basic principle of the Monitor-Actuator Pattern may be summed up this way: If the actuation channel has a fault, the monitoring channel detects it. If the monitoring channel breaks, then the actuation channel continues to operate properly.

9.6.2 Problem

The Monitor-Actuator Pattern addresses the problem of improving safety in a system with moderate to low availability requirements at a low cost.

9.6.3 Pattern Structure

The Monitor-Actuator Pattern structure is shown in Figure 9-10. Both channels run independently and simultaneously.

9.6.4 Collaboration Roles

- *Actuation Channel*
  This is the channel that contains components that perform the end-to-end actuation required by the system. "End-to-end" means it includes the sensing of control signals from environmental sensors, sequential or parallel data processing, and output actuation signals. It contains no components in common with the *Monitoring Channel*.

- *Actuation Data Source*
  The *Actuation Data Source* is the source of sensed data used for control of actuation. This is a physically independent sensor from the *Actuation Monitor Sensor*.

- *Actuator*
  The *Actuator* actor is the actual device performing the actuation.

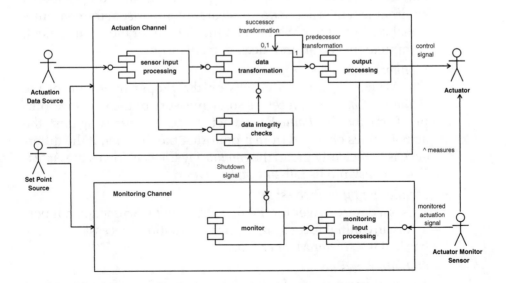

Figure 9-10: *Monitor-Actuator Pattern*

- *Actuator Monitor Sensor*
  This sensor is used to monitor the *output* of the actual actuator for comparison against the expected values. It feeds the *Monitoring Channel* for the monitoring of the success of the *Actuation Channel*. This sensor must be physically independent from the *Actuation Data Source*.

- *Data Integrity Checks*
  This component is used by the *Actuation Channel* to check that its own internal processing is proceeding properly.

- *Data Transformation*
  As in the other patterns, these components process the sensing data in a sequential fashion to compute the ultimate actuation output. This can be done with a single datum running all the way through the channel before another is acquired or with multiple data in various stages of processing simultaneously to provide a serial or parallel *Actuation Channel*, respectively.

- *Monitor*
  The *Monitor* compares the commanded output (received from the *Set Point Source*) and compares it with the actual output (received from the *Actuator Monitor Sensor* and initially processed by the *Monitoring Input Processing* component). This comparison must take into account many aspects of the physical and computational environment in order to do an accurate comparison: the computational lag time, the physical lag time (inertia) of the environment, computational error, and measurement error.

- *Monitoring Channel*
  The *Monitoring Channel* checks on the proper operation of the *Actuation Channel*. It receives some measure of the expected output from the *Set Point Source* actor and compares against the actual values obtained from monitoring the *Actuator*. If the difference is sufficiently great, the *Monitoring Channel* forces the *Actuation Channel* into its fail-safe state.

- *Monitoring Input Processing*
  This is a device driver for the *Actuator Monitor Sensor* actor. It performs any initial formatting or transformations necessary for the particular *Actuator Monitor Sensor*.

- *Output Processing*
  This is a device driver for the *Actuator* actor. It performs any final formatting for transformations necessary for the particular *Actuator*.

- *Sensor Input Processing*
  The *Sensor Input Processing* component is a device driver for the *Actuation Data Source* actor. It performs any initial formatting or transformations necessary for the particular *Actuation Data Source* sensor.

- *Set Point Source*
  This actor is the source of commanded actuation signals. Its purpose is to provide the set point for the actuation control and for its monitoring. It provides the same control signal to both the *Actuation* and *Monitoring Channels.*

9.6.5 Consequences

This pattern is a relatively inexpensive safety solution that is applicable when the system does not have high availability requirements and when there is a fail-safe state. Assuming that its implementation correctly isolates faults, a fault in the *Actuation Channel* will be identified by the *Monitoring Channel*. A fault in the *Monitoring Channel* will not affect the proper execution of the *Actuation Channel*. Because there is minimal redundancy, the system cannot continue to function when a fault is identified.

9.6.6 Implementation Strategies

The *Monitoring Channel* must take into account lag, measurement jitter, control system jitter, computational accuracies (specifically the propagation and compounding of computational numeric error), and other forms of error in determining whether the actuation channel is acting properly. For example, if in an anesthetic agent vaporizer, the concentration of Halothane is increased from 0.0% to 1.5%, the breathing circuit will take time to saturate at 1.5% because of the time necessary to inject that much drug into that much gas volume and the time necessary for it to diffuse evenly into that volume. If the *Monitoring Channel* expects to find the breathing mixture instantly at the proper concentration, it will inappropriately identify a fault. On the other hand, if the concentration never reaches something close to 1.5%, then the *Monitor* should identify a fault. The *Monitor* in this case may require the simulation of the drug delivery and diffusion in order to identify whether the system is achieving the proper actuation. In situations where time lags are irrelevant, it will usually still be necessary to have a band around the commanded actuation set point. For example, if the commanded value of agent is 1.5%, any value in the range 1.45% to 1.55% may be valid.

Another issue with the *Monitoring Channel* is the handling of *transient* faults. In some situations, a single transient fault may not be harmful at all, but *persistent* faults must be identified. In such cases, it may be necessary for the *Monitoring Channel* to maintain a recent history of its monitored values to determine whether an unexpected value indicates a transient or persistent fault.

The system can operate with a fault in the *Monitor Channel,* but if it does so, this is called a *latent fault.* A latent fault is one that by itself does not present a hazard but with the addition of a second fault *does* present a hazard. For this reason, the *Monitor Channel* must be periodically checked. The timeframe for this check must be significantly less than the mean-time between failures (MTBF) of the *Monitor Channel.* In practice, this check is usually done daily or on every startup, whichever is less. It may, at times, be performed during scheduled maintenance of the system but must be done much more frequently than the MTBF of the channel and any of its components. Often, systems using this pattern use a pair set of *life ticks* sent between the channels to indicate the health of the other system. If one channel does not receive a life tick from the other within a specified time frame, then this indicates a fault, and the fail-safe state is entered.

9.6.7 Related Patterns

Sometimes the control signal does not provide the desired end-result to the *Monitoring Channel.* When this is the case, the *Monitoring Channel* must in some sense simulate the processing done in the *Actuation Channel.* When this is done in a lightweight way to get a check on the reasonableness of the resulting actuation output, this is called the Sanity Check Pattern.

A *very* lightweight means of providing monitoring is the Watchdog Pattern. This pattern monitors what the Actuator Pattern *thinks* is the right thing to do and not the actual output of the actuation. If it is necessary to continue actuation in the face of a fault, then a heavier-weight pattern, such as the Homogeneous Redundancy or the Heterogeneous Redundancy Pattern, must be used.

9.6.8 Sample Model

Figure 9-11 shows a straightforward application of this pattern to a drug vaporizer, such as those used in surgical room anesthesia machines. The system works by receiving a drug concentration set point from the physician; this command is sent to both the Vaporizer Actuation Channel and the Vaporizer Monitoring Channel. The Vaporizer Actuation Channel changes its internal set point to what is commanded and acts like a closed-loop control system to infuse more drug into the breathing mixture. The controller itself might try to minimize the time to reach the commanded concentration by inserting a bolus dose into the breathing mixture (via the Vaporizer Hardware) and then lowering in infusion rate, or it may decide to allow a long ramp-up time to achieve the commanded concentration. The Vaporizer Hardware does the actual vaporization of drug into the breathing circuit by controlling the amount of agent in the vaporization chamber and the temperature of the chamber (hardware details not shown). The Closed-Loop Controller of the Vaporizer Actuation Channel gets feedback from the Agent Concentration Sensor 1 actor, which it uses to quickly and accurately converge on the commanded concentration. (We hope.)

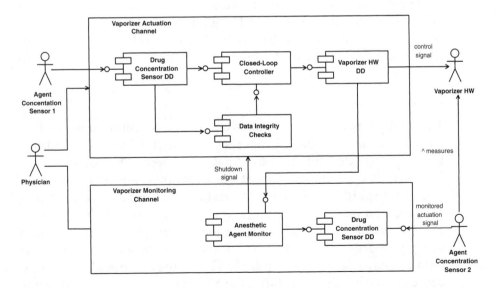

Figure 9-11: *Monitor-Actuator Example*

In the case of a fault, the Vaporizer Monitor Channel monitors the concentration of the drug in the breathing circuit, using a physically different sensor, Agent Concentration Sensor 2. If the Actuation Channel is not acting appropriately, then the Anesthetic Agent Monitor detects the fault and disables the Vaporizer Actuation Channel and issues an alarm to the physician to indicate the fault. As mentioned previously, such a system has a significant lag time between commanding a new concentration and achieving it, so the monitor must take into account time lag, measurement jitter, and the fidelity of control of the closed-loop control system.

9.7 SANITY CHECK PATTERN

The Sanity Check Pattern is a very lightweight pattern that provides minimal fault coverage. The purpose of the Sanity Check Pattern is to ensure that the system is more or less doing something reasonable, even if not quite correct. This is useful in situations where the actuation is not critical if performed correctly (such as an optional enhancement) but is capable of doing harm if it is done incorrectly. It is a variant of the Monitor-Actuator Pattern and, like the that pattern, assumes that a fail-safe state is available.

9.7.1 Abstract

The Sanity Check Pattern is a variant of the Monitor-Actuator Pattern; it has the same basic properties. Where it differs is in the functionality provided by the Monitor Component. The Sanity Check Pattern only exists to ensure that the actuation is approximately correct. It typically uses lower-cost (and usually lower-accuracy) sensors and can only identify when the actuation is grossly incorrect. Thus, it is applicable only in situations where fine control is not a safety property of the *Actuation Channel.* In some extreme cases, the monitor may not even be required to know the commanded set point because it will only ensure that the actuation output is within some fixed range. Usually, however, the *Monitor* will have a "valid range" that varies with the commanded set point.

9.7.2 Problem

This pattern addresses the issue, making sure the "system does no harm" when minor, or even moderate, deviations from the commanded set point have no safety impact, and providing this minimal level of protection at a very low recurring and design cost.

9.7.3 Pattern Structure

The Sanity Check Pattern, shown in Figure 9-12, is virtually identical that of the Monitor-Actuator Pattern (shown earlier) from which it is derived.

9.7.4 Collaboration Roles

- *Actuation Channel*
  This is the channel that contains components that perform the end-to-end actuation required by the system. "End-to-end"

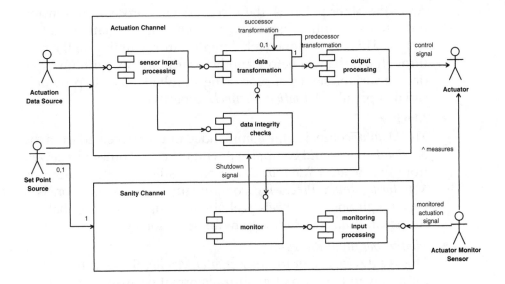

Figure 9-12: *Sanity Check Pattern*

means that it includes the sensing of control signals from environmental sensors, sequential or parallel data processing, and output actuation signals. It contains no components in common with the *Sanity Check Channel*.

- *Actuation Data Source*
  The *Actuation Data Source* is the source of sensed data used to control actuation. This is a physically independent sensor from the *Actuation Monitor Sensor*.

- *Actuator*
  The *Actuator* actor is the actual device performing the actuation.

- *Actuator Monitor Sensor*
  This sensor is used to monitor the *output* of the actual actuator for comparison against the expected values. It is normally inexpensive compared to the *Actuation Data Source* sensor because the accuracy demands on this sensor are not very high. This sensor must nevertheless be physically independent from the *Actuation Data Source*.

- *Data Integrity Checks*
  This component is used by the *Actuation Channel* to check that its own internal processing is proceeding properly.

- *Data Transformation*
  As in the other patterns, these components process the sensing data in a sequential fashion to compute the ultimate actuation output. This can be done with a single datum running all the way through the channel before another is acquired or with multiple data in various stages of processing simultaneously to provide a serial or parallel *Actuation Channel*, respectively.

- *Monitor*
  The *Monitor* compares the commanded output (received from the *Set Point Source*) and compares it with the actual output (received from the *Actuator Monitor Sensor* and initially processed by the *Monitoring Input Processing* component). This comparison is a very rough one with a relatively broad range to ensure that the *Actuation Channel* isn't doing anything obviously bad.

- *Monitoring Input Processing*
  This is a device driver for the *Actuator Monitor Sensor* actor. It performs any initial formatting or transformations necessary for the particular *Actuator Monitor Sensor*.

- *Output Processing*
  This is a device driver for the *Actuator* actor. It performs any final formatting for transformations necessary for the particular *Actuator.*

- *Sanity Check Channel*
  The *Monitoring Channel* checks on the proper operation of the *Actuation Channel.* It receives some measure of the expected output from the *Set Point Source* actor and compares against the actual values obtained from monitoring the *Actuator.* If the difference is sufficiently great, the *Monitoring Channel* forces the *Actuation Channel* into its fail-safe state.

- *Sensor Input Processing*
  The *Sensor Input Processing* component is a device driver for the *Actuation Data Source* actor. It performs any initial formatting or transformations necessary for the particular *Actuation Data Source* sensor.

- *Set Point Source*
  This actor is the source of commanded actuation signals. Its purpose is to provide the set point for the actuation control and for its monitoring. It provides the same control signal to both the *Actuation* and *Monitoring Channels.*

9.7.5 Consequences

The Sanity Check Pattern is meant to be a very inexpensive solution that provides minimal coverage. It has a low recurring cost because cheaper, coarser-grained sensors may be used. It has a lower design cost because the comparison is usually just a simple verification that the commanded set point is somewhere in a relatively broad range, so the design is usually very simple. As a result, however, the coverage is very minimal and does not attempt to replicate the accuracy of the actuation channel. This means that this pattern is applicable in only situations where there is a fail-safe state that the system can be commanded into if the output is grossly in error and that small deviations from the commanded set point that will be missed by the Sanity Check Pattern have no relevance to the safety of the system.

9.7.6 Implementation Strategies

The normal implementation of this pattern will include two different sensors: the high-fidelity sensor used to provide input to the *Actuation Channel* and a low-cost, low-fidelity sensor used for the *Sanity Channel.* The *Monitor* component is often just a simple object with a very simple algorithm. This is most often a simple range comparison. In some cases, it may only need to check that the output is in the same fixed range regardless of the commanded set point, but most often the range will vary with the commanded set point. The implementation usually does not take into account time lag or computational jitter because the check is broad enough to account for those kinds of error sources. In some cases, a slightly more complex algorithm that does take into account time lag may be necessary, but it is almost always a simple computation.

9.7.7 Related Patterns

If a higher-fidelity check on the *Actuator Channel* is necessary, then the Monitor-Actuator Pattern will be more appropriate at the incremental increase in both design and recurring cost. An even lighter-weight solution than the Sanity Check Pattern is the Watchdog Pattern, which provides even less coverage. For more coverage, or when there is no fail-safe state, one of the Homogeneous or Heterogeneous Redundancy Patterns may be used.

9.7.8 Sample Model

The antiskid braking system shown in Figure 9-13 is a good example of a situation that is applicable for the Sanity Check Pattern. As long as the system is working at least somewhat correctly, its use helps in controlling the vehicle. If, however, it fails in a gross fashion, then it could easily lead to a loss of life. If the computer-controlled antiskid braking is shut down in that case, then simple linear force braking remains as the backup system. While this may not be as effective as a correctly functioning antiskid braking system, it may be vastly better than a malfunctioning one.

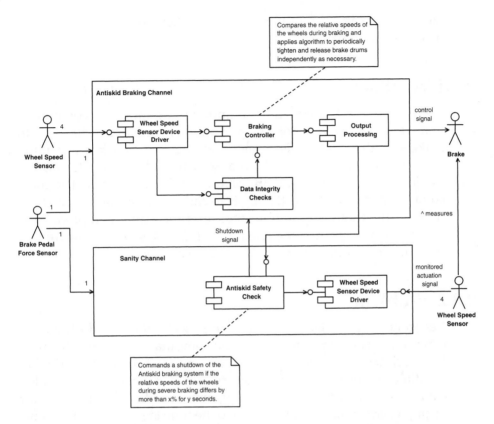

Figure 9-13: *Sanity Check Pattern Example*

9.8 WATCHDOG PATTERN

The Watchdog Pattern is similar to the Sanity Check Pattern in the sense that it is lightweight and inexpensive. It differs in what it monitors. While the Sanity Check Pattern monitors the actual output of the system using an external environmental sensor, the Watchdog Pattern merely checks that the internal computational processing is proceeding as expected. This means that its coverage is minimal, and a broad set of faults will not be detected. On the other hand, it is a pattern that can add additional safety when combined with other heavier-weight patterns.

9.8.1 Abstract

A *watchdog*, used in common computing parlance, is a component that watches out over processing of another component. Its job is to make sure that nothing is *obviously* wrong, just as a real watchdog protects the entrance to the henhouse without bothering to check if in fact the chickens inside are plotting nefarious deeds. The most common purpose of a watchdog is to check a computation timebase or to ensure that computation steps are proceeding in a predefined order. Watchdogs are often used in real-time systems to ensure that time-dependent processing is proceeding appropriately.

9.8.2 Problem

Real-time systems are those that are *predictably timely.* In the most common (albeit simplified) view, the computations have a deadline by which they must be applied. If the computation occurs after that deadline, the result may either be erroneous or irrelevant—so-called *hard real-time systems.* Systems implementing PID control loops, for example, are notoriously sensitive to the time lag between the occurrence of the input signal and the output of the control signal. If the output comes too late, then the system *cannot be controlled;* then the system is said to be in an *unstable region.*

9.8.3 Pattern Structure

The simplicity of the Watchdog Pattern is apparent from Figure 9-14. The *Actuator Channel* operates pretty much independently of the watchdog, sending a *liveness* message every so often to the watchdog. This is called *stroking* the watchdog. The watchdog uses the timeliness of the stroking to determine whether a fault has occurred. Most watchdogs check only that a stroke occurs by some elapse of time and don't concern themselves with what happens if the stroke comes too quickly. Such a statechart for the watchdog is shown in Figure 9-15a. Some watchdogs check that the stroke comes neither

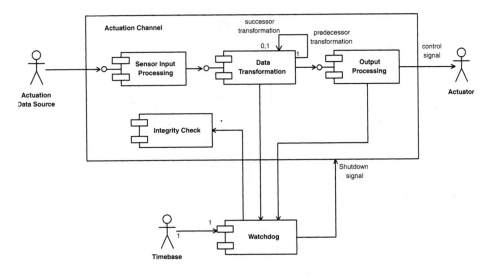

Figure 9-14: *Watchdog Pattern*

too quickly nor too slowly. The statechart for such a time-range watchdog is shown in Figure 9-15b.[4]

For some systems, protection against a timebase fault is safety-critical.[5] In such cases, it is preferable to have an independent time-base. This is normally a timing circuit separate and independent from the one used to drive the CPU executing the *Actuation Channel.*

9.8.4 Collaboration Roles

- *Actuation Channel*
  This is the channel that contains components that perform the end-to-end actuation required by the system. "End-to-end" means that it includes the sensing of control signals from environmental sensors, sequential or parallel data processing, and output actuation signals. It contains no components in common with the *Watchdog*.

---

4. Note that the timeouts in the statecharts are shown with the tm() event transition.
5. It should be noted that *all* safety-critical systems are real-time systems because they must respond to a fault by the Fault Tolerance Time [2].

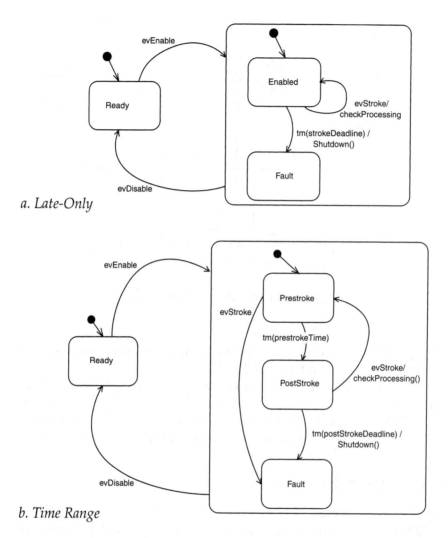

a. Late-Only

b. Time Range

Figure 9-15: *Watchdog State Machine*

- *Actuation Data Source*
  The *Actuation Data Source* is the source of sensed data used for control of actuation.
- *Actuator*
  The *Actuator* actor is the actual device performing the actuation.

- *Data Transformation*
  As in the other patterns, these components process the sensing data in a sequential fashion to compute the ultimate actuation output. This can be done with a single datum running all the way through the channel before another is acquired or with multiple data in various stages of processing simultaneously to provide a serial or parallel *Actuation Channel*, respectively.

- *Integrity Checks*
  This component is (optionally) invoked on every valid stroke of the *Watchdog*. This can be used to run a periodic Built In Test (BIT), check for stack overflow of the tasks, and so on.

- *Output Processing*
  This is a device driver for the *Actuator* actor. It performs any final formatting for transformations necessary for the particular *Actuator*.

- *Sensor Input Processing*
  The *Sensor Input Processing* component is a device driver for the *Actuation Data Source* actor. It performs any initial formatting or transformations necessary for the particular *Actuation Data Source* sensor.

- *Timebase*
  The *Timebase* is an independent timing source (such as an electronic circuit) used to drive the *Watchdog*.

- *Watchdog*
  The *Watchdog* waits for a stroke event sent to it by the components of the *Actuation Channel*. If the stroke does occur within the appropriate timeframe, the *Watchdog* may command integrity checks to be performed. If it does not, then it shuts down the *Actuation Channel*.

9.8.5 Consequences

The Watchdog Pattern is a very lightweight pattern that is rarely used alone in safety-critical systems. It is best at identifying timebase faults, particularly when an independent timebase drives the Watchdog. It can also be used to detect a deadlock in the actuation channel. To improve deadlock detection, the watchdog may require the strokes to be *keyed*—that is, to contain data that can be used to identify that strokes from different computational steps occur in the proper sequence. Such a watchdog is called a *Keyed Watchdog* or a *Sequential Watchdog*.

Because the coverage of the Watchdog Pattern is so minimal, it is rarely used alone. It may be combined with any of the other safety patterns discussed in this chapter.

9.8.6 Implementation Strategies

As mentioned before, if the watchdog is to provide protection from timebase faults, a separate electronic circuit *must* supply an independent measure of the flow of time. This means an independent timing circuit, usually driven by a crystal, but the timebase may be driven by an R-C circuit. Note, however, that the watchdog detects a *mismatch* between the two timing sources but cannot detect whether the fault is the primary actuation channel or the watchdog timebase.

To prevent a fault where the primary actuation channel gets stuck in a loop (so called *live-lock*) that strokes the watchdog but doesn't actually perform the appropriate computation and actuation, the watchdog may require data with the strokes that must occur in a specific pattern. To implement a *keyed watchdog*, the best approach is to *not store the keys in memory* but to have them dynamically computed as a result of the proper execution of the actuation process. This diminishes the likelihood of a live-lock situation not being detected.

When the watchdog is stroked, it is common to invoke a BIT (Built In Test) of some kind to ensure the proper execution of other aspects of the system. These actions can either return a Boolean value indicating their success or failure, or may directly cause the system to shut down in the case of their failure. For example, the watchdog may execute an action on the evStroke transition (see Figure 9-15) that checks for stack overflow[6] and performs CRC checks on the executing application software. If it does a similar check on the application data, it must lock the data resources during this computation, which can adversely affect performance if you're not careful.

---

6. Stack overflow may be checked for by writing a known pattern into the stack of each task beyond the expected stack size. If this pattern is disrupted, then a stack overflow (or something equally bad) has occurred.

When watchdog fires because it hasn't been stroked within the specified timeframe, it invokes some safety measure, normally either shutting down the system or causing the system to reset.

9.8.7 Related Patterns

The Watchdog Pattern is about as lightweight (low effort as well as low protection) as a safety and reliability pattern gets. For this reason, it is normally mixed with other patterns as a way to test the timebase and to drive periodic BITs.

9.8.8 Sample Model

The pacemaker model shown in Figure 9-16 illustrates this pattern. The primary actuation channel controls the pacing of the heart based on time (if the heart doesn't beat on its own quickly enough) or on the heart's intrinsic beat (if it beats faster than the programmed "pace time"). Timing in such a system is crucial to the effective maintenance of cardiac output; in fact, pacing at the wrong time can

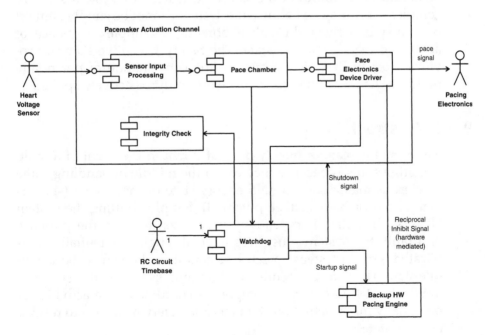

Figure 9-16: *Watchdog Pattern Example*

induce ventricular fibrillation and death. Thus, the Watchdog component uses an RC circuit to maintain its internal timer. If it discovers a fault, then it shuts down the software-driven pacing actuation channel and starts up a simple, nonprogrammable hardware pacemaking engine that serves as a backup. The Pace Electronics Device Driver and the Backup HW Pacing Engine have an association between them so that if one is active, it disables the other. This is done via hardware logic gates to ensure that the pacemaker does not attempt to drive the heart using two different strategies at the same time. Astute readers will note that this example is a combination of the Switch-to-Backup and the Watchdog Patterns.

9.9 SAFETY EXECUTIVE PATTERN

Sometimes the control of the safety measures of a system are very complex. This may be because the system cannot be simply shut off but must be driven through a potentially complex sequence of actions to read a fail-safe state. The Safety Executive Pattern provides a *Safety Executive* to oversee the coordination of potentially multiple channels when safety measures must be actively applied.

9.9.1 Abstract

Systems often cannot merely be shut down in the event of a fault. Sometimes this is because they are in the middle of handling some dangerous materials or a high-energy state of the system (such as high speed or high voltage potential). Simply shutting the system off in such a state is potentially very hazardous. In the presence of a fault, the system must be guided through a potentially complicated series of steps to reach a condition known to be a fail-safe state. The Safety Executive Pattern models exactly this situation in which a *Safety Executive* component coordinates the activities of potentially many actuation channels and safety measures to reach a fail-safe state.

9.9.2 Problem

The problem addressed by the Safety Executive Pattern is to provide a means to coordinate and control the execution of safety measures when the safety measures are complex.

9.9.3 Pattern Structure

Figure 9-17 shows the structure of this pattern. The complexity of the pattern can be seen at a glance. As indicated (via the multiplicity on the association between the *Safety Executive* component and the

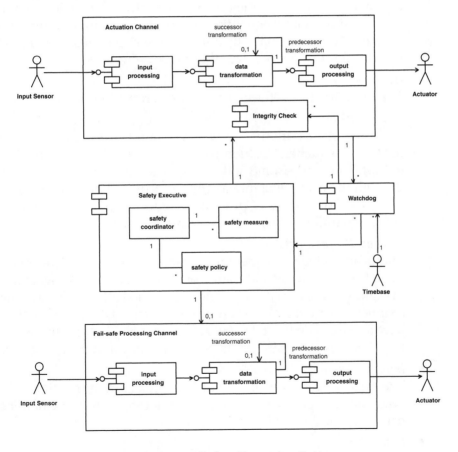

Figure 9-17: *Safety Executive Pattern*

Actuation Channel), the system may have multiple Actuation channels, monitored and ultimately coordinated by the *Safety Executive*. In addition, there may be a *Fail-safe Channel* if the system has an independent fail-safe processing channel (often indicated for highly safety-critical applications).

9.9.4 Collaboration Roles

- *Actuation Channel*
  This is the channel that contains components that perform the end-to-end actuation required by the system. "End-to-end" means that it includes the sensing of control signals from environmental sensors, sequential or parallel data processing, and output actuation signals. It contains no components in common with the *Safety Executive* or *Fail-safe Processing Channel*.

- *Actuator*
  The *Actuator* actor is the actual device performing the actuation.

- *Data Transformation*
  As in the other patterns, these components process the sensing data in a sequential fashion to compute the ultimate actuation output. This can be done with a single datum running all the way through the channel before another is acquired or with multiple data in various stages of processing simultaneously to provide a serial or parallel *Actuation Channel*, respectively.

- *Fail-safe Processing Channel*
  This is an optional channel for systems that have a channel dedicated to the execution and control of the fail-safe processing. In this case, the normal actuation channels are turned off, and the fail-safe channel takes over. It is even more common for systems not to have a channel dedicated to fail-safe processing; instead, the actuation channels have fail-safe states built directly into them.

- *Input Processing*
  The *Input Processing* component is a device driver for the *Input Sensor* actor. It performs any initial formatting or transformations necessary for the particular *Input Sensor*.

- *Input Sensor*
  The *Input Sensor* is the source of sensed data used to control actuation.

- *Output Processing*
  This is a device driver for the *Actuator* actor. It performs any final formatting for transformations necessary for the particular *Actuator*.

- *Safety Coordinator*
  This class controls and coordinates the safety processing (managed in the *Safety Measure* class). The algorithms for control are specified in the instances of the *Safety Policies* class. There is only a single instance of this class in the *Safety Executive* component.

- *Safety Executive*
  The *Safety Executive* is a component that consists of the objects instantiated from the *Safety Coordinator*, *Safety Measure*, and *Safety Policy* classes.

- *Safety Measure*
  The *Safety Measure* class is an abstract class that controls the detailed behavior of a single safety measure. The *Safety Executive* may contain several of these measures[7] controlled by the *Safety Coordinator* class.

- *Safety Policy*
  The *Safety Policy* class specifies a *policy* or strategy for a *Safety Coordinator*. This many involve a potentially complicated sequence of steps that involve multiple *Safety Measure* objects. This is an abstract class that is subclassed for a specific policy. There may be multiple policies concurrently active. This separation of the coordination from the policies allows the policies to be easily adapted and changed as necessary.

- *Timebase*
  The *Timebase* is an independent timing source (such as an electronic circuit) used to drive the *Watchdog*. A single *Timebase* may drive multiple *Watchdogs* as long as they are not used in the actuation channels.

- *Watchdog*
  The *Watchdog* waits for a stroke event sent to it by the components of the *Actuation Channel*. If the stroke does occur within the appropriate timeframe, the *Watchdog* may command integrity checks to be performed. If it does not, then it shuts down the

---

7. Each is a different subclass of the *Safety Measure* class.

Actuation Channel. There may be multiple watchdogs, one per *Actuation Channel*, as necessary.

9.9.5 Consequences

This is a complex pattern to implement with many pieces to design. Therefore, it is usually only used in systems that are both complex and highly safety-critical—especially when the handling of faults is very complex. On the other hand, it can provide excellent fault protection in highly complex systems and environments. Since this pattern was described in my earlier book [2], it has been used in high-speed train control systems and other safety-critical systems.

9.9.6 Implementation Strategies

As with all of these patterns, single point failure safety is key. Any single component, whether hardware or software, should be allowed to fail without creating a hazard. In the systems for which this pattern is appropriate, this means that the channels will each run on their own CPUs with their own memory; safety-critical information must be protected with CRCs or other means to detect data corruption; time-critical processing must be validated as to time-base (via the watchdogs running off an independent physical timebase).

9.9.7 Related Patterns

In some sense, the Safety Executive Pattern is the superset of all the other patterns in this chapter. The other patterns typically describe the inner workings of a single channel, or how a small set of channels work together to improve reliability and/or safety. Each of those patterns can be fitted in to a Safety Executive Pattern, when appropriate. Clearly, this pattern already directly incorporate the Heterogeneous Redundancy Pattern with a "Switch-to-Backup" strategy for the *Fail-safe Channel* and the Watchdog Pattern for the normal *Actuation Channels.*

For simpler systems with a lower safety criticality or where the safety measures are not so complex, any of the other patterns in this chapter can be used.

9.9.8 Sample Model

The example in Figure 9-18 is more complex than the others in this chapter: an explosive chemical production system. The system heats and maintains nitric acid to be titrated with a nitrate to form a

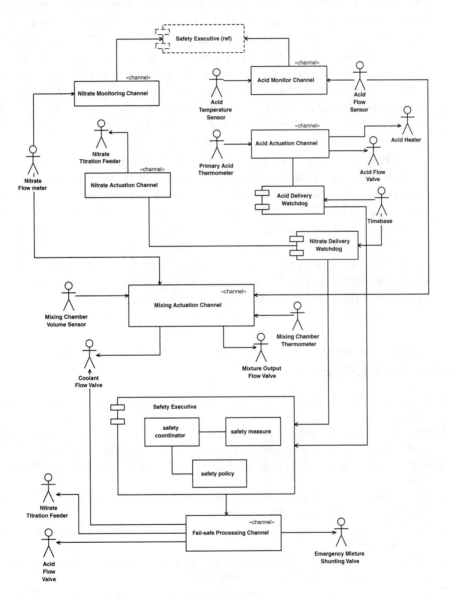

Figure 9-18: *Safety Executive Pattern Example*

mixture in the mixing chamber. The temperature of both the acid and the mixing chamber must be maintained below a specified limit, or bad things can happen (fire, explosion, release of toxic gases, etc.). Both acid and nitrate delivery channels run with a Monitor-Actuator Pattern to detect potentially hazardous faults. Both of these channels also use a Watchdog Pattern as well to ensure liveness and a proper timebase (since the amount of chemical delivered is the time integral of the flow rate). In the event of a major fault, the fail-safe state of the system is to shut down, but since it contains hot acid and nitrate flowing into the system and a mixing chamber potentially full of explosive chemicals, getting to a nonhazardous condition is not simply a matter of shutting down the system. The *Safety Executive* component manages the execution of the safety measures.

The *Safety Executive* identifies a fault through notification by a watchdog, one of the monitoring channels, or from its own monitoring of various sensors. When it detects a hazardous fault, several things happen. The Nitrate Titration Feeder is shut off; the flow of acid is turned off via the Acid Flow Valve; the mixing chamber is rapidly cooled by opening the Coolant Flow Valve; and last, the mixing chamber is emptied via the Emergency Shunting Valve into a large water reservoir. To save space in Figure 9-18, the internal components to the actuation channels are not shown.

9.10 References

[1] Leveson, Nancy. *Safeware: System Safety and Computers*, Reading, MA: Addison-Wesley 1995.

[2] Douglass, Bruce Powel. *Doing Hard Time: Developing Real-Time Systems with UML, Objects, Frameworks, and Patterns*, Reading, MA: Addison-Wesley, 1999.

[3] Storey, Neil. *Safety Critical Computer Systems*, Reading, MA: Addison-Wesley, 1996.

[4] Friedman, M., and J. Voas. *Software Assessment: Reliability, Safety, Testability*, New York: Wiley & Sons, 1995.

[5] Gardiner, Stewart. (Ed.) *Testing Safety-Related Software*, Glasgow, UK: Springer-Verlag, 1999.

[6] Hatton, Les. *Safer C: Developing Software for High-Integrity and Safety-Critical Systems*, Berkshire, UK: McGraw-Hill, 1995.

[7] Kramer, B., and N. Volker. *Safety-Critical Real-Time Systems*, Norwell, MA: Kluwer Academic Press, 1997.

Appendix A

Notational Summary

This appendix provides a summary of the UML notation discussed in this book. It is organized by diagram type to facilitate its use as a reference during development.

Class Diagram

Shows the existence of classes and
relationships in a logical view of a system

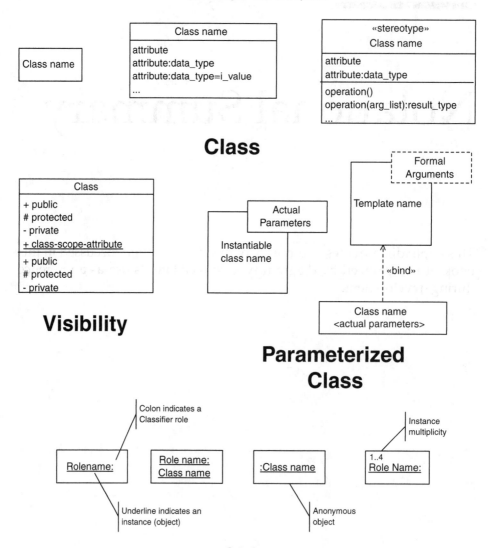

Class

Visibility

Parameterized Class

Object

Class Diagram

Shows the existence of classes and
relationships in a logical view of a system

Indicates speaking
perspective of
association name

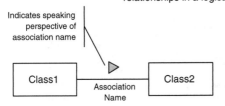

Role multiplicity

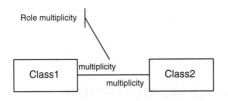

Associations may be labeled using any
combination of names, role names, and multiplicity

Multiplicity Symbol	Meaning
1	Exactly 1
0,1	Optionally 1
x..y	From x to y inclusive
a,b,c	Only specific values of a, b, and c
1..*	One or greater
*	0 or more

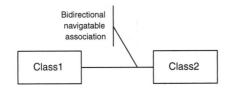

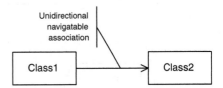

Association

Class Diagram

Shows the existence of classes and
relationships in a logical view of a system

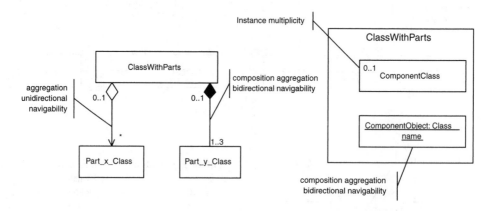

Aggregation and Composition

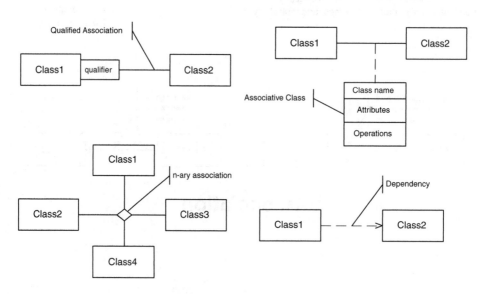

Advanced Associations

Class Diagram

Shows the existence of classes and
relationships in a logical view of a system

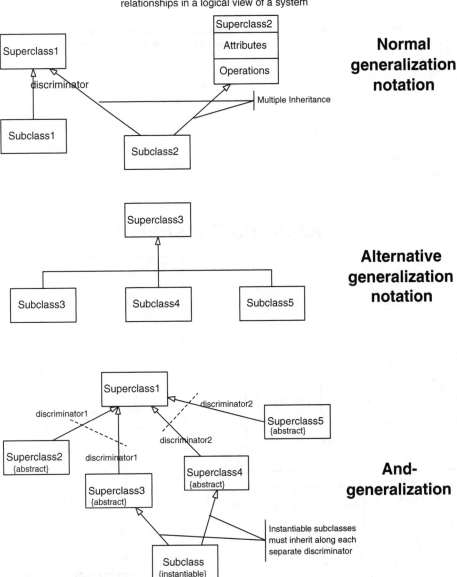

**Normal
generalization
notation**

**Alternative
generalization
notation**

**And-
generalization**

Generalization and Specialization

Class Diagram

Shows the existence of classes and
relationships in a logical view of a system.

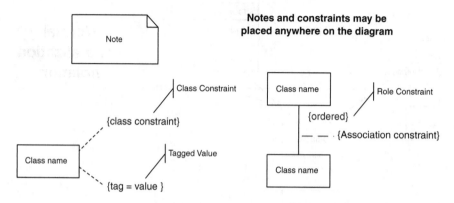

Notes and Constraints

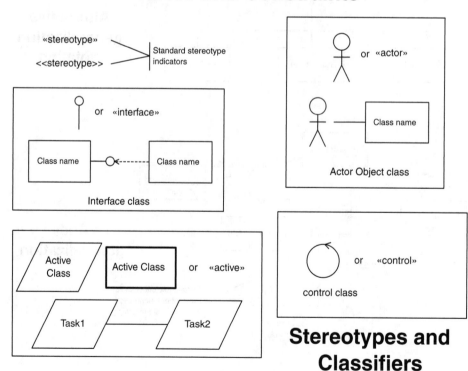

Stereotypes and Classifiers

Collaboration Diagram

Shows a sequenced set of messages illustrating a specific
example of object interaction.

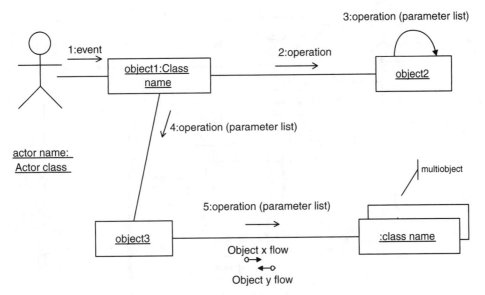

Object Collaboration

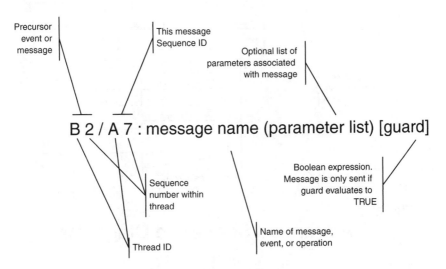

Message Syntax

Sequence Diagram

Shows a sequenced set of messages illustrating a specific example of object interaction.

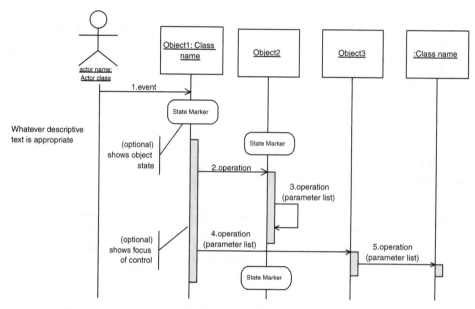

Sequence diagrams have two dimensions. The vertical dimension usually represents time, and the horizontal represents different objects. (These may be reversed.)

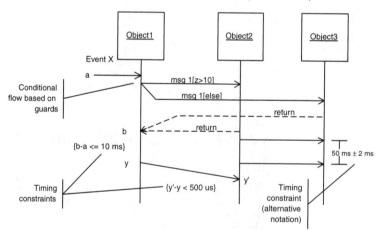

Advanced Sequence Diagrams

Use Cases

Use cases show primary areas of collaboration between the system and actors in its environment. Use cases are isomorphic with function points.

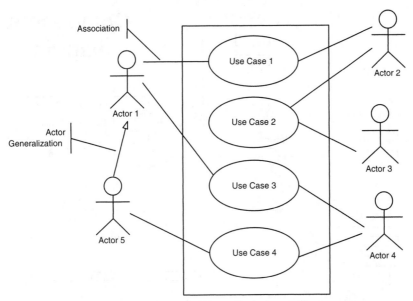

Use Case Diagram

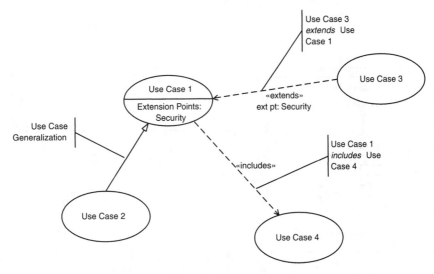

Use Case Relationships

Implementation Diagrams

Implementation diagrams show the run-time dependencies and packaging structure of the deployed system.

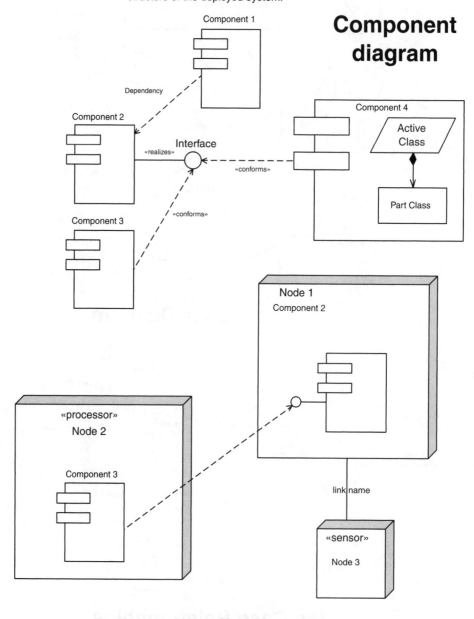

Component diagram

Deployment Diagram

Package diagram

Shows a grouping of model elements. Packages may also appear within class and object diagrams.

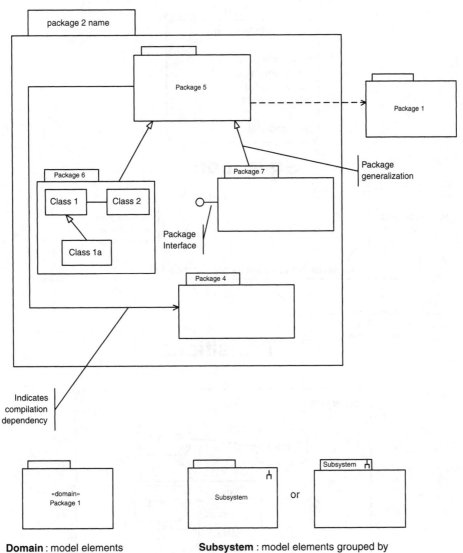

Domain : model elements related by subject matter

Subsystem : model elements grouped by run-time behavior

Statechart

Shows the sequences of states for a reactive class or interaction during its life in response to stimuli, together with its responses and actions.

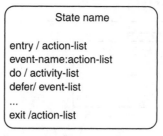

State name

entry / action-list
event-name:action-list
do / activity-list
defer/ event-list
...
exit /action-list

State icon

Name of the event
triggering the
transition

List of actions to be
executed when
transition taken

event-name '['guard-condition']' '/' action-list

Boolean condition must
evaluate to TRUE for the
transition to be taken

Transitions

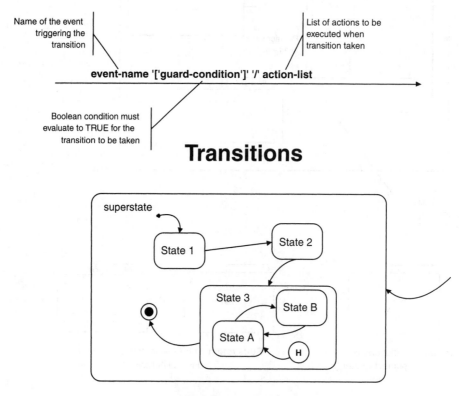

superstate

State 1 → State 2

State 3

State B

State A

H

Nested States

Statechart

Shows the sequences of states for a reactive class or interaction during its life in response to stimuli, together with its responses and actions.

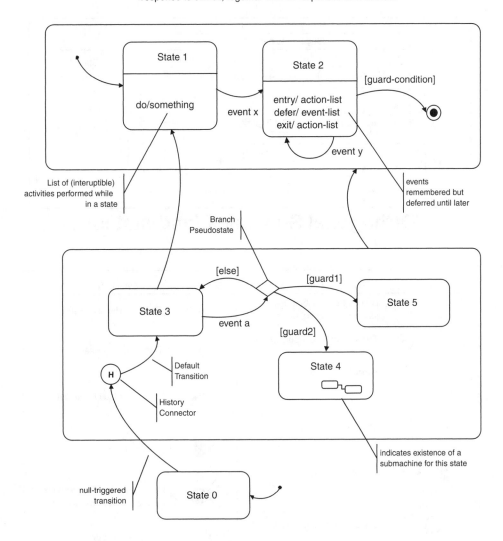

Sequential substates

Statechart

Shows the sequences of states for a reactive class or interaction during its life in
response to stimuli, together with its responses and actions.

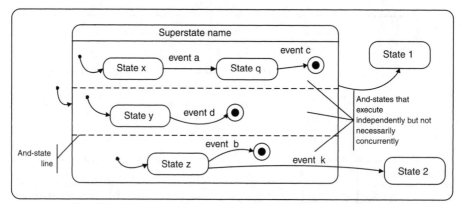

Orthogonal Substates (and-states)

	Symbol		Symbol Name		Symbol	Symbol Name
Ⓒ	or	◇	Branch Pseudostate (type of junction pseudostate)		Ⓗ	(Shallow) History Pseudostate
Ⓣ	or	◉	Terminal or Final Pseudostate		Ⓗ*	(Deep) History Pseudostate
*	or	Ⓝ	Synch Pseudostate		•↘	Initial or Default Pseudostate
			Fork Pseudostate			Junction Pseudostate
			Join Pseudostate			Merge Junction Pseudostate (type of junction pseudostate)
	[g] ⟲ [g]		Choice Point Pseudostate		↘│ label	Stub Pseudostate

Pseudostates

Statechart

Shows the sequences of states for a reactive class or interaction during its life in response to stimuli, together with its responses and actions.

Synch Pseudostates

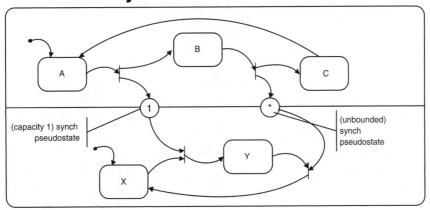

(capacity 1) synch pseudostate

(unbounded) synch pseudostate

Submachines

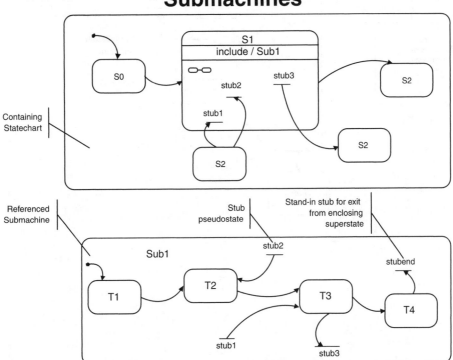

Containing Statechart

Referenced Submachine

Stub pseudostate

Stand-in stub for exit from enclosing superstate

Activity Diagrams

Activity Diagrams are a specialized form of state diagrams in which most or all transitions are taken when the state activity is completed.

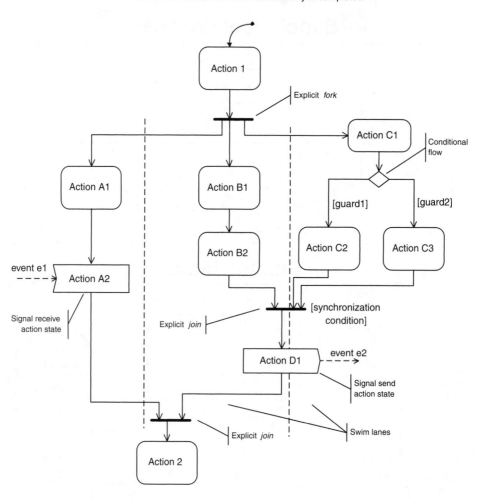

Appendix B

Pattern Index

Index

Note: Page numbers followed by *f* indicate figures and illustrations.

Other Titles by Bruce Powel Douglass

Doing Hard Time

Developing Real-Time Systems with UML, Objects, Frameworks, and Patterns

0-201-49837-5

Real-Time UML, Second Edition

Developing Efficient Objects for Embedded Systems

0-201-65784-8

Register
Your Book

at www.awprofessional.com/register

You may be eligible to receive:

- Advance notice of forthcoming editions of the book
- Related book recommendations
- Chapter excerpts and supplements of forthcoming titles
- Information about special contests and promotions throughout the year
- Notices and reminders about author appearances, tradeshows, and online chats with special guests

Contact us

If you are interested in writing a book or reviewing manuscripts prior to publication, please write to us at:

Editorial Department
Addison-Wesley Professional
75 Arlington Street, Suite 300
Boston, MA 02116 USA
Email: AWPro@aw.com

▲▼▼
Addison-Wesley

Visit us on the Web: http://www.awprofessional.com